PRAISE

LET THE LORD

New York Times Editors' Choice

Winner of the J. Anthony Lukas Work-in-Progress Award

"A searing history of the rise and fall of capital punishment . . . *Let the Lord Sort Them* urges readers to reckon with the ugliest aspects of Texas history, and with how the political debate over the death penalty has elided the long-lasting trauma that executions inflict on everyone involved."
—*Texas Monthly*

"It's a book pitched straight into the gulf between universal theory and individual experience." —JO LIVINGSTONE, *The New Republic*

"An extraordinarily hopeful glimpse of a future in which we are finally beginning to imagine a very different version of justice—one in which the immediate and generational fallout is not so devastating."
—HEATHER ANN THOMPSON, Pulitzer Prize–winning author of *Blood in the Water: The Attica Prison Uprising of 1971 and Its Legacy*

"Texas and the death penalty have a history, as they say. Melding intimate portraits with sweeping scholarship, Maurice Chammah reveals the lies we tell ourselves in the name of justice."
—KEN ARMSTRONG, Pulitzer Prize–winning reporter and co-author of *Unbelievable: The Story of Two Detectives' Relentless Search for the Truth*

"*Let the Lord Sort Them* gives us the story of the death penalty through the eyes of the attorneys, legislators, judges, criminals, and victims for whom one of our oldest and most contentious policy debates became frighteningly real. It's a wonderfully written blend of history and reportage, delivered with sensitivity and grace."
—NATE BLAKESLEE, *New York Times* bestselling author of *American Wolf* and *Tulia*

"It's impossible to understand the death penalty in America without understanding the death penalty in Texas. Maurice Chammah's lyrically written, meticulously researched volume does more to advance our understanding of the state's peculiar devotion to executions than any book before it."

—EVAN MANDERY, author of *A Wild Justice: The Death and Resurrection of Capital Punishment in America* and professor at John Jay College of Criminal Justice

"Nobody, neither death penalty supporter nor abolitionist, will come away from *Let the Lord Sort Them* without having her or his belief in the fairness of the death penalty system utterly shaken if not entirely destroyed."

—DAVID R. DOW, author of *The Autobiography of an Execution* and Cullen Professor at the University of Houston Law Center

LET
THE LORD
SORT THEM

THE RISE AND FALL OF
THE DEATH PENALTY

Maurice Chammah

CROWN
NEW YORK

2022 Crown Trade Paperback Edition

Copyright © 2021 by Maurice Chammah
Book club guide copyright © 2022 by Penguin Random House LLC

Published in the United States by Crown, an imprint of Random House,
a division of Penguin Random House LLC, New York.

CROWN and the Crown colophon are registered trademarks
of Penguin Random House LLC.

Originally published in hardcover in the United States by Crown,
an imprint of Random House, a division of
Penguin Random House LLC, New York, in 2021.

Grateful acknowledgment is made to *The Texas Observer* for permission
to reprint portions of "To Kill or Not to Kill?" (April 23, 2014).
Copyright © Texas Observer.

Portions of this work originally appeared, in different form, in the following
publications: "The Slow Death of the Death Penalty" (December 17, 2014)
and "How Mexico Saves Its Citizens from the Death Penalty in the U.S."
(September 22, 2016) in *The Marshall Project* (themarshallproject.org),
and "Executions Are So Common, Even Protesting Them Has
Become Routine" (November 12, 2013) in *Texas Monthly*.

LIBRARY OF CONGRESS CATALOGING-IN-PUBLICATION DATA
Names: Chammah, Maurice, author.
Title: Let the Lord sort them / Maurice Chammah.
Description: First edition. | New York: Crown, [2021] | Includes index.
Identifiers: LCCN 2020025171 (print) | LCCN 2020025172 (ebook) |
ISBN 9781524760281 (trade paperback) | ISBN 9781524760274 (ebook)
Subjects: LCSH: Capital punishment—Texas—History—20th century. |
Texas—Politics and government—1951—
Classification: LCC HV8699.U6 T435 2021 (print) |
LCC HV8699.U6 (ebook) | DDC 364.6609764—dc23
LC record available at lccn.loc.gov/2020025171
LC ebook record available at lccn.loc.gov/2020025172

Printed in the United States of America on acid-free paper

crownpublishing.com

1st Printing

Book design by Jo Anne Metsch

To Emily

CONTENTS

LET THE LORD SORT THEM

PROLOGUE

ONE AFTERNOON IN NOVEMBER 1982, WARDEN JACK PURSLEY called a meeting of his senior staff. Pursley ran the oldest prison in Texas, which is located a few blocks from the courthouse square in Huntsville, a small city in the eastern part of the state. The Huntsville Unit is nicknamed the Walls because of the tall red brick fortifications that surround its grounds. (The bricks were made by prisoners.) Across the street stood the offices of the Texas Department of Corrections, the agency overseeing the state's prisons. On one side of the street, Pursley gave orders; on the other side, he took them.

The staff had all been told of this meeting by phone rather than the usual written memo, and when unit chaplain Carroll Pickett arrived, he immediately noticed a pinched mood. The typical coffee and doughnuts were absent. Pickett asked the head of the maintenance crew what this was about. He didn't know, and together they asked a major, who didn't know either. After fifteen minutes or so, Pursley appeared, wearing his usual suit, boots, and Stetson hat. His face was grim. As he passed by Pickett, he murmured, "You're not going to like this."

Pursley removed his hat and set it down. "We will soon be having an execution," he said. December 7, shortly after midnight.

Many years later, Pickett could remember the "stunned silence" in the room, the knots in his own stomach. The last time an execution had taken place here was eighteen years ago, and nobody in the room had been around back then. In the intervening years, legal challenges had halted all executions, forcing the state legislature to write new capital punishment laws in 1973. The new death row prisoners began filing appeals. In the meantime, Pursley had been asked to fix up "Old Sparky," the state's electric chair. His work turned out to be unnecessary; the chair was now stored in a wooden crate. State legislators feared electrocutions would be too much of a spectacle—a "circus sideshow," one called it—so in 1977 they adopted a new execution method called "lethal injection." Though the procedure had been developed in Oklahoma, Pursley's team would be the first in the country to put it into practice. Sodium thiopental, a barbiturate, would render the prisoner unconscious. Pancuronium bromide, a paralytic, would freeze his respiratory muscles. Finally, potassium chloride would stop his heart.

"I don't know a thing about what we've got to do," Pursley told the group. "All of us have a great deal of learning to do in a short period of time." He read tasks off a clipboard. Two men would greet the condemned man at the death house. A "tie-down team" would strap him to the gurney. Others would load the body into a hearse and accompany the vehicle to the prison gate.

The warden led the men through heavy iron doors and into the old death house. They walked through a hallway, past several small cells where men had once spent their final days. The atmosphere reminded Pickett of a medieval dungeon: The walls were painted gray, and there was little ventilation, making it feel as if "all of the air had somehow been sucked out of the room." Through another iron door was the death chamber, where Pursley showed them a wheeled stretcher with large leather straps laid across it. (Later, a gurney would be bolted to the floor.) Pickett noticed three small windows, "framed in mint green," behind which the executioners would send the chemicals down tubes connected to an IV line.

The chaplain was not given a task at first, even as he was invited, in the days after the meeting, to watch the preparations. The warden was a former high school football star, fastidious about the smallest details of prison management, and he decided to run drills, requiring the many partial-executioners to complete their assigned tasks over and over until they grew rote. They practiced bringing the prisoner to a cell near the death chamber, a room of less than 200 square feet, and then walking him to the gurney. One young lieutenant agreed to play this role during the rehearsals, allowing each of his limbs to be strapped down.

He played his part calmly—until one day he snapped. With no warning, the lieutenant went into a full panic, fighting off the tie-down team and refusing to go to his own mock death. The team paused briefly in surprise. Then muscle memory kicked in and they managed to force him down.

The warden admitted that this was planned. He had instructed the lieutenant to fight, because "a scene like that is always a possibility." Then he turned to Chaplain Pickett.

"Your job will be to seduce his emotions," he said. Pickett chuckled uncomfortably. The plan was for him to be on hand early in the morning to meet the van from death row; the warden didn't want the condemned man to be greeted by yet another gray uniform. If he arrived ready to fight, hopefully a day getting his spiritual affairs in order would calm him down, making the execution easier on everyone involved. Pickett would later tell this story in many different permutations, slightly altering the dialogue and sequence of events. But that one word, "seduce," was in every telling, a hard pebble in his memory that never dissolved.

Around this time, Dick J. Reavis, a writer for *Texas Monthly*, called the state attorney general's office and asked who would be the first to be executed. He received a list of prisoners whose appeals were near their end, and he drove out to death row to meet them. In the visitation room, he sat down across from a black man named Charlie Brooks. Reavis later described Brooks as "squirming, sparkle-eyed, and full of good cheer," with only a few gray hairs to show for his forty years. There was little to suggest that this man would end up in the history books; others on the row, like Ronald "Candy Man" O'Bryan, who had killed his own son on Halloween, loomed larger in the public imagination.

Prisoners and reporters often have limited time together, so their conversations jump quickly past small talk. Brooks knew that he'd be subject to a new, untested method of execution, and he wanted the public to know whether it was really as "humane" as promised. If he felt pain, he told Reavis, he would nod. Later, Reavis worried that this signal would not be clear enough—it might look like too much like the head tilt that follows a heroin injection—so they agreed Brooks would instead shake his head from side to side.

They ended up having several visits, and at each they reconfirmed this plan. But otherwise, the conversation ranged, and Brooks wanted especially to talk about faith. "I decided to try Islam," he said, "just to see what it would get me. I had tried Christianity before, you know, but it didn't do for me what I wanted." Reavis later wrote, "Charlie didn't pray toward the east, because there was a wall on that side of his cell; he prayed toward the door, as if freedom were Mecca." In and out of prison for various crimes over the years, Brooks had split with his wife, and he had not been around to raise his two sons back home. He was "dating" another woman he had met through letters. Though he reminded Reavis of other self-interested prisoners he had met, who "shave the edges off of everything," he didn't seem like he would lie outright, so Reavis decided to press him on some lingering mysteries surrounding his crime.

Six years earlier, Brooks had been driving around with his friends Woodie Loudres and Marlene Smith when their car broke down. Brooks walked over to a nearby dealership and asked to test-drive a car. He was sent out with a mechanic named David Gregory. Once they left the grounds, he and Loudres forced Gregory into the trunk of the car and drove him to a motel. Gregory was later found gagged and bound with tape and wire from a clothes hanger, with a single bullet wound in his head. Both men were sentenced to death for killing Gregory, even though only one of them could have fired the shot; prosecutors convinced each man's jury that he had been the shooter, which is not uncommon and not against the law.

Over the next few years, both men appealed their sentences, and Loudres caught a break: An appeals court found problems with how his jury had been selected, invalidating his death sentence. He was moved off death row. Brooks, on the other hand, found his appeals rejected by a series of judges, even as he maintained that he had not been the one to shoot Gregory.

Once it became clear that Brooks might be the first Texan up for execution under the new state law, he caught the attention of the national anti-death-penalty community. Because executions were still rare nationwide, a network of skilled lawyers was ready to jump in and obtain a stay. Roughly forty-eight hours before he was scheduled to die, Brooks received a visit from Eric Freedman, a twenty-nine-year-old associate at an elite law firm in New York City, who had spent that Thanksgiving holed up with three thousand pages of court records, looking for any new legal argument that might stall the execution. Freedman had flown to Austin and driven the 150 miles to Huntsville. "You have a lot of people pulling for you," he told Brooks. "This is going to go down to the very last second." There were phones in the death house, with direct lines to the offices of the governor and attorney general. "Until you actually feel the needle in you," Freedman said, "you should have hope that that phone will ring."

Although there were few legal avenues still open to Brooks, Freedman had discovered one argument that might stop the execution. Jack Strickland, one of the prosecutors who had sent him to death row, now felt guilty about the fact that Brooks would die and Loudres would live, despite the continuing uncertainty over who had fired the fatal shot. On the morning of the execution, the prosecutor appeared before the state board that would vote on whether to recommend a reprieve. "I spent a lot of time talking with people and doing some soul searching last weekend trying to determine for myself if this disparity was in some way justified," he said. "I came to the conclusion it was not."

The board was unmoved, voting at 4 P.M. to let the execution proceed, and around 6 P.M. Governor Bill Clements said he would not intervene either. (The governor had been complaining to lawyers representing the state about how long appeals were taking. "The people of Texas want these people executed," he told one.) The Supreme Court also refused to step in, and the justices sounded impatient: "The merits of Brooks' claims have been presented by a total of twelve lawyers, in nine separate hearings, and have by this time been reviewed by 23 judges, state and federal . . . the application for stay is denied." Freedman still had one more move: He could get the troubled prosecutor in front of a federal judge to testify, in hopes that the judge would halt the execution. He found one judge in Fort Worth willing to hold a night hearing, and he put the prosecutor on the last plane leaving Austin.

Brooks knew he might not prevail, and he had been preparing for his death. That morning, he had arrived in a van from death row. Chaplain Pickett was there waiting. Brooks struck Pickett as both nervous and resigned, praying briefly with a Muslim chaplain before asking a guard to bring him a radio so he could listen for news about his case. He'd brought a dozen cans of Dr Pepper from the prison commissary, which the officers let him refrigerate. He asked if anyone played chess. Pickett called the warden's office and had them send an officer good enough to challenge Brooks. He arrived with a small foldable board and plastic pieces, but Brooks was an expert, and after a few games the officer gave up. A prison chef asked Brooks what he wanted for a last meal. He wanted fried shrimp and oysters. The cook said they didn't have any, so Brooks settled for steak, fries, and peach cobbler. "In prison, you've got rights and you've got privileges," Brooks said to Pickett. "I guess shrimp and oysters are considered a privilege."

"I guess so," Pickett said. "This is all new to me."

"Both of us."

Through many sleepless nights, Pickett had come to accept his role in this process. He had always believed that nobody should face death alone, and perhaps God had given him a gift in allowing him to comfort men in their final hours. There was no way he could stop executions, he told himself, but he could offer these men the presence of at least one person who did not stand in judgment.

An imam arrived from Fort Worth, along with Brooks's niece. She smiled at her uncle through wire mesh as they recalled childhood memories. Around sunset, Brooks asked to be left alone to write some letters, all of which began, "If you are reading this letter now . . ." At 10:49 P.M., the federal judge decided the prosecutor's misgivings weren't enough to halt the execution.

Soon after, Brooks received word that his ex-wife and their two sons had arrived. He said he did not want to see them.

Joyce Brooks was at a friend's house in Fort Worth when she learned from the television that her ex-husband was about to be executed. Then she got a call: A reporter had shown up at her own house. She asked the reporter to come over and drive her home. After her interview, she noticed her two teenage sons, Derrek and Keith, were "prancing and going back and forth and crying." The three of them decided to make a last-minute trek to Huntsville, two hundred miles away, and jumped into Derrek's blue Ford Mustang, which had a broken door that clattered to the ground every time they stopped for gas.

When they arrived, they had trouble getting close to the prison due to the crowds. There were at least seventy reporters and hundreds of demonstrators outside. Opponents of the death penalty had driven in from Houston, Dallas, and Austin. College students had also descended from nearby Sam Houston State University, a school known for its criminal justice programs, meaning some of them might eventually work for the prison system. They held signs reading KILL 'EM IN VEIN and JUSTICE FINALLY PREVAILS next to hand-drawn needles. One sign, carried in the hand of a young man whose other hand gripped a Confederate flag, read TO THE RA ON 2ND FLOOR! GOOD LUCK ON YOUR CALCULAS [sic] TEST TOMORROW. When a television crew's lights flicked on, the students clustered in the glow.

Derrek thought about picking a fight, but then he saw all the police nearby and decided against it. As the family approached the prison, the cameras turned toward them and flashed. Once they got inside the building, a state official appeared. They could not visit Charlie, he said, and Charlie did not want them to witness the execution. So the family stood in the foyer and stared at a clock on the wall as it ticked toward midnight.

Around 11:30 P.M., Pickett came to Brooks's cell and said, "It's time to go." Brooks made the short walk to the execution chamber. He didn't struggle as the straps were belted down across his arms, legs, and stomach. The witnesses, including the reporter Dick Reavis, had gathered in a waiting room. Now, accompanied by guards, they trudged down a hallway and through a fenced-in courtyard to the death house. They arrived in the chamber, which was chilly, with green linoleum floor tiles and walls painted the color of red brick. Years later, the prison would install walls and windows between the gurney and the witness area, but for now all that separated them was a black metal railing, beyond which Brooks was lying down, craning his head so he could lock eyes on his girlfriend, Vanessa Sapp. His face was taut with fear. Reavis wrote that his cheeks were "nearly flattened like those of a motorcyclist speeding into a strong, cold wind."

Near him stood the warden, and Reavis noticed he was using a cane. Pursley had been in a car crash a month earlier, which killed a passenger in the other vehicle, and was now facing a misdemeanor drunken driving charge.

Reavis was surprised to see that an IV was already running into Brooks's arm, snaking back into another room. A doctor had checked the prisoner but declined to participate directly, so prison employees set up the injection. It had been hard to find a vein, because of his heroin scars, and he bled when the officers struggled to get a needle in. All of this had transpired before the witnesses entered.

"Do you have any last words?" Pursley asked.

Brooks looked to Sapp, his girlfriend. "I love you," he said. Then he began to chant in Arabic:

"Ashhadu an la ilaha il-Allah" (I testify that there is no god but God).

"Ashhadu an Muhammad Rasul Allah" (I testify that Muhammad is the messenger of God).

"May Allah admit you to paradise," said the imam.

"Be strong," Brooks said to Sapp.

At 12:09, Pursley removed his glasses, a silent signal to begin the flow of drugs. Brooks flexed his right fist open and closed several times. Tears came to his eyes as he began to turn his head from side to side.

Reavis suddenly remembered the deal they'd made. Was this the signal that Brooks was in pain? He couldn't be sure, and he began to silently panic. Brooks opened his mouth and made a sound: "Ahlll." It could have been a yawn or an attempt to gasp, or he could have been continuing his prayer with *"Allahu Akbar,"* God is greater. Then his eyes closed, his fingers trembled, and his stomach heaved. He wheezed several times and then lay still.

A minute or two passed. Two doctors walked in. One pointed a penlight at Brooks's eyes and said, "Dilation, dilation." He walked toward the window and asked, "Is the injection completed?" Reavis assumed the answer was no, because the doctor then said, "Well, we'll just wait a couple of minutes." After a little while, the doctors returned to their work. "I pronounce this man dead," one said.

The witnesses had not been at Pursley's rehearsals, so they did not know what to do next. Reavis heard someone say, "You all will have to leave now."

When Brooks's son Keith saw the witnesses coming out of the chamber, and it dawned on him what that meant, he kicked over a chair and then threw it against the wall. Nobody stopped him.

His father's body was delivered by van to a funeral home in Huntsville, where Joyce was able to touch her ex-husband for the first time in years. His skin was warm and soft. She looked at his hair and noticed bits of gray, the only indication that he'd aged in prison. Then she looked at his face and she froze. He was grinning. As others began to enter the room, Joyce kept staring at that grin, feeling oddly as though at any moment he might open his eyes.

That night, Pickett visited the family at their hotel. Keith and Derrek were angry that they hadn't been allowed to see their father before he died, and Pickett could not bring himself to say it was their father's decision. Brooks's body was taken to Houston, where the prison had contracted with a hospital to conduct an autopsy—this offended Joyce, but there was nothing she could do—and then delivered by helicopter back to Fort Worth, where both Christian and Muslim funerals were held. Keith and Derrek were casket bearers.

The day after the execution, a cartoon in *The Huntsville Item* depicted a row of tombstones toppling over like dominoes, with Brooks's name on the first.

A notable absence in all of these events was the family of David Gregory. It would be many years before the families of victims were invited to witness executions, though reporters did seek quotes. "I didn't know that I would feel this relief," Gregory's mother, Norma Morrison, told one. "Now there is some hope in this society for victims. I think all our pain stems from Charlie Brooks. He hurt his family and he hurt my family. We are all the victims of Charlie Brooks. . . . The burden was lifted off my shoulders today."

For days after the murder, five-year-old David Gregory, Jr., had peered out the window, thinking surely his father's Chevy Bel-Air would soon pull into their driveway. He looked behind doors in their home and asked the adults where his father was hiding. He didn't understand why they were all crying. David's younger sister, Rebecca, was two when their father died, so she had no memories of him, but many years later she would come to understand all the ways her family had been affected by the murder.

Their mother had gone on to live with a man who was violently abusive. Rebecca escaped by becoming pregnant at age fifteen. David began sneaking out of the house as a teenager. Late at night, he would sit across the street from the motel where his father was killed, thinking to himself, *God, take me too.* He had often accompanied his father to work as a child but had faked a stomachache the day of the murder. For years he wondered whether, had he been there, someone else might have been asked to accompany Brooks on his test drive. He drifted toward drugs, alcohol, and violence, and he went to prison on an assault charge, where he joined the Aryan Brotherhood prison gang, inspired by his hatred of the black men who killed his father. He eventually concluded that Brooks should not have been executed; life in prison would have been harsher.

After his own release, David mellowed and abandoned his racism, but he still suffered night terrors. He struggled to raise his own two sons to be good men, the kind of people he thought he might have become had he not lost his role model.

As an adult, Rebecca Gregory sometimes typed her father's name into Google. Eventually, she found videos online of oral history interviews with Keith and Derrek Brooks, along with their mother, Joyce. The three described how Charlie Brooks's father had died when he was thirteen, and how he became addicted to heroin when it swept through their community. As Charlie's own sons grew up, they remembered, he would come home for brief and magical moments, buying them ice cream and clothes, and then disappear again. In their grandmother's freezer sat an uneaten birthday cake, a reminder of the time they all planned to throw him a surprise party and he never showed up. "Now that I'm an adult, I understand that he had a demon that he was chasing—you know, that heroin," Derrek said in the interview, "and no matter how much you love your family, that drug is powerful."

Derrek tried to earn his father's attention with good grades, while Keith reveled in his father's status among sex workers and drug sellers. When Keith was seventeen he was sent to a youth prison, where he joined a weightlifting team that got to travel to other penal institutions across the state. By coincidence, at one of them, he reconnected with his father. They began writing letters, Brooks encouraging his son to never let anyone "steal your cool" and to translate his anger into positivity. A few years later, after his release, Keith started a paving company. He posted his phone number at a parole office and hired men straight out of prison.

Rebecca Gregory had expected Charlie Brooks's sons to be angry at the world, just as she was, but both seemed happy, gainfully employed with families of their own. It felt a little unfair. Would she have run away as a pregnant teenager if she'd felt her father's love as they had? Would her brother have gone to prison? These questions would never go away, but she also felt she could not begrudge these men their successes. "They didn't have a choice in who their father was," she said after watching the videos. Still, it bothered her that, given the drama of the death penalty, history remembered the murderers more than their victims.

Also on Google was the article Dick Reavis ended up writing about the execution for *Texas Monthly*, in which he solved once and for all the mystery of who had really killed her father.

"Who shot that dude," Reavis had asked Brooks, "you or Woodie Loudres?"

"I regret my participation in the events of that day," Brooks responded. Reavis pressed him, and Brooks leaned in close.

"Let's just say that, uh, you know, the gun could have gone off."

When Reavis got home, he read the trial transcript and saw that the murder weapon was a revolver. Reavis knew that revolvers don't typically fire by accident. He went back and confronted him, and Brooks gave an explanation. "In order for a revolver to discharge, you have to either cock the hammer or . . . pull the trigger," he said. "What I'm saying is that okay, like, if you've got the hammer cocked, okay, it can be an accident when you twitch that finger."

Brooks had long maintained his innocence, and perhaps this was as much of a confession as he would ever make, but he added, "I cannot identify with what happened because that was so, you know, it's just like something you do while you're asleep, the sleepwalkers that commit acts. . . . I was so out of it, that I can't even identify with being there." He was desperate for the world to know there was more to him than that awful moment. "I am not a cold-blooded killer," he said. "I know that I am not able to kill someone without compassion."

In every death penalty case, before Charlie Brooks and since, you will find the family members, the lawyers, the journalists, the prison workers—each of them touched, in ways large and small, observable and invisible, by the moment a person takes a life, the moment the state takes a life, and the many moments in between.

To everyone else, the death penalty can feel like an abstraction, a source of dinner table quarrels that reemerge when a major case hits the news and we marshal the arguments we've heard before, citing the Bible or statistics or anecdote to make our case for or against. Capital punishment is a long-standing tradition, close to a cultural universal over the long span of the human experience, but Americans have always viewed it with some ambivalence, and our history is accordingly erratic. Before the Civil War, the French writer Alexis de Tocqueville marveled at the "mildness" of American punishment (for those who weren't enslaved, that is), and Michigan, Maine, and Wisconsin abolished the death penalty for good. Nebraska, meanwhile, kept carrying out executions until 1959, then stopped, then carried out three in the mid-1990s, then stopped again, then formally abolished the punishment in 2015, then voted to bring it back, and finally resumed executions in 2018.

Even amid this turmoil, there was a moment, roughly half a century ago, when it seemed the death penalty would disappear from American society forever. Executions had fallen out of fashion by 1972, when the U.S. Supreme Court decided that the American system of capital punishment as a whole violated the Constitution. Instead of marking the death penalty's end, however, this decision spurred its resurgence. States crafted a new system, and executions resumed and trended upward and the country reached a peak—nearly a hundred executions—in 1999.

This embrace of capital punishment coincided with a historic rise in violent crime that began in the 1960s and trailed off in the 1990s. Seeking to explain this trend, scholars have looked in many directions. Crime is often the product of impulsive decision-making, and young adults with less-developed brains are more likely to act impulsively; as the baby boomer generation came of age, the population of young adults ballooned. The closing of asylums and failure to improve public mental health systems meant that jails often took on the care of those suffering from mental illness. In the 1960s, American society also experienced sweeping transformations in its cultural and sexual mores, which produced new conditions—more unmarried young men, more children without parental stability, more cultural celebrations of violence—that help explain, if only partially, the rise in crime.

But cause and effect, action and reaction, also began to blur in myriad ways. An epidemic of crack cocaine use swept black communities, but political choices criminalized the sale and use of the drug and turned prisons into places where those convicted of nonviolent crimes were acclimated by trauma to violence. The American creed of personal reinvention, which at times had inspired prison officials to focus on rehabilitation and redemption, was shelved as a naive indulgence. (The word "corrections" lingered in the names of state prison agencies, an aspiration for the future or a phantom limb from the past.) As lawmakers made it easier to get sent to prison and harder to get out, the number of incarcerated Americans ballooned from half a million to more than two million. Even at the death penalty's height, it played a role in only a tiny fraction of murder cases, but executions were the ultimate symbol of a national culture that favored retribution, and they rendered sentences of twenty, forty, or sixty years in prison less extreme by comparison. There was no clearer policy expression of the idea that some people were irredeemable.

One state stood at the center of this history. Of the roughly fifteen hundred executions that Americans have carried out since the 1970s, Texas has been responsible for more than five hundred. Oklahoma actually executed more people per capita during this time, while other states sent more to death row, but when *Saturday Night Live* sat a smarmy politician atop a stack of prisoners' coffins, he was a fictional Texas governor, and when a character on *The Simpsons* played an arcade game called "Escape from Death Row," she knew she had lost when the machine spouted "The Yellow Rose of Texas" and an executioner, dressed as a cowboy, danced onto the screen. Across the country, a generation grew up thinking of Texas as the place where the president was shot, and then, soon after, the man who had shot him was shot himself. Years later, on the television show *Dallas*, they watched a conniving oilman take two bullets to the chest in the dead of night. Texas produced outsized bad guys, but also knew how to give them what they deserved.

Texans have relished their reputation for dispensing harsh and efficient justice, amplifying it to guide the country as a whole. Two different Texas governors, running for president in 2000 and 2012, used their death penalty records to appeal to voters in the rest of the country, and the rhetoric trickled down. "If you come to Texas and kill somebody, we will kill you back," said the comedian Ron White. When anthropologist Robin Conley interviewed members of Houston juries for a 2011 dissertation, one told her, "Down in parts of Texas where I work, we would have a room full of eye-for-an-eye people just wanting to hang this guy."

The criminologist Franklin Zimring drew upon this vision when he wanted to explain a seeming contradiction: How could Americans, especially those with conservative views, profess so much distrust for government, but also support the government's efforts to execute people? Zimring's answer was the "mythology of local control." For many Americans, he explained, executions are "expressions of the will of the community rather than the power of a distant and alien government." The death penalty, in other words, is the product of democracy: American voters choose the lawmakers who make the death penalty available, they choose the prosecutors who seek the death penalty in individual cases, and then, as jurors, they choose to actually hand out the death sentences. This sense of ownership is what separates us from other countries that frequently impose the punishment, countries that critics like to bring up, like Saudi Arabia, China, and Iran. Their citizens don't necessarily get to choose whether to have the death penalty, or decide when it should be imposed; we do.

To make such arguments, however, you have to keep one eye closed. Open it and you see a parallel history of American punishment, as present in Texas as anywhere else. Before executions looked like quiet medical procedures, they looked like charred and dismembered corpses, usually of black men, surrounded by throngs of smiling white faces in the courthouse square. Before the days of seemingly endless appeals, there were the days of no trials at all. A community coming together to exercise its collective will can also look like the powerful violently suppressing the weak. Outside the prison cell where Charlie Brooks waited out his appeals, other black prisoners were picking cotton just as their enslaved ancestors had done.

Although the death penalty is rarely used, it wields a special role in our cultural, legal, and political conversations about justice, a word as galvanizing as it is nebulous. Capital cases feature the highest stakes in criminal law, so they attract skilled, ambitious lawyers on both sides, many of whom are driven by something beyond the case at hand, whether an uncompromising ideology or their own political career. Because Texas has been the epicenter of capital punishment, cases from the state have often driven national discussions of how we respond to crime. The case of Cameron Todd Willingham, who was executed in 2004 despite strong evidence of his innocence, awoke many Americans to the possibility that their justice system was failing in its basic tasks of finding and punishing the truly guilty. The case of Karla Faye Tucker, who became a devout Christian while on death row, pushed Americans to consider what role rehabilitation and redemption should play in that system. And the case of Gary Graham was at one time the focal point for America's unresolved tensions over racial injustice, picking up where the O. J. Simpson case left off and foreshadowing the #BlackLivesMatter movement.

In this book, I focus on Texas as I trace the death penalty's national rise, and then examine why the institution is disappearing, and why the trend has been powerful enough to bring Texas along. For all the cultural, historical, and emotional dynamics that swirl around capital punishment, it is ultimately a public policy choice. In the 1970s, we chose to embrace the death penalty as a response to murder, but since the turn of the millennium, we have been deciding—sometimes consciously, sometimes not—to choose other ways. As we lean uncertainly toward ending the death penalty, we can look back at why we embraced it so thoroughly, and what might follow should we embrace it again.

Some of the stories I've selected to illuminate this history cast backward to the defining visions, both real and imagined, of American history: the plantation, the frontier, the courtroom, the halls of political power. Some are about people who became famous, although most are about people whose experiences illustrate the system's day-to-day reality, from jurors to politicians to family members of murder victims to prisoners facing execution. My focus is on lawyers. In the trial transcripts, they do most of the talking. Whether they realize it or not, as they lay out the cold facts and legal principles, they are also helping us answer some of our deepest questions about our own society: Can a person be "evil"? What does "justice" mean? If you look closely you'll see the stories they are telling us about ourselves.

PART
I

RISE

1

ON A THURSDAY MORNING IN JUNE 1972, A DECADE BEFORE THE execution of Charlie Brooks, hundreds of death row prisoners across the country laughed and whooped and rattled their cell doors. They had spent months and even years waiting for the day they'd be led to an electric chair or gas chamber or firing squad or noose, but now the shocking news was making its way down the runs: The Supreme Court had ruled that every death penalty law in the country was unconstitutional; all of their death sentences had been thrown out. In Florida, a prisoner wrapped a guard in a bear hug. In Tennessee, one placed his hands on his hips and scowled as a news photographer snapped his picture next to the electric chair, as though he had conquered this dusty pile of wood and leather.

In Texas, a wave of applause rang through the Ellis Unit in Huntsville, and when Elmer Branch received the evening issue of the *Houston Chronicle*, he stretched his arms out of his cell to show it to his neighbors. The next morning, Branch himself would be above the fold in newspapers across the country, pictured sitting on his neatly made prison cot and gazing through the cell bars. Many of the papers noted his crime: the rape of an elderly white woman. "If I ever get out, I'll try to find a job," Branch, who was black, told a reporter. "I would go somewhere where I could make something of myself."

The Supreme Court's decision in *Furman v. Georgia*—which had been joined by Branch's own case, *Branch v. Texas*—appeared to represent the end of the death penalty in the United States. It was the culmination of a long decline. Since the 1800s, a number of states had been removing capital punishment from their laws or limiting it to rare crimes. In 1959, there had been 124 murders in Harris County, Texas, which encompassed Houston, but only three people sentenced to death, and a candidate for district attorney there openly questioned capital punishment. By 1963, the year a Texan became president, polls showed less than half the country favored the practice, and Lyndon Johnson appointed an attorney general who openly opposed it. The news of American military atrocities in Vietnam—along with the discovery of German death camps a generation before—gave new power to the argument that governments should be restrained in their authority over life and death. Many European countries were abandoning executions as well.

Amid this broad cultural and political shift, there were people nudging history along. In Manhattan, lawyers with the NAACP Legal Defense Fund (which traced its roots to the National Association for the Advancement of Colored People) spent the 1960s mounting an assault on capital punishment, believing the institution to be deeply linked to the history of racial injustice. A key figure in this effort came to be Anthony Amsterdam. A tall and lanky law professor, his eyes sunken but demanding, Amsterdam was famous for working twenty-hour days and appearing to survive on thin cigars, coffee, and diet soda. He was the kind of lawyer who could dictate a brief from memory over the phone and argue in court without notes. In one oft-repeated story, he cited an obscure old case by volume and page number. The judge looked it up and couldn't find it on the page, and Amsterdam brazenly suggested the judge's copy of the volume must be bound incorrectly; he turned out to be right.

In 1963, the LDF's lawyers received a signal that they were uniquely prepared to interpret. In response to an appeal from an Alabama prisoner, three Supreme Court justices signed a brief statement saying the Court should decide whether it violated the Constitution to execute someone for the crime of rape. The justices rejected the vast majority of appeals without writing publicly, so this statement was a quiet bombshell. It implied that if the LDF lawyers challenged the death penalty in the courts, they might succeed.

After the opinion came out, the LDF lawyers sent students across the South to gather data about capital punishment, and produced a "Last Aid Kit," a collection of legal briefs that any lawyer could file to stop an execution. These briefs rarely changed the ultimate outcome of a case, but that wasn't the only goal: The other, perhaps principal, goal was to gum up the legal system. The strategy worked. In part because of their efforts, executions slowed to a halt in 1967. "For each year the United States went without executions," one LDF lawyer recalled, "the more hollow would ring claims that the American people could not do without them." At the end of the decade, the Supreme Court reinforced the trend by giving the LDF a series of victories: In one decision, the justices struck down a federal law that allowed the death penalty for kidnapping, and in another they declared that citizens who had "conscientious scruples" about the punishment should be allowed to sit on juries, even if this gave defense lawyers an edge.

The LDF lawyers knew their successes might not last. In 1968, Richard Nixon took the White House after declaring, "Time is running out for the merchants of crime and corruption in American society," and when the chief justice of the Supreme Court retired, Nixon nominated Warren Burger, a judge known for siding with law enforcement. In 1971, Burger's court ruled against a death row prisoner in California who had argued that his jury had been given no clear legal guidance on how to decide his fate. "This is an oblique attack on capital punishment," Burger fumed to his colleagues. It seemed the Court was done with limiting the death penalty.

So it was all the more surprising when, a few months later, the justices agreed to hear arguments on whether the death penalty as a whole was "cruel and unusual." The move was driven not by those who opposed the death penalty but by those who, like Burger, thought it was perfectly constitutional and wanted to say so, once and for all. Still, they had given the civil rights community a once-in-a-generation opportunity to persuade the Court to do the opposite—to end the death penalty for good.

The justices accepted the appeals of three death row prisoners, which would be argued all together under the banner of the lead case, *Furman v. Georgia*. William Henry Furman had been convicted of murdering William Joseph Micke, Jr., a twenty-nine-year-old father of five. The bullet had gone through a closed plywood door before hitting Micke; Furman claimed to have tripped over a wire, which had caused his gun to go off. He seemed to have little in common with the era's scariest figures, men with epithets instead of names: the Zodiac Killer, the Boston Strangler.

As he stood before the justices at oral argument, Anthony Amsterdam made sweeping arguments about his fellow Americans: Although many might say they believed in the death penalty, he said, in practice they almost never handed it out. If the government started executing "any reasonable proportions" of the people who qualified for the punishment, Americans would be sickened, and it violated the Constitution to execute the random handful who were unlucky enough to wind up in the electric chair.

Even worse, Amsterdam added, that handful wasn't entirely random: The few who were executed were "disproportionately the pariahs, the poor and racial minorities." Amsterdam had the rhetorical skill to pull listeners through a dense argument before slamming on the brakes. "The figures are perfectly plain," he said. "Georgia executes black people." Another lawyer, who argued on behalf of Elmer Branch, the Texas prisoner facing the death penalty for rape, offered proof: A black man convicted of rape in Texas had an 88 percent chance of being sentenced to death, versus 22 percent for other races.

In June, the Court ruled in favor of the prisoners, freeing Furman and Branch and hundreds of other men from their death sentences. Although Branch himself was all smiles when he heard the news, thinking he might now be released, others on Texas death row were apprehensive and even gloomy, realizing they would all likely spend the rest of their lives in prison. Many would have preferred death to such a fate.

Right before the men on Florida's death row learned about *Furman v. Georgia*, they had gathered in a gym to watch the movie *Dirty Harry*. It was an ironic choice. In the 1971 film, a steely-eyed Clint Eastwood struggles to catch a serial killer. He is stymied at every turn, not just by the killer himself, but by his own superiors in the police department, who care—too much, the film suggests—about all the rights guaranteed to criminals by the courts. (At one point, the villain is freed from jail because Harry seized evidence without a warrant.) After the movie ended, the prisoners received word of the *Furman* decision and celebrated, but outside the prison, the public responded just as Dirty Harry himself might have, with righteous indignation.

While the Supreme Court's previous rulings on the right to remain silent and other criminal justice issues sounded abstract, ending the death penalty did not: The Court appeared to be robbing Americans of the ability to fight crime. Among the prisoners the Supreme Court saved from the electric chair were not just obscure men like Furman and Branch, but also symbols of evil like Charles Manson and Sirhan Sirhan. "In outlawing the death penalty, the Supreme Court has removed the shotgun from over the door of civilization," a Dallas judge wrote in the *Texas Bar Journal.* "A sad, indisputable fact of life is that human mad dogs exist. It is not only stupid but is 'cruel and unusual punishment' not to execute them. The doctor's knife must be cruel in order to be kind. If the ruptured appendix is not removed, the patient dies." Americans didn't realize how much they liked the death penalty until they were deprived of it. A year before *Furman*, 49 percent of Americans said they supported the punishment; a few months after the decision, it was 57 percent.

The LDF's identity as a racial justice organization added to the impression, particularly in the South, that the *Furman* decision was part of a wider federal attack on what was sometimes called states' rights, along with *Brown v. Board of Education, Loving v. Virginia,* and the Voting Rights Act. But there was a crucial difference from those other Washington edicts: *Furman* didn't say the death penalty could never exist again. It just said that current death penalty laws were unconstitutional. Read another way, it became an invitation to go back and rewrite those laws.

Almost immediately, state officials around the country got to work.

The Texas Legislature meets for up to 140 days every other year under the pink granite dome of the state capitol in the center of downtown Austin. Texans like to point out that the dome is taller than its counterpart in Washington, D.C.; few of them are aware that the stone was quarried and cut by state prisoners, an effort to undercut union workers, who later called the building a "scab job." Much about the state's politics—including the hostility toward unions—can appear as timeless as that towering dome, but this impression stems from a tendency toward mythology in the state's culture. In truth, Texas can be as politically messy as anywhere else, and the 1973 legislative session was a good example.

Shortly before the 1972 election, a Houston banker named Frank Sharp was accused of making deals with lawmakers, who bought stock in his life insurance company. They pursued legislation to help his business, while he manipulated stock prices to make them all rich. When the "Sharpstown" scandal broke, dozens of incumbents lost reelection, often to young challengers with little or no experience in government. These new lawmakers didn't have much time to set up offices, hire staff, and learn the intricacies of parliamentary debate. In addition to the usual mammoth task of passing a budget, the public was demanding new ethics laws to prevent another Sharpstown. The legislators also had to revise abortion laws in the wake of the Supreme Court's recent decision in Roe v. Wade, as well as remap House districts. For several years, a group of scholars had been preparing an overhaul of the state's penal code, which had grown tangled and bloated.

All that, and a new death penalty law. At more than sixty thousand words—longer than many novels—Furman was among the longest Supreme Court decisions ever published, and each of the nine justices wrote his own opinion. The four-judge minority thought the death penalty was fine as is, while two justices agreed with Amsterdam that Americans had simply moved on from the punishment and nothing could save it. That left three in the middle. Justice William O. Douglas was troubled by the evidence of racial discrimination. Justices Byron White and Potter Stewart voiced concerns that the outcomes—who got the death penalty and who didn't—were arbitrary. Stewart wrote the most famous line of the whole decision: "These death sentences are cruel and unusual in the same way that being struck by lightning is cruel and unusual."

The legislature needed to craft a law that would create some semblance of logic around who would get a death sentence and who would not.

Across the country, state lawmakers were considering a range of potential solutions to this problem. A popular one, adopted by Florida, drew on the work of scholars at the American Law Institute, who thought juries could be given "standards" to guide them. It worked like this: After someone was found guilty of a crime that carried a potential death sentence, the court would hold a second trial to determine punishment. The jury would hear lawyers present cases for and against death and consider specific "aggravating" factors (for example, the defendant killed for money, or killed lots of people) and "mitigating" factors (the defendant had no history of violence, was an accomplice with a minor role in the crime, was young, had a low IQ, or the like). Different states were picking different factors to enshrine in their new laws. Some of these factors were more vague than others, and vagueness always produces debate. What did it mean for a crime to be "especially heinous" or "depraved" or "cruel"? Could you leave it up to juries to define those words? Wouldn't that also lead to arbitrary outcomes, no more meaningful than a lightning strike?

It was all so slippery.

On a Tuesday afternoon in early February 1973, a group of Texas House members gathered on the third floor of the capitol, in an ornate room of walnut furnishings and wool carpet, to discuss another way. House Bill 200 captured an idea that was making the rounds in a few other states. In essence, it removed the problem of arbitrary jury decisions by getting rid of such decisions altogether. Twelve citizens would still decide whether the person on trial was guilty, but then, if their crime was on a short list of those the legislature deemed most heinous, the death penalty would be imposed automatically.

Harsh, yes, but maybe this would make the punishment less arbitrary, and perhaps even reduce the racial disparities: If you committed one of the worst types of murders, then your punishment would be the same whether you were black or white, rich or poor, male or female.

The bill focused just on murder—other states were considering the death penalty for rape—but there was still a debate to be had about which types of murders would make the list. Killing a police officer seemed like a given, but what about killing a child? Killing during a rape? If you lengthened the list too much, might the Supreme Court strike it down? Speaking to the legislators, one prosecutor chewed on the idea of adding to the list murders that were "extremely atrocious," but these words were just so vague. "I would feel personally that if someone murdered me I would think it was extremely atrocious!" he said.

The conversation eventually turned away from which crimes to which criminals: What sorts of people deserved the death penalty?

A prosecutor named John Green had some ideas. He had traveled more than three hundred miles from the oil boomtown of Odessa to tell the legislators about the scariest man he had ever met. In October 1968, a young woman named Linda Cougat had gone missing from a local laundromat. Her body was discovered, hands bound and throat strangled by her own nylon stockings, in a field outside town. A few weeks later, motel owner Dorothy Smith was found dead in her apartment, hands bound with a cable. July 1970: Eula Miller, stab wounds. September 1970: Nancy Miller, abducted while her children were asleep in the next room. January 1971: Ruth Maynard, found in a field. June 1971: Gloria Green, found dead under a rotting mattress in a vacant lot.

A few months later, an itinerant oilfield worker named Johnny Meadows, sitting in a jail cell in New Mexico, began bragging about all the women he had raped and murdered over in Texas. He said he had six separate personalities, and at one courtroom appearance, he ripped off his shirt to show a burn on his back in the shape of Texas, along with initials of his victims, which he claimed were inflicted on him during an interrogation to get him to confess. It was later proven that Meadows had persuaded a fellow inmate to make the burns with a coat hanger.

Green, who had prosecuted Meadows, brought the legislators a television interview with the killer. In the film, Meadows said he had studied *Furman* himself as he weighed his legal options after arrest. He "knows more law than most of my assistants do," said the prosecutor, laughing uneasily. A mandatory law might have deterred such a man, he was suggesting. If Meadows had been sure he would go to his death, would he have killed all those women? Had knowing a jury might spare him given him license to roll the dice? One justice had written in *Furman* that "the death penalty, unless imposed with sufficient frequency, will make little contribution to deterring those crimes for which it may be exacted."

Such thinking has a long lineage. "Of those who have done extreme wrong and, as a result of such crimes, have become incurable, of those are the examples made," Plato quotes Socrates telling his students. "Others are profited who behold them undergoing for their transgressions the greatest, sharpest, and most fearful sufferings." In the Book of Deuteronomy, when Moses tells the Israelites to stone wrongdoers, he adds, "All the people will hear and be afraid."

Public executions have been a common feature of human societies for most of recorded history, though the methods and justifications have varied widely. American thinking on the subject traces back to early modern England, where the "Bloody Code" authorized death for counterfeiting, blasphemy, and sodomy. Immigrants to North America replaced the king with the people as the source of sovereign power, but they preserved public executions as a means of demonstrating that power. Founding Father Samuel Adams even believed that young republics needed public executions more than monarchies did, because they were more fragile. Incarceration was not common practice in the United States until the nineteenth century, so there were few other options for punishing transgressors. A society that embraced slavery assumed the enslaved had little to lose other than their lives.

Because the death penalty was meant to deter people from crime, it had to reach as many people as possible. Masses would gather in town squares to watch executions—groups of as many as fifty thousand people did so in New York in the 1820s—and the executions often took place at night, which "naturally brings with it a kind of Dread that strongly operates upon the Heart of Man," a Virginia newspaper editor wrote in 1752. Preachers delivered sermons from the scaffold, attempting to strengthen the link between what people were seeing and what they should be learning. Broadsides and pamphlets were distributed, usually featuring a lengthy (and almost certainly ghostwritten) statement by the condemned. The narratives, often in verse, followed a formula: good parents, a slippery slope of sin, a warning to others. Here is Levi Ames, hanged for burglary in 1773:

> The dreadful Deed for which I die,
> Arose from small Beginning;
> My idleness brought poverty
> And so I took to Stealing.

In practice, the white and well connected often escaped the gallows; juries might find them guilty of a lesser crime, so as to express their disapproval without exacting the ultimate penalty. Back in England, many men and women had been saved by "Benefit of Clergy," a legal quirk that descended from an era in which clergy members could escape prosecution in secular courts, proving their status through their ability to read. By the end of the Middle Ages, anyone could recite a memorized verse, "Have mercy upon me, O God," and receive a brand on the thumb as a warning. This practice illustrated how British and

American societies could preserve a harsh punishment in the abstract, as a means of deterrence, while granting mercy in a large number of individual cases. A society could want and not want the death penalty at the same time.

The American Revolution featured plenty of wartime executions, but many of the new nation's founders were inspired by the Italian philosopher Cesare Beccaria, whose 1764 *Essay on Crimes and Punishments* argued against the state's right to take a life. George Washington, John Adams, and Thomas Jefferson all read Beccaria, and his arguments were particularly inspiring to the Philadelphia doctor Benjamin Rush, a signer of the Declaration of Independence who argued that executions actually exacerbated violence throughout society. Capital punishment "lessens the horror of taking away human life," he wrote, "and thereby tends to multiply murders."

After the Texas lawmakers finished watching the film of the well-informed serial killer, they faced a group of professors, in a way the intellectual heirs of Beccaria and Rush, who came bearing scholarly analysis showing that executions had no clear effect on homicide rates. The legislators did not seem especially interested, and these scholars could not match the charisma of the man who followed them: a San Antonio defense lawyer named Fred Semaan.

Portly, with a shiny bald head and tortoiseshell glasses, Semaan was descended from a Syrian immigrant family. His last name in Arabic could be translated as "one who listens," but he was more of a talker; he had developed a reputation as a courtroom brawler who could, in the words of a colleague, "devastate a hostile witness and strip him naked in front of a jury." He liked to claim he had defended more murderers than any other lawyer in the history of the state. "No client has ever received the death penalty," *Texas Monthly* said of his record. "Nevertheless, he remains a firm believer in capital punishment as a deterrent—except for his clients."

Now his rhetorical talents would be used not to eliminate the death penalty but to preserve it. He waved off the arguments of the scholars by saying no would-be murderer, scared off by the possibility of execution, would call up a researcher "and say, 'Put that down as a statistic—I was gonna commit murder but the death penalty deterred me!'" A few quiet laughs peppered the room.

A good persuader tells the skeptics some of what they want to hear, and Semaan acknowledged that racism might shape who received a death sentence. "We're all human beings and we're not gonna change," he said. "Some people are going to be prejudiced against black men, and they're gonna give a black man the death penalty when he doesn't deserve it." But a higher court could oversee the process and ensure fairness: "Set up someone somewhere to ride herd on that jury and on that judge. Pick his case apart. And if they find it was given fairly and impartially, let it stick, and if they find it wasn't, do something about it."

One legislator mentioned that Minnesota abolished the death penalty in 1911, and the number of murders subsequently dropped. Could Semaan explain that? "The people in Minnesota, and the state of Minnesota, differ an awful lot from our people and our state," Semaan responded. "I don't think, in Maine, New Hampshire, Vermont, and those states, people go to a beer joint the way some people do here in Texas, sit there and drink beer, and because somebody goes up and puts the nickel in the jukebox and plays a tune that somebody else don't like, kill him for it. That's been done here!"

Amid more chuckling, one lawmaker breathed incredulously into his microphone: "Really?"

In 1857, the writer and architect Frederick Law Olmsted published an account of his travels through Texas. It was a land full of new Anglo immigrants, he wrote, many of whom had left other parts of the South, scrawling "GTT"—"Gone to Texas"—in chalk on their doors, an acronym he called a "slang appendage" given "to every man's name who had disappeared before the discovery of some rascality." The settlers developed a reputation as hotheaded protocriminals, likely to settle their disputes quickly and violently. "Probably a more reckless and vicious crew was seldom gathered," Olmsted wrote.

Even back then, the reality and the perception of Texas were operating on not quite parallel tracks, veering to collide in self-fulfilling prophecies and circular logic; white Texans believed themselves to be self-reliant in matters of law and order, and so they acted that way. Most of the early Anglo Texans came from the South, a region long associated with violence. The historian Edward Ayers argued that while the Northeast's economic and demographic diversity had bred a culture of mutual respect and self-control, the South maintained a culture of "honor" in which the smallest of perceived insults led to duels and barroom brawls. Cultures of honor, he argued, thrived "only in certain kinds of societies, ones that are economically undiversified, localized, explicitly hierarchical—societies where one standard of worth can reign." Ayers found the best explanation in slavery: "Honor presupposes undisguised hierarchy, and a slave society builds an incontrovertible hierarchy into basic human relations." In this view, Texans were the particularly undisciplined children of a particularly violent place, who brought Southern honor culture along with Southern slavery out to the perilous frontier.

Fred Semaan's image of the frontier was similar to the one that had appeared five years earlier in the historian T. R. Fehrenbach's *Lone Star,* an epic survey of the state's history that compared the early settlers to the ancient Israelites. In Texas, Fehrenbach wrote, "the human hallmarks of most true frontiers, the armed society with its almost theatrical codes and courtesies, its incipient feudalism, its touchy independence and determined self-reliance, its—exaggerated as it seemed to more crowded cultures—individual self-importance, and its tribal territoriality, not only flourished but became a way of life." This vision of a place teetering near the abyss, where violence was more justifiable and brutality more understandable, permeated the narrative of the state's origins; generations of elementary schoolers would learn to mourn the defeat of a scrappy band of Texian troops at the hands of the Mexican Army, and to celebrate those who avenged them by declaring "Remember the Alamo!" It also gained purchase nationally. The first working model of the Colt revolver was called "the Texas." The legal doctrine declaring that you had "no duty to retreat"—permitting murder with the thinnest justification of self-defense—was at one time known as "the Texas Rule."

These ideas were between and behind the words of the Texas legislators and prosecutors as they discussed the death penalty in 1973. Houston's top prosecutor wondered whether, if legislators failed to bring back the death penalty, "people would take the law into their own hands and take a gun and go kill the person." One of the House members hearing all this testimony, a freshman state senator from the Panhandle named Max Sherman, had misgivings about executions, but he felt politically vulnerable as a Democrat in a Republican district, and so he came up with a suggestion that tapped into another cultural idea about Texans: They don't outsource responsibility. He wanted the same jurors who declared a defendant guilty to stick around and determine whether they should be sentenced to death, rather than leaving that decision to a different jury. He later recalled, "I thought whoever found guilt needed to, in the old Western saying, 'belly up to the bar.'"

There was little room in all this mythologizing for the history of interactions between the cultures of Mexicans and Anglo Texans that were *not* violent, for the decades of peaceful intermingling across the state between German and Czech immigrants, along with Greeks and Jews and Norwegians and Swedes and Swiss and Chinese. There was an irony in hearing Fred Semaan, a descendant of Syrian immigrants, going on about some mythic Texans settling their disputes through barroom gunfights.

Beyond the rhetoric, capital punishment was also a matter of personal belief, irreducible and idiosyncratic and—more often than most would admit—ambivalent. The longer Semaan spoke, the more muddied his arguments became. He rationalized, pondered, contradicted, doubled back. "I can conceive of a fact situation where a man who kills a policeman ought to get nothing *but* the death penalty," he said. "I can conceive of another fact situation in which a man who kills a policeman, illegally, oughtn't to get that much, because of the facts and the circumstances in that case. And to make it mandatory, I think, would not be right." But he didn't want to limit who could get the death penalty, either. "I want [a criminal] to come to the conclusion that if you kill that policeman, you're going to get the death penalty, and if you kill Fred Semaan, you're going to get it. Or my neighbor, or my brother, or anybody in my family!" But the bill on the table was to restrict the death penalty to murderers of certain types of victims, which did not necessarily include members of Semaan's family. The bill would also make the death penalty mandatory, which Semaan now said he didn't like. After an hour of testimony, he had undercut the very bill he was ostensibly there to defend.

On the other side of the capitol building, across the mosaic-floored rotunda, the thirty-one members of the Texas Senate were also debating how to bring back the death penalty. They were not doing much better. At the center of the discussion was freshman senator Bill Meier from Fort Worth. A conservative lawyer in his early thirties, Meier liked spectacle. Years later he would hold a press conference while hooked up to a lie detector to prove the honesty of his campaign promises. He would also carry out a record-breaking, if unsuccessful, forty-three-hour filibuster, armed with lemon slices, hard candy, and the kind of bathroom bag used by astronauts. But beneath all that showiness was a hard pragmatism; he later worked on a commission that reviewed the work of state agencies and shut down ones that weren't doing enough. His showmanship may suggest why he wanted to be at the center of the death penalty debate, but it was this love of efficiency that explained what he did when he got there. He wasn't concerned with whether the mandatory bill was too harsh, or whether it would deter murderers. He just wanted a bill that the Supreme Court would approve, because it would be a huge waste of time and money if the state voted in a law and sent people to death row only to have the Court strike down the law and free all of them.

Meier didn't think the mandatory bill was the answer. He feared it would alienate some of the justices, including Harry Blackmun, who had written that legislatures should not eliminate "the element of mercy in the imposition of punishment." Meier preferred letting juries decide on life or death and giving them lists of aggravating and mitigating factors to consider, but he struggled to convince his peers. As they saw it, the Supreme Court didn't like that two different people could commit the same crime and one could get the death penalty while the other didn't. Giving jurors too much choice seemed likely to perpetuate that problem.

Meier thought his colleagues were deluding themselves. Even if you made the death penalty mandatory for certain crimes, a jury could still choose to convict a defendant of something less serious than capital murder—perhaps second-degree murder, or manslaughter—if its members were at all queasy about sending that person to die. A savvy defense lawyer (Meier might have been thinking of Fred Semaan) could stoke ambivalence. Such a lawyer could, Meier told them, "lean over the bench, and point to the jury and say, 'And ladies and gentlemen of the jury, if you have a reasonable doubt in your mind and you find this man guilty, he is going to get the electric chair, period.'" The result would be exactly what his colleagues feared: Two people could commit the same crime and end up with different punishments, simply because one had a better lawyer.

The debate had reached an impasse. This created an opportunity for a small cadre of legislators who didn't want the death penalty to return at all. They had no illusions of their strength, but they wanted to go down swinging. Back in the House, Rep. Andrew Z. Baker worried aloud that an innocent person might be executed by mistake and proposed an amendment replacing the death penalty with life imprisonment (such a punishment did not technically exist at the time). Another legislator objected that a life sentence was "more cruel and unusual than the death penalty."

This was Baker's last serious suggestion, but not his last suggestion. He proposed holding executions on courthouse squares: "Invite all the youngsters, have it be a sort of family entertainment on a Saturday afternoon." There was talk of using the rodeo arena in Huntsville, of using lions. "We could sell tickets at twenty dollars a throw," another legislator said, "and we could earmark that for various state funds."

The tone took an abrupt turn as Rep. Craig Washington rose to speak. He proposed that for every execution, the entire legislature should meet, and an electric chair should be placed in the middle of the chamber where they were now sitting. All of the elected officials would then have to vote for the execution directly. "I say the buck ought to stop here," he told them. "If you have the guts to do it there [in Huntsville], you ought to have the guts to do it here."

Some of the legislators laughed. "Mr. Washington," one said, "this isn't serious."

"It *is* serious," Washington insisted. "Have you ever witnessed an execution? Have you ever seen the eyeballs pop out and the blood boil?"

Like many of his colleagues, Washington was new to the legislature, one of a group of black representatives from Houston known as the People's Five. Inspired in law school by legal efforts to force swimming pools and schools to desegregate, he had worked to develop his rhetorical skills, knowing they could be deployed to help people. A few years later, *Texas Monthly* would fawn over this "spellbinding orator," bearded and bow-tied, who "wins admirers even when he loses battles." Like Meier, Washington appreciated spectacle, managing years later to get his peers to raise child welfare payments by holding up a pair of jeans, shoes, two pairs of socks, deodorant, toothpaste, and shampoo, and explaining that buying these necessary items would leave a child just a few dollars left for food.

Though Washington believed a good speech could change minds, he also knew there was little chance of stopping the death penalty from returning. His goal now was to force his peers to go on the record, to acknowledge the grisly reality of their decision. Because to him, the true history of the death penalty in his country, and his state, lay not in Revolutionary-era hangings, nor in a gauzy vision of the frontier, but in the horrors of Southern lynching.

Between 1877 and 1950, more than four thousand African Americans were lynched in the United States. But "lynch" can feel euphemistic and distant; more immediate verbs are necessary. Black Americans were beaten, tortured, hanged, burned alive, dragged through city streets, ripped limb from limb, and castrated. Thousands of mostly white spectators traveled by train to watch. Sometimes they brought picnic food; this was a day's outing and entertainment, like a baseball game or a political rally. They mobbed the bodies of the dead to steal fingers and toes and ears and bits of bone and splinters of wood and links of chain and pieces of rope. They sent postcards with images of bodies torn apart, skin charred, slashed, and stabbed beyond recognition. "The things that influenced my conduct as a Negro did not have to happen to me directly," wrote Richard Wright. "As long as it remained something terrible and yet remote, something whose horror and blood might descend upon me at any moment, I was compelled to give my entire imagination over to it, an act which blocked the springs of thought and feeling in me, creating a sense of distance between me and the world in which I lived."

The true number of victims will never be known. Although black writers like Ida B. Wells wrote vividly of lynchings throughout the South, few scholars or institutions counted them. Even as slavery and segregation were acknowledged in the textbooks of Southern children, white scholars touched lynching lightly if at all. Some sociologists portrayed the killings as the product of isolated, rural backwaters, ignoring how often they struck middle-class, urban communities, while the historian C. Vann Woodward, in his seminal 1951 book, *Origins of the New South*, devoted less than two pages to the subject. When the Equal Justice Initiative, a nonprofit organization in Alabama, began crafting a new list around 2011, they found more than eight hundred lynchings that had never before been recorded.

It was especially easy for white Americans to forget the prevalence of racially motivated lynchings in Texas, where the popular view of the state's origins usually downplayed the role of slavery. Many early settlers to the region had brought slaves with them, but it became clear that the government of Mexico, which controlled the territory, might not continue to support the institution. This was among the reasons the settlers fought for independence in the 1830s. At the same time, one of the state's founding fathers, Stephen F. Austin, worried that someday black slaves might outnumber their white owners and take over; he had a particular fear of black men raping white women.

After the Civil War, violence against freed black people was as vicious in Texas as anywhere else in the South, but Texans had an alternate mythology they could use to sanitize the history: They dressed it up in cowboy hats and set it on open prairies, portraying lynching victims in popular culture as cattle rustlers in the small towns of the West, perhaps denied legal due process but probably not deserving of it anyway, victims only of swift eye-for-an-eye justice. This image of Texas was exported to the rest of the country. "I associated lynching primarily with the frontier," wrote the historian Joel Williamson, trying to account for his profession's lack of interest. Williamson mentioned his own childhood memory of watching *The Ox-Bow Incident*, a 1943 film in which a group of suspected cattle rustlers are stalked by a small town posse, and one man proudly announces, "Down in Texas, where I come from, we just go out and get a man and string him up." Even the word "lynch" derived from the name of a Revolutionary-era judge who allowed for the execution of Tories without robust trials, and had nothing originally to do with the murder of black people in the South.

Lynchings eventually ebbed as Southern elites, hoping to build economic connections to the North, were increasingly embarrassed by these unruly spectacles, finding them difficult to justify on the national stage. Antilynching activists exploited their ambivalence through publicity. In 1916, when a man was lynched in Waco, Texas, the NAACP LDF hired a white journalist to write about how a mob had burned him to death, torn his limbs from his body, and taken photographs in commemoration. Newspapers around the country castigated the city and the state.

Lynchings were not technically sanctioned by the state, but official executions were also held in public, attracting large crowds and spurring similar discomfort among elites. "The great ritual of state could be spoiled by an executioner's incompetence, [by] a condemned man's recalcitrance, or by a disruptive, unruly crowd," wrote the sociologist David Garland. "Instead of affirming state sovereignty the execution could undermine it." In 1922, J. W. Thomas was elected to the Texas Senate arguing that executions should be carried out in the more dignified environment of the state prison in Huntsville, with more modern tools. The legislature appropriated $5,000 to build an electric chair, and the rope that had been used for hangings in San Antonio—"a well oiled and pliable piece of Manila hemp"—was repurposed to tow automobiles. The warden of the prison resigned, telling reporters, "The penitentiary is a place to reform a man, not to kill him." Another warden was hired, and the first closed-door executions in Texas took place in February 1924.

Like the LDF lawyers who fought the *Furman* case, the legislator Craig Washington was deeply aware of the connection between the contemporary death penalty and the lynchings of the past. If his peers saw the connection privately, they would never admit it publicly, and he knew that explicit talk of race tended to make them nervous and less open to discussion. You couldn't convince a man of anything, Washington felt, if he thought that you thought he was a racist. Although Washington dropped references to slavery into his speech, he didn't talk about lynchings, instead attempting to pull his peers toward a higher morality. "You're going to have to face your God one day," he said. "If you believe in your heart and your mind and your soul that the death penalty is right, vote 'aye.' But if . . . it has not been proven to you beyond a reasonable doubt that it is right, and that it is moral, and that it does deter crime, vote 'no.'"

Spectators watching from the gallery above erupted in applause. Some legislators wanted to join Washington, but felt they could not; *The Texas Observer* quoted one anonymous lawmaker: "I can only be thankful that there were statesmen at some times and at some places. But then you can get away with things in the Congress, in the Senate, that you can't get away with in a fucking little state Legislature." After Washington's speech, the debate turned to the Bible. Washington's friend Mickey Leland declared, "And God spake all these words saying, 'Thou shalt not kill.'" He said it again: "And God spake"—louder now, slower—"All. These. Words. Saying, 'Thou shalt not kill.'" Dean Cobb, the bill's sponsor, rose and politely reminded everyone that "there are other Biblical references," including "Whoso sheddeth man's blood by man shall his blood be shed." (Garland, the sociologist, has noted that the death penalty "seems to invite, even to compel, the repetitive restatement of arguments and counterarguments that are all too familiar.")

It was this Biblical debate, with its aura of timelessness, that took over the room, and it made it all the more difficult for them to focus on what the Supreme Court was demanding: a law that wove a path between extremes, that maintained the death penalty but also moderated it. Bill Meier would never persuade people like Craig Washington to vote for a death penalty bill. He could, however, pull his colleagues away from the extreme bill that would make the death penalty automatic for some crimes, if only he could come up with an alternative.

When lawmakers cannot agree, they often procrastinate, and when a session ends, so too does a bill's hope of passage. But the death penalty bill was one they couldn't let expire. The state would not hold another legislative session for two years, and already Texans were demonstrating what they do without capital punishment: A Dallas jury had sentenced two kidnappers to 5,005 years each. The legislature was scheduled to adjourn on the last Monday of the month. With only three days left to go, the divide between the House bill, which made the death penalty mandatory for certain crimes, and the Senate bill, which would allow jurors to make a choice, appeared unresolvable.

On Friday, Dain Whitworth, head of the state prosecutors' association, was doing maintenance work on a new house when his wife appeared with a suit and tie. He'd been called back, she said, by yet another committee. This one was composed of members of both chambers, who would try to hammer out a compromise. Whitworth "took a spit bath" and raced back up to the capitol, where the legislators were gathering at a table. He sat in a chair against the wall, in an outer ring of non-legislators. Others sat on the floor.

Most of the room favored the mandatory bill. But Meier pleaded with them to see that it wouldn't get past the Supreme Court. That night, he searched his mind for a middle way, and the next morning he proposed a new solution: What if the death penalty was mandatory for certain crimes, but you built in "exceptions" for certain people who didn't seem deserving of execution? The group discussed what those exceptions might be, what rare killer of a cop or young child should be spared execution. The consensus was that the murder could not have been committed in the "heat of passion," as the result of some provocation.

The prosecutors played the leading role now—the head of the defense lawyers' association had testified in earlier phases, but by now had abandoned the project—and they recalled the times they'd succeeded in sending someone to death row. Juries, they said, usually needed to believe a murderer would kill again. Their peers in Dallas had begun enlisting psychiatrists to examine the accused and make exactly this point to the jury. Senator Donald Adams liked the idea of enshrining this distinction into the bill, because it would further differentiate a "stone killer" from someone moved by a sudden burst of fury.

The legislators made a limited list of crimes that would be eligible for the death penalty—killing a police officer, killing a young child, killing while committing robbery or rape—and then wrote three questions: Was the murder unprovoked? Was it deliberate? And finally: Was there a "probability that the defendant would commit criminal acts of violence that would constitute a continuing threat to society?" To impose the death penalty, the jury would need to answer yes to all three questions unanimously.

Sometimes a policy compromise is just a tacit agreement not to prod too hard at the vagaries, and this is even more tempting when it will be someone else's job to put the policy into practice. Even decades later, the men who had agreed upon the three questions could not agree about their implications. Some thought invoking "future dangerousness" evened the playing field between prosecution and defense, or even favored the latter. But there is also evidence that the future dangerousness question was meant to be answered "no" only on rare occasions, in order to carve out the few "exceptions" that Meier had in mind, to spare especially sympathetic murderers. *The Houston Post* reported that the committee members "hoped such a system would permit such a small degree of jury discretion that the Court would uphold its legality."

"I'm not sure we did that great a job," one of the legislators present said decades later. But time had run out. The committee finished drafting the bill's language on Monday morning, the final day of the session, and presented it to the House and Senate. Some of their colleagues were openly unimpressed, pointing out that two questions asked of juries—Was the murder deliberate? Was it unprovoked?—were redundant, because the narrow definition of murder used by the courts generally assumed positive answers to both. The new law was also unrecognizable, appearing to have little to do with the two proposals it was meant to combine. To Craig Washington, it was "like the Senate says raspberries are fruit and the House says strawberries are fruit, and then this committee says apricots are fruit."

Washington gave one more speech. With nothing to lose, he invoked race directly: "Show me in this bill how all people will be treated equally. Show me how I can tell . . . that the color of a man's skin will not have a consideration of whether he's executed under this law."

Despite his protests, the law was voted through—114–30 in the House, 27–4 in the Senate—and signed by the governor. Whether it would survive was now in the hands of the Supreme Court, and nobody knew what the justices really wanted.

The justices didn't know, either.

2

THE TOWN OF CUERO, HALFWAY BETWEEN SAN ANTONIO AND THE Gulf Coast, was small enough that a child's disappearance would be noticed quickly. In August 1973, a little after dusk, the grandmother of ten-year-old Wendy Adams arrived to pick her up at the pool in the town park. Her clothes were in her locker, as was some art she'd made during a 4-H event earlier that day. "The child was obedient," her grandmother later recalled, "and I knew that if she had changed her plans she would have called me." She alerted the woman behind the park concession stand, who happened to be the wife of the local police chief. A search began.

Witnesses told police they had seen Adams in the back of a pickup truck, speeding down the road, screaming for help as her long blond hair billowed in the wind. The truck's distinctive homemade paint job—dark blue with a creamy white top—connected it to the Jureks, a white family whose men worked at the local cotton mill. A group of adolescent girls came forward to say twenty-two-year-old Jerry Jurek and his friends had tried to chase them down in the truck earlier that day. At 1:15 A.M., the police picked up Jurek at his parents' house and brought him, shoeless and shirtless, to the local jail. One of the arresting officers was Ronnie Adams, the father of the missing girl.

Jurek, who had recently lost his job at the mill, said he didn't know anything about the disappearance, and he was booked into a cell at 2:30 A.M. A few hours later, he agreed to a polygraph, but there wasn't a machine in town, so the officers drove him 120 miles north to Austin, where he confessed to killing Adams.

Based on his account, sheriff's deputies were able to find her body, floating facedown near the Hell's Gate Bridge. They pulled her into a muddy boat and covered her with a raincoat.

That night, twenty-four hours after Jurek was arrested, he gave a written confession, which was typed up by the district attorney, Wiley Cheatham. Jurek said he'd been drinking with friends. Afterward, he drove to the pool, where he found Adams and invited her to go "riding around" with him. She "crawled into the back of the pick up truck" and he drove her to a bridge near the river. "We sat on the side of the truck and talked," read the confession. "Wendy was still dressed in her bathing suit that she'd had on when we left the park. Wendy told me that I shouldn't be drinking, and that I was just like my brother who drinks a lot; and she also told me that my nieces didn't have a good father because he didn't come home to see them much. I got mad at her and jerked her off the truck and grabbed Wendy around her throat and choked her to death; she tried to talk to me to get me to stop but I wouldn't listen; she was crying when I was choking her; several times while I was choking her she tried to tell me to stop but I was mad and just wouldn't listen to her. Finally she collapsed and fell to the ground. . . . I then picked her up and throwed [sic] her into the river."

Jurek was taken to the jail in Victoria, a half-hour drive from Cuero, so he would not be near the victim's father, who as a police officer regularly entered the local jail. Prosecutors remained suspicious about whether Jurek was telling them the whole truth, and back in Cuero, they continued to press him. At 7:30 P.M., he gave a second confession. "I did not tell the truth about the conversation I had with Wendy at the river . . . and I now herein wish to correct that statement," he said in the new statement. "I asked her if she had ever had sex before and she said yes. I asked her if she wanted to have sex with me but she said no and started screaming and yelled 'help' and 'please don't kill me.' So I started choking her."

Jurek was charged with "murder in the course of kidnapping and attempted rape." A judge appointed two attorneys to represent him: George Middaugh, a part-time lawyer who also ran a lumber mill, and Emmett Summers III, who had finished law school three months before the murder. Summers had grown up with Jurek's older brother and knew the Adams family, too. The more experienced attorneys in town didn't want to be associated with such a horrible crime, he recalled years later, but "a young guy like me could get away with it." Middaugh "was certainly not a criminal law expert, but it was not like anyone else was beating down the door to do it."

At the five-day trial, Jurek's lawyers tried repeatedly to cast suspicion on the two confessions, the first of which had been made after he had spent a night "virtually naked in this cold jail cell." Jurek had scored 66 on the verbal portion of an IQ test, indicating a mental disability, and he had repeated three grades before dropping out of school at age sixteen. And yet the first confession put strangely mature words in the mouth of a ten-year-old, and the second confession—made more than forty hours after his arrest—used words like "herein" and "my prior statement." The pathologist who examined Adams's body found evidence of strangulation, but not of rape.

As the defense lawyers saw it, Jurek had no obvious motive to give a second confession, but the prosecutors did have a motive to get one. Shortly before the crime, Middaugh told the jury, the state legislature had created a new death penalty law that required a second crime along with murder, like rape or kidnapping. The second confession implied rape and also removed the mention of the victim climbing into the truck by choice, implying that Jurek had kidnapped her. Middaugh suggested that the prosecutors knew this and had been lying in bed after getting the first confession and "it dawns on them all at once": "Oh my god. The law's been changed and we don't have this boy accused of kidnapping anybody or raping anybody and we can't get the death penalty."

None of this was enough to sway the jury, which found Jurek guilty of murder "in the course of committing or attempting to commit kidnapping and/or forcible rape." (They didn't need to specify which.) The trial then moved into its second phase, in which the jury would have to decide whether there was a "probability" that Jurek would commit more violent crimes. The district attorney brought up a handful of community members who said Jurek had a "bad" reputation. He'd been accused in the past, though not convicted, of sexually assaulting several other children. A psychiatrist who had met with Jurek described him as "sociopathic, exhibiting a number of antisocial traits." Jurek's father testified that his son had worked—pumping gas, and on oil and construction crews—and gave most of his paycheck to support the family. Neither side presented an especially rich picture, and the jury sided with the prosecution, sending Jurek to death row.

Not long after the trial, Middaugh was disbarred (he had unethically represented both sides in a real estate transaction). So it fell to Summers—still less than a year out of law school—to prepare Jurek's appeal. He knew he could not responsibly do this alone, so he looked for help and found the LDF, which was offering assistance to any lawyer with a death row client, regardless of that client's race. Because Jurek's death sentence was one of the first from Texas to reach the courts on appeal, it was becoming a test case for the new law. The Texas law as a whole, rather than the details of Jurek's case in particular, became the focal point of his defense, folded into the LDF's larger national strategy.

Anthony Amsterdam, fresh off his victory in the *Furman* case, was in charge, but the state laws and test cases were divvied up among the lawyers under him. Jurek's case and the Texas law went to Peggy Davis.

She had little in common with her new client. Davis came from a middle-class black family and had lived in Ohio and Virginia. She'd studied philosophy at a small women's college and considered careers in jazz singing and psychology before attending Harvard Law School and moving to New York City, where she studied psychoanalysis and worked in corporate law. In 1973, she jumped at the opportunity to work at the LDF under Amsterdam, who was one of her personal heroes.

When she arrived, there was still a sense of victory in the air over the *Furman* decision, but her new boss was working as hard as ever, knowing there was a risk the Supreme Court might uphold some of the new death penalty laws. Under his guidance, Davis began studying the Texas law. It was obvious to everyone at the LDF that the question about "future dangerousness" was unique; almost every other state had fully committed to a mandatory law or one that gave the jury discretion to consider aggravating or mitigating factors. Because she'd studied psychology, Davis knew there was a whole academic literature on predicting who would commit crimes, and the consensus was that it couldn't be done. She also suspected that a phrase like "continuing threat to society," as written in the Texas jury instructions, would inevitably lead prosecutors and juries to tag black defendants as more deserving of death than white ones, since they were often perceived, consciously or not, to be more dangerous.

Davis studied the transcript of Jurek's trial, which showed he had been sentenced to death based on hearsay about his reputation, rather than actual facts about his life. Before the case reached her, it had climbed through the courts, and some judges had expressed misgivings about the vagueness of the future-dangerousness question, with its mention of "probability." "We may say there is a twenty percent probability that it will rain tomorrow, or a ten or five percent probability," one judge wrote. Did such small probabilities count? The legislature had never addressed this. And although Jurek's parents had both testified that he was a good son and worker, the Texas law gave the jury little opportunity to consider their testimony as a reason to spare his life. Other states allowed juries to weigh "mitigating factors" against a death sentence, but Jurek's jury simply had to answer three questions.

In the spring of 1975, while Jurek's case was traveling through the appeals courts, the Supreme Court heard the case of Jesse Fowler, a black man who had shot another man after a fight over a dice game in North Carolina. The public backlash to the Court's striking down of the death penalty had created tremendous pressure on the justices to allow the punishment to return—both presidential candidates, Gerald Ford and Jimmy Carter, supported such a move—and Fowler's case would be a crucial indicator of how they would respond to the new laws.

North Carolina had enacted the kind of law that Texas had narrowly scrapped, deciding the death penalty would be mandatory for any first-degree murder. Anthony Amsterdam returned to the Court, now arguing on Fowler's behalf. It would have been natural for him to attack the law as too rigid, too harsh, and explain how the law robbed jurors of the ability to show mercy, to consider whether the murderer really deserved to die.

But Amsterdam did the opposite.

North Carolina's law, he said, actually involved too much discretion. Prosecutors were still choosing whom they would charge with first-degree murder, he explained, and if jurors didn't want to sentence someone to death, they could convict them of a lesser crime like manslaughter. North Carolina's governor had the power to commute death sentences and could choose to spare whichever death row prisoners they wanted, for whatever reasons they wanted. With so much human decision-making baked into the process, the outcomes for defendants would be just as random, just as much like a lightning strike, as they had been under the old laws. "Whether you get sentenced to death is a luck of the draw, at best," Amsterdam said, "and invidious discrimination at worse."

That was the most directly he ever touched on race, but it turned out he didn't need to say more: After Amsterdam finished, North Carolina's assistant attorney general Jean Benoy got up to defend the law, explaining that the state constrained the decisions of its prosecutors far more than Amsterdam suggested. Sure, an individual prosecutor or judge or even the governor might violate the law by discriminating based on race, but that did not invalidate the whole system.

Justice Thurgood Marshall, the nation's first black justice, wouldn't let this pass. "What's the percentage of Negroes in North Carolina?" he asked.

"I believe it's about . . . twenty or thirty percent of the population."

"And what's the percentage on death row?"

"It's about fifty-fifty, as I understand it."

"It gives you no problem?"

"No, sir. It doesn't give me a bit of a problem, Your Honor. There are things far more important in the State of North Carolina—"

"Than race . . ."

"Than the race of a man who kills and rapes."

Marshall kept at her. "How many Negroes do you have on your judicial system?" he asked.

"I believe there—I don't know if the last Negress, there was a Negro woman who was a judge."

"A neg-what?"

"A Negress, a Negro woman who was a judge in Guilford County . . ."

"You still use the phrase 'Negress'?"

"Well, Your Honor, I'm a Caucasian, and I see nothing wrong with using the word 'Negro,' that's the name of a race of people."

Marshall had made his point and let the subject go. It was lucky for Benoy that she was not the only person defending the North Carolina law that day. She was joined by Solicitor General Robert Bork. Deep-voiced and jowly, Bork was a widely respected legal scholar. He had famously been tapped by Nixon, a year and a half earlier, to step in and fire the special prosecutor investigating the Watergate break-in, in an event known as the Saturday Night Massacre. Years later, during his own confirmation hearings for a spot on this Court, his conservative views would be tagged as too extreme, but for now he was a powerful spokesman for the death penalty, which enjoyed widespread public support. He had submitted a "friend of the court" brief in support of the new laws, and the justices invited him to deliver an argument against Amsterdam.

Stepping up to the lectern, Bork immediately undermined Amsterdam's central point about human decision-making by noting that the criminal justice system "breathes discretion at every pore." In every case, not just those involving capital punishment, you needed to give jurors and prosecutors choices, because that's how you created opportunities for them to be merciful. "The discretion which is in the system is not the defect of the system," he declared. "It is indeed the genius of the system."

Amsterdam, when he returned for rebuttal, responded that "when you regard something as a genius or a defect depends on whether you're standing at the long end of the stick or the short end of the stick." Giving people the choice to be merciful sounded good until they chose not to be merciful to you. Still, he needed a way to argue that he was not condemning the workings of the criminal justice system as a whole. His solution was simple, even elegant. He captured it in three words: "Death is different." You could give average citizens, whatever their biases, the ability to send people to prison, but if you were going to give them power over life and death, you needed to exercise more over-sight.

This argument turned out to be a prelude. The Court put off ruling because of Justice William O. Douglas, who had suffered a stroke shortly before the arguments. He was becoming mentally erratic, his eyes glassy and his speech slurred, and the other justices, who were deadlocked 4–4, did not feel comfortable giving him the deciding vote. In the meantime, they ordered Court staff to gather the full list of death penalty cases that had made their way up from the states. In the next session, they would tackle the subject directly.

The justices decided to hear five cases that would allow them to rule on the full range of laws that states had passed in the wake of *Furman*. Their selection mirrored the central tension in the Texas legislature: Should the death penalty be mandatory, or should juries and judges be given guidance in their decisions through lists of aggravating and mit-igating factors? They picked cases from North Carolina and Louisiana, which had opted for mandatory laws, and Florida and Georgia, which allowed jurors to weigh different factors and make a choice for them-selves. The Texas law, with its three questions, was a unique compro-mise between these approaches—the Court's staff lawyer called it "quasi-mandatory," while one clerk thought it left a lot of room for jury choice—and the justices added it to the list.

Oral argument for the five cases was scheduled over two days in March 1976. (By this time, Justice Douglas had retired, and Justice John Paul Stevens had joined the Court.) Each case involved a lawyer, often Anthony Amsterdam, representing a defendant, and a state attorney general defending the state law. Robert Bork was invited to present separately on behalf of the federal government. Complicated as the agenda appeared, it would again boil down to an intellectual showdown between two lawyers at the peak of their influence.

Many of the justices' clerks were convinced Amsterdam would lose—surely the Court would uphold at least one of the new laws. At the LDF, Peggy Davis was discouraged by how strongly Americans seemed to support the punishment. "Maybe (I doubt it, but maybe) the public can be convinced the death penalty is a bad thing," she wrote in a letter to the ACLU, "but they cannot be convinced in the next four months." But there was plenty of room for a partial victory: The Court might keep one law while striking down others, letting the death penalty return but severely restricting its use. Amsterdam himself was optimistic that the LDF could get the Court to strike down all five laws, effectively shutting down the death penalty in the United States forever. "We were sure if the Supreme Court had any balls we would win," he told the scholar Evan Mandery years later. (He was a saltier talker outside the courtroom.) "Even after our exposure to the reality that shit happens, we had some hope."

Amsterdam planned to continue down the path he had begun in the Fowler case, arguing that every single one of the new laws involved too much human decision-making, and that as a result executions would remain arbitrary. This would give the justices an easy intellectual route toward a sweeping decision against all of the laws.

It was also risky. If the justices didn't buy Amsterdam's reasoning, he could lose everything. A safer option might be to focus on the laws in North Carolina and Louisiana, which made the death penalty mandatory for certain crimes. One of Amsterdam's assistants thought this would be a good move, since the Georgia and Florida laws, with their lists of aggravating and mitigating circumstances, were novel and might sway the justices no matter what Amsterdam said.

But if Amsterdam attacked only the mandatory laws, he would risk making matters worse for other death row prisoners. Jurek's case illustrated the problem clearly. If Jurek had his own lawyer, who was looking only to save his life, the best argument may well have been that the Texas law was practically mandatory—that the three questions would almost always be answered the same way—and that the jury who sentenced Jurek had therefore never been given a robust opportunity to weigh whether, given his mental limitations, perhaps he deserved mercy. But if Amsterdam made this argument, he would be tacitly approving the laws in Florida and Georgia, imperiling people who had been sentenced in those states. Representing everyone on death row meant taking an all-or-nothing approach.

Might this mean that one lawyer shouldn't be representing five defendants with five different sets of interests and potential legal strategies? There is no evidence that Amsterdam and his colleagues ever considered this question.

Jerry Jurek, living in a prison cell sixteen hundred miles from the LDF office, could hardly have known he was at the center of this conundrum. Peggy Davis, though she was responsible for his case at the LDF, was unable to visit him. "There were conversations about whether you attack the death penalty overall, or whether you attack just the case and do what's best for Jerry," his local lawyer recalled. "Jerry would not have been able to participate in the conversation." He could barely spell the names of his own family members.

As Amsterdam set his strategy for the argument, he relied on Davis, along with David Kendall, who had been a clerk at the Supreme Court before joining the LDF. They rehearsed arguments, Amsterdam smoking a cigar and working out how to make himself appear reasonable to the justices. He agreed with Davis and Kendall that he needed to grant that the death penalty could be legal for certain rare crimes that elicited public outrage, like airplane hijackings and political assassinations. He would concede what they called the "exotics."

Still, Amsterdam did not let the younger lawyers seriously challenge his plans. Not that they would have. "I didn't feel like I could disagree with Tony," Davis later said. "He was a phenomenon."

On the day oral arguments began, in March 1976, dark rain clouds veiled the Supreme Court building. *Jerry Lane Jurek v. Texas* was argued first, but Amsterdam's opening was not about Jurek or Texas: He began with an overview of the new capital punishment laws across the country and said that for all of their superficial differences, in every state, prosecutors, jurors, judges, and governors were still exercising too many human, and therefore possibly arbitrary, decisions about who would be executed and who would be granted mercy.

One justice wrote a note to himself: "Amsterdam doesn't like these 'elaborate' opportunities for mercy." Another asked Amsterdam if he thought a death sentence to be cruel and unusual no matter how serious the crime and no matter how fair the trial. Amsterdam said yes.

Now the chief justice, Warren Burger, stepped in, rephrasing the question: Could *no* law actually save the death penalty? He was giving Amsterdam an opening to concede the exotics, to say it might be all right to execute airplane hijackers and presidential assassins. It was a chance for him to look like a compromiser.

He didn't take it, again describing how all five laws featured some human decision-making and would thus create arbitrary outcomes. As an example, he brought up the future-dangerousness question in Texas. "The thing that is most devastating is that you can't even challenge the jury's finding because the question to which it responds is so meaningless," Amsterdam said, noting that Jurek had been sentenced to die on the testimony of a few community members who just didn't seem to like him. Justice Lewis Powell, Jr., wrote down that he found Amsterdam's views on the Texas law "fairly persuasive." But as the argument continued and Amsterdam continued to talk abstractly about all the laws, Powell added to his notes, Amsterdam is "not interested in the fairness of procedure in a particular case." He also wrote down that Amsterdam didn't "believe" in the "right of legislatures in [democratic] society" to make a "moral judgment" about capital punishment.

Before Amsterdam's opening argument ended, he was confronted with the slippery slope his argument might be inviting: A justice noted that human decision-making existed throughout the criminal justice system, not just in death penalty cases. Was Amsterdam saying the whole system violated the constitution?

"No," Amsterdam said.

"And why not?"

"Our argument is essentially that death is different," Amsterdam said, laying it all on the line: "If you don't accept the view that for constitutional purposes death is different, we lose this case; let me make that very clear. Death is factually different, death is final, death is irremediable. . . . It goes beyond this world. It is a legislative decision to do something and we know not what we do."

After this subtle reference to Jesus's statement of forgiveness on the cross, Amsterdam stepped down and was followed by John Hill, the attorney general of Texas. Hill was a former plaintiff's attorney with a lispy twang and a love for courtroom battle.

Hill pounded Amsterdam as an extremist who was trying to foist his personal opposition to capital punishment on the American people. He later wrote of this moment, "My trial lawyer instincts pushed me toward reduction of the complexities, to simplify an audience's job, and toward hyperbole, to implant a vivid image of my argument that would upstage Amsterdam's performance in my listeners' memories when they later formulated their ruling. . . . They were going to hear a jury speech."

Amsterdam "stands utterly alone," Hill said. "The theory seems to be, let *me* say what this case is about, let *me* say what the Texas case is about and what the facts are, and let *me* say where we draw the line, let *me* determine what offenses should come within the purview of capital punishment in this country, let *me* decide what constitutes proper social goals, let *me* decide where retribution is possible and proper and where it isn't."

To show that the Texas law and its three questions were fair, and that Texas juries were careful in deciding who deserved to live and who should die, Hill relied on statistics. Among sixty reported cases in which juries had been asked the three questions, fifteen juries had answered no to at least one. He brought up the case of a young black man who had killed a white police officer. The jury thought this man would not present a "continuing threat to society" and spared him the death penalty. "There is no evidence that, once our system begins, there is racial discrimination," Hill said.

As for Jurek himself, who was white, Hill reminded the justices that this man had taken Wendy Adams to a bridge, "got her out of the truck, undertook to have sex with her, choked her until she fell into unconsciousness and threw her in the river and left her there to die" and then "went back with his friends and his beer with no remorse."

"Strong jury speech!" Powell wrote in his notes. Hill would have taken this as a compliment, but it wasn't meant as one. The justices didn't like hearing emotional descriptions of the crimes; they wanted intellectual parsing of the law.

They got it the next day, when Robert Bork stood before the justices. He jumped on the weakest part of Amsterdam's argument: By saying that human decisions were a problem, he explained, Amsterdam was actually implying the solution would be a law that totally removes human decisions, that is "so rigid and automatic and insensitive that it would be morally reprehensible." Then Bork made his most sweeping argument—that the death penalty was a sign of a healthy democracy at work: "These five cases are about democratic government, the right of various legislatures of the United States to choose or reject— according to their own moral sense and that of their people—the death penalty."

Amsterdam had one more opportunity to speak directly to the judges. He was called up later that day on behalf of James Woodson, who had been sentenced to death under North Carolina's mandatory law. Again, Amsterdam had a chance to go after the law for being severe and rigid. And again, he didn't take it.

Turning to the new federal death penalty law, which focused on the rare crime of airplane hijacking, Powell asked, "Can you conceive of any crime to which you would consider the death penalty an appropriate response by society?"

Amsterdam could have made concessions, saying one law was slightly preferable to another. But that would mean throwing some potential future defendant under the bus. He couldn't do it.

"No," he said.

"Let me put a case to you," Powell said. "You read about Buchenwald, one of the camps in Germany in which thousands of Jewish citizens were exterminated. . . . If we had had jurisdiction over the commandant of Buchenwald, would you have thought capital punishment was an appropriate response to what that man or woman was responsible for?"

Powell had recoiled at the emotionally charged description of a murder by the attorney general from Texas, but now he was bringing up, unprompted, one of the worst atrocities in human history. Amsterdam, who is Jewish, responded, "We have an instinctive reaction that says 'Kill him,'" but "at this point in time my answer would be no."

Amsterdam might better have acknowledged the belief in evil held by many Americans, but Powell was also letting emotions get the best of him. In the Supreme Court, just as in the Texas Legislature, the death penalty had a way of hardening positions and destroying good faith. "So if some fanatic set off a hydrogen bomb and destroyed New York City," Powell said, "still you think the appropriate remedy for that would be to put him in prison, perhaps out on parole in seven years?"

Amsterdam now attempted to calm down the conversation. "It seems to me we are getting constitutional and normative questions mixed up," he said, suggesting they had moved from the question of what the Constitution said to how Powell wanted to interpret it. Powell then gave Amsterdam one more chance to make a concession: "Well let's assume for the moment that someone, somewhere, had to choose among the five [laws]," Powell said. "Which . . . would be most likely to minimize the elements of discretion and arbitrariness that are so offensive to you?"

"None of them is close enough so that I can give a meaningful answer," Amsterdam said.

Forty years later, pondering the what-might-have-beens with the historian Evan Mandery, Amsterdam would note that there may have been some value in changing course completely and trying to turn the justices against one law in particular, the law that pretended to give juries a choice but restricted that choice so much that it was practically mandatory—the one from Texas.

.   .   .

"Now I know what it's like to hear Jesus Christ," William Brennan fumed to his clerks once he returned to his chambers. Brennan was one of the Court's most liberal justices, and he hated the death penalty, but he was angry at Amsterdam for giving up so many opportunities to appear pragmatic.

When the justices gathered two days later, Brennan told his colleagues he'd vote to strike down all five laws and keep the death penalty from returning. Thurgood Marshall agreed. At the other extreme were four justices whose support for the death penalty was firm and who wanted to uphold all the laws: Chief Justice Burger, along with Justices Byron White, Harry Blackmun, and William Rehnquist.

That left three whose votes were still in question: John Paul Stevens, Lewis Powell, and Potter Stewart. They were all willing to accept the Georgia and Florida laws but were troubled by the "mandatory" laws in North Carolina and Louisiana. Powell said to his colleagues that executions should be public, since only then would legislators in these states realize just how many people they had chosen to condemn to death, and how bloody the results of full implementation would be.

Texas, with its three questions and talk of future dangerousness, fell awkwardly between the two approaches. Stevens called the mandatory laws a "lawless use of the legal system." The North Carolina law, in particular, was a "monster" (it featured a broader definition of "first-degree murder" than the Louisiana law). Afterward he told his colleagues he'd originally seen the Texas law the same way, but he had come to feel it was acceptable because jurors would still have a separate discussion about punishment, however constricted. Powell also approved of the Texas law. Stewart said he was "not at rest as to its validity" and declined to cast an official vote, but it did not matter—Texas now had six justices (Blackmun, Burger, White, Rehnquist, Powell, and Stevens). Powell, despite his ambivalence, voted for the Louisiana law.

So every state law had a majority except the one in North Carolina, which had a tie of four to four (with Blackmun abstaining). Chief Justice Burger picked Byron White to write the opinions.

But all was not settled; Powell was having second thoughts. He was listening to one of his law clerks, Christina Whitman, who felt it was necessary to preserve an element of mercy in the system and that both the Louisiana and Texas laws, like the one in North Carolina, restricted that mercy too much. She had long thought the Texas law was effectively a "mandatory" death penalty.

Powell was an establishment figure from Virginia whose quiet demeanor obscured his leadership abilities. Years earlier, in his fraternity, a pattern had emerged, which his biographer later summed up: "Wait until everyone else has spoken, incorporate their views, then propose a decision." Now, with multiple justices unsure of their views, there was room for someone to take over the process and shape a final compromise.

But Powell was also cautious. He had voted to uphold the death penalty in *Furman*, believing it was obvious that the Constitution allowed the punishment. The Fourteenth Amendment said the government could not deprive you of life without due process of law, which implied that it could still deprive you of life. But during his four years on the Court, Powell had come to see more nuance on the issue. The year before he'd joined the Court, his peers had ruled in *McGautha v. California* that states did not need to give juries "standards" for deciding who should be sentenced to death. The debate over how to square that with *Furman*, which did seem to demand standards, had produced some of the more complex moments of the oral arguments. There was no clear path here.

And perhaps there never could be. The justices seemed to want to let juries make individual decisions about each defendant while also ensuring their decisions, in aggregate, were not arbitrary—a tension that was unresolved then and remains so today. Most Americans are familiar with the idea that "the punishment must fit the crime," suggesting that two different people who commit the same crime must suffer the same consequences. Many Americans also believe in mercy—that judges and juries should be able to show leniency based on what they learn about the individual person before them. But how should we respond when their decisions fall along lines of race and gender and class that trouble us? In Mandery's elegant formulation, "a person cannot be both unique and equal."

Given how much Amsterdam had focused on race four years earlier, telling the justices in the *Furman* case that "Georgia executes black people," it was notable that he said little on the subject this time around. Such arguments had not found much traction at the Court in the past, and besides, Jurek himself was white. At the same time, because Amsterdam said so little, Bork was able to say, virtually unchallenged, "Capital punishment has not been shown to be inflicted on the basis of race." In the end, race would play almost no role in the justices' deliberations about whether to bring back the death penalty.

Powell, Stewart, and Stevens had lunch at the Monocle, a restaurant near the Supreme Court building. As they ate, they worked out their differences and devised a plan: All three would oppose the Louisiana law and uphold the Texas one. Afterward, they informed their colleagues that the votes had changed, and took over the assignment to write the opinions. (White, who until then had been working on them, was furious.)

On a Friday morning in July, the Court announced that the death penalty would return, upholding the laws in Florida, Georgia, and Texas and striking down those in Louisiana and North Carolina. The overall message was that juries should be allowed to choose whether a specific person should receive the death penalty, considering the particulars of the crime (Did the defendant seem especially cruel while committing it? Did he show remorse right away?) and of the defendant (What was his childhood like? Had he struggled with poverty or addiction or mental illness?). Defendants should be treated, in Stewart's words, as "uniquely individual human beings." In an early draft of the decision striking down the mandatory law in North Carolina, Stewart wrote that jurors should be able to consider "the frailty of human actors," but he cut the phrase and replaced it with something a bit more poetic and sweeping: "the diverse frailties of humankind."

The three justices believed the questions devised by the Texas Legislature would allow the jury to weigh these factors. Ironically, it was

William Rehnquist, a conservative who approved of all the laws, who disagreed. Although he thought the Texas law was constitutional, he also thought his colleagues were fooling themselves by believing the law would really give juries the opportunity to consider the "diverse frailties of humankind" and spare some people from the death penalty. The Texas law, he thought, was going to turn out to be just as unwavering as the "mandatory" laws his colleagues had voted to strike down.

The final majority opinion, upholding the new laws from Texas, Georgia, and Florida, described the death penalty as "an expression of society's moral outrage at particularly offensive conduct." The justices pointed out that murders were on the rise, and they gestured at a vision of the frontier: "The instinct for retribution is part of the nature of man, and channeling that instinct in the administration of criminal justice serves an important purpose in promoting the stability of a society governed by law. When people begin to believe that organized society is unwilling or unable to impose upon criminal offenders the punishment they 'deserve,' then there are sown the seeds of anarchy—of self-help, vigilante justice, and lynch law."

The announcement of the death penalty's return was made on July 2, 1976, two days before the United States of America was due to celebrate its two hundredth birthday. Marshall and Brennan dissented from the bench, Brennan raising the ghosts of slavery: "The fatal constitutional infirmity in the punishment of death is that it treats 'members of the human race as nonhumans, as objects to be toyed with and discarded.'" Shortly after the announcement, while delivering a speech to a group of lawyers, Brennan gave up in the middle and sat down without finishing. Over the following week, Marshall's physical health took a turn, as he suffered multiple heart attacks.

But these two had no regrets about their own opinions; what of the crucial three justices? As Stewart publicly read the opinions, paving the way for executions to begin, his voice cracked and his hands trembled. Powell had tried to find a way to make the new decision apply only to future cases, seemingly concerned that he had just consigned hundreds of men on death row to their executions, but he couldn't find constitutional backing for the idea. Stevens's reckoning would not take full form until three and a half decades later, when, in an interview, he brought it up without prompting: "I think upon reflection, we should have held the Texas statute . . . to fit under the mandatory category and be unconstitutional," he said. "In my judgment we made a mistake on that case." He said it was the only decision of his entire career that he regretted.

Later scholars were rough on Amsterdam, calling his legal strategy "a cautionary tale about cause lawyering" and his attitude "tone deaf to the changing tune of the country." But he had no time to look backward. He began writing a guide for lawyers on how to attack the individual death sentences that were sure to begin flooding the courts. At the same time, he wrote up a request for the Supreme Court to reconsider its decisions. Such "petitions for rehearing" are seldom granted, but it was one more opportunity to argue that the Texas law was mandatory—and thus should have been struck down along with those of North Carolina and Louisiana—and that Jerry Jurek had not been given a robust opportunity to present a case to spare his life.

Peggy Davis pushed her boss to take this route. She had not slept well in the days after the decision. "Over and over again, during the last week I have thought: What kind of rehearing petition would I write if I represented only Jerry Lane Jurek?" she wrote to Amsterdam in a memo. "And every time I think about that I am troubled because I think that a much stronger attack on the Texas statute could be made." She thought the Texas law was "unconscionably mandatory" and would not allow a jury to consider the "diverse frailties of humankind" mentioned by the Court. Amsterdam did write in his petition that the Texas law was "Draconian" and "forbids the consideration of any but the narrowest factors of mitigation," but he declined her suggestion to fully separate the Jurek case from the others.

Gary Gilmore faced the firing squad in Utah in 1977, after having given up his appeals, and then John Spenkelink sat in the electric chair in Florida in 1979, the first person to be executed after submitting all the appeals to which he was entitled. In 1982, Charlie Brooks became the first killed in Texas, by lethal injection, and then the numbers swelled—five in 1983, twenty-one in 1984—and the individual names and crimes became a blur to all but close observers.

But Peggy Davis did not need to worry: Jerry Jurek survived. Even after Davis left the LDF, in 1977, the organization kept fighting his case. A couple of years later, the Fifth Circuit Court of Appeals agreed that he should have been appointed a lawyer after his arrest, that his two confessions were "involuntary," and that his words did not sound like his own. "A person like Jurek, whose verbal intelligence is limited, is less likely to be able to understand his right to remain silent," the judges explained. "The statements used against Jurek were apparently not his own words. They are written in complete sentences, mostly grammatical, with even a touch of legalese."

His death sentence was thrown out, and the same year that lethal injections began, in 1982, Jurek pleaded guilty in exchange for a life sentence. Though his name was attached to one of the most significant moments in the country's legal history, Jerry Jurek himself faded into the growing wave of American incarceration, one of thousands of men marking days, sleeping and eating and working on former slave plantation land. As his hair turned gray and wispy, he continued to slick it back into the style of his youth. He worked in a prison kitchen—avoiding the dayroom because the televisions and loud fans and shouting prisoners stressed him out—talked to his cellmate, and wrote letters with doodles of cartoon dogs along the bottom of the page. He spoke with a clipped, wised-up drawl, though his mind had departed significantly from reality. "Mine is the [case] that got everyone off death row," he recalled incorrectly in 2015. He maintained that he was totally innocent of killing Wendy Adams, and that he had been the victim of a conspiracy between his lawyers and local authorities. He said there is a missing document that will prove it, if only someone will go find it in a town called Eldorado. "If everything goes right," he said, "I might be out of here pretty soon."

Every so often, Jurek would come up for parole, and Brandi Adams

Garza, his victim's little sister, would write a letter to the parole board describing the toll the murder took on her family; her father quit his job as a police officer, and her mother suffered a mental breakdown. "I think that the death penalty was appropriate to start with and, had it been followed through with," Garza told a reporter, "it would have eliminated a lot of stress on my dad, my family, myself, my brother."

As the death penalty system ground into motion in the late 1970s, the LDF realized its work was only beginning. Every case would now be a smaller battle in a bigger war of attrition. Hundreds of men and women sentenced to death would need lawyers to attack those sentences one by one—arguing the finer points of how a jury had been selected, or how evidence had been gathered—and stave off execution. Sometimes their cases would end up back at the Supreme Court, which would be tasked with deciding not whether the death penalty as a whole was constitutional, but rather whether one element of a trial or police investigation had violated a defendant's rights. The Supreme Court would go on to rule in ways big and small that both helped and hurt death row prisoners, but the overall effect would be to further entrench the punishment.

In a death penalty system so bound up with the courts, there would be a lot of relationships like the one between Peggy Davis and Jerry Jurek. Often the racial dynamic would be flipped, with white lawyers and black clients. Almost always the lawyers would come from far more privilege. The lawyers would develop arguments and study arcane legal precedents while their clients sat in death row cells for years and years, waiting for the day they'd lose their case and their lives. And what haunted Peggy Davis would haunt the many lawyers who would come after her. They would wonder, as she had wondered: What else could be done?

3

WHEN DANALYNN RECER TELLS THE STORY OF HER LIFE—OR AT
least of her career, though she seldom makes much of a distinction—
she begins with a phone call. At the time, she was an extremely busy
twentysomething, working on both a law degree and a master's in history at the University of Texas at Austin. Some lawyers called the history department and invited her to an office with an oddly vague name:
the Texas Resource Center. They represented men on death row, and
the name served to camouflage such unpopular work.

One of their clients was black and had been sentenced to death for
shooting a white man, by an all-white jury, in a county where black
men had once been victims of lynching. That last part would not have
surprised Recer, since she was writing her master's thesis on lynchings
in Texas. The surprise was that these lawyers thought her research on
the past might bolster their modern-day legal claims. She printed out
some of her findings on zigzagging dot matrix pages and made her way
to an old house downtown, not far from the capitol building.

It was a homey warren of little offices, with a big white dry-erase
board displaying a calendar of upcoming execution dates. Everywhere
you looked, banker's boxes full of court records were stacked high,
overflowing with trial transcripts, police reports, and other documents.

Scrawled across the sides of the boxes were the names of death row prisoners. When one received an execution date, the center would try to find him a lawyer, but if they couldn't, they would jump in themselves. Amid the boxes, young lawyers raced around, speed-reading transcripts, debating which legal claims to make, sending faxes, and fielding calls from colleagues conducting investigations around the state. The lawyers were interested in Recer's research, but their conversation was cut short: There was a deadline in some other case and they needed to get a document to a FedEx office. Since she had nowhere to be, Recer offered to take it. Many years later, Recer would pluck this story out of many others and hold it out as pivotal, explaining, "I still haven't come back from that run to FedEx. I ran away with the circus."

At the time, she had two clear professional paths: continue her master's research in a Ph.D. program, or take the bar exam and practice law. It was a stark choice between analyzing the world and trying to change it directly. She had long displayed an impulse toward the latter. Her father, Paul Recer, was a journalist, and he had once covered a civil rights rally in Tulsa during which several African Americans tried to get into a cafeteria and white people tried to keep them out by pushing against the door to keep it shut. He had arrived early, managing to make his way into the cafeteria before the protest started and get material the other reporters couldn't. When he later told the story, his daughter wasn't impressed. "What the hell, Dad?" she said. "You're just sitting there and writing? Why didn't you help?"

In 1979, when Recer was fourteen, her mother died, leaving her father to finish raising her and her younger sister. Soon after, he was transferred from Houston, where he had spent years covering the space program, to Virginia, to work as a science editor. Recer had just finished her sophomore year, and she was desperate to finish high school quickly and return to her friends back in Texas. So she took some tests and skipped her junior year. As a senior, still in Virginia, she took a job at Hardee's and ended up marrying a co-worker, but they divorced after a few years. In order to move up to a management position at one of her fast food jobs, she started taking night classes in accounting at a community college. Her professor saw a spark. "What the hell are you doing here?" he asked her. In 1984, she enrolled at the University of Texas and moved to Austin.

Like many Southern university towns, Austin was a haven for lefty misfits from conservative high schools throughout the state. The campus was just blocks from the state capitol, making it fertile soil for each generation's activists, as these almost-adults found their peers and voices and causes. Confronting the end of the Reagan era, they struck out in many directions, attacking the university's role in the "military-industrial complex" and investments in apartheid South Africa. They would later remember a young woman, fiercely well-spoken, with a rattail hanging down from the short hair she piled up haphazardly on her head. "The Left is full of all these people who are very rigid, follow so many rules," Recer's friend Carey Hattic recalled. There were the vegans, the boycotters, "and then here is Danalynn, going around with this humongous Super Big Gulp full of Diet Coke. Doesn't give a shit." It was rare to meet someone, amid the earnest crusaders, who could laugh at herself: "Unlike many on the left, she admits to her flaws." Though her friends were impressed by her lack of ego, Recer didn't see herself quite the same way, at least in retrospect: "It's not all altruistic, there is maybe some vanity there. I got to lead organizations because I liked to be a speaker and I had a flair for it."

She rose quickly to the top of the university chapter of the National Organization for Women, where she pressured university administrators to take claims of sexual assault more seriously. But she also tried to bring the group's influence to other causes, like electing a black, openly lesbian student as student body president. "When you're young," Recer recalled, "it feels like all these issues are of one cloth."

But the more you burrow into a political movement, the more you see the cracks within it. By the mid-1980s, feminism was confronting new political dynamics that would test its relationship to other progressive causes. Recer was bothered that the national feminist movement, in its fight against sexual assault, was pushing for longer prison sentences for rape. This put the movement into conflict with racial justice groups, who advocated for a less punitive justice system. To Recer, it felt like women were turning their backs on other oppressed groups and embracing solutions, like prisons, handed to them by men.

Recer started to find answers, or at least new ways of asking questions, in her academic work. One of her first freshman-year classes had been with George C. Wright, a professor of African American history. In high school, history was a numbing series of dates, but Wright taught social history, pushing his students to examine the lived experience of ordinary people. Recer loved it, and she decided to major in African American studies. Often, she was the only white student in her classes.

As she neared graduation, it was clear that she'd spent more time planning how to influence the university and her peers than finding a vocation. She decided to stick around for a master's degree and then perhaps a Ph.D. But there was another part of her that didn't want to end up with a quiet life of research and teaching. She thought about paths to carry her activism past college and decided to enroll in law school, too. It was an ambitious plan, but it was also a way of not having to commit. Some of her friends thought law school was a sellout move, a way of turning into the Man while talking naively about fixing the system from the inside, but Recer told herself she could still be an outsider to power.

In the meantime, Wright hired her as a teaching assistant, and she eventually helped him collect information on lynchings in his native state of Kentucky. She decided to focus her own master's thesis on lynchings in Texas.

In order to gather historical data, Recer traveled to Alabama and rented a hotel room by the week near Tuskegee University, where lynching records had been gathered since the days of Booker T. Washington. She spent days there photocopying and retyping old newspaper articles into the blue screen of a boxy little computer.

In these archives was a Texas far more Deep South than Old West. Lynchings often targeted black men who appeared to challenge the racial hierarchy—refusing to work without pay, trying to form a union, or appearing, at least in a white person's mind, to be acting somehow "uppity"—but the crime that defined lynching, the transgression that tapped something deep in the cultural id of Southern life, was the rape of a white woman by a black man. Only about a quarter of lynchings followed rape accusations, but, as the historian Jacquelyn Dowd Hall wrote, it was the rape narrative that "gripped the southern imagination"—even lynching victims who weren't accused of rape were portrayed in sexual terms. The victims were often described as "lustful black brutes," as "beasts" and "denizens of the underworld." They "ravished" white women. "A new generation of blacks, born in freedom and less willing to act out the etiquette of obsequiousness, seemed to many whites to betoken a society whirling away into the unknown," Dowd Hall wrote. "The ideology of racism reached a virulent crescendo, as the dominant image of blacks in the white mind shifted from inferior child to aggressive and dangerous animal." After the Civil War, many white Americans believed the newly freed would fall back into a precivilized, violent state, and that lynching was necessary to scare them back into subservience.

Lynching was also a way of teaching young white people, and especially young white women, how society was supposed to work. In an era when Northern feminists were demanding suffrage and equal pay, white Southern men needed to justify their power over women, and they did so by portraying themselves as protectors, as the only thing standing between these women and the black men who wanted to victimize them. Recer noticed that the white women appeared to be more than just silently complicit in lynchings; they were actively involved, accusing black men of rape and then watching them be publicly killed. Recer was herself a white woman, confronting the fissuring of the feminist movement around crime, and she came to see that it was not so strange for a white woman to be in an African American history program. Studying lynchings actually involved studying white psychology—or, as she put it, "what the hell is wrong with white people."

She found some answers in a book called *Killers of the Dream* by Lillian Smith, a scathing 1949 memoir and psychological profile of the South. Smith wrote of poor white men who clung to a sense of racial superiority because it "made you forget that you were eaten up with malaria and hookworm; made you forget that you lived in a shanty and ate pot-likker and cornbread, and worked long hours for nothing," and of white women "who have rarely felt esteemed or beloved" and "are suddenly caught up by a vision of themselves as Sacred Womanhood on a Pedestal, as Southern Madonnas, and though in a few hours they will be back totin' slops to the pigpen, milking cows, cooking supper, yet for one miraculously sweet breath of time they are transfigured by this image of themselves and they will never forget it." Smith's analysis implied that the accusations made against black men by white women were not always true. Smith was herself from Florida and spent much of her life running a summer camp in Georgia. In her writing was a model for how a person could look at their own role in an oppressing majority and fight the culture around them. Many white liberals had fled the South, but Smith had stayed.

Recer found that Texas lynchings were especially grotesque—the state led the country in burning victims alive—and she developed a theory about the state having a "siege mentality." She eventually wrote in her thesis that in 1860, while Texans debated whether to secede from the Union, they "felt besieged by enemies on all sides: Mexicans to the south, Comanches to the west, Republicans to the north, and, most alarming, the blacks among them." The result was an "identity forged in fear," a culture that blended "frontier vigilante justice with the ritualized codes of Southern Honor into a uniquely Texan formulaic tradition of the most sadistic and most public lynchings of any state."

This tradition did not target only black Americans: Between 1848 and 1928, at least 282 people of Mexican origin or descent were lynched in Texas. Many were murdered by the Texas Rangers, a law enforcement organization that is still venerated in state myth but has been responsible for numerous atrocities, including the 1918 shooting of fifteen unarmed Mexican men and boys in the village of Porvenir. (The shooting was supposedly in retaliation for cattle raids, though there was no evidence that these villagers had been involved in them.)

Whereas Texas legislators a generation before had ignored Southern racial injustice and embraced a sentimental vision of the frontier, Recer was crafting a theory that fused these two images and cleaned out every scrap of romance.

After researching in Tuskegee, she drove two hours south to a wooden duplex in Headland, a tiny town near the Florida border. Her academic mentor, George Wright, used the term "legal lynchings" to describe officially sanctioned executions that were virtually indistinguishable from the mob killings they were supposed to prevent, and she wanted to learn more about them. She'd received a tip that she could see records in the living room of a man named Major Watt Espy, Jr.

Espy was famously eccentric, working from one in the afternoon to three in the morning most days in his pajamas and keeping the blinds closed because he didn't have air conditioning. He decorated the walls with photos of people who had been executed. The walls were yellow because he chain-smoked, although tilted pictures allowed glimpses of the original white paint. For much of the twentieth century, his house was the unlikely epicenter of death penalty history in America. He'd loved true crime magazines, and during his career as a traveling salesman—of encyclopedias, insurance, and cemetery plots—he made stops at libraries and courthouses, tracking down trial records and newspaper clippings. At one point the University of Alabama briefly gave him a full-time position, but when students were hired to help him computerize his records, he found them sloppy and disrespectful, and he took the files back to the house in Headland. So he wasn't well disposed to this college kid from Texas, who, standing amid the dusty boxes, stacks of magazines, and scampering cockroaches, tried to negotiate access to his collection.

"Let me take these records to Kinko's and copy them," Recer pleaded. "I'll help you digitize them."

That suggestion didn't take, but she did persuade Espy to let her hang around and look at his notecards about Texas executions. For the next two weeks, she appeared each day with a computer and a stack of floppy disks and retyped his information manually.

Her thesis was supposed to be about lynchings performed by mobs, not official executions conducted by state officials, but the more cases she looked at, the more the lines blurred. In case after case, there were vivid stories of local authorities trying to keep an accused man safe from a mob so that he could be killed "properly under the law." But there were also stories of sheriffs "failing" to stop the mob from taking the man anyway. When officials did manage to hold on to the man and give him a trial, the trial itself was hardly an image of measured justice. Among Espy's records, Recer found the story of Dick Garrett, a black preacher accused of a minor crime in Center, Texas, in 1906. While running from law enforcement, Garrett shot a white man. During his trial four days later, a crowd—"so thick it was difficult to move a hand or arm," by one account—gathered in the courthouse square. Children were let out early from school so they could attend. While facing trial inside the courtroom, Garrett could hear hammers and saws outside; on the courthouse lawn, they were already building the scaffold.

After the Supreme Court allowed the death penalty to return, in 1976, Anthony Amsterdam and the NAACP Legal Defense Fund kept trying to keep race in the picture, to show the Court and the public that while white Americans had abandoned chattel slavery and legal segregation, racial injustice still saturated American life. The brutality of the criminal justice system was but one illustration, executions only the most extreme symptom. To them, when President Nixon had spoken of the "first civil right" being freedom from crime and violence, he was speaking in code, and the translation could be heard in a statement attributed to one supporter of Alabama governor George Wallace: "Y'all know about law and order. It's spelled n-i-g-g-e-r-s." Many years later, Nixon aide John Ehrlichman would tell *Harper's* that his boss "had two enemies: the antiwar left and black people. You understand what I'm saying? We knew we couldn't make it illegal to be either against the war or black, but by getting the public to associate the hippies with marijuana and blacks with heroin, and then criminalizing both heavily, we could disrupt those communities. We could arrest their leaders, raid their homes, break up their meetings, and vilify them night after night on the evening news."

Over time, the racial undertones of conversations about crime became so quiet they could barely be heard at all, unless you were listening for them. In 1977, the Supreme Court finally banned the execution of people who had committed rape but not murder, explaining that such a punishment was "grossly out of proportion" to the crime. The vast majority of people executed for rape had been black men, and yet the Court made no mention of this history, issuing the ruling in the case of a white male defendant. Still, the LDF spent the next decade building toward a broad challenge to the death penalty that focused explicitly on race. In 1987, the Court decided to hear them out. The case concerned Warren McCleskey, who had shot and killed a white police officer during a robbery. The LDF argued that McCleskey had been unfairly sentenced to death because he was a black man, and data showed that black defendants were slightly more likely than their white counterparts to receive death sentences, controlling for other factors. Another finding was even more stark: Nationwide, defendants of any race were 4.3 times more likely to be sentenced to death if their victim was white. A Texas study found that the disparity there was even higher.

Justice Lewis Powell wrote for the majority that McCleskey's "claim, taken to its logical conclusion, throws into serious question the principles that underlie the entire criminal justice system." Judges and jurors made decisions in every case. If the Court ruled for McCleskey, he reasoned, what would stop a small army of statisticians from chipping away at every decision about punishment? Powell wrote that in order to prevail in an argument about race, a death row prisoner would need to prove that discrimination had infected his case specifically. For the vast majority of prisoners, this would be impossible. Amsterdam later called the opinion "the Dred Scott decision of our time," referring to the landmark 1857 case that validated slavery. As the LDF saw it, the Court had finally been forced to look the country's violent, racist history in the face, and had once again looked away.

Over the preceding decade, the LDF's staffers had been part of a network of lawyers in New York and Washington, D.C., who made it their mission to overturn individual death sentences. They grew used to taking panicked calls in the middle of the night from lawyers, most of them in Southern states, who needed help getting a stay of execution. Despite the growing number of executions, the network was surprisingly successful. By the late 1980s, courts were reversing one Texas death sentence for every execution the state carried out.

Defense lawyers obtained a major victory in 1989, when the Supreme Court forced Texas to substantially change its death penalty law for the first time since the Jurek decision thirteen years earlier. It was in the case of Johnny Paul Penry, a white man who had been sentenced to death in Livingston, a small town deep in East Texas. He had forced his way into the house of twenty-two-year-old Pamela Moseley Carpenter, where he raped her and stabbed her with scissors she'd been trying to use to fight back. Penry had already been to prison for rape, and he was paroled not long before this new crime. But on appeal his lawyers learned that he was severely mentally impaired; he couldn't name the days of the week, and at age twenty-three he still believed in Santa Claus. When he was a child, his mother had beaten him with a belt and locked him in a room for extended periods without letting him use the toilet. His lawyers argued that the Texas law, with its emphasis on future dangerousness, limited their ability to present this mitigating evidence and push the jury toward mercy.

The Court agreed, writing that the future-dangerousness question had turned evidence of intellectual disability into a "two-edged sword." Jurors might decide such a person was sympathetic, and thus deserved to be spared, but they also might think he was unable to control his conduct and would therefore be more likely to kill again. The decision forced the Texas Legislature in 1991 to go back and rewrite the jury questions. The question about future dangerousness was still key, but the lawmakers cut the other two questions, about whether the crime was deliberate and unprovoked. They added explicit language saying defendants could be sentenced to death even if they did not commit the murder directly but "anticipated that human life would be taken." Most importantly, jurors would now also be specifically asked to consider the circumstances of the crime, along with the defendant's "character and background" and "personal moral culpability," in deciding whether a life sentence was more appropriate than death.

The law still had flaws. The instructions given to juries were confusing, stating that ten or more jurors would need to agree on their votes to trigger a life sentence. This was not technically true—a single holdout juror could stop a death sentence—and yet by law, jurors were not to be informed of this, so potential dissenters, thinking incorrectly that they would need to convince nine others to their position, sometimes just went along with the majority and voted for death. Also, the new law would govern only new trials. There were hundreds of men already on death row in Texas who had been sentenced under the old law, and it was unclear whether and how the Penry decision would apply to them. They would all need lawyers.

In Texas, a long-standing distrust of centralized authority had led to a decentralized justice system in which, at any moment, a judge in a remote, rural county could set an execution date. (In other states, execution dates were set by a governor's office or state supreme court.) In the 1980s, a Texas death row prisoner who received an execution date might go to the prison library, pull out a legal directory, and start writing letters, pleading with lawyers to take his case without pay and file a last-minute appeal to stop the execution. If he had a little commissary money, he could beg by phone. The few lawyers in Austin and Houston who agreed to work on these cases found themselves inundated. There was little incentive beyond a feeling of nobility, and there was plenty to keep you from doing it. Houston lawyer Carolyn Garcia found that her children were taunted by other kids for having a mom who helped murderers.

The leaders of the national capital defense community were watching grimly from afar. Robert McGlasson was eating Mexican food with his colleagues in Atlanta one night in 1987 as they discussed the lack of capital defense lawyers in Texas. "There was a lot of tsk'ing, lamenting," he recalled, "and someone looked at me and said, 'Hey, you're young, you're arrogant, you have no rational fear, and you're from Texas!' . . . I thought, Well, hell, I can do this!" He prepared to move back to his home state. From Washington, D.C., the ACLU sent its own emissary, who visited judges and found they were frustrated. They were getting lots of hasty midnight pleas for stays of execution from lawyers who had signed on at the last minute. Relationships were fraying: A federal judge snapped at one lawyer for making her miss a birthday party.

Although the lack of lawyers was especially bad in Texas, the problem of death row defense plagued every state that practiced capital punishment, and in 1988 the federal judiciary responded by funding statewide offices to specialize in death row appeals. They were dubbed "resource centers," the idea being that they would help to recruit, train, and advise lawyers for people on death row. Death penalty supporters, including judges, liked the idea that these prisoners would no longer be able to endlessly stall their executions by claiming they couldn't find a lawyer.

The average salary at the resource centers was $30,000, so it was impossible to attract seasoned criminal defense lawyers, especially those from the big cities. But there were plenty of recent law school graduates who felt called to the mission of death row defense. George Kendall and Steve Bright, two of the lawyers who had persuaded Robert McGlasson to go to Texas, spoke with evangelical fervor about their work to students at Harvard, Yale, and Columbia. One of Bright's protégés, Bryan Stevenson, was an especially charismatic representative. (Many years later, running the Equal Justice Initiative in Alabama, he would inspire a much larger audience through his book *Just Mercy*.) Northern law students could see themselves as latter-day Freedom Riders, packing their bags and heading south.

The resource centers also attracted homegrown liberals. A young University of Texas law professor named Jordan Steiker, fresh off a clerkship with Supreme Court Justice Thurgood Marshall, funneled students over to the Texas Resource Center, which began in an office in Austin. Satellite offices eventually sprang up in Houston and San Antonio. The center's staffers drove to death row to ask who needed representation, and would take calls from lawyers who were already assigned to a death row case but felt they needed help. There was no shortage of tasks, and the payoff was so beyond anything they'd learned to expect in law school: Even winning a stay of execution represented, however momentarily, the saving of a person's life. "We were so green," one of these lawyers recalled. "A green bunch of troops."

While visiting the Texas Resource Center to make copies for her thesis research, Recer found herself addicted to the atmosphere. She began volunteering. Many nights, she would descend the staircases, peering into whichever offices had a light still on, and ask how she could help. The lawyers would ask her to pick up a pizza, or drive someone to the airport, or sort documents, or make copies. The office saw a constant churn of students, but the dedicated ones stuck out, and eventually Recer's tasks grew more substantial. One evening, she returned home from school to a voicemail. A center lawyer needed her to go to Houston to meet a witness. There was no time to spare—this concerned a pending execution date—and the lawyer had already bought her a plane ticket for 6:00 A.M. the next morning. She was proud to know he thought he could count on her, though she knew the fact that they were sending a student meant this effort was a long shot.

The prisoner facing execution was Eddie Ellis, who had been convicted in 1983 of strangling an elderly woman named Bertie Elizabeth Eakens and leaving her body in her bathtub. He'd been fired from his job as a maintenance worker at the apartment complex where Eakens lived. His fingerprints were on her door, and he'd been seen driving a car that resembled her yellow Cadillac. Recer was paired up with Joe Ward, an investigator originally from Idaho who was known at the center as Idaho Joe or sometimes just Idaho. When they arrived at the apartment complex, they saw gang graffiti on the walls of the buildings, and dozens of shell casings littered the ground. "Be aware of your surroundings," Idaho told her. To his eye, she didn't seem fazed.

They found the woman they were looking for, Esperiridiona Alonzo, known as Dora. She told them that her husband, Pablo "Lucky" Alonzo, an acquaintance of Ellis's, had died a couple of years before. But for years before his death, she said, Lucky had threatened her with violence to keep her from telling anyone a secret—that he, not Eddie Ellis, had killed the old woman. "I feel sick about it," she told them. "I remember when that woman was killed in her bathtub and how Lucky acted that day. . . . He looked scared and real nervous and upset. . . . He said something ugly had happened and that I would read about it in the newspaper. . . . He saw the article and got real scared and nervous again, and said, 'I thought I told you I didn't want to talk about it. Don't be bothering me with this, bitch.' . . . Then he said something like, 'Besides, I told you Eddie was going to go down for it.' . . . He was very angry and pushing me and shouting."

Over the years, every time she heard about someone else being executed, Dora would fight with her husband over Ellis's fate. Lucky had eventually grown ill, and shortly before he died in a hospital, he wrote her a letter apologizing and fully confessing to the crime. But, she told Recer, she didn't know where she had put it.

Recer helped her search her home, then accompanied her to an old storage locker. They dug through a bag of mildewed papers from his hospital stay. Eventually, they found a crinkled, handwritten note in broken English:

Feb 20, 1990: Dora as time went by I didn't have time to tell you but I have done a lots off thinks that you were against me I am sorry for all the thinks I done to you—I can't express but we had good times and bad but most of the time bad. Here is sometime I have to say I killed the poor woman that Eddie blame for only God will fine a place for forgiveness I hope he well forgive me because I know you won't.— Lucky

The center enlisted a document examiner, who found that the handwriting matched other samples of Alonzo's writing. The whole thing felt to Recer like a movie moment when, as she put it later, "Barbra Streisand starts singing and the gates of the jail open up and it's blue skies forever." Lawyers at the center quickly wrote a new appeal, citing the letter "found only hours ago" by a "student from the University of Texas Law School." They submitted it around four o'clock, roughly eight hours before Ellis would be strapped to the gurney. In the meantime, Recer remembered she knew someone who knew Governor Ann Richards, and she started working the phones.

The Harris County District Attorney's office, which had prosecuted Ellis, stood by the conviction. A lawyer from the state attorney general's office, which had opposed his appeal in federal court, was not convinced that Lucky had written the letter, and told a reporter that his widow was "borderline mentally retarded." But for the moment, the question was not whether Ellis was innocent; it was whether he was entitled to a stay of execution, which would allow the courts to open the case back up.

The answer was no. In fact, it was worse than no.

At a last-minute hearing, federal Judge David Hittner told the resource center lawyers they were developing a reputation for showing up with dramatic claims at the last minute. "It is not your role to sabotage the efficient administration of justice," he said, admonishing the lawyers for submitting the petition by fax forty minutes late. (Page one, according to a lawyer's account, had been on time; the problem was a slow fax machine.) The court above him, declining to stop Ellis's execution, wrote that "federal courts do not retry facts already found by state courts" but added that "Ellis's evidence of actual innocence is so riddled with holes that it will not hold water." They simply didn't believe Dora's letter. And it wasn't clear that the press did either. The first sentence of a *Houston Chronicle* article about the execution quoted a prosecutor's description of Ellis as a "self-perpetuating crime machine."

Ellis was executed that night. In his final statement, he called the men who'd sent him to death "sorry sons of bitches." Recer was furious. The state's arguments seemed disingenuous to her, and the judges seemed uninterested in the truth; it felt as if they were personally accusing her of having concocted a scheme, when in fact she'd seen Lucky's confession herself.

A year later, the Supreme Court ruled against another Texas prisoner, saying his evidence of innocence wasn't enough to stop his execution.

By the time Recer went to Houston, Ellis had already been through the entire appellate process, which had become tremendously labyrinthine. After someone is sent to death row, he is appointed a lawyer for a first appeal, called a "direct appeal." The lawyer is supposed to scrutinize the transcript from the trial, looking primarily for errors made "on the record" (Did the judge incorrectly overrule an objection? Did the jurors see grisly crime scene photographs that unfairly swayed them?) as well as whether the evidence was sufficient to support the conviction and death sentence. The lawyer comes up with a series of claims, the state responds, and the statewide Court of Criminal Appeals decides whether to uphold the conviction and sentence. If the court rules against the prisoner (and it usually does), he can ask for review from the U.S. Supreme Court, which virtually always declines cases at this stage.

This is just part one. Next is the "post-conviction" stage. The prisoner gets a new lawyer, who is supposed to "expeditiously investigate the law and facts of the case" and might find serious problems: Perhaps the trial defender failed to properly investigate and did not learn some relevant facts before the trial started, or the prosecutors withheld evidence they should have shared with the defense, which might have led to a lesser sentence, or even an acquittal. The lawyer files a "petition for a writ of habeas corpus." Habeas corpus, which can be translated from Latin as "You may have the body," is supposed to be a check on the power of the government—or, in earlier eras, a monarch. It's technically a civil lawsuit rather than a criminal appeal: The prisoner is suing the head of the prison system and arguing that he shouldn't be incarcerated.

This lawsuit goes first to the trial court, then the state appellate court, then the U.S. Supreme Court again. Assuming they all side with the state, the prisoner may then file a new petition in a federal district court. The losing party can then go to a federal appeals court—Texas is handled by the Fifth Circuit Court of Appeals, based in New Orleans—and then the U.S. Supreme Court. This is all difficult for most people to follow, much less a prisoner with limited education and access to law books, so it is important to have a knowledgeable lawyer. The resource center was officially supposed to handle the federal stage, though they often filed in state courts as well.

In all, a case can cross the desks of more than a dozen judges, and on paper, it looks like a system that bends over backward to give the condemned a chance to have his death sentence examined closely. Unless, of course, each court rubber-stamps an injustice without really examining it, and the judges take the state's arguments at face value and the defense lawyers are paid such paltry sums that they cannot develop the strongest possible claims. A system can look robust from one angle and empty from another.

Recer's wake-up moment came in the field; for many of her peers it came in the big house on San Antonio Street, opening up the banker's boxes of trial transcripts, grabbing yet another Diet Coke or coffee, and reading. They were looking for problems that might be convincing on appeal. You didn't really need to be a lawyer to do this, because the problems were often so obvious.

In one trial, a defense lawyer's entire closing argument—his final chance to ask the jury to spare his client's life—consisted of asking his client to stand up and then saying, "You are an extremely intelligent jury. You've got that man's life in your hands. You can take it or not. That's all I have to say." In another trial, a lawyer failed to raise a single objection. One attorney called his client a "wetback" in front of potential jurors.

But at least these lawyers had been awake.

In three separate cases, the defense lawyer had fallen asleep through parts of the trial. In one, a resource center lawyer had discovered this fact during an investigation, when a former juror let the fact slip, but in another case the *Houston Chronicle* had reported on a sleeping lawyer while the trial was still under way. This lawyer was named John Benn, and his client, George McFarland, was facing the death penalty for a robbery-murder. Benn fell asleep when one witness was on the stand and woke up to find someone else there. Much of the cross-examination fell to his assistant counsel, and together they had spent fewer than ten hours preparing for trial. Neither visited the crime scene or interviewed witnesses. The *Houston Chronicle* reporter couldn't believe what he was seeing, so during a break he asked Benn why he was sleeping.

"It's boring," Benn said.

The reporter asked the judge why he was allowing the trial to continue. The judge said the Constitution guaranteed you the right to a lawyer, but not necessarily one who was awake.

Such stories were not unique to Texas, but the state featured a number of political and cultural dynamics that made them especially likely. Part of the problem was money; counties were not paying enough to attract top shelf talent. In 1984, an El Paso trial lawyer received $11.84 per hour as he worked to defend a client from the death penalty. In Houston—which by 1992 was responsible for 10 percent of all executions nationwide—the pay was $600 a day for time in court, and judges had a reputation for appointing defense lawyers who would not pad the bill by stretching out the trials. Joe Frank Cannon, who also fell asleep in court, once bragged that he tried cases "like greased lightning."

The Supreme Court had famously guaranteed a lawyer to anyone facing a felony charge in the landmark 1963 case of *Gideon v. Wainwright,* but two decades later the justices scaled the ruling back, deciding that these lawyers did not need to be especially effective; in a Florida death case, the Court ruled that a prisoner could get a new trial only if he could show that, had his lawyer not made an error, there was a "reasonable likelihood" that the result would have been different. A "strategic" choice could not be considered an error, even if it was clearly a poor choice in retrospect. The courts overseeing Texas used this standard to uphold death sentences in which the lawyering had been especially shoddy. The Fifth Circuit called the "You are an extremely intelligent jury" closing argument a "dramatic ploy." Judge Michael McCormick, who presided over the state's Court of Criminal

Appeals from 1989 to 2000, later wondered whether lawyers who fell asleep during the trial might be doing so intentionally, as a tactic to get juries to feel sorry for their clients. In a 2017 interview he said, "Maybe the point was to have the jury see the sleeping lawyer and think, 'Well, he's not going to help the guy, so maybe it's up to us.'"

Scouring the trial transcripts, Danalynn Recer saw beyond the violations of these prisoners' rights, beyond crappy lawyers and miserly judges and ignored evidence of innocence. "We've lost the streets to them," one prosecutor had said in 1974 while asking a jury to hand down a death sentence. "The whole community is in fear of them. Every one of us who puts bars on our windows, and loaded our guns, and every one of you ladies who has refused to go to the convenience store after dark, and every one of you men who refuse to let your wife go out at night, you're a hostage." The word "them" ostensibly referred to violent criminals, but for a researcher who had read hundreds of newspaper accounts of lynchings, who understood the blurry line between such lynchings and legal executions, and who believed that racism had not disappeared in American politics but had just gone underground in coded language about crime, the implications of this rhetoric were unmistakable. When a prosecutor said of one defendant, "He had a predisposition to kill, he was ready to kill very easily," Recer believed that the argument, as she eventually wrote in her thesis, "resonates clearly and convincingly against white Texans' long-held perception of criminality as an immutable characteristic of black men."

While reading transcripts from the resource center, she found that the old archetypes of white female victims, robbed of their virtue through rape, shape-shifted but didn't disappear. "Sweet and innocent as a child," a prosecutor had described one victim.

Recer decided to extend her thesis beyond lynchings and early executions and into the present. At the same time, she kept getting asked to jump into cases, kept finding herself willing to help out. Although the center had initially been set up to recruit and train other lawyers, the number of executions continued to grow—twelve in 1992, seventeen in 1993—and as the well of lawyers ran dry, the center itself took the cases, often with only weeks or even days to go before a scheduled execution, as had happened with Eddie Ellis. In 1993 alone, Texas judges set one hundred execution dates. By the end of that year, the center had sixteen lawyers. What had struck Recer her first day as excitement was really its twin: panic.

BY THE TIME ELSA ALCALA WAS BORN IN KINGSVILLE, A SMALL city in South Texas, few of her neighbors remembered the days of lynchings and racial violence that historians sometimes call La Matanza, or "the slaughter," when ethnic Mexicans were killed in staggering numbers—sometimes by mobs and other times by law enforcement officers, sometimes under the guise of legality and sometimes not. From the earliest days of the frontier up through the 1920s, as the border was defined through the push and pull of armed colonization and resistance, Mexicans living in the region were often gripped by fear of Anglo settlers, and especially of their law enforcement officers. "It seems only necessary for that some one to whisper our names to an officer, to have us imprisoned and killed without an opportunity to prove in a fair trial, the falsity of the charges against us," the residents of Kingsville wrote to President Woodrow Wilson in 1916. "Some of us who sign this petition may be killed without even knowing the name of him who accuses. Our privileged denunciators may continue their infamous proceedings—answerable to no one."

Alcala was born in 1964, so although some of her older neighbors may have remembered this era, she did not need to fear the lynch mob; the inequality that shaped her early life was more a matter of economic opportunity and subtle social prejudice. One of her earliest memories is of her mother telling her that she would always need to work much harder than her white peers to get the same opportunities. Her sister would recall being followed around a hardware store by a clerk, who seemed to assume she was going to shoplift. Perhaps it was her looks, or perhaps it was her age, or perhaps it was nothing—perhaps he wasn't following her at all.

Alcala grew up with three sisters and a brother in a two-bedroom house, living with the sort of functional poverty in which day-to-day life was livable but small problems could erupt into big ones. She remembers reading Archie and Richie Rich comics at the corner store where her mother worked as a cashier. Then she remembers, during elementary school, seeing her mother leave on a bus to go to a hospital in Galveston, where she underwent a hysterectomy. Her oldest sister was in college, so the second oldest, Rita, then fourteen, was left to pay the bills and feed the siblings while their father worked.

When their mother returned, she went back to work, but soon had trouble breathing. She went to a local hospital, where she was diagnosed with blood clots in her lungs. It was a complication from her surgery. Soon after, Alcala learned her mother had died.

Her father was left with five kids and an elderly mother-in-law. The siblings remember him drinking and smoking a lot, but still keeping up with his work as a carpenter to support everyone, spending long hours under the hot sun in their backyard. Alcala remembers the hammers and nails and ladders. She remembers the moment she was watching TV at home one day when she heard a knock at the door.

It was a police officer. Their father had suffered a heart attack while driving. Alcala's sister drove to the site, where she learned he was dead.

Their father had paid off the house, so the Alcala children did not need to fear a landlord. Alcala's older sister Rita, who was fifteen years old, found a lawyer to help them designate their grandmother as their guardian, but it quickly became clear that the kids were the ones taking care of her rather than the other way around, and she moved in with extended family. Rita became the parent. Sometimes the younger ones would buck her authority and say, "You're not my mother," and she would respond, "I'm the one who is here."

Rita had strong memories of her mother, how she would never use a pejorative word like "gringo," how she'd say that no job was without honor, how she'd participated in boycotts to support striking farm-workers, how she had cried while watching news reports about the 1970 shooting of college students at Kent State University. "They're just kids!" she exclaimed. In later years, Rita would speculate that perhaps she had managed to pass along some of these impulses toward fairness and empathy to her younger siblings, who could not remember their mother as clearly.

Elsa Alcala and her siblings worked at sandwich and pizza shops while staying in school, in part because they had to be students to receive Social Security benefits stemming from their parents' deaths. If this had all happened in a later era, perhaps Child Protective Services would have put them into foster care, but they were left alone; their extended family checked in on them, but day to day they lived on their own, buying groceries, making simple meals of macaroni and cheese and tuna—Alcala ate so much tuna that in later years the sight of it would make her sick—while working and studying and dating and learning to drive. Years later, she would still find herself amazed that none of them ended up in serious trouble with the law, or worse. She remembered how her grandmother had read to her from a Spanish-language Bible, and it felt now as though the angels from those stories had made their way to Kingsville to look out for these orphaned siblings.

Toward the end of high school, Alcala learned that the Reagan administration was pushing to eliminate Social Security benefits for students with deceased parents but that she might be grandfathered in if she was attending college, so she drove across town to the local branch of Texas A&M and enrolled. She found a job at a urologist's office to help with tuition. She had been mentored by a speech teacher in high school, and in college she found she had a knack for competitive debate. Law school seemed to be the place where public speaking skills were rewarded, so she applied to the University of Texas at Austin, where she thrived in mock trial and moot court.

At one competition, she caught the eye of the guest judge, a prosecutor working for the Harris County district attorney. He invited her to apply for a job in his office, and she was hired. After graduation, she moved from Austin, where she now had friends and mentors, to Houston, where she knew nobody. But she got lucky: The office was like a family.

This was partly because the young lawyers had no time to meet anyone else. They arrived early in the morning and stayed late into the night, working misdemeanors while waiting for a promotion to the courts that handled felonies. Whereas many prosecutors' offices put a premium on winning convictions through plea bargains, Harris County prosecutors were measured on how many cases they won at trial. The record—forty-four felony cases in a single year—belonged to John B. Holmes, Jr., who was now the boss.

Alcala saw Holmes in the hallways and hoped he didn't know her name, since that would probably mean she had done something wrong. Johnny Holmes had been district attorney for a decade at this point, and his power was as fortified as his Old West image: the long handlebar mustache, the rich drawl, the tobacco pipe, the deer rack and animal hides that lined his office walls. None of this had much to do with his past; like Alcala, he had not let his origins define him, though he had come from the opposite direction. The heir to an oil fortune, Holmes had learned to fly while in middle school and after college piloted private charter planes. His father quipped, "You're nothing but a fuckin' bus driver," and then paid for law school.

During an internship with federal prosecutors, Holmes learned two things about himself: He loved prosecuting, and he hated federal bureaucracy. He was now a Republican, and a Southern man typical of his generation, skeptical of the feds but unlikely to talk directly about race (although as an undergraduate in 1961, he had written an op-ed opposing integration in college athletics). Hired by the former DA, he flew up the office ranks while spending his nights riding shotgun with police officers. Now, as an elected official, he spoke to voters about personal accountability and community control in a language that synced seamlessly with his handlebar mustache and rascally sense of humor: the big-city prosecutor as small-town sheriff. Defending the death penalty, he evoked the frontier. "We've got to scratch the retribution itch," he once said. "Otherwise people will do it themselves."

Holmes was famously incorruptible; he made hiring and firing and promotion a committee process so he couldn't be accused of nepotism. Even Craig Washington, the black state legislator who had so vehemently opposed the death penalty in 1973, once admitted that Holmes "would indict his own mother." He was sometimes accused of playing politics—getting his employees to run against judges he didn't like, for example—but Holmes disputed this. "If I had a hit list, I would damn well put it in plain view."

More than nine hundred thousand people moved to Houston in the 1970s, attracted by jobs in the petroleum industry and a broader economic upturn across the Sun Belt. The larger population coincided with a nationwide rise in crime, and the police department was overwhelmed as the number of burglaries alone nearly doubled. In the DA's office, however, the deluge created a sense of mission, a feeling that the city was desperately counting on them to get all these bad guys off the streets. "Johnny used to say, 'Don't you feel guilty for getting paid to do this?'" prosecutor Lyn McClellan recalled. "I'd say, 'Yeah, but pay me anyway!'" The office would circulate statistics showing how many convictions each prosecutor had obtained. They talked constantly about their cases, asking one another for advice over meals. They came in on Sundays to prepare for trial.

It surprised Rita Alcala that her sister was working for a Republican. Their mother had been a staunch Democrat. Their aunt had even been a prison reform activist. At one point, when Elsa visited Rita in Los Angeles, they got into a fierce argument stemming from the O. J. Simpson trial—Rita thought racism had tainted the case—and Elsa defended the prosecutors. Rita told her, "Not all prosecutors are like you." On other occasions, though, they did not fall into their expected roles.

Rita became a humanities professor, and at one point during a car ride, the two argued about the death penalty: Rita thought men like Jeffrey Dahmer and John Wayne Gacy didn't deserve to live. She remembers her sister taking a surprisingly pragmatic position: "All those cases do is clog up the court system, and they get so many appeals, they live in prison forever, and it's better to just do life sentences."

But work was work. As Alcala climbed the ranks in her office—Holmes was considered especially progressive for his era when it came to hiring and promoting women—Harris County was on its way to becoming the death penalty capital of the United States. In 2001, the county accounted for more than 150 prisoners on death row. This was more than the total number of death row prisoners in thirty-one other states. By the end of that year, a county with 1 percent of the national population had produced nearly 10 percent of the country's executions. Holmes didn't see these numbers as saying something about his own taste for the death penalty; if anything, they said something about Harris County. "If [in] ninety-five percent of the cases where you seek death, twelve citizens say 'Kill him,' how do you go and say 'We're not going to do that'?" he explained. "Is that not democracy in action?"

When a murder came in that qualified for the death penalty under the 1973 law, the prosecutor assigned to the case would fill out a questionnaire and then discuss it with Holmes. Often, when they didn't agree, it was because Holmes thought the death penalty was too harsh. "I think juries would have given more death sentences," one recalled, "but Johnny picked and chose." A prominent defense lawyer saw it differently: "Johnny is a west-of-the-Pecos kind of guy. . . . He is not a Renaissance man. His theory is, 'Let's kill 'em all and let God sort 'em out.'"

One study spanning 1974 to 1988 found that prosecutors across Texas were more likely to seek the death penalty in murder cases involving a rape or multiple victims, or in which the victim and defendant were strangers. Another analysis found that the "sexual degradation" of female victims led to more media coverage, which put pressure on Harris County prosecutors to seek death. Many prosecutors have also said they are more likely to seek death when the evidence of guilt is stronger, and in Houston it was known that Holmes wanted to see whether the defendant had committed crimes in the past. At this time, Texas didn't have a life-without-parole sentence, so if a murderer did not receive the death penalty, he could someday be back on the streets. A later analysis would find that Holmes was three times more likely to seek the death penalty when the defendant was black than when he was white, controlling for other factors. He made his decisions case by case, a method that has fueled racial disparities in many policy areas, not just criminal justice.

After five years in his office, Alcala had become the chief prosecutor of the 178th District Court, which was presided over by a somewhat eccentric judge named William T. Harmon. A former colleague of Holmes's in the DA's office, Harmon made no secret of his support for the death penalty, having once said in earshot of defense lawyers that he was "doing God's work" in helping execute their client. (He later said this was a joke.) He once displayed on his desk a postcard depicting Judge Roy Bean, a legendary Old West barkeep who turned his saloon into a court, requiring the jurors to buy drinks; he was dubbed the Hanging Judge. Harmon had replaced Bean's name with his own.

Defense lawyers complained about Judge Harmon's bias toward the prosecution, but it wasn't particularly easy to be a prosecutor under him, either. He often insisted on working through lunch, eating a sandwich at the bench. This was good for Alcala's advancement—lots of time in court meant lots of trials and lots of opportunities to win them—but it was also grueling. She would get to work at six or seven in the morning so she could read police reports and call crime victims. Then Harmon would keep her long after work, and he didn't seem to care when she said she couldn't see straight. Sometimes, late at night, her fellow prosecutors would be hanging out. "Where is Elsa?" one would ask. "She's still in trial," another would respond.

In Harmon's court, Alcala was assigned her first death penalty case. Her superiors had already made the decision to go for the punishment, but it was not hard for her to see why.

One night, Gerald Eldridge kicked in the apartment door of his ex-wife, Cynthia Bogany. Their daughter Chirissa, age nine, was sleeping on the couch in the living room. He approached her, raised his gun, and shot her between the eyes. Then he pointed the gun at his son Terrell's head and fired. The bullet hit his shoulder.

A cousin named Tomika, age thirteen, was staying with them and managed to get into a closet before Eldridge could find her. Cynthia and her new boyfriend heard the gunshots and bolted into the room. The boyfriend, who was naked, tried to wrestle the gun away from Eldridge, felt a bullet graze his neck, and then escaped by jumping through a second-story window.

Cynthia tried to run too, but she tripped on some stairs and Eldridge caught up with her. She begged him: "Don't kill me. Don't kill me. Don't kill me." He fired twice.

At a hearing before the trial, a psychologist hired by the defense testified that Eldridge did not understand his charges. In some states, the question of whether someone is "competent" to stand trial is answered by a judge. In Texas and others, it is left up to a jury, and it becomes a battle between experts for the prosecution and experts for the defense over who is more credible. An expert for the state countered: "I think most of his unusual behavior is saved for the doctors who interview him, then [the] rest of the time he is pretty much kind of just behaving himself or at least is quiet. . . . I interpret that as malingering. He is faking mental illness." A second psychologist agreed. Alcala believed them rather than the defense expert.

Even as her memories of the case thinned out over the next two decades, one remained vivid. As they were selecting the jury, the courtroom had settled into a dull, sleepy routine when all of a sudden, the table next to Alcala's slammed to the floor. Eldridge had flipped it over. Papers were everywhere, people were scattering, and the bailiffs were rushing over to restrain him. As the trial began, Eldridge cursed loudly and often, standing up and knocking over cups and pushing paper off his table. He complained that his own lawyers were failing him. "I got inassistance of counsel," he said. "When I start talking, they get up and walk off." Not that he made it easy for them; he gave first or last names of witnesses he wanted called but then provided no other identifying information about them. At one point the judge told Eldridge that the jurors were "physically frightened" of him.

Eldridge was at the defense table when his son Terrell Bogany, age nine, got up on the stand. Bogany had watched his father point a gun at his sister and fire, and then fire at him. He still had a bullet in his shoulder. "How you doing?" Alcala asked him.

"Fine."

Having lost her own parents at a young age, Alcala appeared to have a natural ability to make a traumatized child feel more comfortable in the harsh atmosphere of the courtroom. She asked him to name his elementary school, his teacher, his siblings. She explained what it meant to tell "the truth." She asked him to describe how one night he'd gone to sleep, lying on the floor while watching television. "What happened when you were on the floor?" she asked him.

"Gerald Eldridge came by and shot me." He called his father by his first and last name.

After the shooting stopped, his cousin Tomika had called out from the closet, "Boobee, is that you?"

Alcala stopped the narrative for a moment: "People call you Boobee?"

"Yes, ma'am."

The jury would probably not have questioned this boy's youth and innocence, but by picking up his nickname, Alcala intensified those themes. She asked the boy to step down from the witness box and lie on the floor. She stood where Eldridge had been, so the jury could see just how close the two had been to each other.

Prosecutors laid out their cases like horror movies, the kind in which you knew how the story was going to end, and it was sickening to watch the path there, and yet you couldn't look away because there were going to be ghastly surprises. Terrell, it turned out, had lived only by luck: He'd tilted his head just slightly, causing the bullet to enter his shoulder instead of his skull. Alcala showed him pictures from the crime scene, one of which depicted a bloody T-shirt. "What is the red stuff?" she asked.

"Blood."

"Blood. Whose blood is that?"

"Terrell's."

"Who is Terrell?"

"Me."

"Boobee. Okay."

The jury found Eldridge guilty. Alcala had little time to celebrate before launching into the punishment phase of the trial. For weeks her office desk had been surrounded by boxes of evidence detailing Eldridge's past. Prosecutors could rely on allegations against a defendant that had not ever been proven in court, an advantage that made defenders furious. But Eldridge had been convicted of numerous crimes, so Alcala didn't need to rely on hearsay as she tried to prove he'd be dangerous in the future.

In response to the legislature's 1973 death penalty law, many Texas prosecutors enlisted expert witnesses, usually psychiatrists, to lend a scientific veneer to the argument that the defendant would kill again. Many doctors took on the role, but only one earned the title of Dr. Death.

James Grigson—Jim to his friends, and he had many—was a forensic psychiatrist with a salesman's relentless cheer and a country doctor's kindly bedside manner. In the 1960s, he had specialized in examining defendants to see whether they were mentally competent to stand trial. Sometimes he testified about why particular murderers were incorrigible and deserved the death penalty. One lawyer recalled seeing him talk to strangers at a hotel bar, asking them what they'd need to hear from an expert witness in order to return a particular sentence: "It was like we now do with focus groups . . . but thirty years ahead of his time." His skills indirectly influenced the legislature's decision to include "future dangerousness" in the 1973 bill, and as it became the most important question in death penalty cases, Grigson solidified his role in Texas courtrooms. By 1978, he had testified against twenty-six of the eighty-six men on Texas's death row.

The NAACP Legal Defense Fund fought back. They found a defendant, Ernest Benjamin Smith, who had entered a grocery store to rob it and then stood by while his accomplice shot and killed a clerk. Smith had been arrested only once before, for possessing a tiny amount of marijuana. Still, Grigson interviewed Smith and then popped up at the punishment phase of the trial to tell the jury he was a "very severe psychopath." (He told one lawyer that all he needed to do to know the truth was look into a man's eyes while asking about the crime.) The LDF lawyer argued before the Supreme Court that Smith's "right to remain silent" meant that he should have been able to refuse a conversation with the doctor. He won unanimously.

Prosecutors needed a new way to bring in Grigson's testimony, even if he wasn't allowed to interview the defendant, and a strategy emerged in Bell County, a rural community north of Austin. At first, the young district attorney there, Arthur "Cappy" Eads, was stumped. How could you get a psychiatrist to testify about someone he had never met? One assistant told him that in civil cases an expert often responded to a "hypothetical," or a question that laid out a series of suppositions. At the trial of Thomas Barefoot, who had shot and killed a police officer, the prosecutors called Grigson to the witness stand. "Sit back and relax," Eads told him. "I'm going to ask that you assume that all the facts in the hypothetical situation that I give you are true." According to the transcript, he went on:

> Dr. Grigson, I will ask you to assume that Thomas A. Barefoot, who was convicted on the 24th day of October, 1975, in the Western district court of the Western District of Oklahoma, for the offense of the possession of an unregistered firearm, and that his punishment was assessed at one year in prison. I would ask you to further assume that Thomas A. Barefoot was convicted on the second day of December, 1974, in the 15th district court of Lafayette Parish, Louisiana, for the offense of distribution of marijuana, and his punishment was assessed at five years in prison at hard labor probated and one year in the parish jail. Further assuming Thomas A. Barefoot was convicted . . .

On and on Eads went, listing Barefoot's résumé for more than half an hour—it was, in truth, hardly hypothetical at all—winding up to the moment Barefoot "pulled a gun from his pocket, pointed it to the head of Carl Levin, and pulled the trigger, causing a bullet from the gun to enter the brain of Carl Levin from a distance of no more than six inches." No detail was too small. Then Eads asked Grigson for his assessment. "This would be a fairly classical, typical, sociopathic personality disorder," Grigson said. If they ranked sociopaths from zero to ten, Barefoot "would be above ten."

But would he "commit criminal acts of violence that would constitute a continuing threat to society?"

"He most certainly would."

In prison or out?

"It wouldn't matter if he was in the penitentiary or he was free."

And what was the degree of "reasonable psychiatric certainty" to this prediction?

"Well, yes, sir, I would put it at one hundred percent and absolute."

A second doctor, named John Holbrook, answered similarly. The defense objected continuously. They noted that the American Psychiatric Association had said that it was impossible to predict whether someone would be violent, and that most psychiatrists agreed they couldn't give opinions about people without actually meeting them in a clinical setting.

Grigson had a retort ready. "This is that same group," he said, "that found homosexuality was not an illness."

Barefoot's death sentence ended up at the Supreme Court in 1983, a few years after the justices heard about Grigson's testimony in the Smith case. "Are you using just Dr. Grigson in *all* these cases?" one justice asked the state's lawyers. "He has been here in every case we have had from Texas." But a majority of the justices thought psychiatrists should be permitted to testify, even if they had never met the defendant. Barefoot was executed, Eads was elected president of a national prosecutors' association, and Grigson began his golden age.

In 1990, the writer Ron Rosenbaum profiled the doctor for *Vanity Fair* on the occasion of a new feat: testifying at two trials, seventy miles apart, on the same day. He was a journalist's dream, offering up tidbits like his family's business when he was young: manufacturing tombstones. Once, Grigson told Rosenbaum, he was testifying and a particular woman on the jury struck him as skeptical. He thought she might be a holdout, ruining the jury's unanimous vote for death. During a coffee break, Grigson alerted the prosecutor, and they studied the questionnaire she had filled out. It turned out she had a fourteen-year-old daughter. "I got back on the stand," Grigson recounted, "and had the prosecutor ask me . . . 'Is this the kind of man that would rape and kill fourteen-year-old girls?' And we went into that. And she uncrossed her legs."

Grigson was from Dallas, and some prosecutors called his style of hypothetical testimony the Dallas Way. The Dallas County DA's office was run from 1951 until 1987 by Henry Wade, another larger-than-life good ol' boy whose folksy charm belied his legal brilliance. (His name is famously associated with his defense of a Texas law prohibiting abortion, in the case *Roe v. Wade*.) Whereas critics of Holmes could still be found crediting his honesty, Wade earned no such admiration. His deputies were often accused of withholding evidence from the defense that they were legally supposed to hand over. More than one former Dallas prosecutor would later relate a joke made around the office: "Anyone can convict a guilty defendant; convicting the innocent bastards is the trick."

Many former Dallas prosecutors have denied this characterization, saying there was no "win at all costs" mentality. Part of the problem was that Wade let too much get into writing. Though he denied having ever made the statement attributed to him by an underling—"If you ever put another nigger on a jury, you're fired"—there was a 1963 memo on how to pick citizens for a jury, written by an assistant, that was nearly as damning and remained in use in Wade's office for decades. The memo went into personality ("You are not looking for a fair juror, but rather a strong, biased and sometimes hypocritical individual"), political views ("Look at the panel out in the hall before they are seated. You can spot the showoffs and the liberals by how and to whom they are talking"), looks ("Look for physical afflictions. These people usually sympathize with the accused"), weight ("Extremely overweight people, especially women and young men, indicates a lack of self-discipline and often times instability. I like the lean and hungry look"), dress ("Conservatively, well dressed people are generally stable and good for the State"), age ("People over forty are more settled and more ready to believe that criminals should be punished"), gender ("I don't like women jurors because I can't trust them. . . . They do, however, make the best jurors in cases involving crimes against children. . . . It is possible that their 'women's intuition' can help you if you can't win your case with the facts"), cosmetics ("Old women wearing too much make-up are usually unstable, and therefore are bad State's jurors"), and race ("Minority races almost always empathize with the Defendant").

In 1986, the Supreme Court declared that a person could not be excluded from serving on a jury purely because of their race. Prosecutors began training one another on all the different ways you could strike a juror without mentioning race explicitly. A statewide training document from a Dallas prosecutor included a number of them, some of which suggested race ("Agreed with O. J. Simpson verdict") while others were so broadly applicable as to be useful workarounds ("Chewing gum"). Prosecutors argued that these justifications weren't intended to target potential black jurors—that they had simply been listing judicially approved reasons to cut people from the jury pool—but in 2005, the Supreme Court struck down a Dallas death sentence after prosecutors used a training manual with racial stereotypes to strike ten of eleven potential black jurors from the pool. (In Houston, Johnny Holmes was also accused of keeping black residents off juries; he said his prosecutors were cautious about black jurors because they were perceived to be more sympathetic to defendants and skeptical of police, but he denied ever instituting a ban on their service.)

Wade's right-hand man through many of these years was Doug Mulder, who was credited with inventing the line about "convicting the innocent," though he denied it. He obtained twenty-four death sentences during his career, and he noticed that this became easier to do so in 1973 when the legislature handed down the "special questions."

"I think they were trying to make it more difficult [to get a death sentence]," he said in a 2017 interview, "but they didn't know what they were doing."

Mulder was friends with Grigson—he threw the doctor's retirement party—and it was a case featuring them both that cast a pall over the entire Texas death penalty system.

In the late 1970s, the filmmaker Errol Morris read about Grigson in *Texas Monthly*. He'd long abhorred the death penalty, and he thought the doctor would make a good subject for a documentary. Grigson agreed to an interview and encouraged Morris to meet some of the men he'd helped send to death row. He warned Morris, however, that these men were "different than you and me." They were psychopaths, and would probably profess their innocence.

Morris played along, telling Grigson he could be his "guide" to the mysteries of the criminal mind. One of the men Morris interviewed was Randall Dale Adams. As the doctor predicted, he proclaimed that he'd been framed for the murder of a police officer.

Morris found Adams's many assertions difficult to follow, but when he visited a courthouse in Austin and read the trial transcript, he became obsessed with the case, convincing himself through a detailed investigation that Adams was in fact innocent. A movie about "Dr. Death" became a movie about the railroading of an innocent man. Grigson didn't even make the final cut. After Morris's 1988 film *The Thin Blue Line* was released, Adams was freed.

The last time Morris saw Grigson was at a court hearing in Dallas. "I'm sorry about all of this, but I really do believe he's innocent," Morris told the doctor.

In his memory, Grigson's face broke into a "hideous grin" as he responded: "Super good, super good, super good."

"It was like contempt," Morris recalled later. "A form of 'Fuck you.' "

In 1995, the American Psychological Association officially expelled Grigson. A few years later, researchers looked into the prison records of 155 people on death row who experts said would be dangerous in the future; only eight had engaged in "seriously assaultive behavior" (though the data did not include attempted assaults, and it is impossible to know what prisoners would have done had they not been under a death sentence). The doctors who came after Grigson were not as adept at charming juries, and eventually prosecutors stopped using them. Grigson himself died in 2004. An obituary read, "He always had a good word to say to everyone."

As his punishment trial began, Gerald Eldridge made a decision that could only be explained by mental illness, a bizarre effort to fake mental illness, or just a profound lack of wisdom: He refused to be in the courtroom. This meant that any time a witness needed to complete the ritual of formally identifying him, Eldridge had to be escorted into the room and then back out again. For Elsa Alcala, his absence was a gift, because she could proceed without the interruptions that had marred the first part of the trial.

In Houston, the ethos among prosecutors ran against using psychiatric experts. They tried instead to show that the defendant made active decisions rather than responding to outside influences. For example, a PowerPoint slide from a later training for prosecutors across Texas listed the following themes that might sway the jury toward death: "Number of Blows Wielded," "Motive: Sexual, Financial, Sport/Fun," "Biding His Time," and "Efforts to Hide Handiwork." Alcala focused on Eldridge's past, showing how these murders, although his first, had been the culmination of a slow, steady rise in violent behavior. He had bought a gun at age twenty and often waved it around to scare people. He once attacked a man who had accused him of wearing fake gold jewelry, and he later shot the boyfriend of his ex-girlfriend eight times. The man survived, and Eldridge went to prison, where he constantly got into fights. When he was released, he beat up his young son Terrell and went back to prison again. When he was released a second time, his ex-wife was so afraid of him she put her bills in the names of family members so he couldn't find her.

"Do you have an opinion as to why Gerald is as violent as he is?" Alcala asked his friend from elementary school.

"Gerald likes to control things," the friend said. "I think he is a control freak."

Just as Alcala had drawn out the full horror of the shooting, she now lingered on this theme, feeding the jury the message in small bites.

"He wants things his way—"

"His way."

"Or no way?"

"Or no way."

"Are you afraid of him?"

"Yes."

The defense team countered by showing that Eldridge came from a family of imperfect but decent people. Eldridge's brother said they'd been beaten up a lot by other kids. His mother had been married five times and often fought with her husbands. She admitted that she'd raised Eldridge as well as she knew how, and "whopped" him with a belt when he misbehaved. In high school, Eldridge had excelled in football, but an injury ruined his hopes of using the sport as a way out of poverty. "It affected the way, you know, he felt, because this was something he really wanted to do," she said.

Alcala had taken the lead throughout the trial, but she let her co-counsel Don Smyth cross-examine the defense witnesses, including Eldridge's mother. He managed to turn her parenting against her son. Under his questioning, she said she worked nights so she could be home when her kids finished school during the day. "You didn't just run off, [leave] them unattended, let them roam across the street?" he asked.

"No. I also had help from grown-up people that I knew and trust."

"You tried to teach your kids right from wrong, did you not?"

"I did the best I could."

"I'm sure that you did the best you could. There's no doubt in my mind about that. . . . When you found your son might be headed in a direction that he should not be headed in, did you try to straighten him out?"

"Sure. I talked to my children, but God gave them a mind of their own."

In other words, Eldridge had nobody to blame for his crime but himself. Over the long history of the Texas death penalty, this was not the only time a prosecutor would use a mother's testimony to help send her son to death row.

"People have choices in this life and certainly Mr. Eldridge had that choice and decided not to go one path," Alcala told the jury during her closing argument. "He decided to go the other path." She picked out moment after moment when he could have abandoned violence but had instead gone further. Why had he made that choice, over and over again? "Because he is a power hungry, evil, mean person."

Not every prosecutor asking for the death penalty used the word "evil," but a theological strand cut through their rhetoric. The epigraph to a Texas District and County Attorneys' Association 2004 guide to getting a death sentence was Ecclesiastes 8:11: "Because sentence against an evil work is not executed speedily, therefore the heart of the sons of men is fully set in them to do evil." Good defense lawyers made the defendant into the protagonist of their stories, but prosecutors made him the villain—and not the complicated, secretly human style of villain who would later become popular in television characters like Tony Soprano and Walter White, but rather the unflinching, mysterious style epitomized by Hannibal Lecter and Anton Chigurh. Around the country, defendants were called monsters and menaces and animals, and though appellate courts might sometimes reverse if the language, in their view, crossed into racism ("King Kong"), the line was seldom clear or consistent.

Evil also meant you didn't need to explain why the crime had taken place, for evil is mysterious. All you could do was work to make sure such evil was contained. In her closing argument, Alcala listed nineteen people killed or injured by Eldridge and allowed the jury to write its own end to an already terrifying story. "Are we going to let there be a twentieth?" she asked. "How many people do we let this man hurt before at some point we decide to use society's right to self-defense?" This sort of rhetoric was used in many American courtrooms, but in Texas the "future dangerousness" question invited it directly.

Eldridge's jury took thirty minutes to answer the questions and sentence him to death. Alcala's fellow prosecutor Don Smyth told her, as she later recalled, "I'm going to go out tonight, I'm going to buy a bottle of wine, I'm going to put today's date on it. Then when they put the needle in him I'm going to open that wine and have a drink." The office was known for celebrating its victories. Men executed for crimes in Harris County were referred to as the Silver Needle Society, and several prosecutors started a party band called Death by Injection.

Alcala didn't feel that kind of jubilation. She felt she'd done her job well, and if anything she just felt sad that people did things like shoot their own children. After the trial, Johnny Holmes himself called her on the phone and asked to see her. She nervously walked into his office.

"Congratulations, killer," he said, handing her what looked like a small plastic syringe. It was a novelty pen.

5

THE DRIVE FROM AUSTIN TO HUNTSVILLE TOOK ABOUT THREE hours without traffic, and there was seldom traffic. For most of the route, one-lane roads cut through grassland dotted with barbecue restaurants and junk-cluttered porches. This journey became a ritual for the young resource center lawyers as they traveled to the Ellis Unit, where death row was housed in the early 1990s. A sign out front made a cheery, unintentionally ironic acronym from the unit's name: EVERYONE LIVES LONGER IF SAFETY IS FIRST. Another sign warned not to spit on the cactus. After parking, the lawyers approached a guard tower with a red bucket hanging from a rope down the side. They dropped their driver's licenses and state bar cards into the bucket and watched it ascend.

Inside, they passed a LIFE GIVER AWARD plaque, celebrating prison employees who had donated to a blood drive, as well as glass cases full of leather and wood craft items made by prisoners, much of which was for sale. They arrived at a long, narrow room separated into individual booths, with visitors on one side, prisoners on the other, separated by Plexiglas. Their new clients sat in cages wearing thin white uniforms. Some had shaved their heads—death row wasn't air-conditioned, so this was a way to keep cool—and the lawyers could see their scars, evidence of a childhood beating or a long-ago fight. Many death row prisoners didn't understand the convoluted arguments being made on their behalf, so conversations tended toward food, weather, the latest Dallas Cowboys game. It could get noisy, because everyone had to speak loudly in order to be heard through the Plexiglas. This made it all the more difficult for the lawyers, many still in their twenties, to gain the trust of their new clients, who were by now used to lawyers making empty promises.

Shortly after Danalynn Recer finished law school in 1992, she was hired by the resource center, and she made the journey to Huntsville to meet one of her first clients, a black prisoner named Carl Kelly. He had been on death row since his early twenties for the murders of two men. One was Steven Pryor, a teenager who had disappeared, along with his Camaro, from a 7-Eleven in Waco where he was working the night shift. Police put out an all-points bulletin for the car, and it turned up in a nearby town, being driven by another teenager named Thomas Graves. Inside the car were two guns, a green canvas sack filled with money, bloodstained towels, limestone dust, and Carl Kelly's billfold.

The dust led investigators to a cliff in a Waco park—popularly known as Lover's Leap—at the foot of which Pryor's body was found along with that of a hitchhiker named David Riley. Both had been shot, presumably before they were thrown over the cliff.

Kelly was already known to police: He had shown up at the 7-Eleven while officers were looking for clues, belligerently asking whether they had found fingerprints, as well as whether he could purchase a Slurpee. They arrested him and he confessed, saying Graves had shot the two men but he had helped push their bodies over the cliff. Kelly later said he'd fired a gun but missed, although this did not technically matter because in Texas, as in many states, a person who "solicits, encourages, directs, aids or attempts to aid" a murderer can be prosecuted for the murder himself. Graves pleaded guilty and received a life sentence, but Kelly went to trial and received a death sentence. A Waco lawyer had shepherded Kelly through the entirety of the appeals process, but when a judge set his execution for a night in February 1990, the lawyer called the resource center, where a staff lawyer named Rob Owen began working frantically and managed to get a stay of execution.

Owen was twenty-seven, a wiry and bearded Georgia native just out of Harvard Law School who was known, despite the gravity of his work, for his quick wit, which could defuse tension among his overworked peers. After reading about Kelly's weird behavior at the crime scene, he called a neuropsychologist. He eventually learned that Kelly had an intellectual disability. In the words of one doctor who evaluated him, he had "approximately the same understanding of the world around him as the average twelve-year-old," even though he was then in his thirties. In addition, a brain injury had made him impulsive and also severely limited his ability to think abstractly.

These insights would be crucial to the legal effort to save his life. Less than a year before Owen started looking into Kelly's case, the Supreme Court had ruled that the jurors who sentenced Johnny Paul Penry to death had not been given an adequate opportunity to consider his "mental retardation." They had only been asked the three questions that the legislature had written in 1973: Was the crime deliberate? Was it unprovoked? Was there "a probability" the defendant would be a "continuing threat to society"? The Texas Legislature had responded by adding a question for juries about "mitigating evidence," but what about all the other cases of men on death row, like Carl Kelly, whose juries had similarly been restricted?

Owen read the transcript from Kelly's 1981 trial, which had taken place two years after Penry's. The evidence was limited: Kelly's stepfather, Richard Stanford, said he was a good son and hard worker but had struggled in school and dropped out, and the jury learned that Kelly was high on drugs when he committed the crime. But the prosecutors pushed jurors away from considering this evidence, saying they only needed to answer whether the crime was deliberate and whether Kelly would be a danger in the future. The implication of the *Penry* decision was that prosecutors shouldn't be allowed to limit jurors like that.

The Court of Criminal Appeals agreed to halt Kelly's execution in 1990 in order to examine his lawyers' arguments. But two years later, they rejected them. The Texas law had asked the jury to decide whether Kelly would be a "continuing threat to society," and the court thought this question would allow the jury to consider mitigating evidence; if Kelly had been a dutiful son, the jury might decide his crime had been an aberration, unlikely to be repeated. The state's highest court for criminal cases was growing increasingly conservative, ruling in other cases that mitigating evidence was only relevant if it had some "nexus" to the crime, meaning it helped explain in a direct way why the crime had been committed. The defendant being high on drugs was relevant, for example, but not a story about his father beating him as a child. To Owen, it seemed the court was desperate to interpret the Supreme Court's decision in the *Penry* case narrowly, so that they wouldn't have to overturn lots of death sentences.

Kelly got a new execution date: July 31, 1992. Owen suddenly had to shift from slow, steady labor to a binge of deadline work. It was still unclear whether or how the Supreme Court would step in, clarifying what the *Penry* decision could mean for older Texas cases, so Owen and the other lawyers had to strategize about what arguments might convince a federal court to interpret the *Penry* precedent favorably for their clients. Chess metaphors abounded in talk of defense strategy, and Owen used them when talking about Kelly's case to a reporter: "Every move you make has consequences," he said. But with this new date looming, he was growing pessimistic.

"You've been through this before," he told Kelly during a visit. "It can get kind of close. You just have to hang on." Privately, he agonized over whether he was giving his client too much hope, knowing as he did that most men, even if they managed to fight their case for years, would eventually lose. Court after court, judge after judge, all had said no to him.

And then one said yes. Without explanation, the Supreme Court halted Kelly's execution. Owen thought perhaps it was because of another resource center case, in which the defendant was seventeen years old at the time of his crime; the Court had agreed to hear arguments on whether his age had been properly considered by the jury as a reason to spare his life. Kelly had been older, but it was still a good sign that the courts wanted to reexamine how Texas laws handled mitigating evidence. The chessboard had briefly shifted in Kelly's favor.

It became Recer's job to further explore Kelly's family background, in order to show judges what other mitigating evidence his jury had never heard. But first she had to meet him.

When she did, she found it easy to establish a connection. It was a little like speaking to someone very young—the same emphasis on concrete details, on favorite colors, favorite numbers. He noticed when she'd gotten her teeth cleaned, when they shone particularly bright. She noticed that he liked to talk about the lottery and guess the numbers that might win. She promised him she'd buy a ticket with whatever numbers he wanted.

She asked him, "What would you do if you hit the lottery, if you won?"

"Well," he said, in her recollection, "I wouldn't be here, because rich people don't come here."

He had been steeling himself for execution since his arrival, back in 1981, when he had seen a raised-up red chair near his cell. At first he'd been terrified, thinking he'd die in that chair within the week. But then he was told it was for haircuts. As it turned out, he'd have time for many of those over the next dozen years, as four execution dates came and went. As these dates approached, he would write letters to his family ("If you don't hear from me . . ."). He liked to play basketball and was allowed to dribble and shoot for three hours a day, alone in the prison gym. "Michael Jordan is unbelievable," he once said, "and the man to slow him down is on death row."

He also practiced what the prisoners called "piddling," taking long, thin strips of wood, cutting them into small pieces, and carving and gluing them together to make objects. Brewing coffee in his cell, he'd dip the wood strips into the liquid in order to dye them, varying the shades to create subtle gradients. Along with another prisoner, he built a clock for Owen, writing in a note, "I hope you will displace it in your office." Kelly noticed that Recer smoked cigarettes, so he made her a box to hold them. It was taller than normal, she realized, because he had noticed that she smoked 100s.

As Owen plotted how to make the best of the quickly shifting legal landscape, Recer learned about Kelly's life. In other states, mitigation specialists were often enlisted by defense lawyers at the earliest stage of the case, long before the trial began. But in Texas, the 1973 death penalty law, under which Kelly was sentenced, had failed to mention the idea of "mitigation" at all. With so little funding for the defense, a culture of looking for such evidence before trial never developed. So the resource center often gathered this information for the first time, using it to bolster various legal arguments in their appeals. If all else failed, the evidence would be vital for the clemency application, the last chance to persuade the governor and her board of appointees to stop the execution.

Getting that information meant going to the family members and friends of the man on death row. Recer had shown a knack for getting people to open up. She'd learned from Idaho Joe that you couldn't call ahead; you had to just show up. It also helped that Recer didn't dress fancy. It seemed to Recer that many of her peers had attended elite law schools and wanted to *look* like lawyers, but this could be intimidating to a family member of a prisoner. At one point, walking into a trailer park, Recer had to practically order a lawyer to leave his suit jacket and briefcase in the car, and for God's sake not let the first words out of his mouth be "I'm a lawyer." For a lot of these family members, it had been lawyers who put their loved one on death row, and lawyers who had kept them there. Recer's jeans and ratty T-shirts could quietly induce trust. "You're their only hope," recalled Idaho Joe. "That's a big responsibility, and you can only do that by sharing some of yourself. And in theory, at some point, you'd done this so many times you don't have anything left to give. But Danalynn always found something to give."

In Waco, the team looked for anyone who had known Carl Kelly growing up. It didn't take long to see that his trial lawyers had not dug very deep. His stepfather, Richard Stanford, whose testimony was supposed to inspire sympathy, was far from an ideal witness. It was Stanford who had driven Kelly out of the house. (Kelly's biological father had disappeared when he was too young to remember.)

The team spoke to Kelly's brothers and sisters, along with administrators at his school and his prison pen pals. They often referred to him by his nickname, Gene:

> "I remember Richard whipping Gene with a leather belt. He could hit awful hard, I tell you that. Sometimes the boys would wear two pairs of pants for extra padding against a whipping."

> "Richard hit Gene with anything, a horseshoe once. And when Gene was about eleven or twelve, it was a big old board knocked him flat."

> "He wouldn't let Gene and Rochelle eat sometimes for two-three days—it was a long time. He locked them in the closet."

> "Our stepfather tried to hit Mama and Gene would fight him. . . . We would run up and grab the legs of Richard's pants and cling to them and try to keep him from hitting my mother, but it didn't help."

> "When Gene worked, Richard took all his money."

His elementary school principal recalled that Kelly was a "slow learner." In high school, he would act out so he'd be sent to the principal's office instead of having to read aloud in class. He was embarrassed and frustrated by his own limitations.

At home, he was far more at ease, cooking for his siblings and teaching them to swim and fish. He was good with his hands, fixing their bikes and even building a go-cart. "He used to wake us all up for Christmas and we would sneak in the front room to check the presents," his brother Gerald recalled, "but if my daddy heard us, there would be a whipping." As a child, his sister, Laura, underwent surgery on her leg, and she lived for a time in a cast that ran from her ankle to her hip. Kelly would pick her up and carry her around the house. When she couldn't play with the other children, he would entertain her inside and spend his own money to buy her dolls.

But there was a darker side to his innocence:

"Carl was known for being a follower, not a leader, among the guys we hung out with. First, Carl didn't have the brains to lead. Besides, he wanted to be liked and to be included in the things we were doing. The fact that he was so slow in school made him more eager to be part of the crowd outside. It got him into trouble more than once. . . . Because he was so big and strong physically, people would take him along if they thought there would be trouble or a fight. Guess he thought those people were his friends, but they were just using him."

Numerous family members confirmed that Kelly's trial lawyers had not asked them about any of this, even when they had explicitly offered to testify about his past. Would hearing these memories have convinced the jurors to spare Kelly's life?

If not, then what if they had known that his criminal life had begun with the theft of a jar of pig's feet after his stepfather refused to let him eat the family's food? What if they had known that he'd been hit by a car at age fifteen, slamming his head on the pavement, and that afterward he'd get dizzy and black out? That his brain damage, coupled with his intellectual disability, had combined to create a tendency toward impulsive behavior? That he had sought to escape his suffering through substances and on the night of the murder had been on Valium and barbiturates and marijuana and alcohol?

The jury might have seen all that as a series of excuses, to be sure, especially the drug use. But Owen and Recer grew convinced that confronted with all of these stories, all of this evidence of struggle and pain, a jury might come to see Kelly not as a monster who killed in cold blood, but as a broken man who had made a terrible decision in a moment of weakness, who was capable of redemption and worthy of mercy.

Because that's how they saw him. And that is how many of the resource center lawyers were coming to see these men behind the Plexiglas on death row. In order to defend someone properly, you had to study the "diverse frailties" that had produced the act of violence the state was now seeking to punish. And once you did that, you no longer saw these men as monsters; you saw the state as a monster, for refusing to look as you had looked, for turning its head in order to placate the same kinds of public impulses that had created lynchings decades earlier. "I realized fairly early on they were being killed because their lives hadn't worked," one leader at the center later told an interviewer. "They were an inconvenience to everybody else because of how their lives had unfolded and the violence that had come out of their lives. And I found a kind of work that called for every resource and talent that I had and more, working with the people who needed my help the most." After executions, some of the older lawyers would tell the younger ones that there was a value in telling these stories of broken people, of creating a written record of what the state had done. Sometimes you had provided a therapeutic, nonlegal service, finding a long-lost sibling or child and giving your client some comfort and peace before death.

Some saw themselves in line with a long tradition of lawyers who defend the least popular clients—mafiosi, Communists, terrorists. But underneath the pariah pride was a blooming trauma. The writer and therapist Susannah Sheffer interviewed many of these lawyers for a book, and one told her that he pictured himself as a surgeon: "But there's another surgeon in the room who's trying to kill the patient while you're trying to save him, and you have no idea that they're not going to knock you backwards over a crash cart and kill the person while you can't react." One would wake up in the middle of the night and look over at her husband and think: "That's not him. He's been killed, and the murderer is in my bed." She would touch him to prove herself wrong before falling back to sleep. Another would dream of being a death row prisoner "and I'm awaiting the certainty of this fate with these other people who are all awaiting the same fate, and it's this sense of despair, that you're alone, and you're going to die essentially alone."

All around them the politics of criminal justice were growing harsher. "We've carried out thirty-two [executions] since I have been the attorney general of Texas—more than any other state," Jim Mattox said at a Democratic primary debate while running for governor in 1990. "I don't think it's anything to brag about, but just to say that Texas is a very violent society and I do think the death penalty does keep people from going back and committing crimes."

The debate audience broke out in laughter. Had Mattox meant to make a macabre joke about the inability of a dead man to commit murder? His face didn't suggest so at first, but then a mischievous look passed across it. "No doubt about it," he said. "When they ask you if it's a deterrent, it's a deterrent to *some* folks."

Not to be outdone, his opponent Mark White released a campaign ad in which he walked down a corridor lined with photos of men who had been executed while he was governor. The stridency of all this rhetoric caught the attention of *Saturday Night Live*, where "Wade Hammond," a fictional Texas governor, announced, "Death penalty is my middle name!" The camera zoomed out to show that he was sitting atop a pile of coffins: "You fellas comfortable? Now that's what I call cheap housing!" Mattox and White lost the Democratic primary to Ann Richards. She was no great fan of the death penalty, but her aides told her she had no room to maneuver. "I recommend that your response to any questions regarding this issue should be that as governor you would uphold the [death penalty for] juveniles and mentally retarded killers," one advised her in a memo around this time. As governor she oversaw nearly fifty executions, as well as a massive boom in prison construction.

At the same time, in Washington, D.C., the Supreme Court was shifting to the right as Presidents Reagan and Bush appointed a string of conservatives from 1980 to 1992: Anthony Kennedy, Antonin Scalia, Sandra Day O'Connor, David Souter, and Clarence Thomas. These justices tended to rule against death row prisoners, and the message they sent was that federal judges should rarely question the decisions of state judges. Concerned about death penalty cases dragging on forever, the justices restricted the ability of prisoners to submit multiple appeals.

These decisions paved the way for more executions, but only in states where the pathway was otherwise clear. Each state had its own death penalty system, and they varied widely. In some states, particularly outside the South, prosecutors and juries sentenced dozens or even hundreds of people to death, but well-funded public defenders' offices, liberal judges, and a general political ambivalence about executions produced an environment in which few people were actually put to death. This was the case in California, where the page limit for a prisoner's first appeal was more than twice the limit in Texas, and where a defense lawyer could get $50,000 for investigation alone. The whole system was oriented toward slowing things down.

In Texas, the highest court for criminal appeals was separate from the state supreme court, which handled civil cases (in most states, one "supreme court" does both), so death penalty appeals were not as likely to get stalled in a queue. With the Supreme Court's blessing, the federal courts were moving toward letting states do what they wanted with the death penalty, and what everyone in Texas professed to want—from the governor to the attorney general to the many elected judges and district attorneys across the state—was more executions.

Everyone, that is, except the resource center.

In every other criminal case, a prisoner files his appeals as soon as he can, so he can get out of prison as quickly as possible should the courts rule in his favor. In death penalty cases, the incentive is flipped: taking as long as possible to file an appeal, and filing as many as possible, become means to stop the state from carrying out an execution. This practically invites defense lawyers to push the system to its limit.

Judges had supported the Texas Resource Center at first because they were tired of the chaos of last-minute appeals on execution nights. But the center's lawyers, convinced they had an ethical obligation to do everything possible to save their client, filed new claims as aggressively as they could, no matter how close to the time of execution. This created lots of work for the judges, clerks, and prosecutors, many of whom grew resentful. "I think their strategy was just to overwhelm the judiciary so that the judges would say 'There is no way we can review three hundred pages in fifteen minutes; we have to issue a stay!' I thought that was offensive," recalled Rick Wetzel, a senior court staffer at the time. Combined with life-and-death stakes, these chaotic moments frequently led to accusations of bad faith. Prosecutors and judges began accusing the center's lawyers of lying.

While representing death row prisoner Robert Black, one center lawyer had gotten in touch with a man named Grady Deckard, who had been in jail with Black and had testified at his trial that he'd heard Black planning an escape. This helped prosecutors prove that Black would be dangerous in the future. But when the center approached Deckard, he admitted he had lied in order to get more jail privileges and favorable treatment from prosecutors in his own case. (Such use of "jailhouse informants" was common, although usually they testified at trials about how they'd heard the defendant confess to the crime in question; Deckard's tale was more creative.) When the center made this known, the DA charged Deckard with perjury and blasted the center in the press. In 1992, Harris County DA Johnny Holmes filed a complaint with a federal appeals court, claiming the center was making up facts. Numerous prosecutors wrote letters, later cited in congressional reports, accusing center employees of misrepresenting themselves to witnesses, filing false claims in court, and manipulating the legal process to stall executions. One judge banned the center from his court. Another judge, approached by a resource center lawyer, said, "I think your whole place ought to be wiped out and defunded. Now, what do you want?"

The Texas State Bar Association to this day has no public record of any disciplinary sanctions against a resource center lawyer. But some center lawyers did feel justified—even took a kind of pleasure—in making prosecutors and judges sweat. Every little victory, every stay of execution or gesture of interest from a new court, was more than just an excuse for patting yourself on the back: You had saved a life, if just briefly, from these callous political forces.

The emotional toll of this work could breed a certain puckishness. At one point Rob Owen described himself, to a newspaper reporter covering the Kelly case, as a "leftist radical nut." He was reprimanded by his bosses at the center; this was precisely the reputation they were struggling to avoid.

Nobody promoted this reputation as forcefully as Jerry Patterson. A first-term state senator from Houston with libertarian views, he had become aware of the center after the actor Danny Glover appeared at the state legislature claiming that a man represented by the center was innocent and facing execution. Patterson was horrified, but then he spoke with prosecutors from Houston who assured him Glover was mistaken and the man was plainly guilty. The execution was eventually stayed, and the case returned to the courts, but Patterson was indignant. He believed the resource center was trying to manipulate public opinion through celebrity power and abolish the death penalty by any means necessary. He set up a 1-800 hotline, advertising on the radio that citizens could call and be sent pamphlets about the center. "All of a sudden we have a new level of due process and that's the Hollywood jury, the celebrity jury," he declared in the press. "They can come to Texas and tell us what to do."

Years later, pressed to clarify his views, Patterson said he believed the center should not be trying to help every single death row prisoner who had already been through a full round of appeals; they should instead focus on the cases that featured real constitutional violations, real claims of innocence. Within the center, some of the lawyers also thought they should focus more on particular cases rather than spread their resources so thin. But if there were legitimate policy questions to answer, they were buried under anger and distrust. That fall, Patterson tried to prove that the center was using its federally funded budget of $4 million to mount a political crusade to abolish the death penalty. He asked them to open their books.

When they refused, saying it would break attorney-client privilege, he showed up at their door, tailed by TV cameras. He never made it in, but he took the center to court, winning at first and then losing on appeal, all the while drumming up publicity. The *Houston Chronicle* took his side in an editorial and dispatched a reporter to produce three thousand words that blended the era's anticrime righteousness with a muckraking tone usually reserved for crooked politicians. "Thanks partly to high-profile cases and its own efforts to turn executions into public relations extravaganzas, these death row angels are sweating under an increasingly warm spotlight," the reporter wrote. "Prosecutors call them liars and cheats. Judges accuse them of manipulating the courts." The center's leaders got to respond in the article with "sighs of exasperation" and "earnest explanations" of how they were victims of the political climate. After all, before they were around, hundreds of people had faced execution without any representation, and even now the center was barely staying afloat as it tried to make sure these men had their legitimate claims heard by courts before they were killed. Patterson would later recall that after losing his legal battle against the center, he sent them flowers.

Politicians, prosecutors, state court judges—all of them could be ignored as long as federal judges continued to grant stays of execution. But in September 1993, even that wall started to crack, when the center filed an appeal for a prisoner named Lesley Lee Gosch two days before his execution date. The center lawyers explained that they had been trying to find him an outside lawyer and, having failed, were now stepping in to get him a stay so they could represent him themselves. This had worked to stop an execution multiple times in the past, but this time, a series of judges ruled against him, until one stepped in with only a half hour to spare.

This issue ended up before the Supreme Court, where resource center leader Mandy Welch argued on behalf of another prisoner, Frank McFarland, who had asked for his own stay of execution. Welch had just begun her second sentence when Justice Antonin Scalia interrupted her to ask how long the center had waited before stepping in as his lawyer, and suggested they had intentionally held off from doing so. "I find it extraordinary to think it was something you did not want to happen," Scalia said. This was a common accusation leveled by Texas judges and prosecutors: that the center wanted to create chaos to shame the system. Now it was in the mouth of a Supreme Court justice.

Welch tried to keep her cool, countering with statistics: The center, she said, had eighteen lawyers, five of whom had only two years of experience. They were involved in the cases of at least 220 of the 376 prisoners on death row in Texas. The month of McFarland's execution date, ten executions were scheduled, seven of them for men without lawyers. Scalia responded, "Don't waste any more of your argument time on this. I just want you to know that I am not happy with the performance of the Texas Resource Center in the cases that come before me."

"I understand," Welch said.

"Try harder."

As a bunker mentality set in, the resource center lawyers pushed themselves to the brink. They came to see themselves as the only thing standing between the poor, broken souls they represented and the gurney. In that environment, why wouldn't they stay up all night working, neglecting their families and their friends and their health? Why wouldn't they get nasty with judges, seeing them as accomplices to state-sanctioned murder? The young lawyers at the Texas Resource Center had moved there right out of law school and had never made time for friends outside the center. Those with families struggled to be spouses and parents. Many quit. When a couple of Colorado lawyers came down with the intention of volunteering for a year, one didn't last more than a few days, and he spent them curled in a fetal position on a couch in a colleague's office.

Rob Owen bought a white '65 Ford pickup truck from a farmer on the rural outskirts of Austin, and the young lawyers would pile into the bed of the truck to go out to lunch before heading back to pull an all-nighter. Sometimes at night they'd descend upon the Texas Chili Parlor in Austin for drinks—sometimes too many—and one night an investigator for the center almost ended up in a fistfight with a prosecutor. On another evening, lawyer Brent Newton realized he was sitting and eating with a colleague while their friends were back at the office working all night, and he asked why they weren't helping. She said to him, "Well, in ten days it could be your guy, and if you help now you won't have the energy."

When they lost, it meant going back out to Huntsville. It meant telling their clients that they had done everything possible but it wasn't enough and now death was coming.

During the summer of 1993, the Supreme Court lifted the stay in Carl Kelly's case. His execution was set for August 20. Owen tried to slam through one final appeal, arguing that Kelly's mental impairments had made it impossible for him to truly understand the right to remain silent when he was first arrested, so his confession should have been thrown out. Owen cited the fact that Jerry Jurek, even after the Supreme Court used his case to uphold the Texas death penalty law, had been freed from death row on a similar argument.

In the meantime, Recer filled Kelly's clemency application with stories about his childhood, but she knew these applications were virtually never granted. And the family members of Kelly's victim Steven Pryor wanted to see the execution through. "I know you're not supposed to hate, you're supposed to forgive people," his sister told a reporter. "I don't think I could. . . . I think he deserves to die." Kelly decided it would be too shattering for his own family to watch the execution—"My grandmother, she'll be crying before she gets in the doors," he had told a reporter—so he asked his lawyers to be there. On the one hand, it was the last thing you could do for your client; on the other, it was the worst imaginable illustration of your failure, with a three-hour drive to think about it.

In August 1993, Recer drove to Huntsville with her girlfriend and got a hotel room. She had never seen an execution before. The first few executions after Charlie Brooks in the 1980s had brought out crowds, but by 1993, executions in Huntsville had become just common enough to go mostly unnoticed in the town. A writer for *Harper's*, in town to witness Kelly's execution, took her own informal survey and discovered that off-duty prison guards at the Dairy Queen, as well as college students at a pool hall, had no idea it was happening. Across the street from the prison, in a parking lot, a small group of anti-death-penalty protesters banged on pots and pans and played wooden flutes. For a moment, they were joined by two pickup trucks, which zoomed into the lot, filled with college kids who heckled the protesters by belting out, "You're on the highway to hell!"

Recer wore a yellow dress, because Kelly had said it was his favorite color. Owen joined her, wearing a rumpled blue pinstripe suit, his face pale, his beard and hair matted with sweat. He had gotten to spend a final half hour with Kelly. The idea was to tell him he was out of options, but Kelly already knew. He was smoking cigarette after cigarette. "I don't want you to get the idea that I'm chain-smoking," he told Owen. "I just don't have any matches. I have to light one off the other." Owen told him he loved him and walked out, nervous that when the time came for the execution he would let Kelly down one more time, by falling apart in the witness room and making Kelly feel sad on his behalf.

When they entered the execution chamber, Kelly was already on the gurney. Owen noticed the bright, gleaming white of his new tennis shoes, which he had been allowed to buy at the commissary. A microphone hung down over his face to pipe his last words into the witness room, which was now separated by glass from the chamber. He turned his head. "Hey, Rob," he said.

There was no visible microphone in the witness room, but still Owen responded, "Can you hear us, Carl?"

"Oh, yeah. I can hear you."

An hour before, Owen had accepted that he had spoken to his client for the final time. Now he had to improvise. "How are you doing, Carl?" he asked.

"I'm doing all right. You the best, Rob."

"Thanks, Carl."

At Kelly's head and feet were Jack Pursley and Carroll Pickett, the warden and chaplain who had been in this room for virtually all of the sixty-three lethal injections since Charlie Brooks.

"Do you have any final statement?" Pursley asked.

"I'm an African warrior," Kelly said. "Born to breathe, born to die."

Owen was confused; he had never heard Kelly say this sort of thing before. Recer wondered if it was something he'd picked up on death row, where a type of black nationalism had been spreading among some of the men. It was one more sign of what his family had told her, about how he tended to be a follower. He must have thought this would be a dramatic thing to say in his final moments.

"I feel the poison running now," Kelly said.

"Won't be but a minute, Carl," Owen said. "Don't forget that we love you." Recer was silent. Kelly's eyes locked on the ceiling. He coughed and gasped, and his eyes slowly appeared to glaze over. Rob closed his own eyes. His ears filled with the now deafening sound of the reporters' pencils, scratching against paper.

By twelve thirty, Owen and Recer were back outside, where they met several colleagues. Recer was in a state of shock, and channeled it toward anger. She did not blame herself, because she had not made any of the decisions about litigation that had led to this moment. That was Owen's burden; it would be hers later.

Owen's memory fuzzes out here. He remembers picking up Kelly's prison property, which had been left in several orange mesh bags on a curb outside the unit. Kelly had asked him to deliver his belongings to his family, but to first remove some inappropriate photos. Along with old holiday cards and letters, there was a shoebox, which had held his new tennis shoes. Owen remembers buying a beer, but not drinking it, and he does not remember the three-hour drive home to Austin in the middle of the night, but he does remember waking up in his own bed the next morning, and then sleeping through the whole next day. He does not remember talking to Recer about what they had witnessed.

Years later, describing how they handled the emotional burden of seeing their clients executed, lawyers from the center would speak in sweeping terms of the supportive community of fighters who held each other up, who would always put aside their banker's box of papers to lend an ear. "There was also a sense you could go into anyone's office and confide in them in your moments of despair," one recalled.

But sometimes, recalling the very hardest moments, the tone would shift, and they would admit that it was more complicated, that actually they did not always share their deepest traumas. "People didn't really know how to console each other," one said. "I suspect there was an assumption that if we go too far down that road, either the bereaved or the consoling, it may be too much for us to do the work. It would make it too difficult to go on to the next case, to do what you had to do." After his own client was executed, this lawyer wrote a long, vulnerable email to a colleague and barely received a response. "I remember needing somebody to hear me out, and realizing that it felt too dangerous for this other person to go there." Perhaps Owen did not remember talking to Recer about Kelly's death because they never did.

Some managed to keep the trauma from ruining their home lives, but many did not. Some marriages failed. Others—between center lawyers—were born. Recer, as was her tendency, intellectualized the trauma and channeled her rage into an ever more grueling work ethic. She noticed one rare point of agreement between her fellow defense lawyers and the prosecutors and judges who hated them: It was crazy to put so much of the emphasis on the appeal rather than the trial, which was supposed to be the main event in these cases. As prosecutors saw it, if a defendant received better representation at trial, there would be fewer good arguments against his execution at the end of the appeals. As Recer saw it, if he had received that better representation, he wouldn't have gotten the death penalty in the first place.

Owen's last act on Kelly's behalf was to deliver his property to his family, and his grandmother insisted on showing him the box that now held his ashes. Back at his office, he placed a photo of his former client on the wall. Recer kept buying lottery tickets. She was still technically enrolled in her graduate program in history, but she had no plans to go back and write a dissertation, so she finished her master's thesis. Her advisers had allowed her to extend her analysis into the present, meaning it could crystallize her years of immersion among the resource center lawyers.

While some of her prose drifted toward the academic and theoretical, some passages displayed the radicalization of her time at the center, conveyed through a literary tone that was overwrought but vivid:

One need only drive through the gates of the Ellis I Unit, past the lush azaleas of summer, fresh spring pansies and dazzling fall mums, all tended by rows upon rows of inmates, their prison whites startling against inky flesh, toiling under the direction of pale and flabby armed horsemen, to understand with clarity the racial dimensions of criminal justice in Texas. Only a glance at the stacks upon stacks of caged and condemned men within the walls is needed to know surely, viscerally, that capital punishment is genocide.

Her thesis made scant mention of the crimes committed by these defendants; to her, the far greater horror was her society's effort to portray them as monsters. In her final chapter, she described Kelly's execution, comparing it to a lynching: "The ancient spectacle continues today in the urban setting of downtown Huntsville, with drunken crowds singing, dancing, and brandishing placards outside the Walls Unit, cheering the demise of their prey and hurling epithets at abolitionists who congregate on the opposite street corner for candlelight vigils." The 231-page text of her thesis ends abruptly, with a newspaper reporter's account that names her and describes her reactions to Kelly's execution in the third person. Suddenly the omniscient narrator of the text is a player within it: "Owen hugged Recer, who quietly wept . . . [Warden] Pursley turned to the witnesses. 'The time of death is 12:22 A.M.' " At the beginning of the thesis, which sits to this day on a shelf in a library at the University of Texas, she placed a dedication:

CARL EUGENE "BO" KELLY,

BORN "AN AFRICAN WARRIOR," MARCH 27, 1959
KILLED BY THE STATE OF TEXAS,
12:22 CST, AUGUST 20, 1993.

YOUR DIGNITY ELEVATES US ALL.

6

SCATTERED AMONG THE PAGES OF THE *HOUSTON CHRONICLE* WERE brief, cold write-ups, seldom more than a couple hundred words, each telegraphing oceans of trauma: the two runaway girls, ages twelve and sixteen, promised tattoos by men at a bus station who instead raped them; the store clerk beaten with a shotgun during a robbery; the boys, ages one and five, shot and drowned by their father; the homeless veteran fatally stabbed by teenagers who had decided to go "bum bashing." At the beginning of 1995, the country's fourth-largest city was experiencing levels of violent crime on par with New York City and Los Angeles, and the prosecutors working for Johnny Holmes had their hands full with murders, rapes, and robberies.

But this was all easy to ignore in the suburbs, where those with some money could move their families away from that senseless, terrifying violence, so that they encountered it only while thumbing through the *Chronicle* or flipping channels and seeing the B-roll footage of yellow caution tape and flashing police lights.

On a cool evening in January, in a house twenty miles from downtown, amid the manicured lawns and tall, skinny pine trees that lined Apple Valley Lane, Allison Vickers and her best friend, Kim Williamson, weren't watching the news; they were folding laundry. Kim was staying there temporarily. The house belonged to Vickers's father, but he was out of town on a business trip to Louisiana, so the kids had the place to themselves.

Earlier that evening, Allison and her twin brother, Matt, along with Kim and their younger brother, Jack, had spent the evening at their mother's house, eating fried shrimp and playing with the puppies they had recently adopted. They mostly talked about the future. Kim, who was twenty, was about to move in with her father in Michigan, where she would pursue her dreams of going to college and becoming a pharmacist. The twins, who were nineteen, had taken a semester off after high school and were two days away from starting classes at a nearby community college. The evening was a bit of a celebration: Kim moving, the twins starting school. "It was the most perfect night," their mother later recalled. She had recently been divorced from their father, Steve, and it seemed to her that her children were finally growing comfortable living between two households. She was thrilled that they were going back to school, was excited by their excitement. Much of the dinner was spent discussing their schedules, which Matt had written down in a notebook. He was already thinking about how he might celebrate the end of the semester a few months later, perhaps with a camping trip.

After dinner, Allison and Kim drove to a Dairy Queen for dessert, and then to Allison's father's house, where the twins lived most of the time. Kim needed to get her things together; she was planning to begin her drive to Michigan the next morning and wanted to get an early start. Allison helped her pack.

Allison's brothers Matt and Jack arrived later. Matt invited over his friend Grant. Upstairs, the two girls folded clothes; downstairs, the three boys watched television.

At a nearby apartment complex, another group of high schoolers were also making plans, discussing how they might raise $500 to buy a pound of marijuana to sell. One wanted to rob someone at an ATM machine, but the others didn't like that idea. Another owned a .38 revolver and a scale for weighing drugs, and they talked about selling these items. Michael Wilson said he knew a kid named Matt Vickers who might be interested. He went to a payphone and called him. Vickers told Wilson he didn't want either item, at least not tonight. But Wilson told his friends that Vickers usually had a pound or two of marijuana with him, and lately he had been talking about how he had received a thousand dollars in insurance money from a car accident. The idea emerged: They should go to Vickers's house and rob him. As they stood in the complex parking lot, another friend showed up. His name was Edward Capetillo, but he went by Eddie.

The group drove to Capetillo's house so he could pick up a .22 rifle he owned. Wilson, the one who knew Matt Vickers personally, drove to the house on Apple Valley Lane to scout it out while the others waited at a park. He didn't want to go in himself, since Vickers would recognize him. The plan was to ring the doorbell, and then Capetillo would hit whoever answered with the butt of his rifle. Then they'd all go in and round up everyone else and find the money and drugs.

After they split up, two of the boys went toward the backyard, where they saw a short iron fence they could hop over. But as they approached, they saw several dogs. They turned back and decided to make a wide circle back toward the front door, where the others had already entered.

When they rounded the corner of the house, something flashed before them: a person running.

Kim Williamson stepped out of the room where she was packing a suitcase with Allison Vickers to take a call from her father. From inside the room, Allison heard the front door open downstairs, and then footsteps coming up to the second floor. When a figure came into the room, at first her brain registered it as her brother Matt, but then she saw a second person behind him. One of these not-Matts, she now realized, was holding a rifle.

He walked toward Williamson in the hallway. "Get downstairs now," he said. "I am serious." He grabbed the phone from her.

"What do you think you're doing?" Williamson said.

He threw the phone on the floor.

Williamson screamed: "Dad!"

Now Allison stood up and the other young man, who was short and skinny, with dark skin, came toward her. "Get downstairs now!" he said.

She felt a foot on her back; he was kicking her. She stumbled toward the door and made her way to the stairs. As she reached the bottom, she realized she was right by the front door. She unlocked it and bolted out, feeling the wet ground soak into her socks. She prayed: *God, just put wings on my back.*

She made it to a neighbor's house and called 9-1-1. While she waited, she heard several loud pops coming from her house. When the police arrived, the intruders were gone, and Vickers was escorted to a police car, where she was told to sit in the back seat.

She started picking up fragments of the detectives' conversation: The brother, they said, and a girl unrelated to the family were dead. Allison sat in the car, in a state of shock, for more than an hour while they investigated, wearing a T-shirt and shorts and wet socks. Before she knew it, she was being driven to the police station, where she was asked to talk to a sketch artist. She was inundated by books, full of samples to choose from: eyes, eyebrows, noses, lips, hairlines, cheeks. She sat with the artist until six in the morning. She learned that after she'd escaped, the young man with the rifle, Eddie Capetillo, had shot Matt Vickers in the head. Another boy had shot Matt's friend Grant, but he had survived. When Kim Williamson tried to escape, she tripped, and then Capetillo shot her several times, in the chest and throat.

At her twin brother's funeral, Allison thought she saw Eddie Capetillo again. It was just a young man who looked like him, but she insisted he be asked to sit out of her view. A detective told her she should leave town; the young men had not been caught and might know she could identify them. Who knew if perhaps they were looking for her already? What if they had friends who could track her down? Her father had a friend pack a bag with her belongings, and then he drove her to her grandmother's home in Louisiana.

Her grandmother slept with her in the same bed at first. It was many more months before she could sleep with the light off. Any little noise could make her nervous, could make her think, if just for a second, that someone was kicking in a door.

She knew that sitting in her grandmother's house with nothing to do would make her dwell on what had happened, so she enrolled at McNeese State University in Lake Charles. She moved into the dormitories and started classes, but she still tried to let herself grieve in whatever way felt natural; one time she left the campus and went to her aunt's house nearby, where she spent the rest of the day lying on a couch and crying. She had gone to church occasionally growing up, but her survival had given her a strong sense that God had saved her life for a reason, and she joined the Baptist Student Union.

At night, she learned to tell herself that little noises were nothing to be afraid of. On visits to Houston, she sometimes held herself back from mentioning Matt around her parents. They were struggling, too, and she didn't want to further burden them. Already divorced, they were now even more at odds. Since their father had been out of town when Matt was killed, their mother blamed him in part for what had happened, as had the family of the other victim, Kim Williamson, who decided to sue him. In order to heal, Allison needed other people to confide in. At the courthouse, she would deal with various officials, and one emerged as someone she could rely on, someone who would ask how she was doing and really seemed to mean it. It was the woman who would be prosecuting Capetillo, Elsa Alcala. She looked to be in her early thirties. As she visited their home, showed Allison around the courtroom, and prepared her to testify, Steve Vickers noticed his daughter warming to this woman, who was about the age an older sister might be. Alcala said that she'd lost both her parents at a young age. She would always be there to talk to, she said, handing over her personal phone number.

The parents of both Matt Vickers and Kim Williamson wanted the young man who had killed them to get the death penalty, and Alcala told them that her boss, Johnny Holmes, was committed to seeing him executed. But behind the scenes, she was ambivalent. There was no question that Capetillo had killed two people in a vicious way, but he was also seventeen, a high school kid, with very little in the way of a criminal history. There were flashes of violence in his past—he was known to push other soccer players, and once, when he received a red card, he punched the referee—but was that enough to convince a jury he would be dangerous in the future? In Alcala's first death penalty case, the defendant, Gerald Eldridge, had stalked and attacked many people over many years.

Though Capetillo's age could be seen as a sign of rehabilitative potential, it could also suggest he had a long career of violence ahead of him. The latter interpretation was far more in sync with the national consensus. Shortly before the trial, the criminologist John DiIulio published an influential article called "The Coming of the Super-Predators," in which he described "kids who have absolutely no respect for human life." Perhaps Alcala could show the jury that Capetillo was one of these super-predators. Her co-counsel, Lyn McClellan, was another one of Johnny Holmes's top deputies. She didn't know what a red card in soccer meant, but he told her, "That's a big deal." He knew what their boss would think was heinous, and the case stuck out to him because crimes like this just didn't happen out in the suburbs, on streets like Apple Valley Lane. Alcala would later admit that this sounded a little classist—she would stop short of saying another word—but she agreed that the brutality of the crime felt heightened by its quiet surroundings. The prosecutors did not dwell on the fact that Matt himself dealt marijuana, a fact that, had he been black or Latino, might have made the crime appear less shocking.

As Alcala prepared for trial, she felt herself growing emotionally connected to Allison Vickers and her parents. The court documents would read "The State of Texas vs. Edward Capetillo," but the first of these, which Alcala represented, was an abstraction. The Vickers family, and their pain, were right in front of her. The twins' mother said she kept imagining the life she'd always pictured, with Matt grown and kids of his own running around. Meanwhile, Matt and Allison's younger brother, Jack, had to live with the fact that he survived by the dumb luck of having driven back to his mother's house, and had returned to see his brother lying in a pool of blood.

In October, nine months after the murder and four months before the case was set to go to trial, Allison Vickers was asleep in her dorm room when she received news that her grandparents were downstairs in the lobby. This was strange, so late at night, and she asked her suitemates to walk down with her. On the stairs, she started to feel nauseous, thinking perhaps one of her cousins had been in a car accident. When she got downstairs, they told her that her brother Jack had taken his own life.

Alcala agreed with her bosses to seek the death penalty, and she knew it would please the family, but something still nagged at her. It was the way the mother appeared desperate for the result. It seemed as if she thought Capetillo's death would mend the hole left by the disappearance of her two sons. Alcala knew this was a mistake. She had known from a young age that when you lose so much of your family all at once, the hole might get easier to manage, but it never goes away.

In many times and places, it has been up to victims of crime to respond to those who have harmed them. In colonial America, you would pay a watchman to arrest someone, and then pay a constable to process the case, and then a lawyer to prosecute. The process was more akin to suing, and often the point was restitution: The victim could force the defendant to work off his debt. In sparsely populated regions like Texas, giving the government the power to prosecute and punish simply wasn't practical, and the residue of that reality—the phrase "frontier justice"—long outlasted the formal establishment of law enforcement throughout the West.

Inspired by the Enlightenment, Americans eventually came to view crime as a violation of a social contract, and the response to it as the job of the state, but the romance that accrued around vigilantism never totally dissipated. As crime and a corresponding social anxiety rose in the 1970s, movies like *Death Wish* and *Dirty Harry* updated and urbanized the archetype of the lone man who seeks justice when law enforcement fails. In 1984, when Bernhard Goetz felt threatened by four young African American men on a New York City subway and responded by shooting them, he became a folk hero.

Throughout the 1970s and 1980s, the tension between these two strains of American culture—one celebrating vigilantism and the other law and order—was resolved by a new idea: that victims of crime should play a role in the state's administration of justice. A movement coalesced from many directions. There were feminists who believed that rape victims should be given a stronger voice in prosecutions, and civil rights leaders who wanted the same for victims of crimes motivated by hate. Law-and-order conservatives thought the courts had spent too much energy on the rights of criminals and felt the rights of victims would offer a counterbalance.

Crime victims themselves were complaining that they didn't find out what happened in court until they saw it in the newspaper, and that they weren't informed of hearings about their attackers' parole; they literally wanted their voice heard in such forums. In 1982, President Reagan appointed a Task Force on Victims of Crime, which recommended that victims be allowed to speak at sentencing hearings. It was, in a way, the flip side of the mitigation argument: If the defendant was allowed to present personal information to the jury in hopes of sparking sympathy, the victims should be able to do the same.

The Supreme Court zigzagged on the issue, ruling that family members of victims could not testify in the punishment phase of trials in 1987, and then overturning its own opinion in 1991. "You know one of the purposes of retribution was to prevent people from taking law into their own hands," Justice Scalia said at the oral argument in *Payne v. Tennessee*, "saying the State will avenge you; you need not avenge yourselves." Victim impact testimony—the image of a grieving parent or sibling on the stand—helped turn the victims into the protagonists in media coverage of crime, and the death penalty could now be viewed as a service to those left behind. Often, prosecutors would say as much to the jury, presenting justice as a zero-sum game in which giving a defendant a life sentence instead of death was tantamount to spitting on the victim's grave.

The public symbols of the victims' rights movement were usually the white parents of young children who had been murdered. Many of the laws the movement inspired were named after individual victims stripped of a last name, evoking a sort of innocent everychild: "Marsy," "Jessica," "Adam." Critics like the law professor Lynne Henderson complained of how the victims valorized in the public sphere were never "prostitutes beaten senseless by pimps or 'johns,' drug addicts mugged and robbed of their fixes, gang members killed during a feud, or misdemeanants raped by cellmates." Defense lawyers argued that their clients shouldn't be sentenced more harshly based on the identity of the person they killed—and that the trend might further exacerbate another trend, in which people who killed white and female victims received the death penalty more often than those who killed minorities and men.

These dissenters gained little traction. Crime victim groups had lobbied successfully at the Texas capitol for rights and compensation throughout the 1980s, but in the early 1990s, Houston—with its high crime rate and large, conservative suburbs—became an epicenter of the movement. One of the most publicly visible of these family members was Randy Ertman, whose daughter Jennifer was raped and killed, along with her friend Elizabeth Peña, by a group of young men on a June evening in 1993. It took days to find their bodies. President Bill Clinton wrote letters to the families. The conservative columnist William F. Buckley penned a column, "Brutal Urban Frontier Terrifying as the Old West," in which he suggested that the young women should have been allowed to carry guns. Harris County DA Johnny Holmes told the Peña family, "I hope to God that I'm still alive when they execute the sons of bitches. I will make it a point in my life to see these bastards fry."

A judge allowed Randy Ertman to speak directly to the defendants at several of their trials. Facing the man believed to be the ringleader, he said, "You can look at me if you want." When the defendant did not, he shouted, "Look at me!" Several people in the courtroom started crying. The defendant turned his head. "You're not even an animal," Ertman said. "You're worse than that. You're a piece of shit." The Ertman-Peña murders helped bolster the power of a new victims' organization called Justice for All, which was far more explicitly political than its predecessors. With three thousand members, it became a key endorsement for anybody running for office in Houston and ran attack ads against candidates they perceived as weak on crime.

Lawmakers in the state legislatures and Congress also cited the interests of victims when they restricted the ability of death row inmates to endlessly appeal their sentences. The term "closure" grew in usage; in 1989, the word was used a single time in an American news article about the death penalty, but a decade later it was showing up hundreds of times a year. "As families of victims we can never find any closure, when we know that we have to continuously worry about the appeals after appeals," Linda Kelley told Texas legislators in 1995, the year before Eddie Capetillo killed Matt Vickers and Kim Williamson. "I know people that have had someone on death row for sixteen, nineteen years and I just don't know if I'll live that long to see him pay for the crime that he did to me." Kelley's son and daughter had been murdered at a pawn shop in Houston, and as it turned out, she did live long enough to see their killer, Leo Jenkins, die: Soon after her speech to the legislature, the state prison system gave victims' families the option to witness executions, and the Kelley family became the first.

Robin Kelley, the sole surviving child in the family, hoped she and her parents could set a standard of decent behavior—if the first family to witness an execution caused a scene, she feared, state officials might change their minds about letting future families in. Although her family had spent years hoping to see the execution, she was spiritually conflicted. "If Jenkins did anything to make us feel sorry for him," she recalled thinking, "how will that change my grief process?" She prayed: "Hey, God, is it okay for me to watch it?"

She decided to attend, and when the family arrived in Huntsville, prison officials gave them a tour of the death chamber and told them a counselor was available if they needed to discuss the experience. Once they were in the chamber, Kelley watched Jenkins's body closely and witnessed his soul leave it.

She found the experience to be healing. Then she looked over at her father. He was smiling. It was a stunningly quick transformation. For years, he had been a shell, rarely talking, slumping and frowning. But after the execution they went out to eat Mexican food in Huntsville and he was his old voluble self. He seemed to walk faster, to break into a grin with less effort. It was as though, she later said, "the bowling ball attached to the back of his neck was gone."

The Kelleys allowed an HBO crew to follow them. After the documentary on their experience aired, they were approached by producers from major talk shows. But it quickly became clear there were preconditions. Linda Kelley spent two hours on the phone with an *Oprah* producer who told her they didn't want her onstage unless she forgave Jenkins. She refused to go on the show.

In polls, many Americans have said they support the death penalty because it offers "satisfaction and closure" to the families of murder victims, and more than a dozen states have allowed families to witness executions. (There has been very little scholarly research on the subject, though one study found that victim families in Minnesota, which does not have the death penalty, described "higher levels of physical, psychological, and behavioral health" than their counterparts in Texas, in part because they felt they were not subject to an unpredictable appeals process.) But the rise of victim impact testimony, coupled with the power of groups like JFA, also shrouded the existence of another group of victims: those who didn't favor the death penalty and didn't think it was healing.

Other organizations with names like Murder Victims' Families for Reconciliation and Murder Victims' Families for Human Rights were complaining that prosecutors and other state officials would ignore them while tacitly or even explicitly favoring victims who wanted the harshest punishments available. Jeanette Popp, whose daughter was murdered in Austin in 1988, found that when prosecutors learned she didn't want the man responsible to get a death sentence, they stopped telling her about his court dates. In 1992, Houston's mayor hired a former parole officer named Andy Kahan to head up a new Mayor's Crime Victims Office. He was the one who lobbied the state to allow families to witness executions. He was also accused of showing favoritism to pro-death-penalty victims, though he denied this.

Victims who opposed executions felt that state officials ignored them, just as victims who supported executions thought the media was unfair to them. Each endured the pressure to perform to the expectations, and for the ideological satisfaction, of others.

Allison Vickers testified in the first phase of Capetillo's trial, but after he was found guilty and it was time to decide the punishment, her mother took the stand. "So within the past year you have had your two sons die; is that correct?" Elsa Alcala asked her.

"Right," she responded.

She was clearly struggling, and Alcala tried to comfort her. "I know it's hard. We're just going to have to get through it, okay?"

"Okay."

Alcala asked about the dinner they'd had before the murder. "They were getting older and growing up," the mother said, "you know, getting over the divorce, and all of the things that happened in their lives . . . it was just . . . it was just . . . it was perfect." She described the care with which Matt planned his college schedule, the way he wrote it down in his notebook. Later, that same notebook would be repurposed, its pages filled not with lecture notes and homework assignments, but instead with funeral arrangements.

Alcala turned the conversation to Jack, her other son, who had taken his own life in the wake of the murders.

"He seemed to hold up pretty good for a few weeks," she said, "but then he said every morning when he woke up the first thing he saw when he opened his eyes was Matt laying there dead."

Alcala asked how this all affected her.

"You think a lot about your future, that you had thought would be, with the grandchildren and children around you," she said. "It feels like your life has almost been taken completely away. . . . It makes me angry at almost everything. . . . You feel some things that other people don't or can't relate to . . . you feel very alone."

She was followed on the stand by Grant Barnett, Matt's friend who had been shot and narrowly survived. "Basically this killed the person that I was," he told the jury. "I was forced to grow up. . . . I don't feel comfortable doing the things my friends do every weekend. It's no fun to go out anymore, I don't like other kids my age being around me, being behind me." The smallest social interactions could fill him with a piercing nervousness: "I have to have my back to a wall just about anywhere."

He concluded with a question that continued to haunt him: "How could God have let this happen?"

Even Capetillo's lawyer, during his closing argument, told the jury, "I hope that each one of you will remember Kimberly and Matthew and Grant the rest of your lives." But he noted that the testimony from the survivors had nothing to do with the questions the jury had to answer about future dangerousness and mitigating circumstances. And then he seemed to undercut his own argument, telling them, "You can consider whatever you want to consider as jurors."

In Alcala's closing argument, she discussed Capetillo's red card for punching a referee and obvious proclivity toward violence. Then she contrasted the survivors' wrenching testimony with Capetillo's way of talking about the victims. After the murders, Capetillo allegedly told a friend, "If the girls had been prettier, I would have raped them."

This statement had so disturbed the friend that it prompted him to turn Capetillo in to the police. Now, before the jury, Alcala repeated it, and she pointed out that one of those girls, Allison Vickers, was in the courtroom.

"It's so offensive I even hate repeating it," Alcala told the jury. "I was not happy that she had to hear this." But she repeated it nonetheless because "if that's not the most callous, cruel, vicious comment that somebody could say, after executing two people in cold blood, I don't know what is."

After the trial, a male juror approached Allison and Matt's father, Steve Vickers, and told him that another juror, a woman, had not wanted to sentence Capetillo to death. This juror told the woman that he would sit in a corner of the jury room and read a book until she changed her mind. Eventually she did.

After two death penalty trials, Alcala went to work for the "special crimes" unit handling complex drug and corruption cases. Soon after came another death penalty trial, her last. The defendant, Enrique Mosquera, owed $80,000 to Hurtado Heinar Prado for cocaine, but rather than pay, he hired a hit man to kill Prado. Multiple people were killed in the chaotic shooting, including the target's three-year-old nephew. Alcala prosecuted Mosquera, and the jury chose to give him life in prison rather than the death penalty. The case barely stuck in her memory, after two decades, she could scarcely remember the defendant's name. Her colleague who prosecuted the hit man was convinced Alcala's "heart wasn't in it," though she was willing to "toe the party line." In an office where prosecutors handed out syringe pens and called their band Death by Injection, even a bit of ambivalence stood out.

Nearly a decade into her career, Alcala faced a decision. Would she compete for the highest ranks, like division chief or first assistant? Would she run to replace Johnny Holmes someday? Any job in which the boss is elected presents a risk: Holmes's replacement could always choose to fire the old hands like her. A common career path was to work as a defense lawyer, promising inside knowledge of the other side. Another path was to become a judge. You could run for these spots, but when someone retired and there wasn't an election coming up, the governor would appoint the replacement.

When a spot came open, in 1998, Alcala's new husband, Dan, a fellow lawyer and former police officer, encouraged her to apply. Even if she didn't get this one, he said, the process might set her up to get the next. She was interviewed by an assistant to Governor George W. Bush. She was a member of the Republican Party, and she knew the party was eager to cultivate Latinx leaders. It was becoming clear that the electoral math would soon favor whichever party appealed to this demographic. Her inspirational life story didn't hurt either. Still, she was surprised and delighted when she learned she had been picked. At thirty-four, she would become one of the youngest judges in the state.

Alcala spent three and a half years presiding over a criminal district court in downtown Houston. She oversaw only one trial that led to a death sentence, but it was also her job to make recommendations to the Court of Criminal Appeals on how to rule in cases that had passed through her court before she'd gotten there. She would assess the arguments of defense lawyers and the responses from prosecutors. She tended to take the views of prosecutors at face value. This practice infuriated defense lawyers, but it was common among busy judges— many of them former prosecutors—who would sign appeals effectively ghostwritten by their former colleagues. (Sometimes they would even fail to correct misspellings.) In 2002, the new governor, Rick Perry, elevated Alcala to the First Court of Appeals, which oversaw cases from all over Houston, though not ones involving the death penalty.

Through all of this, Alcala remained in touch with Allison Vickers. They would talk by phone and send each other letters, discussing their families and professional lives. Steve Vickers remained comforted by his daughter's enduring relationship with the prosecutor who had shown such care for their family. In the meantime, the two death sentences Alcala had won were appealed up through the courts. Gerald Eldridge's lawyers argued he should be disqualified from execution because of his mental limitations. With Eddie Capetillo, the case hinged on a single number, his age at the time of the crime: seventeen.

7

DURING EDDIE CAPETILLO'S FIRST WEEK ON DEATH ROW, HE SAW two men get into a fight in the caged outdoor basketball court. He was not surprised. At the jail in Houston he had witnessed a fight nearly every day among the teenagers housed on the "Gladiator Floor." Sometimes he was the one doing the fighting—nobody would hesitate to challenge someone so small and skinny. These men were facing execution, he realized, so of course they had nothing to lose.

But it turned out this fight was an exception; he never saw another one. Teenagers in adult prisons are often raped and beaten into sexual and financial subservience, but nobody came for Capetillo. Instead, soon after he arrived, in February 1996, a prison porter arrived at his cell with a welcome basket. Men along the tiers, knowing it took a while for commissary accounts to come online, had tossed in whatever they had lying around: shower shoes, stationery, stamps, chips, coffee, shampoo. These men couldn't be bothered with the usual politics of prison life because, as Capetillo soon learned, they actually did have something to lose. Most of them were appealing their sentences, which meant they had a chance of seeing their sentences overturned, and maybe even a small chance at freedom.

Until 1965, Texas's death row was located near the execution chamber at the Walls Unit, but as appeals grew longer and longer—owing in part to Anthony Amsterdam and the NAACP Legal Defense Fund—Texas prison administrators needed more space, so they secured several wings of the Ellis Unit. This massive prison was set on more than 11,000 acres just outside Huntsville, where prisoners spent their days harvesting crops and tending to chickens, cows, and pigs. Even in the 1960s, many Texas prisons retained the feel of the slave plantations they had replaced. (In some cases they were actually on the same land.) One prisoner, Anthony Graves, wrote that "coming to death row is like stepping back in time a few hundred years." A couple of months before Capetillo's arrival, at the end of 1995, Texas had 408 prisoners on death row, including six women who were housed elsewhere; 68 were Hispanic, 242 were white, and 162 were black (some identified as more than one race). This meant that for all of the racial inequities faced by the state's Hispanic population, their numbers on death row were much smaller, proportionally, than in the state as a whole (17 percent of death row, 27 percent of Texas). The black population of death row, on the other hand, was disproportionately large (40 percent of death row, 12 percent of Texas).

In Texas, death row prisoners were not allowed to do the agricultural work other inmates did. They were referred to as DRs and required to walk between two bright yellow lines that ran down the middle of the walkways. Upon arriving at the Ellis Unit, Capetillo was placed in solitary confinement. Many on death row lived in lockdown, which meant they were in their cells more than twenty hours each day. At times, the lights on top of the wing—comprised of several stacked tiers of cells—would never be turned off, which made it more difficult to sleep but did allow men to read at night. During the day, it could get so hot that men would pour water on the concrete floor, strip naked, and lie down until the water itself grew too warm to offer relief. They could usually spend a few hours in a communal room or outside in a small, enclosed yard. The worst section inside death row, for prisoners tagged as troublemakers, was known as the Dungeon. It smelled like feces, and rats skittered up and down the run. The cells were covered with black steel mesh, and because light barely made it through the windows, it was hard to tell night from day.

Breakfast here started at three thirty in the morning; lunch came around ten o'clock, and dinner around three thirty in the afternoon. "The food wasn't quite rotten, but it wasn't not rotten, either," Anthony Graves wrote. "The smell suggested the advanced age of the chicken that had lost his life to make that meal." In the early 1990s, Texas prisoners were also fed VitaPro, a soybean-based powder, as a meat substitute, and one defense lawyer recalled that men on death row were afraid it was slowly poisoning them.

Since commissary food was also available for those with money, it was not uncommon for men to scrape this greasy mush into their toilets before shoving the tray back under their doors. Throughout mealtime, the row filled with banging and flushing and scraping. This was on top of the usual ambient noise, which in any prison is far louder than outsiders usually imagine. Doors slid and slammed over the din of televisions and radios. Each cell could access three stations—soul, country, and rock—and often all you heard was a jumble of all three. Many of the prisoners had delusions and would stay up all night talking to imaginary friends.

Bruce Jackson, an anthropologist and photographer who interviewed and took pictures of many of the prisoners in the 1970s, made a list of everything a death row prisoner at Ellis could do to pass the time in that era: sleep, eat, watch the television sets bolted to the wall across from the cells, listen to the radio, read or write, work on their legal cases, roll or smoke cigarettes, make art, use the toilet, practice hygiene, masturbate, have sex with another prisoner or maybe a guard, go to recreation or the shower, pray, get into a fight, fall into mental illness, self-harm, or attempt suicide. You could receive visits, but calls were rarely allowed.

In such limited circumstances, ingenuity flourished. The prisoners would attach small mirrors to sticks and poke them through the cell bars so they could see down the run. Some made chessboards out of cardboard and tied them to the bars so they could play against their neighbors. Some adopted the ever-present rats as pets. They passed notes via long wooden sticks dangled down into the air vents that separated the back sides of two cells. One man sold his drawings of horses to magazines for money. Another converted to Judaism and was visited by a rabbi who prayed with him in the visitation room.

The death row prisoners literally had a space of their own, but they also inhabited a different sense of time. Jackson called it "timeless time," a kind of limbo. One man described it this way:

When you go through life out there, time is like air to you. You breathe it in and you breathe it out; it passes through you, and you sort of pass through time. But when you're here and it's final . . . time doesn't go anywhere. It comes and it stops. It builds up inside, and it's actually like a weight after a while. Ten years weighs an awful lot. It just builds up, and there's times in the morning when . . . you almost literally feel it crushing you when you wake up and you have to look around and see the same things in here and you are in the same cell and doing the same things that you did years ago, and nothing's going to change.

Capetillo noticed that much of life on death row consisted of waiting—to leave your cell, to shower, to eat, to get mail delivered—and against the monotony, little moments of levity stood out. Decades later, he would vividly remember playing basketball during the hours he was allowed out of his cell, when a man in the game looked down and saw that his own teeth were on the ground. Nobody had known this man had dentures. They all burst into laughter. Capetillo later wondered if laughter was so rare because prisoners were so accustomed to projecting a kind of steely pride.

The other event that could break monotony was learning that someone had an execution date set. A year after Capetillo arrived, he got to know David Herman, who lived in the cell next to his. Herman liked to draw, and he showed Capetillo his work. After about a week, Capetillo woke up in the morning feeling unsettled. He saw several officers escorting Herman away. A janitor walked into Herman's cell, and Capetillo grabbed his mirror, stuck it out through his own bars, and held it at an angle. The walls of Herman's cell were streaked with blood. He had tried to slash his throat and wrist with a disposable razor. Less than two days later, after his wounds were stitched up, Herman was executed.

The very first man to be sentenced to death under the 1973 Texas law hanged himself with a bedsheet. Over the next few decades, roughly a dozen death row prisoners in Texas also took their own lives. More than thirty gave up their appeals and let the state execute them. Some of these "volunteers," as lawyers called them, undoubtedly suffered from mental illness; in order to stop appealing you had to be deemed "competent" by a court, but the bar was low. In 1983, a death row prisoner named Charles Rumbaugh said at a hearing, "If they don't want to take me down there and execute me, I'll make them shoot me." Then he charged at a deputy U.S. marshal, who shot him. He survived, only to be executed two years later.

Researchers tried to understand the motivations of these "volunteers." One found that they shared many traits with those who died by suicide in the free world: They tended to be white and male and have a history of substance abuse, mental illness, or both. Another scholar studied the public statements of Texas volunteers and found that some believed that death was a fair punishment for their crimes, some spoke of a desire for spiritual rebirth in the next life, and many just didn't see value in living in brutal prison conditions. The phrase "death row syndrome" gained academic currency.

But seeing a man try to end his life had the opposite effect on Capetillo. He resolved to do anything he could to avoid death and hopelessness. He had never read a book in its entirety, but now he dove into any text he could acquire, from *1984* by George Orwell to the *Dune* series by Frank Herbert to countless fantasy paperbacks. He found that every book, no matter the subject, would have at least one sentence that would stick with him and teach him something new. Often, his mother would read the same books, and their visits would become a two-person book club meeting. Living among men whose childhoods had been marked by abuse and neglect, Capetillo came to realize how lucky he was to have such a supportive family. They had stuck with him.

The families of death row prisoners had few places to turn for support. Few scholars studied them, few journalists profiled them, no politicians gained by advocating for them, and no institutions officially considered their needs. Their grief was, in the academic parlance, unacknowledged and disenfranchised. They watched their children and siblings be portrayed as vile monsters and then lived with the possibility that they would have to watch them be killed. Capetillo's mother, Leonor, was once interviewed by a filmmaker. She told him:

> My impulse is to hug, to hold, and I haven't been able to do that for ten years, and it tears me up. Because my instinct is to throw my arms around my child and say, "It's going to be okay, it's going to be okay." But I can't do that. So I have to go and see him and I have to smile and talk about everything under the sun, and let the guys [my husband and Eddie] have their guy time, and I can't cry, I can't do any of that, because it would make him feel even worse. . . . He tells me in his letters, each time, "Walk with your head up high, Mom, don't let them hold you down. . . ." It lifts my spirits to see he is that strong.

In addition to the emotional support of his family, Capetillo enjoyed that of his peers. Those going to their death often bought their fellow prisoners ice cream or other treats as a way of encouraging them to celebrate being alive. Prisoners commemorated the departed with prayers and moments of silence. Some drank prison wine at the moment they knew the last meal was being served. Others refused their own meal and fasted in solidarity. They'd stay up late, listening to their radios to see if the courts would step in. When someone won at the Supreme Court, they cheered. Some found mentors who would instruct them in legal research or spiritual matters; one prisoner held his friend to a commitment to send out ten letters a week to lawyers and organizations that might help him, and gave him stamps when he didn't have enough.

The high point of death row solidarity had come a few years before Capetillo's arrival, when prisoners organized to publish newspapers. In the pages of *"What's Happening . . . ?,"* the *Texas Death Row Journal,* and the *Endeavor,* they updated one another on individual cases and legal developments, reviewed new books about capital punishment, reported scores from the latest death row handball tournament, held writing and art contests, arranged carpools and lodging among their family members in distant cities, and organized hunger strikes. The tone sometimes felt like a neighborhood newsletter. "For some time now, a number of [death row] prisoners have been harassed—and sometimes jumped on—by the guards here," wrote John Kennedy Barefield, who was executed a year after Capetillo arrived. "The sad part is that a great number of us . . . sometimes encourage such action because of our dislikes, hatred, and petty jealousy of one another. . . . Not long ago here on J21, officers Tunner and Hicks jumped on C.C. Some of us thought it was funny. But if it would have been one of your roaddogs, I bet it wouldn't have been so funny. . . . We're all in this boat TOGETHER!" Sometimes they wrote obituaries of one another. By 1991, the men of Texas's death row were organized enough to publish writers from death rows in Arizona and Connecticut. The issues were printed and distributed by the Missionary Sisters of the Immaculate Conception Convent, a group of retired nuns in West Paterson, New Jersey.

Capetillo wrote, too, mostly in letters home and later to a Parisian pen pal named Nathalie Pias. Lots of prisoners on death row had European friends and even lovers, owing in part to the Continent's widespread opposition to capital punishment (Italians at one time lit up the Colosseum when an American death sentence was commuted or a state abolished the penalty). On visiting days at death row, the motels nearby were often full of women from Switzerland, Norway, and other European countries.

Pias could never quite explain why she felt moved to write to Capetillo, and once they began corresponding, she realized she needed to know the basic facts of what had gotten him to death row. *I'll only ask this once*, she wrote. *I won't judge you.* He said he'd killed two people in a home invasion. But what really devastated her was something he didn't say, which she learned from reading news articles online: The brother of one victim had died of suicide. She also read that Christmas lights were still up when Capetillo committed the murders, and she found herself holding back from responding to him around the holidays. She thought sometimes about the parents of his victims, about the unimaginable horror of losing a child.

Still, she felt Capetillo had a humanity that could not be reduced to his past actions, however terrible, and she came to discover they had a lot in common. She had health problems that made it difficult for her to leave her home, so they were both unable to live as fully as they would like, if for different reasons.

In letters to her and others, Capetillo developed his personal voice, pondering how he had been shaped before he could fully think for himself, by media portrayals of criminals and movies that glorified violence and power like *The Godfather* and *Scarface*. He often spoke and wrote about how as a young man he'd "reacted" without thinking and slowly drifted to darker versions of himself, and about how he had now accepted his actions and was working to make peace with what he had done. (Criminologists speak of people "aging out" of crime as their brains develop and they become less impulsive.)

But Capetillo never discussed his crime with the depth that would satisfy an outsider's curiosity. Other death row prisoners proclaimed their innocence to any pen pal or journalist or activist who would listen, with varying degrees of credibility. When asked about his crime, Capetillo did not shy away from admitting to it—but that was all he did. He didn't want to dwell on it. He offered many explanations for this: It was in the past, and he wanted to focus on the future. He didn't want to revive the tragedy for his victims or appear to be minimizing the enormity of what he'd done. Pias wondered whether this was a coping strategy to get through the difficulty of living in such a harsh environment; perhaps he could not steel himself to survive death row while also fully confronting what he had done to get there.

Capetillo explored his feelings in poems, some of which he sent to Pias, including this one:

INNER SIGHT

I close my eyes
and see myself
in the mirror of the mind
unclouded by sight
the darkness reveals the light
that part of ourselves that made
the world
Seeking, searching, working
to find a way out.

At moments, Capetillo would offer a flush of the kind of comfort with violence that had marked his teenage years. He could tell the story of how he punched a soccer referee with no trace of remorse, suggesting he had not totally abandoned the side of himself capable of harming others. In an untitled poem, Capetillo wrote, "Always a sinner, I can sin no more. I've been there and done that, I'm rotten to the core." But he did manage to curtail this tendency in prison, because after about a year at the Ellis Unit he was given a privilege offered to the best-behaved prisoners: He could work in the death row garment factory.

The garment factory, which had opened in the early 1980s, was a large industrial space, where spools of thread hung from the ceiling and more than a hundred men sat at wooden tables operating sewing machines, wielding needles and large pairs of scissors. Capetillo's job was to sew pockets onto the gray uniform pants worn by corrections officers. Some men refused to work in the factory, even if they qualified; as one put it, "I don't like working for the man who's gonna kill me." But Capetillo enjoyed the perks. If he completed his quota quickly enough, he could skip work later in the week, and he used the earned time for visits with his family. Now he could be out of his cell from six in the morning until late into the night. After work, he played basketball or handball, or just sunbathed outside. On the weekends, he would pool commissary purchases with his friends and make tacos in the day-room. A common topic of conversation was escape: how they'd do it, where they'd go, what they'd do.

To Capetillo it was all talk; everybody had a plan, but nobody was all that serious about it.

On a foggy Thanksgiving Day in 1998, after dinner was served, seven death row prisoners stuffed makeshift dummies under their sheets and went to the outdoor recreation area. Taking advantage of the diminished holiday security, they climbed a fence and cut it at the top with a hacksaw, peeling the metal back just far enough to allow them to squeeze through and climb up to the roof. They wore long underwear colored black with markers, which helped them avoid notice as they crawled to a hiding spot. Shortly after midnight, they used the prison chapel's sloped roof to slide to the ground and started running. Guards in towers saw the men as they scaled the two layers of perimeter fence and began shooting. Six of them dropped to the ground in surrender, but one, Martin Gurule, continued until he disappeared into the fog.

By the next day, five hundred people were searching for him. Huntsville residents were terrified, Governor George W. Bush was furious, and prison officials were embarrassed. Gurule was otherwise obscure, sentenced to death for killing two people at a diner, but his disappearance reactivated the long American romance with prison breaks. (Even the city where he was incarcerated had once marketed itself with the phrase "Escape to Huntsville.") Reporters marveled at how the details—dummies in beds, a pilfered hacksaw—seemed straight out of Hollywood, as did the searchers' use of helicopters and dogs. One columnist at *Time* admitted to rooting for Gurule's success. After a week, nobody had found him. The television show *America's Most Wanted* ran a segment, posters with his mug shot were scattered along the Mexican border, and police staked out his grandmother's house in Corpus Christi.

The hunt ended when two correctional officers, who were fishing near the prison while off duty, happened upon a bloated body in the still water of a creek. They tied a rope around one wrist and dialed 9-1-1. An autopsy later revealed that a bullet had grazed Gurule's back while he was climbing the fences. He had worn a layer of cardboard under his clothing, which had helped him get over the razor wire, but it soaked up too much water and he drowned. Before a bank of news cameras, Texas Department of Criminal Justice spokesman Larry Fitzgerald ripped a picture of Gurule in two and announced, "He's no more."

Capetillo was skeptical; he thought the authorities had probably killed Gurule when they found him and made up this story about fishing. But whatever the truth of what happened to Gurule, the political implications were clear: No longer would Capetillo be able to come and go so freely, to make tacos and use scissors.

He soon learned it would be much worse. TDCJ announced that it would move death row from the Ellis Unit to the newly built Terrell Unit, about an hour's drive north in Livingston. (The town was next to an idyllic lake that attracted vacationers from around the region. The prisoners were driven there in buses; many had not seen cars and houses, much less a lake, in years.) The agency issued conflicting rationales for the move, at times saying it was a response to the escape and related concerns about security, at others noting that death row had simply grown too big for the dedicated wings at Ellis. As the decision was being made, Charles Terrell, the agency board member for whom the prison had been named, said he did not want his name attached to the place where people were warehoused before their deaths. Another member, Allan Polunsky, had no such qualms.

At the Polunsky Unit, prisoners were alone in a cell smaller than a parking space for at least twenty-two hours a day, surrounded only by a sink, toilet, and steel bunk. Each cell had a small window, but you had to stand on something to see out of it. There was no more garment factory or group recreation or religious services or regular phone calls or television. They were now allowed outdoor recreation by themselves for only a few hours per week in a cage topped by a metal grate and surrounded by concrete walls; they felt the sun's rays only if they happened to catch the right weather. The white prisoners grew pasty from the lack of sunlight. Their bodies aged more quickly than they otherwise would have, owing to the poor nutrition and limited movement, while their minds struggled to advance past the age at which they'd been arrested. Capetillo slowly came to feel as if he was surrounded by teenagers in the bodies of older men.

These changes tracked with the larger spread of such conditions for many prisoners—not just those on death row—across the country. In 1995, 57,591 inmates were in some form of restrictive housing. By 2000, that number had grown to 80,870. Every state had its own rationale for the change, whether an escape or a riot or just a general political atmosphere of punitiveness, but everywhere the results were the same. Prisoners started feeling more depressed, experiencing memory loss, anxiety, paranoia, and hallucinations. They could not keep track of time. They grew unused to human touch, never feeling the skin of another person unless that person was a guard applying handcuffs. Suicides increased. Those who were already mentally ill found their conditions worsened, and otherwise healthy prisoners struggled to stay afloat. Lawyers and journalists who visited these men found they looked dazed and withdrawn. They complained about the guards: saliva and dead cockroaches in their food, being body-slammed for no good reason, finding the heaters turned on in the summer. One wrote in a letter that at Ellis "the guards looked at us as guys they had to baby-sit until our dates. Here, we are guys that need to be *punished* until our dates."

The guards, for their part, argued that they, too, were molded by the inhumanity of the environment, at both Ellis and Polunsky. They didn't write the policies that required them to watch men constantly strip down to dehumanizing nudity, to see visiting children struggle to understand why they couldn't touch their fathers across the glass that separated them, to escort men to their final shower and meal. With little training, and certainly no counseling, they were thrown into a place where they were the enemy—the wildly outnumbered enemy, subject to black eyes and chipped teeth and stabbings. They exhibited symptoms of post-traumatic stress disorder, but they seldom had the clinical language to make sense of their nightmares and cold sweats and surges of adrenaline and high blood pressure.

Some of the prisoners found strategies for making it through time at Polunsky. Others saw them as monsters or victims, but many, like Capetillo, preferred a different self-image: survivor. Some created schedules for each day, while others let time grow fluid, sleeping all day so they could stay up late and take advantage of the rare quiet hours. The daytime noise, which had already been bad at Ellis, was even more intense here: The easiest way to communicate was to yell. Chess now involved setting up boards in two cells and screaming the moves—"PAWN TO ECHO FOUR!" Others used the role-playing game Dungeons & Dragons to take one another on adventures. One prisoner, Anibal Canales, learned to vividly describe his own mental journeys to the cliffs of South America, or to bodies of water full of dolphins and whales.

Though television was banned at Polunsky, each man was allowed to own a small radio, and some learned to tinker with the electronics. The most creative strategy for coping with the environment was to rewire the radios so they could transmit as well as receive. In an unpublished memoir of his time at Polunsky, Robert Pruett wrote:

> We listened to sports and music together, shared our deepest thoughts, darkest fears and all of the good and bad times of our lives. We played games like Risk, Monopoly, chess, checkers, trivia, hangman, and derivatives of them all. We went on mental excursions together, turning out our lights and closing our eyes as we went out hunting, fishing, skateboarding, swimming, fighting in wars, and even heading out to the club to meet chicks. We invented a game called Death Row Idol in which we competed with songs, poetry, jokes, skits, and stories, then we all casted our votes to see who'd be voted off the gurney.

Pruett's account offers a rare image of solidarity on the Polunsky Unit; other prisoners felt as though the solidarity that had once marked their ranks was subsiding, that newcomers were no longer able to get care packages, that hunger strikes and moments of silence were fewer and farther between. The activists who had written the internal newspapers were dying out, and the new environment seemed designed to keep projects like that from emerging. When a prisoner received an execution date, he might get a supportive little note, tied to a string and slid under his cell door, but otherwise you were on your own. "Guys have no fight left in them," one prisoner wrote in a 2016 letter. "Just eating, and gaining weight—waiting on their demise."

When Capetillo's appellate lawyer, Elizabeth DeRieux, would visit him, she would find him cold and uncommunicative. "He could write letters and express things but he couldn't function in person," she later recalled. "My impression of Capetillo was he hated seeing me, and not because he hated me, but I was asking him over and over about vulnerabilities, mitigation, and he was like, 'Don't touch that.' It was like I was asking him to go to places he didn't want to go. I'm not a psychologist. I could be misreading. Or I was trying to tell a story that he thought was wrong. Maybe I *was* wrong."

8

SIXTEEN YEARS BEFORE EDWARD CAPETILLO ARRIVED AT THE ELLIS
Unit, on a Saturday morning in April 1981, a non-death-row prisoner
named Eroy Brown was working in the unit's tire shop, fixing flats on
farm equipment and complaining about his situation. Although he
would soon be eligible for parole, and he had a good job by Texas prison
standards, he had been trying and failing to get a furlough, a brief release to the free world. Brown was angry that the prison farm manager,
Billy Moore, wasn't doing more to convince higher-ups that he deserved this reward. "After all I done for Billy Moore," he said, "I don't
see why I can't get no furlough."

Brown spoke loudly enough that another prison employee, Bill
Adams, perked up at three key words: "all I done." Was Brown making
a threat? Adams and Moore had been enlisting Brown in a variety of
illicit schemes, including stealing tires and mounting them on non-
prison vehicles, and giving free oil changes to their friends. It sounded
like Brown was threatening to snitch. Adams ordered Brown into a
truck and brought him to Moore, who called in the unit's warden, Wallace Pack. The three white prison officials and the one black prisoner all
convened at a creek. By early that afternoon, Moore had been shot in
the head and Pack had been drowned.

Brown faced the death penalty, and the lawyers appointed to represent him knew they needed a skilled courtroom orator who understood the racial dynamics of Texas prisons, so they called Craig Washington.

In the years after his failed 1973 effort to stop the death penalty, Washington often represented men facing the punishment at trial. He was known as masterful on the subject of race, specializing in getting potential jurors to betray their prejudices, even the unconscious ones, so that he could prevent them from serving. In the case of Eroy Brown, he went further, weaving the history of Southern racism and slavery into the narrative presented to jurors.

In Washington's telling, a black prisoner was convinced these three white men were going to kill him so he couldn't report their grift, and he fought back only to save his own life. When Adams—the surviving employee, who had initially ordered Brown into the truck—took the stand, Washington's first question was whether the prisoners under his charge called him Boss Adams. No matter how Adams answered, according to the journalist Michael Berryhill, "Washington wanted the jury to understand that the language of prison was the language of the slave plantation." Washington asked Adams if he had ever called a prisoner "boy," and he denied it, but later, under Washington's skilled questioning, he slipped, using the word in front of the jury.

"Everyone wants to live," Washington told the jury. "No one wants to die. It was like being at the end of your rope." He called the state's version of events, in which Brown had planned to kill the men, a lie—and "no lie can live forever." This last phrase was borrowed from a 1965 speech, given in Montgomery, Alabama, by Dr. Martin Luther King, Jr.

The jury's deliberations ended in a mistrial—eleven of the jurors wanted to acquit Brown, but one held out for conviction—and the case went to trial again. This time Washington and his team prevailed, with no holdouts. The two trials had been for the drowning of Warden Wallace Pack, but then prosecutors sought the death penalty a third time, for the shooting of Billy Moore. Washington beat them a third time. Brown remained in prison, but he would never face execution. (State officials named prisons after Billy Moore and Wallace Pack.)

Every two years, Washington would leave his home in Houston for a few months to attend the legislative session in Austin. "His mere association with a bill helped lend it legitimacy," *Texas Monthly* marveled in 1981. But after being elected to the state senate in 1982, Washington began to flounder. The House was more like a courtroom, in which a good speech could win you support, but the Senate was dominated by backroom wheeling and dealing, and Washington had never been much for compromise. "Seldom has a member fallen so far, so fast," said the same magazine that had so recently praised him. He missed meetings, got thrown out of others, and recklessly called his peers racists. He "haunted the House floor like an unhappy ghost, lurking near the back mike, scene of his former triumphs."

In 1989, Washington's friend Mickey Leland, who was serving in the U.S. House of Representatives, died in a plane crash. Washington was elected to his seat. He didn't fare much better in the nation's capital, finding himself dispirited by the way lawmakers voted against their own principles for political purposes. He was criticized for missing meetings and votes, and for using taxpayer dollars to rent office space from his ex-wife, while also putting the mother of one of his children on his payroll. None of this was illegal, but it didn't look like the behavior of a moral crusader. A couple of years after the election, he filed for bankruptcy, claiming to be $1 million in debt and owing $250,000 in back taxes. The *Houston Chronicle* called him an "embarrassment and an affront to his constituents." Washington was convinced that the city's elite had turned on him because he voted against money for NASA—a major local employer and source of pride—as well as against the First Gulf War.

When the situation called for Washington's courtroom abilities, he was as strong as ever, testifying forcefully against Clarence Thomas's nomination to the Supreme Court. But when it came to crime, one of his signature issues, his lack of interest in compromise and his tendency toward stridence were unhelpful in a Congress in which his views were so wildly out of step with those of his peers. In 1991, he pushed provisions to let defendants avoid the death penalty if they could prove that members of their race were disproportionately sentenced to death, and to strengthen their ability to challenge prosecutors over race during jury selection. "Give 'em a fair trial before we lynch 'em," he said. Both ideas failed resoundingly.

Still, Washington managed to exert some influence by pressuring centrist Democrats from the left. As Senator Joe Biden pursued what would become the 1994 Violent Crime Control and Law Enforcement Act (better known as the Crime Bill), Washington offered a wide-ranging alternative bill that would aim to prevent crime by improving police-community relations and school safety, implementing gun control measures, and increasing confidence in the system among African Americans by removing disparities in punishments for crimes involving crack and powder cocaine. Washington's bill earned the support of the ACLU and the *Washington Post* editorial page, and by the time Biden's crime bill passed, it did include prevention programs like Midnight Basketball, which made basketball courts available to young men late at night, during the hours when it was believed they might otherwise commit crimes. "We are trying to promote an enlightened discussion to get at the root causes of crime," Washington told reporters.

These successes were short-lived. In 1994, as unpopular as ever back in Houston, he lost the Democratic primary. He moved to Bastrop, a quiet town near Austin, and resumed his career as a lawyer for hire, occasionally taking on clients facing the death penalty and managing, as he had in the case of Eroy Brown, to beat the odds.

It was increasingly important to win at trial, because lawmakers, in both Austin and Washington, D.C., were looking for ways to restrict appeals and speed up executions.

In the run-up to the 1994 congressional election, Republican leaders unveiled a list of promises that candidates could sign called the Contract with America. "There are always loopholes that benefit the criminals, not the victims," said Michigan congressional candidate Megan O'Neill at a rally on Capitol Hill. "Our contract will make the death penalty real. No more endless appeals." President Bill Clinton had tried to bolster the image of Democrats as equally interested in punishment, celebrating the 1994 Crime Bill as a major achievement, but Republicans continued to assail him, criticizing the types of prevention programs that Craig Washington had argued would address the "root causes" of crime, like Midnight Basketball. When the Republicans passed a bill to dismantle some of these policies, Clinton found himself in a political bind: He could veto the bill, but it would allow the Republicans to tag him as "soft" ahead of the 1996 election.

Meanwhile, in Texas, the families of murder victims were complaining that the long appeals process was emotionally grueling. Democrat Pete Gallego, a former prosecutor chairing the state House committee on criminal jurisprudence, found their arguments compelling. As a Latino man from a border district, he was also sympathetic to the argument that minorities suffered unfairly in the justice system. But he felt that everyone would benefit from faster appeals: In addition to the families of victims, death row prisoners would not live without resolution for so long.

Gallego oversaw the writing of a bill that would make two forms of state appeals run concurrently, meaning one defense lawyer didn't need to finish analyzing the trial transcript before another began reinvestigating the case. Barring rare exceptions, prisoners would be allowed to file only a single state habeas petition, meaning they would have just one shot to make arguments based on the new investigation—saying their trial lawyers were ineffective or prosecutors had failed to disclose evidence, for example. "What we're attempting to do here is to say 'raise everything at one time,'" Gallego explained. "You get one bite of the apple."

The bill also required that the state recruit, appoint, and pay lawyers for the first state habeas petition, so it wouldn't fall to the resource center (which was supposed to confine its work to the federal courts, anyway). Judge Michael McCormick—who had helped write the 1973 death penalty bill as a prosecutor and was now the chief judge of the Court of Criminal Appeals—offered that his court could oversee payments to lawyers. Gallego had overseen a compromise: Victims would see executions faster, but prisoners would get better representation.

Some in Congress took notice of what was happening in Texas. Senator Biden, himself a former public defender, had for years been trying to broker a similar compromise that would both speed up federal appeals and guarantee lawyers to everyone on death row. He solicited data from Columbia law professor James Liebman, who discovered that more than two-thirds of death penalty sentences featured a "serious, reversible error," in the opinion of judges who reviewed them. Some people thought appeals took too long, while others thought capital trials were full of problems. Liebman concluded both were right: They took so long because there were so many problems to root out.

To Republican supporters of the death penalty, this just meant judges were overstepping their bounds, reversing otherwise solid jury verdicts. Republican senator Bob Dole introduced a bill to restrict appeals, which gained traction in early 1995. Clinton and his aides had problems with Dole's bill, but the landscape changed irrevocably on April 19, 1995, when Timothy McVeigh detonated a truck full of explosives outside a federal building in Oklahoma City, killing 168 people, including many children. The Democrats' interest in the right to appeal suddenly looked like an effort to help a mass murderer.

This was ironic, because McVeigh was a "volunteer" who gave up his right to file a habeas petition, and he was executed after just a few years. But Clinton appeared to have been deeply affected by meeting family members of the Oklahoma victims. When an adviser sent him a memo urging a more cautious approach, Clinton handwrote the words "No. Oklahoma." When the Anti-Terrorism and Effective Death Penalty Act of 1996 was finally passed, he signed it.

AEDPA ("ed-pah," as it was usually pronounced) set strict time limits: Death row prisoners would have a year to file a federal habeas petition, requesting a federal judge to overturn their sentence. Except in rare cases, they could file only a single one. A federal judge could not free a death row prisoner unless a state court had made a decision that was "an unreasonable application of clearly established Federal law" or involved "an unreasonable determination of the facts." Practically, these were very high burdens for death row prisoners to meet. More than ever, they would need lawyers to navigate the complex new restrictions on their ability to appeal. It would have been a new challenge for the resource centers.

Only there would be no more resource centers. The complaints that had plagued the center in Texas—that they were radicals, using taxpayer money to try to abolish the death penalty—had spread throughout the country, and the same Republican-controlled Congress that passed AEDPA also voted to defund them.

The money ran out in October 1995. In Texas, there was a bit of extra funding to pass off cases to other lawyers, box up papers, and close down the office. Center lawyers found themselves in limbo. Some had completely burned out. One became a minister, another a therapist, another a journalist, another a professional chef.

Those who still wanted to work with death row prisoners, like Carl Kelly's lead lawyer, Rob Owen, looked for positions at law schools. Some relied on spouses or altruistic law firms to float them as they went into private practice and continued taking cases. Mandy Welch, who had run the center and been berated at the Supreme Court, joined Timothy McVeigh's defense team. She also established a nonprofit organization, funded by donations and court-appointment money, to carry on as much of their work as possible. The new Texas Defender Service would never be able to take many cases, but it planned to hold trainings and lobby the legislature on behalf of death row prisoners.

The new restrictions on appeals, along with the absence of resource centers, helped produce a surge in executions, from forty-five in 1996 to ninety-eight in 1999. By 2006, the rate at which judges reversed death sentences had fallen by 80 percent. There were all kinds of new ways for a habeas lawyer to screw up. Many lawyers missed the one-year deadline demanded by AEDPA. In two Texas cases, federal judges granted lawyers extensions and then, after the appeals were filed, enforced the original deadlines and ruled them inadmissible. Prosecutors could seize on minor errors in how a document was filed to persuade a federal judge not to entertain its arguments at all.

AEDPA also restricted the ability of federal judges to overturn state death sentences, which put more pressure on state judges to closely examine whether trials had been fair. This meant that it was crucial for death row prisoners to have a capable lawyer in state court, but the new Texas system for appointing lawyers quickly proved disastrous.

The Court of Criminal Appeals, which was now supposed to oversee appointments, sent out postcards to defense lawyers around the state, promising good pay. The Texas state bar committee had estimated the cost of doing one of these appeals at $35,000, a number far below what the national capital defense community considered reasonable, given that the work could take months, if not years. But then, after the law was passed, the court dropped the pay to $7,500. "It might be my imagination, but I remember a hush fell over the room" when the number was floated, one lawyer recalled. The hundreds of lawyers suddenly were not so keen to volunteer, and the cap was raised back to $25,000. But the court and the lawyers continued to quibble over expenses in each case. The bill's drafters had asked for $4 million in taxpayer funding for the first two years, to be doubled as more lawyers got involved, but then the legislature cut that number in half and never increased it. "None of us had any idea what we were doing," recalled Rick Wetzel, a court staffer. "There was some slash and burn on those bills. . . . I look back and think we didn't treat those lawyers fairly."

Poor defense lawyering existed before the new law, of course, but the resource centers had demonstrated what good lawyering could look like. The Texas Defender Service, with a fraction of the resource center's staff, was reduced to commenting on the problems rather than fixing them. In a 2001 report titled "A State of Denial," they tracked 84 cases in which a Texas law enforcement official presented false or misleading testimony or concealed evidence that the defense should have been able to see, 160 cases involving forensic science of dubious credibility, and 6 cases of men executed despite clear doubts about their guilt. Another study, "Lethal Indifference," examined 251 habeas petitions—almost every single one filed between September 1995 and December 2001—and found many lawyers were not doing any investigation at all. Where the resource center had often filed petitions totaling more than a hundred pages, many now came in under thirty. One was just two pages. The study also found two petitions, submitted on behalf of two different prisoners, that appeared to contain the same text; the proof that their lawyer had copied and pasted his work could be found on page 17, which in both appeals featured the same error of capitalization.

The Texas Criminal Defense Lawyers' Association began urging members in 1998 not to accept death penalty appointments, believing the system was totally broken and their members would only be helping the state perpetuate unjust executions. But many did not listen.

The lawyer for Johnny Joe Martinez—who, at age twenty, shot and killed college student Clay Peterson while robbing the convenience store where he worked, and had been sentenced to death despite having no prior criminal record—spent less than fifty hours on his habeas petition. The state bar had suggested lawyers spend at least four hundred hours. Many on death row did not understand that they were being poorly served by their attorneys; they'd been poorly served at trial, so why would they expect anything different now? Some had mental illnesses or disabilities that kept them from understanding.

But Martinez understood.

In June 1997, he received a letter from Nathaniel Rhodes, who had been appointed to represent him despite having no relevant experience. Martinez tried to call him collect from death row, but Rhodes didn't accept the charges, so Martinez sent a letter. "I am wondering about the due date on my appeal," he wrote. "Have we had an opportunity to hire an investigator to search issues or run down leads to save my life? . . . I have not heard from you in a long time and this makes me wonder if this is a bad sign, is there something wrong? . . . Sir what is going on. . . . Please get back with me and let me know! . . . I am not trying to sound pushy or anything like that, it's just that I'm in the dark here and my life is on your hand. . . . Sir I do not want to die and you are the only one that can help me and prevent this, please do your best. . . . Take care o.k. and God Bless!"

He never received a reply, and so a few weeks later he wrote again.

After several letters, he learned that it was too late: The court had ruled against him. Rhodes had filed a habeas petition—with legal claims totaling just seventeen lines of text—without talking to him at all. Martinez wrote to the judges, explaining that he needed to "refile [the appeal] because my lawyer was incompetent." The judges were unmoved.

Martinez was executed in 2002. "I know I'm fixing to die," he said from the gurney. "But not for my mistakes. I'm dying for the mistakes of my lawyers."

The new Texas law, passed in 1995, stated that lawyers must "investigate expeditiously . . . the factual and legal grounds" for a habeas petition, but the Court of Criminal Appeals did little to ensure lawyers did even that. The year of Martinez's execution, Judge Cathy Cochran wrote for a majority that although lawyers must be "competent" when appointed, their clients had no constitutional right that they be "effective." Even when the lawyers were effective—investigating and finding out about police misconduct or prosecutors hiding evidence or a defense lawyer having fallen asleep—the court seldom ruled in their favor. Often, the judges would agree that there had been an error in the original trial but then would rule that the error was "harmless," that the final result of the trial would have been no different.

This was a judgment call, of course, since it was impossible to know how the jury would have responded to information it had not seen. A good example of just how strongly the court embraced the doctrine of "harmless error" was a 1996 opinion in the case of Cesar Fierro. Fierro had been sentenced to death in 1980 after confessing to the murder of an El Paso taxicab driver. He went on to recant and claim innocence. In the early 1990s, lawyers from the resource center had discovered that the confession was tainted in a particularly shocking way. Across the border in Juarez, the Mexican police had taken Fierro's mother and stepfather hostage and were threatening to torture them with an electric generator attached to their genitals.

Later on, an El Paso detective, in a deathbed confession of his own, admitted to colluding with the Mexican police and telling Fierro that confessing to the murder would free his parents. By the time the case reached the Court of Criminal Appeals, both the prosecutor and the El Paso judge overseeing the case were pushing for a new trial.

The court found that the coerced confession was a "harmless error," using the case to set a new, higher bar for defense claims. Four of the nine judges dissented, but over the next few years, two of them lost reelection and the other two retired. Under AEDPA, Fierro lost in federal court. As the years wore on, he let his hair grow wild and began to mumble to himself and spread feces on the wall of his cell. "I used to think Fierro would walk out of prison because I thought it was quite likely that he is innocent," his lawyer David Dow wrote in a memoir. "Now I hope he is not. I hope I was wrong and that he committed the murder, because the alternative is that he has spent the last twenty-five years of his life going insane in a sixty-square-foot cell for a crime he had nothing to do with."

Danalynn Recer wanted to work for the Texas Defender Service, where some of her former colleagues were finding a professional home, but it seemed to her that every time a new position came open, someone else would get it. As the post-resource-center era dawned, she traveled to Airlie, a conference center on a large, verdant estate in Virginia, where the national network of capital defense lawyers—many of whom could trace their professional family tree back to Anthony Amsterdam—met each year to strategize, commiserate, and look for jobs.

There she met Clive Stafford Smith, a British lawyer running a death penalty defense organization in Louisiana. He had been trained by Millard Farmer, a contemporary of Anthony Amsterdam's who, critical of the LDF's emphasis on postconviction work to stop executions, instead chose to stop the death penalty from being imposed, by mounting a vigorous defense at the trial stage. This appealed to Recer: If one lesson of the resource center was that men were being killed because of their inept defense lawyers at trial, then why not try to arrange better representation for them in the first place?

Stafford Smith saw a bit of himself in his new employee. Both were workaholics and informal dressers, without the Harvard and Yale pedigrees of many of their peers. Although his accent marked him as an outsider in Southern courtrooms, it didn't seem to elicit the same distrust that greeted "Yankee" lawyers. (Once, a judge told him his country had helped "us" in "the war," a reference to British support for the Confederacy.) But of course Stafford Smith couldn't charm everyone. Defense lawyers for unpopular clients were prone to receiving death threats, and when he started an organization of his own, he called it the Louisiana Crisis Assistance Center so that nobody would know what they actually did.

As with the resource center, the office was ramshackle, the salaries low. When they rented houses during trials outside New Orleans, Stafford Smith slept under the dining room table, sometimes draping a blanket over it for privacy. In the courtroom, he played a lack of pretense to his advantage. He appeared totally devoted to his clients, sometimes crying during closing arguments, an image all the more impactful given stereotypes of British stoicism. Recer saw how effective it could be to "unlawyer," to present yourself as a human asking for mercy on behalf of another human rather than as an "attorney" working for a "client."

At the resource center, her job had been to convince a judge that jurors would have shown her client mercy had they seen certain evidence. Now she was simply showing the jurors that evidence. The pressure was immense: If she won, it would vindicate the arguments the resource center had made—that better lawyers could change the outcomes of trials—but if they lost, there was no previous lawyer they could blame.

Recer also became close with Scharlette Holdman, a friend of Stafford Smith's and the doyenne of the field of mitigation. Though she had not invented the idea of finding evidence to convince a jury to be merciful, Holdman had refined the practice into a unique blend of art and science, coining the job title "mitigation specialist." She was also happy to insult people if it would shake them into doing a better job. Once, Recer was meeting with a client in jail when he abruptly walked out on her. She called Holdman. The man was mentally ill, Recer explained, and she had told him he could tell her how he felt no matter what; there were no right or wrong feelings. Later on, when he described his remorse, Recer tried to comfort him, saying he shouldn't feel guilty. Hearing this, Holdman burst into laughter.

"Danalynn, you dumbass!" she said.

"What?" Recer said. "What'd I do?"

Holdman pointed out how she had contradicted herself, telling this man he could share any feelings, but then telling him not to feel a certain way. Why should he trust her? Trust was everything to someone who had probably been failed many times in his life.

Once you had that trust, you became a biographer, ethnographer, therapist, and friend. The terrible stories of abuse and mental illness that could help explain a crime and elicit mercy were not easily uncovered; they might be so shameful that they emerged only after months of jail visits.

One of Recer's first clients with Stafford Smith was Allison Scott Thibodeaux, a man with multiple convictions for child molestation who, in 1993, broke into the home of his on-and-off girlfriend Nancy Melton and slit her throat, and then killed her friend Sadie Landreneau. The case featured an endless stream of sickening details that would test the most empathetic of lawyers: Landreneau's nine-year-old daughter had awoken to see blood everywhere and Thibodeaux pinning his girlfriend to the wall, and when police arrived, they found Melton's breasts severed and stuffed in her mouth and vagina.

Recer did the same sort of obsessive digging she'd done at the resource center, seeking out anyone who had ever known Thibodeaux. She spent hours with Louis Bellard, a step-uncle who had babysat Thibodeaux and was now himself in prison for murder. He admitted to molesting Thibodeaux regularly from the ages of five to fourteen. "I feel that I'm partially to blame for the crime he committed—you know, that maybe affected him some kind of way," he eventually said on the witness stand. Recer also found many people who had gone to church with Thibodeaux and watched him struggle over the years, drifting back and forth between alcoholism and a fervent devotion to his faith.

The jurors were evidently moved by this complicated portrait: It took them less than an hour to decide he should spend his life in prison rather than be executed.

Recer also worked with Stafford Smith in other states. In Mississippi, they represented Sabrina Butler, who had spent several years on death row for the murder of her nine-month-old son before her conviction was overturned due to a prosecutor's improper statement. When she faced death at a new trial, Recer helped Stafford Smith show the jury that the baby had in fact died from a kidney disease and not because Butler had physically abused him. Butler was the first woman in the country freed from death row as the result of proof of innocence, and Recer got to greet her when she walked out of jail. Executions were ramping up in Texas, and her peers from the resource center were burning out as they visited prisoner after prisoner with bad news, but Recer was seeing what it felt like to win. It was healing. It was also infuriating, because it proved that the judges who talked of "harmless error" were wrong—that when defense lawyers did a thorough job, they really could save people.

Still, she wasn't totally satisfied. She wanted to return to Texas. The state was still the epicenter of the death penalty, the place she felt her skills were most needed, the place that was still in a sense her home—she'd kept her Texas driver's license and an apartment in Austin. She pushed Stafford Smith to let her take on Texas cases, and he did let her help TDS with some of their research. During this time, she fell in love with a postconviction lawyer named Morris Moon, who lived in Florida. He got a job with TDS in Houston, and they began looking for a way to live together, despite their commitments in neighboring states. Eventually, Stafford Smith allowed Recer to move to Houston and commute back to Louisiana for work, but it was clear this solution wouldn't last forever.

PART
II

FALL

9

A MURDER IS PHYSICAL AND INTIMATE. SOMEONE PULLS A TRIGGER, or thrusts a knife, or wraps a hand around a neck. Police work is physical and intimate, too; detectives take photographs, label pieces of evidence, question suspects and witnesses, and then shackle wrists. The police might devise a theory about what happened, but it's when the lawyers arrive that words and ideas take over, as prosecutors and defenders place the evidence in service of a narrative. When the question is life or death, the lawyers try to establish not only what people did but also who they are, and they speak of good and evil.

After the death sentence is handed down and the case climbs through the appeals courts, it grows increasingly cerebral. A person without a law degree, who would have understood most of the plain-speaking witnesses in the trial transcript, is now confronted with dense jargon and a great deal of Latin. At the top of the system, the Supreme Court works out constitutional interpretations that apply to thousands of cases, and abstraction prevails. When the Court was listening to arguments in 1976 over whether the Texas death penalty law was constitutional, and the state's attorney general told the justices the story of how Jerry Jurek had strangled his victim Wendy Adams, Justice Lewis Powell had bristled at the intrusion. He and his colleagues were supposed to decide whether the Texas death penalty law comported with the Constitution. The grisly details of one murder could only be a distraction.

But when a case has finally been rejected by the highest court, it returns, for a moment, to the intimacy with which it began.

The governor—or, in a federal case, the president—decides whether to grant clemency, holding singular and total power over a person's life. Defense lawyers shift their arguments from the legal to the personal. Danalynn Recer submitted her client Carl Kelly's artwork and interviewed his family to demonstrate his struggles and his moments of kindness. If journalists cover the case, the public gets to know the murderer again, often for the first time since the trial, and if there are doubts—about his guilt, about whether the crime was really the worst of the worst, about redemption—they now appear, turning the question of life or death from a legal fight to a political one. If celebrities or activists are going to get involved, this is their cue.

If the final push for clemency fails, and it usually does, the center of action shifts suddenly from the highest realms of politics, from the governor's office on the second floor of the capitol building in Austin, 150 miles east, to a room at the Walls Unit in Huntsville, where a group of men are given a task as intimate as the original killing: another killing. They strap the body of a man, or occasionally a woman, to a gurney, insert a needle into their arm, and then send chemicals through the needle and wait for their heart to stop. Then they unstrap the body and lift it into a casket and place the casket in a car that will leave the prison grounds. Beginning with Charlie Brooks's execution in 1982, they performed these tasks four times a year, on average, in the 1980s. In the 1990s, they carried out one execution per month. In 2000, the year that executions peaked in Texas, they executed forty people, including, in a few instances, three men in a single week.

Carroll Pickett, the death house chaplain, worked nearly a hundred executions, from 1982 to 1995, and grew ever more sophisticated at "seducing" the emotions of the prisoner. "I realized that the attitude of each inmate brought to Huntsville to be executed was likely to be different," he later wrote. "While one might be arrogant and flippant, another would be somber and anxious. Some arrived in a reflective mood. It was important to recognize the state of mind quickly and adapt to it." In the death house there was one small window, and Pickett had thought it might be nice to let in some sun. But over the years he learned that it made the men feel worse to see the sun go down and the shadows lengthen, so he asked that the window be painted black.

Pickett was there when James Autrey smoked a cigarette while strapped to the gurney, waiting for the courts to rule, the needle already in his arm when word came down that the execution was stayed and they had to unstrap him. He was there when Johnny Paul Penry, with his IQ of 60, received a last-minute stay as well, having arrived at the death house with comics he could not read; he would thumb through them and laugh to himself. "Those innocent, childlike sounds chilled me," Pickett wrote. He was also haunted by the execution of Carlos DeLuna, who had always claimed that another man, also named Carlos, had actually committed the murder for which he was sentenced. (Researchers later made an extremely thorough case for his innocence.) DeLuna, though he was twenty-seven, acted like a teenager and took to calling Pickett "Daddy." Pickett told him the execution would be quick and painless. It was neither, and after it was over Pickett couldn't shake the image of DeLuna's eyes, which seemed to accuse him of lying.

Still, Pickett continued to do the work. "How could I be a party to something that I judged so un-Christian, so barbaric?" he wrote. "I asked myself, was it possible that even by ministering to a condemned man, I would be viewed as a willing participant to his death?" But he made peace with his role; people needed comfort in their final hours, and he was good at providing it. "No one, I had long believed, should face dying alone. Not even a hardened criminal about to be executed."

As Pickett gained expertise, he and his colleagues were contacted by men tasked with carrying out executions in other states. At least fifteen states, including California, Pennsylvania, and New Mexico, took lessons from Texas as they developed their own lethal injection protocols. Many sent officials to Huntsville. In Florida, a man caught fire in the state's electric chair, causing the witness room to fill with the smell of burnt flesh, and afterward the state's governor sent a warden named Ron McAndrew to the Walls Unit. He told him not to write anything down, in McAndrew's memory, because "if someone sees you writing something down, it immediately belongs to the press." McAndrew took notes anyway, because there was simply too much to memorize: the specifications of the syringes and IV lines, the way industrial tape was used to keep the two IVs in the two arms, and then covered with hospital tape "to make it look pretty."

In earlier times, making executions "look pretty" would have cut directly against their purpose. They were both public and gruesome—drawing and quartering, breaking on the wheel, burning at the stake—in order to display and reaffirm the power of the king, the monarch, the sovereign, or the people. But the Supreme Court began to apply the Eighth Amendment's ban on "cruel and unusual punishment" to executions, writing in 1890 that the word "cruel" "implies there is something inhuman and barbarous—something more than the mere extinguishment of life." A long line of decisions dovetailed with a steady improvement in technology, as courts and public officials sought to reduce the number of executions that were "botched" in some way. (The scholar Austin Sarat placed roughly 3 percent of American executions between 1890 and 2010 in this category.)

As a return to executions began to look likely in the 1970s, a television reporter from Dallas asked prison officials to let him film them. They refused, and the reporter sued. A judge ruled in his favor in January 1977, and the parties tussled through most of that year before the agency finally won. But while the final result was in question, state legislators in Austin began looking for a method of execution that would not look so grisly on camera. "We've gone from stoning to crucifixion, to quartering, to burning people at the stake, to hanging," said Rep. Ben Grant, passing out pictures of Ol' Sparky, as the electric chair was known. His problem was that electrocutions had a tendency to "become a circus sideshow."

Following Texas, other states came to hold rehearsals like the ones Warden Jack Pursley organized in 1982. Alabama copied the Texas practice of automatically allowing an Associated Press reporter to witness the execution and then picking other reporters through a lottery. New Mexico copied the microphone in the execution chamber and speakers in the witness rooms, so everyone could hear the last words.

Still, there was always tension between the professionalism and care that state officials tried to project and the fact that there was no medical basis for the process; prison employees were ultimately making things up as they went along. A pharmacy director in Louisiana once spoke over the phone with a counterpart in Texas and asked him why Texas used five grams of sodium pentothal when other states used two. He laughed, telling her, "When we did our very first execution, the only thing I had on hand was a five-gram vial. And rather than do the paperwork on wasting three grams, we just gave all five."

Pickett could help these men and women with the mechanics of the process, with the division of labor and the contingencies it was necessary to consider. What he could not do was prepare them adequately for what it felt like to play a role in killing someone. Over the years, he had learned that although his official task was to minister to the condemned, he would need to be a minister to the executioners as well.

In early 1998, Pickett received a phone call from Fred Allen, who had served on the "tie-down team" more than a hundred times. Allen had been working in his shop at home when news of an execution came over the radio. He started shaking and sweating, as tears streamed down his face. He started seeing in his mind all the people he had helped to strap down. Pickett came over the next day.

As they sat on Allen's porch swing, Pickett told him you could pour a drop of water into a vase, and it would not seem to matter, but after enough drops the vase would overflow. Allen later said the execution that triggered this reaction was "no different than anyone else's." This might have been true for him. But other members of the tie-down team would later say this execution was especially difficult, because, for the first time in more than a century, the person they were helping to kill was a woman.

On a January evening in 1998, Karla Faye Tucker sat across from Larry King, as her soft voice and bright eyes took over CNN for a full hour. Her execution date was less than a month away. "Does it get worse every day?" King asked her.

"No," she said. "It gets a little more exciting every day."

"Interesting choice of words, Karla."

"Yes."

"Exciting, how?"

"Just to see how God is unfolding everything."

Tucker's name was already well known in Texas. Fifteen years earlier, she had been arrested along with her boyfriend, Danny Garrett, in Houston for killing two people—Jerry Lynn Dean, her roommate's ex, and Deborah Thornton, who was in bed with him—with a pickax, while trying to steal Dean's motorcycle. The mitigating circumstances were known, too: Tucker had been exposed to heroin by age ten and followed her mother into sex work as a teenager. The view of the world emblazoned on a T-shirt she wore—KILL THEM ALL, LET GOD SORT THEM OUT—seemed handed to her rather than chosen. But was a bad upbringing an excuse for leaving a pickax in someone's chest? Prosecutors found a recording, from after the murder, in which Tucker said, "I come with every stroke." A story about her in the *Houston Chronicle* was headlined THE EMBODIMENT OF EVIL?

In jail, after attending a puppet show put on by a Christian ministry, Tucker stole a Bible, not realizing that they were free. "I hid way back in the corner so nobody could see me, because I was, like, really proud," she told Larry King. "I didn't know what I was reading and before I knew it, I was just—I was in the middle of my cell floor on my knees and I was just asking God to forgive me." She agreed to testify against her ex-boyfriend. On death row, she connected with Linda Strom, a volunteer who ministered to women in prison, and the two became close. Women were rarely sentenced to death in the United States, and female death rows never housed more than a handful of prisoners. In Texas, at a prison in Gatesville, they had a much easier experience than their male counterparts, with wide access to books and magazines. In a dayroom, they could eat together and watch television. They crocheted tablecloths and constructed dolls called Parole Pals, which were sold to prison employees.

Most of the women avoided media, but Strom was friends with Terry Meeuwsen, the former beauty queen who by then was hosting *The 700 Club*, a television show at the center of the growing evangelical political movement. The show sent an interviewer to Gatesville, and Tucker's radiance was undeniable. Evangelical Christians in the United States had largely supported the death penalty since the 1970s, but Tucker showed that their support might conflict with their other views on life and death. "I personally don't believe in capital punishment," she told Larry King. "I don't believe in abortion or euthanasia." Even if Christians were not prepared to totally abandon the death penalty, it was easy to support mercy for an individual whose redemption appeared so complete and convincing. She appeared to take ownership of what she'd done ("I can give you all kinds of excuses . . . but I don't want to do that"), establishing distance from her previous life ("Your boyfriend was proud of you?" "Yes. Isn't that sick? That's crazy"), and tapping the vivid metaphors of born-again faith ("God reached down inside of me and just literally uprooted all of that stuff, and took it out, and poured himself in").

Everyone had something to gain by promoting Tucker and her story. Christians saw it as proof that anyone could find faith and redemption. Journalists saw a powerful onscreen presence, a brilliant narrative contrast between dark and light. Tucker's lawyers could use the attention to convince Governor George W. Bush that she should be granted clemency. It seemed so clear that the primary basis for the death sentence—future dangerousness—had vanished.

If any Texas governor seemed likely to consider a story of Christian redemption, it was Bush. He had made his own born-again narrative central to his political identity, repeating in speeches and interviews and his 1999 book *A Charge to Keep* the story of how he'd been inspired by the pastor Billy Graham to give up drinking and give his life to Christ. "Faith changes lives," he wrote. "I know, because faith has changed mine."

Still, there was not much for a governor in Texas to gain politically by commuting a death sentence; in the 1980s, Mark White had rarely done so, and in the early 1990s, Ann Richards never did. When Bush took the governor's seat in 1995, he told his staff he would consider only two questions when deciding whether to stop an execution: Were there doubts about guilt? And had the courts had "ample opportunity" to review the case? It was not the traditional way of thinking about clemency, a power that, going back to the time of monarchs, was not about rubrics but about mercy, which is by nature not logical. But this approach offered Bush the appearance, if not the reality, of consistency, and it would insulate him politically.

Bush also had an extra layer of political protection compared with his counterparts in other states. In Texas, decisions about clemency technically belonged to the Board of Pardons and Paroles, an eighteen-member body that had been established in the 1930s after one governor was found to be selling pardons. A majority of the board would have to vote to spare a death row prisoner before the governor could grant clemency.

The governor appointed the board members, and Bush openly admitted that he could tell them how to vote if he so desired (although he denied doing so). One woman who served on the board during this time said in 2017 that members of the governor's staff had made it clear she was not to vote for clemency often, if ever, and certainly not in the case of Karla Faye Tucker. "They didn't tell me to change a vote, but it's what they meant," she said. "There was a sense of: Don't upset the status quo." Those who did go on record while still serving said they had no interest in harming the political career of the man who had appointed them.

In 1998, a few resource center alumni mounted lawsuits against the board on behalf of their clients, including Karla Faye Tucker, and forced board members to admit in a testy hearing that they could not articulate what would sway them to recommend a commutation. Board chairman Victor Rodriguez said the point of the board's decisions was "not about guilt or innocence," which flatly contradicted Bush's emphasis on that question, while other members said they did consider evidence of innocence. One witness admitted that the board members occasionally voted before receiving the full clemency application, and some members admitted to skimming the applications. They seldom if ever met in person and sent their votes in by fax, a process that some later called "death by fax."

The effort to make the board more transparent failed—the board members pointed out that if they *did* start giving explanations, they could be challenged in court over them—and Bush continued to deflect in public, saying all he could do was issue a thirty-day reprieve, which was technically true but failed to account for his formal and informal power over the board.

Still, Bush took direct responsibility for the Tucker decision. He was troubled by her *Larry King Live* appearance, and he was getting lots of pressure from his fellow evangelicals to save her life. Tucker herself wrote Bush a letter. "If my execution is the only thing, the final act that can fulfill the demand for restitution and justice, then I accept that," she wrote. But she wanted to live so she could help divert other women in prison from returning to crime when they were released: "I can't bring back the lives I took. But I can, if I am allowed, help save lives. That is the only real restitution."

By his own account, Bush was moved by her words, but he also feared that saving her would set a problematic precedent: What would happen when a Muslim or Jew—or even a Christian man—wrote something similar? It was a conundrum like the one the Supreme Court confronted in the 1970s: Giving humans the power to make life-and-death decisions meant those decisions could never be entirely rational and were likely to be swayed by our biases. Perhaps you could set rules to avoid disparities based on race, gender, or religion, but what about on-camera poise? If Bush saved Tucker, he felt, it would be difficult to respond to the argument that he had done so for the wrong reasons. (Tucker's lawyer, Walter Long, thought Bush should have focused on whether she would be dangerous in the future, to which the answer appeared obvious.) By saying no every time, though, Bush could make himself look unflinching and apolitical, a leader who stuck to his principles even when tested. He later described the act of announcing Tucker's denial as "one of the hardest things I have ever done."

During her final moments in her cell at the death house, Tucker spoke with Kenneth Dean, a leader of the tie-down team. "This isn't your fault, it's my fault," she said. "I'm not mad at any of your staff for what you have to do." Many people on the outside had come to her for advice on forgiveness, and now she was preempting the inevitable moment in which they would seek forgiveness for what they were about to do. They were standing in her cell, and Dean was shocked by how, unlike most prisoners on the brink of death, she seemed to be at peace.

This was in clear contrast to his fellow officers. The agency had decided to bring in some of the staff from the female death row, to let them sit with Tucker in the death house. When it was time for her to be taken away, "they just fell apart," Dean later recalled. He realized it had been a mistake to involve them precisely because they knew her so well. Where chaplains like Carroll Pickett had spent so many years learning how to comfort prisoners before their executions, now Tucker was the one doing the comforting, telling the executioners, "Don't worry, you are going to be okay." After skipping down the hallway to the gurney, she leapt on with no assistance and whispered, "Lord Jesus, help them to find my vein."

Then she spoke her final words: "Everybody has been so good to me. . . . I love all of you very much. I am going to be face-to-face with Jesus now. . . . I will see you all when you get there. I will wait for you."

As a devout Christian himself, Dean felt sure she was right about where she was going. He had witnessed her faith up close. But at the same time he felt that if Tucker had been released from the prison that day instead of killed, she would have lived a productive, nonviolent life.

A quiet, husky man with kind eyes—his fellow officers teased him with the nickname Teddy Bear—Dean had joined the agency in 1984, while getting his degree at Sam Houston State University in Huntsville, and slowly worked his way up the ranks. Only high-level officers were allowed to work executions, and so it was many years before his superior asked if he would be interested. It was totally voluntary, and it seemed clear he wouldn't be penalized for saying no. There was no extra pay.

Dean talked to his pastor. There were numerous Bible verses that spoke in both directions about the punishment, but his pastor said the important thing was what the scripture made his heart feel. He felt he could handle this duty.

At his first execution, he was assigned to the prisoner's head. It was not really a job, because the head itself was not tied down; you would only need to touch it if the man started to resist, which was rare. He kept wondering to himself how he would react, whether he would feel bothered, but by the time it was over and he had helped load the body off the gurney, he realized he had not felt much. It had all gone like clockwork. As he was given more responsibilities, he found the routine itself was the best way to cope. The team would buckle all the buckles, across the wrists and ankles and stomach and chest, the same way every time. They would wait in another room while the actual execution took place, and then return to help load the body into the hearse.

But of course it wasn't all predictable. Execution team members often had to spend time with the condemned man, playing checkers or dominoes with him, getting him some coffee or one of the pastries laid out on a table in the death house, and most importantly explaining what to expect. The most common question Dean found himself answering was a strange one. A rumor spread on death row that the executioners were going to place a plug into their anus, to keep them from defecating on themselves when they were killed. Dean would have to explain that this was not true.

Eventually Dean rose to the level of major and was given the job that Warden Jack Pursley had performed more than a decade earlier: selecting new members of the execution team. Dean was cautious about approaching officers, and often would let those interested approach him. He would then invite them to executions without giving them a task, gauging their reactions. They had to be dignified, not the type who would say a crass or vicious word to the prisoner. They could not be especially cold or insensitive. But they also had to be stoic; once a sergeant asked to be on the tie-down team, and he let her practice, but when she watched an execution and he saw tears streaming down her face, he decided she was not the right fit. Once someone was on the execution team, there was no shame in being human, and Dean watched the faces of the officers to see how they were faring. Occasionally, a particular execution would bother them. When they executed Betty Lou Beets, a sixty-two-year-old woman convicted of killing her husband, Dean debriefed some of the officers and learned they had been thinking of their own mothers.

Dean himself prayed before and after every execution. As executions grew more frequent, the work was simply exhausting, and the team was growing irritable and zombie-like. It became Dean's job to escort the family of the prisoner for their final visit, which he found difficult. Dean had two little kids himself at this point, and he found himself wondering, if he were going to be executed, what his last words to his loved ones might be, what he'd want them to "hang on to."

For Dean, the comfort offered by routine gave way to another worry: Why *didn't* he feel more bothered? He wondered if his emotional detachment suggested he had changed for the worse. He found himself becoming more withdrawn, more sealed off, outside the tight, brotherly circle of his fellow executioners. The tie-down team would sometimes hang out at the warden's house after an execution and debrief, but when the agency leadership asked if they wanted to speak to a psychologist after executions, they refused. They didn't talk to their families about it, either; Dean definitely didn't want his kids to be able to picture what he was doing. When other officers would ask questions, he wouldn't go into detail. Dean would think, as he put it, "That's a person's life that we were a part of, and I think some dignity should be left there with that." Fred Allen started talking to the media about his mental breakdown following the Tucker execution, and some of the other officers were bothered, as if he was betraying their unspoken pact to stay quiet.

But like Allen, Dean had been especially troubled by Karla Faye Tucker's death, feeling as though she could have improved the world had she continued to live. He still supported the death penalty, but what was the point if there were more people on death row like her? He reminded himself that his own task was very limited, that by the time he was involved, the decisions of lawyers, judges, and state officials all the way up to the governor had come together to produce this result. He also looked to his faith. He noticed that prisoners who expressed religious conviction, like Tucker, seemed to die in a more peaceful way. Those who didn't seemed to have an inner struggle, as though seeing something they did not like. The prisoners with faith just eased off.

Dean's colleague Buster McWhorter took particular comfort from the biblical passage of Romans 13:04: "For the one in authority is God's servant for your good. But if you do wrong, be afraid, for rulers do not bear the sword for no reason. They are God's servants, agents of wrath to bring punishment on the wrongdoer." McWhorter, a ruddy-faced, affable man who liked to draw comics in his spare time, also sought comfort in the words of Jim Willett, one of the wardens he worked under, who said that some of those executed might not have found God if they were not facing death.

McWhorter started seeing his role as a little like the chaplain's, helping the prisoners get right with God before the end. For a while, he drove the van from death row to the death house, and he'd sometimes talk to his passengers about faith. He'd tell them about Luke 15:7: "There will be more joy in heaven over one sinner who repents, than ninety-nine righteous persons who do not need repentance." One day, a man he was driving told him he was involved in a Bible study on death row. Later that day, the man received a stay of execution, and McWhorter told him, "The Lord's not through with you."

Tucker's death was the first in a run of news events out of Texas that scrambled the usual narratives about capital punishment. For much of the 1980s and 1990s, stories about death sentences and executions had fallen into patterns: the monstrous murderer and the undeserving victim, the steely-eyed prosecutor delivering justice, the governor soberly overseeing the execution. There were occasional challenges to this script, including Errol Morris's movie *The Thin Blue Line* and the subsequent exoneration of Randall Dale Adams, as well as the news reports about sleeping defense lawyers. But these stories came and went. Now, with increasing competition in the twenty-four-hour news cycle—both Fox News and MSNBC went on air in 1996—an unusual or evocative case could stick around, challenging the conventions of the execution story genre and pushing politicians and the public to think about the death penalty in new ways. This was especially difficult, politically speaking, for Governor Bush: Whereas his predecessors could score easy points by giving the public what it wanted, now it was increasingly unclear what the public, or at least the majority of it, actually did want, and what role in the drama the governor was supposed to play.

A few months after the Tucker execution, Bush was confronted with another case that was garnering national interest. A serial killer named Henry Lee Lucas was set to be executed for the murder of a young woman who had been found dead on Halloween 1979 in a culvert off a highway about an hour north of Austin. She had never been identified, so she was named for the only clothing found on her: Orange Socks.

Lucas had confessed to the killing after being arrested for two other murders. (He had already served time in prison for the murder of his mother.) And now he kept confessing to other crimes beyond the "Orange Socks" murder. Eventually, the Texas Rangers set up a Lucas Task Force Office at the Williamson County Jail, north of Austin. Lucas referred to it as "my office." He realized that if he kept talking he would keep drinking milkshakes and watching color TV rather than be sent to death row. His confessions grew increasingly outlandish. He said he had killed the union boss Jimmy Hoffa, and that he was a member of a Satanic cult that sold babies into slavery in Mexico. He said he'd delivered poison to Jim Jones in Guyana and had been paid to assassinate President Jimmy Carter.

His claims were greeted with a stunning lack of skepticism from law enforcement officers, who traveled from around the country to ask him about unsolved murders. The Rangers admitted that they "refreshed" his memory by sharing information about victims and letting him look at crime scene photos. Through his confessions, he helped police close more than two hundred murders—despite a dearth of physical evidence—and was interviewed about thousands more.

Many reporters took these claims by law enforcement at face value. But the Dallas journalist Hugh Aynesworth started tracking down Lucas's work records, along with eyewitness accounts from landlords and employers that placed Lucas hundreds of miles from the murders to which he had confessed. Having collected all this evidence, Aynesworth finally asked Lucas how many murders he had actually committed, and Lucas held up three fingers. He had grown skilled at gleaning details from crime scene photos and parroting them back as if he had just remembered them. A psychologist interviewed Lucas and decided that "the most prolific serial confessor in the world" had a personality disorder and low self-esteem. "Lucas told me that in the eyes of the media he became the biggest monster alive and it made him feel good," the doctor wrote. "Everybody was paying attention to him." Lucas himself described his false confessions as a service to the public—he wanted to expose law enforcement misconduct. "They think I'm stupid, but before all this is over, everyone will know who's really stupid," he said. "And we'll see who the real criminals are."

Aynesworth's reporting pushed the state attorney general's office to enlist an investigator, who found witnesses and documents, including receipts with Lucas's signature, demonstrating he was nowhere near where he had supposedly killed the vast majority of his victims. By the summer of 1986, the Texas Rangers' confession mill had been exposed as a fraud.

And yet, a dozen years later, he was still facing execution based on a set of facts that strained credulity. When Lucas first confessed to the "Orange Socks" murder, he had gotten many details of the crime wrong, including the cause of death, saying he had stabbed the woman when really she had been strangled. At his 1984 trial, a job foreman from Jacksonville, Florida, told the jury he had seen Lucas several times on the day of the murder. Prosecutors had laid out an elaborate time-line that would involve Lucas driving from central Texas to Jacksonville without a moment to spare. Given incomplete and misleading evidence, the jury decided he was guilty. Or maybe they didn't: Jim Boutwell, the sheriff who took the confession, was heard to say during the trial, "Even if they don't believe Henry did this one, they know he done a lot of them." At Bush's request, the Board of Pardons and Paroles reexamined the case, and Hugh Aynesworth, whose journalism on the case was a finalist for the Pulitzer Prize, wrote Bush a long letter urging him to stop the execution. Bush's own advisers told him something was amiss.

Still, Lucas's lawyers needed a way to make clemency look politically tenable for Bush. When lawyer Rita Radostitz, a resource center alum, announced to her colleagues, "They can't kill Henry, he's innocent!" one of her fellow lawyers laughed. Such an argument had proven inadequate so many times before. So they whittled the message down to something a little more subtle and harder to refute: It would be an embarrassment for the system to be so sloppy.

Eventually the pardons board voted 17–1 in favor of commuting the death sentence. At the board's news conference, one of the state's lawyers said to one of Lucas's lawyers, "We just dodged a bullet." Bush approved of the board's vote, telling himself the clemency system was a safety valve for "unusual or exceptional circumstances." "I take this action so that all Texans can continue to trust the integrity and fairness of our criminal justice system," read his statement to the public. It was the first death sentence commutation in Texas in many years, and it helped Bush demonstrate that he was willing to make unpopular decisions. He scored even more political points when Garry Mauro, his Democratic opponent for governor in 1998, said Lucas should have been executed because he was "guilty of enough of the murders he confessed to." Bush's campaign called Mauro's "disregard for the law" an "alarming" indicator of how he would govern.

But the Lucas case also proved that if Bush really wanted to, he could push the pardons board to look deeply at a case and give him cover to grant clemency; it made his claims of personal limitation ring a little more hollow.

A few weeks before the Lucas commutation in June 1998, the national news cycle was taken over by another Texas murder, a tragedy that raised the specter of racial violence that some Americans wanted to believe was far in the past and other Americans knew wasn't. In the east Texas town of Jasper, a forty-nine-year-old black man named James Byrd, Jr., was walking home from a party when three younger white men offered him a ride home. Shawn Berry, Lawrence Brewer, and John King attacked Byrd, beating him and defecating on his body before tying him to the back of a truck and driving several miles. His limbs and head were later found strewn along country roads. Forensic analysis showed that he had remained alive for much of the dragging, and had managed, at least for a moment, to raise his head.

The perpetrators were open white supremacists; King had a tattoo of a black man hanging from a tree. Law enforcement leaders in the town brought in the FBI to help investigate. At the time, the town had a black mayor and school superintendent and a tightly knit, politically active black community. "We had to satisfy them that this was not 1920," the white district attorney, Guy James Gray, later said, referring to a long-ago incident in a neighboring county where another black man had been dragged to death behind a truck and nobody was ever arrested for it.

Most black Americans opposed the death penalty, including those who lived in Jasper, but the special historical resonance of this murder led many to set aside that view when it came to these three men. A black reporter named Joyce King (no relation to the perpetrator) moved briefly to the town to write a book about the case and later wrote, "Black residents who had never supported the death penalty in their lives urged the DA to find a legal way to seek the death penalty in this case." It was necessary now, they felt, to send a message to other white supremacists. And symbolism mattered, too. No white man had been executed in Texas for murdering a black man since 1854, when it was a punishment for killing another white man's slave. Sentencing these men to death would signify that the life of a black man had more value now, in the eyes of the state, than it had in the past.

John King and Lawrence Brewer were sent to death row and eventually executed, while Shawn Berry received a life sentence. This outcome could be interpreted in two ways: Either America was still a place of lynchings and racial terror, or America was working very hard to relegate such crimes to the past by taking them seriously on the rare occasion they still happened. "The world press beat a path here," the comedian and civil rights activist Dick Gregory said approvingly. King, the reporter, noticed that the death sentence functioned as a sign of racial healing, an outcome that both black and white residents of Jasper could rally around together.

This was awkward for the national anti-death-penalty community. A representative of the NAACP Legal Defense Fund argued in the media that the death penalty itself was a tool of racial injustice, with clear historical ties to the long-ago lynchings evoked by Byrd's murder. At the same time, if prosecutors had not sought the death penalty, they would have been accused of bigotry themselves. The death penalty had become so entrenched in American life, so thoroughly severed in people's minds from the lynchings of the past, that now it could be seen as a redress for racially motivated violence.

Some in Byrd's family would come to oppose the death sentences. "You can't fight murder with murder," his son Ross Byrd said when an execution date was set for Lawrence Brewer in 2011. But by the late 1990s, retribution had become an organizing principle of the American criminal justice system. Even those who opposed the death penalty back then could simultaneously support harsher treatment for perpetrators of hate crimes.

Byrd's murder inspired public support on the left for longer prison sentences for those who committed crimes out of bigotry, and bills to this effect were introduced in Congress and the Texas Legislature. Governor Bush declined to support these measures, and it appeared to liberals that it was because they also increased penalties for crimes related to the victim's sexual orientation (inspired by the murder of Matthew Shepard, a gay college student in Wyoming). The press characterized the Texas bill as an "awkward political decision" for Bush, because signing it might alienate Republican voters uncomfortable with homosexuality, but a refusal to do so would further unite Democrats against him.

The bill never made it to Bush's desk, so he didn't have to resolve this dilemma for now, but it was yet another example of how political calculations around crime and punishment were growing more difficult to make. Bush stepped even deeper into this thicket when, in the late spring of 1999, he announced his run for president.

10

IN THE FALL OF 1999, A PROFILE OF GEORGE W. BUSH WAS PUBLISHED in a now defunct magazine called *Talk*. The writer was Tucker Carlson, who was already gaining popularity as a conservative pundit on television, but here his ideological commitments gave way to his journalistic instinct to embarrass the powerful. "Bush's brand of forthright tough-guy populism can be appealing, and it has played well in Texas," Carlson wrote. "Yet occasionally there are flashes of meanness visible beneath it." He described their conversation about the execution of Karla Faye Tucker. Bush said many people had come to Austin to ask him to spare Tucker's life. "Did you meet with any of them?" Carlson asked.

> Bush whips around and stares at me. "No, I didn't meet with any of them," he snaps, as though I've just asked the dumbest, most offensive question ever posed. "I didn't meet with Larry King either when he came down for it. I watched his interview with Tucker though. He asked her real difficult questions, like 'What would you say to Governor Bush?'" "What was her answer?" I wonder. "Please," Bush whimpers, his lips pursed in mock desperation, "don't kill me." I must look shocked—ridiculing the pleas of a condemned prisoner

who has since been executed seems odd and cruel, even for someone as militantly anticrime as Bush—because he immediately stops smirking. "It's tough stuff," Bush says, suddenly somber, "but my job is to enforce the law."

Carlson pointed out that Tucker had never said anything close to "Please don't kill me" in her interview, meaning that in addition to being callous, Bush was loose with facts. The conservative columnist George Will wrote that the profile "suggests an atmosphere of adolescence, a lack of gravitas—a carelessness, even a recklessness, perhaps born of things having gone a bit too easily so far." Bush's campaign book came out a couple of months later and pushed back with a sober account of his emotional struggles with the Tucker and Lucas cases, but it was too late. It was by now clear that Bush's opponent would be Al Gore, and that part of Bush's strategy was to show that he was folksy and relatable, while Gore was heady and wooden. Now liberals had one clear line of attack: They could show that Bush was a fraud. Other presidential candidates had approved executions as governors, and Gore himself did not oppose the death penalty, but Bush had overseen a system so large and active that it represented a curiosity on the national stage. He would inevitably become the face of that system.

One night outside the Walls Unit, during an otherwise quiet execution, the sounds of cheerleaders and a marching band pierced the air: "Florida oranges, Texas cactus. We kill convicts just for practice!" Members of the victims' rights group Justice for All initially cheered along. "You could actually see the realization come over the faces of those in the pro-death-penalty camp," a reporter observed, as the chants grew more extreme: "Who's the best on the killing scene? George Bush, he's a killing machine!" It turned out this was a Houston theater troupe, hired by a producer for liberal gadfly Michael Moore's television show *The Awful Truth.* The idea of the segment was that Bush was "competing" with his brother Jeb, the governor of Florida, to see who could carry out more executions.

This stunt may have further enraged liberals who already did not like Bush, but it was unlikely to damage him politically. Sixty percent of Americans supported the death penalty, and most condemned prisoners were not Karla Faye Tucker. In order for liberals to successfully paint Bush as a villain, the person facing the gurney could not be a villain himself: He needed to be a victim of the system, someone executed despite his innocence.

Such a figure had long been a cultural idea. "The vision of American criminal law as a ravening monster, forever hounding innocent people into the electric chair, is one with which emotional persons like to chill their blood," a *New Yorker* writer had written in 1935. Arguments about innocence emerged sporadically around famous cases like those of Nicola Sacco and Bartolomeo Vanzetti, and Julius and Ethel Rosenberg. Errol Morris vividly demonstrated in his 1988 film that a man had been wrongly condemned to death in Dallas. But for the most part, the innocence claims of prisoners were a cultural cliché, which people would expect to hear but seldom have reason to believe.

Then came DNA. Beginning in the 1980s, the analysis of genetic material started to be marshaled by defense teams to prove, with an unprecedented degree of scientific certainty, that their clients could not have committed the crimes for which they were sitting in prison. The legal system had always aspired to establish truth, while hedging with language about "reasonable doubt." Now the actual truth appeared within reach, and the public and politicians could no longer dismiss innocence claims as desperate efforts to avoid execution. In case after case around the country, men were freed from death row when DNA helped them prove their innocence, and in late 1998, at a conference on wrongful convictions at the Northwestern University School of Law, more than two dozen people exonerated from death row appeared together on a stage. "Had the state of Illinois gotten its way, I'd be dead today," one said. The political implications were big: Even if the justice system had not killed someone innocent yet, it had gotten awfully close, over and over again.

The New York Times explicitly called the Northwestern conference a "public relations counterattack" by opponents of capital punishment, and some conservatives saw a conspiracy. In *The American Spectator,* the columnist Byron York depicted philanthropists George Soros and John R. MacArthur as a "new breed of death penalty abolitionists" who manipulated public opinion by funding the Death Penalty Information Center, a think tank in Washington, D.C., and driving a new focus on innocence. "It was less moralistic—no candles, please," he wrote. "It was designed to appeal to the public's sense of fairness without appearing squishy on violent crime." Whether the linking of innocence to the death penalty was deliberate or organic or some combination of the two, it represented a seismic shift, as the image of an innocent person facing execution was seared into public consciousness. Two Hollywood films, *True Crime* and *The Green Mile,* dramatized the idea. The founders of the Innocence Project worked with a writer to publish *Actual Innocence: Five Days to Execution, and Other Dispatches from the Wrongly Convicted.* George Will, in a positive review, offered his fellow conservatives a way to link their reactions to their ideology: "Capital punishment is a government program, so skepticism is in order."

In 1999, the *Chicago Tribune* put several of its best reporters on the death penalty beat. Together, they produced a multipart series that showed how an innocent person might end up on death row as a result of problems that pervaded the system, from unreliable detective work to weak defense lawyering to misconduct by prosecutors. In Illinois, more men had been released from death row than were actually executed. Shaken by what he learned, Illinois governor George Ryan declared a moratorium on executions. "I cannot support a system, which, in its administration, has proven to be so fraught with error and has come so close to the ultimate nightmare, the state's taking of innocent life," he said.

His decision put pressure on Bush. On *Meet the Press,* the presidential candidate was asked if he would follow suit and halt executions in Texas. "No, I won't," Bush said. "Because I'm confident that every person that has been put to death in Texas, under my watch, has been guilty of the crime charged and had full access to the courts."

After seeing this answer, *New York Times* reporter Raymond Bonner approached his editor. "Boy," he said, "that's really throwing down the gauntlet." It was as if Bush was asking to be proved wrong. Bonner and a colleague were sent to Texas, where they tracked down witnesses and collected court documents and spread them out over hotel beds, debating whether all the evidence in this case or that really added up. The *Chicago Tribune* reporters who had documented the system's flaws in their own state came down as well. They hunkered down in the basement of the Court of Criminal Appeals in downtown Austin, reading case after case and finding dozens of egregious examples of bad lawyering and tainted evidence, all ignored by ideologically motivated judges.

Seeing the media's interest, the national community of anti-death-penalty lawyers began discussing how the innocence issue could be harnessed to gain public support for their cause. Some weren't sure the focus on innocence was the best move. They feared it would distract the public from bigger questions of fairness and racial injustice, and from the ultimate question of whether the death penalty is just even for the guilty. Others felt too overwhelmed with fighting individual executions to even think on such a broad, strategic level.

And would it even work? Alabama senator Jeremiah Denton argued that "saying that we should not have the death penalty because we may accidently [*sic*] execute an innocent man is like saying that we should not have automobiles because some innocent people might be accidentally killed in them." In polls, Americans tended to say they believed at least one innocent person had been executed, but also that they supported the system in place. Although the questions were not asked in relation to each other, it was possible many Americans would learn that Bush had overseen the death of an innocent man and just shrug.

And then there was the practical problem: It is very difficult to prove with complete certainty that a person did not commit a crime. In many cases DNA is not collected or does not offer clear answers. Even if a new person confesses to a murder—and there were plenty of cases in which someone claiming to be the real perpetrator did confess—the case now relies on the credibility of someone who had (maybe) committed murder. Defense lawyers began receiving flurries of calls from television producers asking if they knew of an innocent person who had been executed under Bush. "How would we know?" lawyer Maurie Levin asked in response, raising her hands in frustration.

Even without a single media-ready case, the messaging was effective: Gallup polls showed that support for the death penalty had dropped from 80 percent nationally in 1994 to 66 percent by early 2000. In January of that year, *Frontline* aired an hourlong special on innocence, focusing on the Texas case of Roy Criner, who had received ninety-nine years for aggravated sexual assault before a DNA test proved the semen found with the teenage victim had not come from him. The Texas Court of Criminal Appeals had denied him a hearing on this new evidence, with Presiding Judge Sharon Keller writing that Criner might have used a condom, or not ejaculated. On national television, she called the victim "a promiscuous girl." Another judge complained she'd turned her court into a "laughingstock."

Bush kept the issue alive by failing to dispel the image of himself as both heartless and blithe. At a Republican primary debate, he was told that a Texas prisoner had been released because his lawyer had slept through his trial. Bush appeared to laugh. (A spokesman said later he was merely incredulous at the question.) "Well, you just made your case," he said with a defensive tone. "The man is out. I'm sorry, he's out—he's a really violent person. I hope he gets retried soon. But the system worked in this case."

Bush looked a little petulant, and as the campaign continued he kept trying to calibrate his tone. At first he failed: During a debate with Gore, he appeared to smile when discussing the death sentences handed out to the men who killed James Byrd, Jr. (Byrd's daughter emerged months later, in a NAACP-funded ad, to say she had pleaded for tougher sentences for hate crimes, but Bush had not supported her.) On late-night television, David Letterman said, "We make a lot of jokes about you electrocuting people in Texas." The crowd laughed, and Bush now grew serious. "I hope you're not laughing at the expense of victims or people who are put to death," he said.

In June, the cover of *Newsweek* featured a previously obscure death row prisoner named Ricky McGinn. He had been convicted of raping and murdering his twelve-year-old stepdaughter, but biological material on her clothing had not been matched to anyone, meaning DNA testing might prove his innocence by implicating someone else. Bowing to the political pressure, Bush used his authority to stop the execution for thirty days so the testing could be completed. When the results came back, they all matched McGinn—or, to be exact, there was a 1 in 65 quadrillion chance that the semen on the victim's shorts belonged to someone else. McGinn was executed soon after, and Bush could use the case to show the public that he was careful.

But there were many more executions scheduled before election day, and one of them was for a man with a far bigger national profile.

By 2000, Gary Graham was already among the most famous death row prisoners in the country. He had been sentenced to death in 1981 for the murder of Bobby Grant Lambert, a fifty-three-year-old man from Arizona. He maintained his innocence, and there was never a clear motive; Lambert still had $6,000 in his pocket when the police found him outside a grocery store. The prosecution had focused on a single eyewitness, Bernadine Skillern, who had been waiting in the car for her daughter to buy school supplies. After her daughter returned, she saw a man approach Lambert and press a gun to his head and fire. She blew her car horn, and the man backed off and looked her way. He took off running, and she followed him briefly in her car before driving away.

Graham had the good fortune of finding a pen pal, a woman from California, who begged lawyers and activists to investigate his claim that he didn't shoot Lambert. In the early 1990s, his case became the focus of lawyers from both the NAACP Legal Defense Fund and the Texas Resource Center. They found numerous problems with his case. It turned out that Skillern, the key eyewitness, had been unable to pick Graham out of an initial photo lineup, but then did pick him out of a live lineup; he was the only person to appear in both lineups, which meant she might have been subconsciously led to identify him. They found other eyewitnesses who were convinced they also had seen the shooting, and that it was not Gary Graham they had seen.

Why hadn't these other witnesses been called to the stand at his trial? Because Graham was represented at the time by Ronald Mock, a lawyer so famously ineffective that part of death row was dubbed the Mock Wing, since it was full of his clients. He had told his own investigator not to spend too much time on the Graham case because he thought he was guilty.

When Graham faced an execution date in 1993, his new lawyers worked to get media attention for the case—if the public believed he was innocent, perhaps the governor, Ann Richards, would feel political pressure to commute his sentence. (Danalynn Recer was briefly involved in this work, interviewing the jurors who had sentenced Graham, some of whom now had misgivings.) The center enlisted Steve Hall, a former journalist, who brought on Amnesty International and Riptide Communications, a public relations firm in New York. The Graham case began showing up everywhere: *The New York Times*, *The Washington Post*, the *Los Angeles Times*, *The New Yorker*, *People*. The Congressional Black Caucus asked for a stay of execution, as did former first lady Rosalynn Carter and more than a dozen Roman Catholic bishops in Texas. The singer Kenny Rogers offered to pay for a second trial.

Graham did manage to get a stay of execution in 1993, and the case went back into the court system. His lawyers continued to build a detailed argument for his innocence. They argued that Graham had no reason to kill Lambert, while others did: Lambert had once been arrested for piloting an airplane carrying forty thousand Quaaludes and some cocaine, and he had made a deal with prosecutors to testify against others involved in the trafficking. But Graham's lawyers had been stymied at every turn by increasingly unfriendly judges and the onerous legal hurdles set up by Congress. No court would grant him a hearing.

Graham's execution—scheduled for a Thursday evening in June 2000, nearly five months before election day—was a perfect news peg for the issues the *Chicago Tribune*, *The New York Times*, and other newspapers had been reporting on. Instead of a backward-looking effort to prove Bush was responsible for an innocent person's death, here was a real-life battle to the end, featuring a black man who claimed he was being railroaded. Protesters began showing up at Bush's campaign events around the country. A few interrupted his remarks at a $1,000-a-plate fundraising dinner in Silicon Valley, shouting, "Don't kill an innocent man!" In Houston, members of the New Black Panther Party, toting guns and driving an open-top Hummer stretch limousine, demonstrated outside the state Republican Party's convention. The interest from black public figures like Al Sharpton and Jesse Jackson amplified the idea that Bush had tolerated, and even championed, a racist system.

Texas attorney general John Cornyn stepped in to take some of the political heat off Bush. Less than a month before Graham's execution date, the Supreme Court had overturned a death sentence in a case in which the expert witness said the defendant was more likely to be dangerous because he was Hispanic. Although it was usually Cornyn's job to argue for upholding death sentences, he agreed that such testimony was indefensible, and his team looked for other cases in which the same expert had testified. They found six, and Cornyn said he wouldn't object if those defendants sought to have their sentences overturned. Bush was able to sell Cornyn's decision as further proof that the system had safeguards.

If opponents of the death penalty had hoped to use innocence concerns to undermine public support for the punishment, Graham's case appeared ideal because the evidence of his guilt was so weak. At the same time, the man himself was an unsympathetic protagonist, especially to the white conservatives who had flocked to Karla Faye Tucker two years prior. Graham had admitted to many violent crimes, claiming to be innocent of only the worst of them, and his living victims were vocal. Greg Jones, whom Graham had robbed and shot in the throat, said of him in *USA Today*, "I could see that smile, that little snicker, and then I felt the explosion. I will never forget that smile."

Graham did not seem to be helping his case, either, though how much his personality was filtered through the preconceptions of reporters is difficult to gauge in retrospect. "Visiting days here at the rural Ellis Unit of the Huntsville State Prison have turned into weekly press conferences," one had written back in 1993. "Graham, displaying the kind of vanity usually reserved for film stars, admonished a photographer not to take a picture while he was talking." If there was ever a chance of white Bush voters thinking about the death penalty through the lens of racial injustice, it was unlikely they would be swayed to do so by a man like Graham. He spoke boldly of black power, and because he didn't want to be remembered by his "slave name," he changed his first name to Shaka (for a Zulu chief) and his last name to Sankofa (a Ghanaian word that served as an exhortation to remember the past).

As Graham's execution approached, the question of race was overtaken in the press by the perennial, abstract question of whether the death penalty was a just punishment. On the Maury Povich show, the Gary Graham case was framed not as a question of innocence, but as a "highly charged debate" between two conflicting sides: Graham's famous supporters and the victims of his other crimes. Povich made prominent mention of the "celebrity question," implying there was something inorganic and staged about the whole media circus.

On the eve of Graham's execution, anyone who tuned in to CNN would have seen defense lawyer turned pundit Alan Dershowitz, television star turned activist Mike Farrell, and Baptist leader Albert Mohler steer the argument away from the particulars of Graham's case and toward the death penalty in general. In an effort to frame this as a culture war with two sides, the coverage focused on Skillern, the eyewitness, who again repeated on national television that she was sure Graham was guilty, and David Spiers, whom Graham had shot in a separate crime. "He pulled out a 12-gauge shotgun and put it to my chest," Spiers recounted on CNN. "He pulled the hammer back of the shotgun and blew my leg in half. . . . I almost died. I got my last rites. After that, I didn't walk for two years. I still don't walk properly today. . . . And when I see him on TV today, nineteen years later, and I look at his eyes, I see violence."

It is impossible to know how Graham would have been viewed had he been white, or had his criminal history been less scary, or had he presented himself as a born-again, redemption-seeking Christian, or had the victims of those prior crimes not gone on television themselves. But as it stood, Graham's innocence claims, though they came at a time of increasing attention to wrongful convictions, struggled to stick amid the amorphous and fickle and racially biased rules of public sympathy, which were ready to make space for Karla Faye Tucker, no matter how terrible her crime, but not for a black man, no matter how questionable his guilt. The Graham story resonated subtly with the trial of O. J. Simpson five years prior: To many black supporters, he was a hero, while to white viewers he was a villain and a grandstander.

On the day of the execution, hundreds gathered in the streets of Huntsville. Two hundred state law enforcement officers were brought in to manage the crowds, and businesses closed for fear of violence. The cameras turned to the extremes: the Ku Klux Klan men with their white hoods and Confederate flags, and the New Black Panther Party men with their berets and military guns. Law enforcement tried to keep them separated, but still they found ways to each other. Quanell X, head of the New Black Panther Party in Houston, shouted "Fuck you" in the face of a white man in a Confederate bandana as the two were swarmed by cameramen. A parade of Graham's supporters banged hand drums and cowbells and then lit an American flag on fire, shouting, "We fired up! We ain't takin' no more!"

Tie-down team leader Kenneth Dean found Gary Graham to be arrogant. Graham had already made it clear he wouldn't go to his death without a fight. During an earlier execution date, in 1993, he had spat in Chaplain Pickett's face. Now, when the van door opened at the Walls Unit, Dean told Graham, "You can step out and walk inside, or you will be carried." Graham—outfitted in leg irons, handcuffs, and a shackle around his waist—didn't respond. "There's nothing in his eyes but pure hatred," Warden Jim Willett later wrote in a personal journal. "His body is tense. Rigid. Like a cornered animal." A group of officers suited up in riot gear carried him into the death house, where they removed his uniform and gave him paper clothing to wear. He shouted and cursed.

The men on the tie-down team did not discuss whether the men they helped execute were guilty or innocent, believing that was the job of the courts. Sometimes they would tell a story about one man who had proclaimed his innocence loudly in the media. But when it came time for the execution, he told the chaplain that he'd been lying, that he had in fact committed the murder, but he wouldn't admit this from the gurney, because it might devastate his family to hear his reversal after backing him for so long. (It was also out of concern for the family that the executioners did not share the man's name.) His last words were another proclamation of innocence, but the executioners knew the truth.

Sometimes they were more cavalier about the issue. Earlier in Dean's career, a prisoner delivering food to the death house came to him in terror. He said he was clairvoyant and could hear three distinct voices proclaiming their innocence. Dean knew there had been well over a hundred executions by then, and responded, "Only three innocent, that's pretty good odds." If there was room for ambivalence on Graham, these men did not embrace it. They resented the activists who showed up to protest outside the prison, parachuting into their community to score points by calling them murderers.

When word came down that Graham had no more pending appeals, the tie-down team suited up in their riot gear. Graham stood at the back of the cell. "I need you to move up to the bars, and put your hands through the slot, so we can handcuff you," Dean told him. Graham shook his head, clenched his body, and narrowed his eyes. "Come on," he said.

An officer unlocked the door and Dean, shield in hand, barged in, with several more officers holding on to one another's shoulders and waists. A prison official standing nearby later said he could not hear any words—just "grunts, breathing, the sound of a struggle." Dean knocked Graham down, and Graham raised his leg, nailing Dean in the gut and knocking the wind out of him. Dean recovered and pinned Graham's head to the side so he could not spit upward at them.

One witness, seeing Graham on the gurney, noticed bruises on his arm. Usually the prisoner could move his head freely, but Graham's was strapped down with Velcro. He was covered with a sheet; his paper clothing had ripped in the scuffle, nearly exposing his genitals. Looking through the glass at his chosen witnesses, who included Bianca Jagger (the ex-wife of Rolling Stones singer Mick Jagger), Jesse Jackson, and Al Sharpton, Graham said, "What is happening here is an outrage for any civilized country." He mentioned Malcolm X and Martin Luther King, Jr., and the history of slavery. "This death, this lynching will be avenged," he said. He spoke for more than six minutes before the warden let out a sigh and made his trademark gesture, lifting his glasses up from his nose. Within a minute, still in midspeech, Graham appeared to fall asleep.

Dean left quietly, trying to avoid the crowds, though he knew nobody would recognize him.

Some reporters tried to set up Graham's death as the first in a long line of horrid spectacles that would bedevil Bush up to election day. But others were skeptical about whether this all mattered that much to the voters; a *Houston Chronicle* columnist argued that the obsession with executions shown by some press outlets sounded "like anti-death-penalty wishful thinking." Polls showed Bush leading Gore by eight points around the time of Graham's death, and the issue failed to penetrate his lead.

After all the buildup, the Graham execution had little afterlife in the media landscape, which was soon overwhelmed by the legal fight over ballots in Florida, by Bush's eventual victory, and then a year later by the attacks of September 11, 2001, which shifted the focus of his presidency, and of the country, far from the criminal justice system. A couple of years later, *The Atlantic* obtained confidential memos sent to Bush during his governorship by his general counsel, Alberto Gonzales, which showed that the information he relied on in clemency decisions was scant and heavily tilted toward the prosecution. Although opponents of Gonzales's bid to become U.S. attorney general tried to use these memos against him, he was still confirmed easily.

With Bush in the White House, journalists now steeped in the workings of the Texas justice system continued to follow their curiosities, publishing the sorts of feature stories that would not have been possible during the heat of the campaign. A few months after the Graham execution, Kenneth Dean received a call from a spokesman for the prison agency, asking if he would make the tie-down team available for interviews with a reporter from National Public Radio. "No, we're not doing it," he said.

"You might want to think about it," the spokesman responded.

An hour and a half later, Dean's phone rang again. It was the prison system's executive director, Wayne Scott. "I think it would be a positive thing for our agency," he said. Dean got the meaning: He had no choice.

"Yes, sir," he said.

The night the radio story aired, Dean locked his doors, nervous that for the first time his name would be identified in public. But in the following days, supportive letters arrived from around the country, even from listeners who opposed the death penalty. When *The New York Times* called about a print story, Dean let reporter Sara Rimer follow him around and opened up about his personal struggles, telling her how his seven-year-old daughter would ask him about his work and he wouldn't know how to respond. "All of us wonder if it's right," he told Rimer. "I know how I feel, but is it the right way to feel? Is what we do right? But if we didn't do it, who would do it?"

Rimer portrayed Dean and his colleagues as decent people handling a task most would not want, with the unspoken suggestion that it would be unfair to blame these men personally for strapping prisoners down and killing them. Buster McWhorter's wife, Phyllis, wrote a letter to *Texas Monthly*, which the magazine published, that took issue with how some protesters portrayed her husband as bloodthirsty. "The people who participate in executions for the State of Texas are no different from anybody else you know," she wrote. "My husband is no villain. In fact, he's a hero, not because he carries out a job few want to do and a portion of our society wants him to feel ashamed of, but because he works hard serving the people of the state, then comes home, pays his bills, goes to church and parent-teacher meetings, and takes his kids to school, ball games, and out for snow cones. And then he has the courage to get up the next day and do it all over again." The men on the tie-down team, like the prosecutors and jurors and judges, and even like the governor himself, were just bit players, acting at the behest of the public. Blaming them was a way of outsourcing our own responsibility.

As the national media disappeared and the tensions cooled and Huntsville returned to its quiet execution routines, it became clear that something in the state's political atmosphere had cracked. "I think we had all realized that mistakes had been made," State Representative Pete Gallego recalled.

The change in mood began the day after Gary Graham's execution, in a case that had nothing to do with the death penalty. On June 23, 2000, *The Texas Observer* published "The Color of Justice," a story by Nate Blakeslee about a town called Tulia, up in the Panhandle. The year before, roughly forty black men had been arrested and convicted of drug crimes based on allegations from an undercover federal agent. Tulia was tiny, and these men represented more than 10 percent of the entire town's black population. Blakeslee reported on a number of troubling details, including the total lack of drugs, money, or guns seized when the men were arrested. The agent, Tom Coleman, had a checkered past. His ex-wife claimed he was a member of the Ku Klux Klan.

The Tulia story hit a new set of notes. Here was government overreach, a classic theme of conservative rhetoric; many of the people arrested were hardworking, law-abiding citizens without criminal records, far more sympathetic than Gary Graham. Even conservative lawmakers were willing to support restrictions on testimony from undercover agents, and a "Tulia bill" passed in the state legislature.

With reform in the air, progressive bills that had fallen flat in the past now gained traction. Democrat Rodney Ellis pushed through the Fair Defense Act, which vastly improved the quality of court-appointed trial defense lawyers for all criminal cases. The legislature explicitly banned prosecutors from putting on evidence that painted a defendant as more likely to be dangerous in the future because of his race or ethnicity. Ellis became friends with Robert Duncan, a Republican supporter of the death penalty who nevertheless felt strongly that the state should never execute an innocent person. He pushed a bill that would give death row prisoners the opportunity to seek DNA testing.

Not every proposal survived—the new governor, Rick Perry, vetoed a bill banning the execution of the intellectually disabled—but the stories of potentially innocent people being executed cast a new light on the old problems. No matter what you thought of Gary Graham, it was clear that the Tulia men were innocent, as was Roy Criner, the man freed from prison after a DNA test proved he had not committed rape. The Republican governor of Illinois had halted all executions because so many men on death row in the state had been proven innocent, and whatever George W. Bush had claimed in order to get to the White House, it was no longer realistic to believe that the system could get it right every time. In light of that understanding, many other problems in the criminal justice system began to take on a new hue. In the past, the public could see a defense lawyer's midtrial nap, or a confession obtained by police without proper procedures, as errors that might be regrettable but did not demand a major response. Now, it was clear that those problems might condemn an innocent man to death.

Some in law enforcement failed to acknowledge the shift in tone— and they paid for it. At one meeting, Williamson County prosecutor John Bradley argued before a room of Senate staffers that making DNA testing too easily available would lead to an onslaught of new court battles, that it would upend the "finality" of death sentences. A defense lawyer named Keith Hampton asked him whether finality should be more important than innocence. Bradley said it should. The room went silent. He was implying that it was okay to execute an innocent person. "It was a staggering statement to make," Mike Charlton, another lawyer in the room, recalled.

In the midst of these changes, the case of Calvin Burdine returned to public awareness. Sentenced to death for stabbing his lover in 1983, he was one of several death row prisoners from Houston whose lawyer had slept through parts of his trial. His case was moving through the federal courts and gathered some press attention during Bush's campaign. The case featured other damning details: A prosecutor had argued to the jury that they should send Burdine, who was gay, to his death because life in prison for a gay man would not be sufficient punishment, given that he'd be surrounded by men. Burdine's lawyer did not raise an objection—perhaps because he wasn't awake.

In August 2001, a federal appeals court finally overturned Burdine's death sentence. His lawyer, Robert McGlasson, received a sympathetic audience on CNN. The newspaper columnist Leonard Pitts sarcastically compared Burdine to O. J. Simpson, saying both had been represented by a "dream team." (Harris County prosecutors disputed that it was ever clearly established that the trial lawyer had been sleeping.) Burdine's case was mentioned by the legislators who pushed the Fair Defense Act, but once the act was passed and he was given a new sentencing hearing, he faced a terrible irony. The new law required that anyone who wanted to do capital cases be added to a local list of qualified lawyers. McGlasson had been representing Burdine for years—he began working the case shortly after he helped found the Texas Resource Center—but he had since moved to Atlanta. A judge now told him that he was not on the list of approved local lawyers and thus could not represent Burdine. Burdine wrote to the judge, begging her to appoint this man who had seen him through so much already. "After my first trial, it took me a very long time to be able to trust even Mr. McGlasson," he wrote. "I know that I will not be able [to] trust another lawyer very quickly."

In the meantime, McGlasson needed a lawyer with a Texas bar card whom he could rely on, and who in turn could gain the trust of his jittery client. He called an old colleague from his days at the resource center, Danalynn Recer.

Recer was already living in Houston, traveling regularly to Louisiana to work cases. In 2000, Johnny Holmes retired from his two-decade tenure as Harris County DA, and his longtime assistant Chuck Rosenthal was elected in his place. As Recer took on the Burdine case, she tried to convince Rosenthal that, should he seek Burdine's death again, he'd be signing up for a pitched and draining fight. When the judge tried to give Recer only a few months to prepare for a trial, then balked at her request for more time, Recer went to a federal court. She also rounded up fifty Houston lawyers to sign a letter demanding the judge acquiesce, which embarrassed her in the local news. Over the course of a year, she filed motion after motion. Eventually, Rosenthal agreed to let Burdine plead guilty and take a life sentence. "I owe you a great big hug," Burdine wrote to her in a letter.

Taking the Burdine case gave Recer enough momentum to start her own organization. She found a house in the shadow of Houston's downtown skyscrapers and moved in with her boyfriend and fellow lawyer, Morris Moon. They converted the attic apartment into an office. She called it the Gulf Region Advocacy Center, or GRACE, and she solicited supplies from her former colleagues. Jim Marcus, the head of the Texas Defender Service and a fellow veteran of the resource center, donated a futon, which interns slept on. The interns themselves came from England and Australia, furnished by a human rights organization called Reprieve, which had been founded by Recer's former Louisiana colleague Clive Stafford Smith.

When twenty-three-year-old Elizabeth Vartkessian told Stafford Smith that she wanted to fight the death penalty, he gave her a few names. Recer was the first to respond, asking how soon Vartkessian could be in Houston. She bought a car in Washington, D.C., and spent two days driving south. She arrived at the address Recer had given her. It was an "intern house." Vartkessian couldn't find a mattress. "Oh, we'll find you one," Recer told her. The next morning, Vartkessian arrived at the tiny attic office, maybe four hundred square feet, where at least seven people were working amid file cabinets and piles of documents and hamburger wrappers and Recer's endless supply of Diet Cokes.

In sporadic newsletters, Recer railed against the injustice of individual cases, thanked people for donations, and pleaded for more ("Even with the generosity of all these folks, we are still in need of a photocopier, two more licenses to use Microsoft Office XP, a laptop, and various other office supplies"). She was proud of her ragtag approach, calling it "bakesale justice." She made an Amazon.com wishlist, and asked death row prisoners to help design the logo. Her writing was full of her breathless optimism ("We have temporarily rented some extra rooms while we prepare for our big move into a place of our own!!!") but also barbed humor: She invented the "Fall from GRACE" award and gave it to the Harris County DA's office. Many newsletters featured obituaries for "our friends"—men who had been executed.

The meager digs and chaotic rhythm were not for everyone. Vartkessian found that many promising new faces didn't stick around, turned off by what sort of felt like hazing, as Recer would make the culture of the office revolve around her own taste for last-minute binges of work. Whereas some lawyers would get 99 percent of a five-hundred-page petition completed and then tinker until the clock ran out, Recer was the type to wait until two days before the deadline to do much of the writing, even if they'd been working for months. She was known to be demanding, and because she was often on a tight deadline, you had to be persistent to get her attention and then, once you had it, be very concise. She had trouble retaining other lawyers far along in their careers to work at a more senior level, and even lower-level employees left due to the poor compensation. Eventually, the organization would have trouble making payroll, begging supporters for $6,800 so staff could get their paychecks. The resource center had jumped from crisis to crisis due to circumstance, but it had molded her into the kind of person who did this by design.

11

IN THE TOWN SQUARES AT THE CENTER OF MANY TEXAS COUNTIES, the courthouses tend toward opulence: delicate cupolas, tall white pillars, regal arches and spires and clock towers, window shutters painted in rich blues and reds and greens. In the 1960s, the population of Matagorda County, a community of fewer than thirty thousand farmers and fishermen near the Gulf Coast, abandoned this tradition, knocking down their Second Empire–influenced behemoth because it was too expensive to maintain, and hiring architects to produce a sleek modernist box, with a parking lot underneath and vertical slats over the windows to limit the heat coming in.

The same impulse against pretense and ostentation was reflected in Steven Reis, the man elected in 1992—and then reelected every four years for the next three decades—to serve as the community's district attorney. With a sweep of white bangs and the occasional trim goatee, Reis exuded none of the good-ol'-boy swagger of his big city peers—no handlebar mustache, no big talk of locking up criminals, no cigars or syringe-shaped pens. Those men were politicians, overseeing hundreds of lawyers confronting waves of urban crime, whereas Reis handled many cases personally, making decisions that affected his literal neighbors. He could prosecute a man in the morning, agree to probation, and then run into him at a Little League game later the same day.

In another life, he might have been a writer. Having studied journalism in college, he practiced a yearly ritual of writing a short story on Christmas, to read aloud to his family and email to friends. ("I never know for sure what will appear on the pages as I let the story write itself," he explained in one year's message.) He drifted for a while in search of a career. After working as a deckhand on a tugboat and serving in the Air Force, he married his high school sweetheart and took over his father-in-law's loan business. He studied counseling on the side, and then business, and then he worked in real estate. He often talked about going to law school, and shortly after he turned thirty, his wife, fed up with his lack of direction, gave him an ultimatum: Go now, or wait until their youngest child turned eighteen. (This would have been a significant wait; Reis and his wife eventually had a total of seven children.) Reis's wife took over the breadwinning while he attended law school in Houston, eighty miles to the north, and commuted home on the weekends.

By age thirty-five, he had hung a shingle in town, and a couple of years later, he began prosecuting misdemeanors for the county attorney. Soon after, the county was hit by a major scandal when a probation officer was raped at a party attended by some local leaders, many of whom left office. Reis's friends began encouraging him to run for district attorney. He found he hated campaigning, and yet he was elected. He was four years out of law school and had never before won a trial by jury.

He found he hated the ferocity of real courtroom conflicts. At one point, a defense lawyer screamed in his face, nearly spilling coffee over both of them, and Reis felt bothered by the expectation that he respond with similar fury. "Maybe law is not where I need to be," he would think. "I'm losing cases. I'm being yelled at. I'm expected to be mean to people." But over time he came to realize this wasn't necessary; he was the one in charge, so he could set the tone. He started telling defense lawyers he would never want their relationships to sour to such a point that they couldn't enjoy a meal together.

That was easy enough when handling DUIs and small drug cases, but less so when a crime was violent, and it was virtually impossible when capital punishment was on the table. DAs in small counties knew that very rarely—maybe never, maybe only once in their career—would they have to decide whether to seek the death penalty in a case that qualified. Big-city DAs would rely on whole panels of prosecutors to help them make these decisions multiple times per year, but in a small town you mostly had to rely on your own judgment, and the rarity of the decisions only added to the pressure: People would talk about it for years to come.

In 1998, after Reis had been in office for five years, tragedy struck close. Two young men broke into the trailer home of twenty-eight-year-old Linda Malek. They raped her and then shot her in the head before making off with her purse and jewelry. Her children, ages six and eight, had witnessed all of this. One of the men, Michael Jimenez, admitted to a friend that they had wanted to kill the children as well, but the "gun messed up." Jimenez was sixteen, and in Texas someone had to be seventeen to face the death penalty. His co-defendant, Kenneth Parr, was eighteen, so he qualified.

Reis had personal ties to both sides of the case: The victim's mother had recently been hired by his office, and her father and boyfriend both worked for the local sheriff's department. Kenneth Parr's mother had long ago rented a house from Reis when he worked in real estate. He remembered her warmly, as someone he would allow to pay less than full rent when she couldn't afford it.

Although the victim's family wanted to see Parr executed for the murder, as did many of Reis's own employees, he tried to remain dispassionate. He thought a lot about the state's Code of Criminal Procedure, which stated that the job of a prosecutor is "not to convict, but to see that justice is done." The meaning of "justice," such a nebulous word, was not always obvious, and in death penalty cases there were myriad factors that Reis felt he should consider: Did Kenneth Parr seem fully culpable for his actions? How would the jury respond to sympathetic material about him brought forward by his lawyers? Was the victim's family, despite their support for the death penalty, prepared to weather years of appeals and uncertainty before an execution? Would the death sentence itself survive all those appeals?

To Reis, the facts of the robbery suggested that Parr knew what he was doing. If not for a stroke of luck—a gun's malfunction—he might have slaughtered two young children. He decided to seek death, and given the small size of his office, that meant he'd be the one making the argument before the jury.

At Parr's trial, Reis proved that when the moment called for it, he could be as ruthless in the courtroom as the best urban prosecutors. The defense tried to make Parr more sympathetic by portraying his mother as a weak parent who had failed to teach him right from wrong. But when it was Reis's turn to cross-examine the mother—his own former tenant—he pushed back against this narrative. "You tried to teach your children to learn some responsibility?" he asked.

"I've talked to them about being responsible," she responded. "I've talked to them about . . . making something out of theirselves."

He was using her pride in her parenting to bolster her son's blameworthiness, and to show the jury why he deserved death. After her testimony, he went to her and apologized, and they both cried. The jury sentenced Parr to death.

Nine years after his trial, when Parr ran out of appeals, Reis decided he would travel to Huntsville and witness the execution himself. This is unusual for prosecutors, though not unheard of. Reis wanted to prove to himself that he was capable of doing his job, even if it meant sending someone to his death. Whereas most people in the death penalty system, from prosecutors to jurors to politicians to executioners, could see their own role as limited and shift responsibility to someone else, Reis found he could not. "Let's not mince words . . . we're killing a human being," he said years later. "Would you look him in the eye? Would you blow his brains out and watch him die? That has to be the visceral picture of what you're doing. Can you cold-bloodedly kill this human being? If you cannot, why would you ask twelve people to make an executioner do that?"

As Parr lay on the gurney and the drugs began to flow, Reis watched him. He tried to see some sign of spiritual deliverance in this man, who was still only twenty-eight years old. He thought to himself that he was responsible for sending Parr to the execution chamber, but that everything after that moment was up to God. When he realized that Parr had died, he began to feel uncomfortable, because he had seen no sign that Parr had "made peace" with some higher being before his death. Later, sitting with his minister and describing the scene, Reis broke down in tears.

Still, he also came out of the experience feeling a kind of resolve. He could handle seeking the death penalty again if another case came along, though he felt that he should do so only in extreme circumstances. Other prosecutors, like Johnny Holmes in Houston, might seek it more often, and that was acceptable: Each had been elected by his fellow county residents to decide what it meant for justice to be "done." Each was following laws written by legislators, who were themselves elected. This, Reis felt, was democracy in action.

In 2005, a couple of years before Parr's execution, Reis was called out to a weed-clogged alley half a mile from his office, where police had found the body of four-year-old Sanjunita Stephanie Gaona. Reis saw her small body lying still, with stab wounds in the neck and chest.

Her uncle Francisco Castellano had been left to take care of her. When his sister, Gaona's mother, returned home, he said the girl had disappeared. A search party formed, and Castellano joined it. After her body was found, he confessed, telling police he'd tried to rape his niece. "I continued hitting her on the floor with her head," he said, through a translator. "I don't know what came over me to grab a knife." There was no doubt this would all horrify jurors. The girl's mother wanted the death penalty, as did Reis's own investigator and assistant DA.

As the case proceeded toward trial, Reis had court dates to check in with the judge and the defense team. Initially, a judge had appointed a lawyer named James Sidney Crowley to defend Castellano, but another lawyer, Danalynn Recer from Houston, kept showing up at the hearings. She said Castellano was a Mexican citizen, and she was there to represent the Mexican government's interest in the case. She persuaded the judge to kick Crowley off the case, and then she enlisted another Houston lawyer named James Stafford to represent Castellano. Reis knew Stafford's reputation and felt they would have an easy rapport, which he appreciated, because Recer's combative style tended, in his words, to "chill negotiation." Years later, he would describe Recer as "determined." He was much too decorous to use any other word.

By the mid-2000s, GRACE had emerged under Recer's leadership as a scrappy but potent force in the defense community, working alongside the Texas Defender Service and the NAACP Legal Defense Fund. The benefit of having so little money and an inexperienced staff was that you could turn on a dime, taking on unique tasks that fell outside the mandates of bigger organizations.

After saving Calvin Burdine from death row, Recer continued to take on "resentencing" cases. It was delicate work: Many of the men would be scarred and paranoid after living for decades under a death sentence, and she knew how to help them open up and revisit their often traumatic early lives to show judges, prosecutors, and juries that they were deserving of sympathy. She would do the deep investigations into mitigating evidence that the original lawyers had not done, in order to prove to prosecutors they would surely fail to get a new death sentence at a trial and had better make a deal so as not to waste the massive resources involved.

There were more and more of these cases, in part because her former colleagues were managing to persuade the Supreme Court to overturn Texas death sentences. Although President Bill Clinton had signed a law that made it more difficult for death row prisoners to appeal, he had also appointed two justices to the Supreme Court, Stephen Breyer and Ruth Bader Ginsburg, who appeared open to defense arguments. Justice John Paul Stevens was not ready to admit that he regretted voting to uphold the Texas death penalty law back in 1976—he wouldn't do that until 2011—but he was often ruling in favor of death row prisoners, as were his fellow Republican presidential appointees David Souter and Sandra Day O'Connor.

In 1976, a majority of the justices had ruled that death penalty juries should be able to consider the "diverse frailties of humankind."

Over the years, they had expanded the meaning of this phrase, allowing defense lawyers to bring in anything that might cut against a death sentence, no matter how seemingly unrelated. They also ruled in favor of death row prisoners who said their trial lawyers failed to present such evidence. These cases suggested that the work done by Recer and her peers had become not only accepted, but expected of all competent lawyers. Still, defense lawyers complained that Texas lagged far behind other states; mitigating evidence had not been mentioned in state law until 1991, and even then, the state and federal courts overseeing the state tended to approve death sentences stemming from trials in which such evidence had been restricted. In the 2000s, the Supreme Court finally took note— scholars noticed that Justice Anthony Kennedy, a swing voter on many issues, appeared to have a "change of heart"— and freed a handful of prisoners from Texas death row. (The Court also made it easier to challenge ineffective trial defense lawyering, although they declined to protect death row prisoners whose lawyers had made errors at later stages of appeal.) Some of these new cases had been argued by Jordan Steiker, one of Recer's professors in law school, and Rob Owen, with whom she had worked on the Carl Kelly case.

Although their run of victories was well received by the old resource center gang, they were also tinged by the cruelty of time. In 2002, the Supreme Court abolished the death penalty for people diagnosed with "mental retardation," in the parlance of the time, because they were less "culpable" for their crimes. Carl Kelly was executed in 1993, and had his appeals stretched on for another decade, he might have been saved. Rob Owen still kept a picture of Kelly in elementary school in his office, to remind himself, as he told a reporter, "that the person they killed had the mind of a child."

Recer also filled much of her fledgling GRACE budget with a new and surprising player on the scene: the Mexican government.

The Mexican public had long been outraged by American executions of their fellow citizens. This stemmed in part from a Catholic opposition to the taking of life, and in part from a sense that the United

States was using the punishment to be an imperialist "bully." As far back as the 1920s, the American journalist Alma Reed had campaigned to save the life of a Mexican teenager on death row in California, and her efforts earned her an audience with Mexican president Álvaro Obregón. In 1997, the body of executed prisoner Irineo Tristan Montoya was greeted by crowds and a mariachi band at the border. After the execution of another Mexican national in 2002, the country's president, Vicente Fox, refused an invitation to President Bush's ranch in Texas.

Mexican officials also fought in court. At the International Court of Justice, they claimed that U.S. officials violated previous treaties by failing to tell Mexico when its citizens had been arrested on capital charges. The court ruled in their favor in 2004, but it had little power in the United States, where the Supreme Court ruled it was not binding on state courts. (The U.S. government position was argued by then solicitor general Ted Cruz.) Still, there were other ways for the Mexican government to fight back. Beginning in 2000, the country's foreign ministry started the Mexican Capital Legal Assistance Program, which paid lawyers to track capital cases around the United States and step in as the country's representative. Eventually, the program claimed a 95 percent success rate in keeping Mexican nationals from execution.

Recer received one of these Mexican government contracts. She saw an opportunity in this money: It could help her prove that what she'd seen in Louisiana would work in Texas—good lawyering could stop a death sentence even in a case with a very heinous murder. A case like that of Francisco Castellano.

Once she heard about Castellano, Recer repeatedly called the defense lawyer appointed to represent him, James Sidney Crowley, but could not reach him. When she finally showed up at a pretrial court date, she found Crowley there. He looked disheveled. She asked him to file some motions and he demurred. Back in Houston, she directed her interns to scour the court calendars in other counties in the area, and they proved her suspicion: Crowley had agreed to defend so many different people in so many courtrooms that there was no way he could meet his obligations. She filed a motion in the court demanding that

Castellano get adequate representation—implying Crowley should be fired.

The judge ruled in her favor, and then asked if she'd take the case instead. She teamed up with James Stafford, who brought something to the effort that she could not: He had a good rapport with Matagorda County DA Steven Reis, the man deciding whether Castellano would face the death penalty. Recer had already presented herself as combative, and Stafford realized that Reis didn't really enjoy talking to her. So she would pressure Reis through aggressive litigation, pushing him to the negotiating table, while Stafford would wait at that table with a friendly face. It was a classic approach: good cop, bad cop.

Steve Reis knew it would not be difficult to prove to a jury that Francisco Castellano had killed his niece, but a trial would still be grueling. There was some indication that Castellano might be intellectually disabled, and in 2002 the Supreme Court had ruled it illegal to execute these defendants. This meant Reis's office had to pay experts to determine Castellano's IQ, to see if he was covered by the ban. The two he hired ended up disagreeing, one saying Castellano was mentally fit to face the death penalty, the other saying he was right on the line of intellectual disability. Even if Reis decided he agreed with the former, who could predict where the jury would land? And even if the jury agreed with the prosecution and sentenced Castellano to death, what about all those judges who might question his mental fitness later? If one of those judges reversed the death sentence, would the victim's family be further traumatized?

The defense team was looking into Castellano's past in Mexico. Reis wanted to do the same—he might learn about previous crimes that would mark Castellano as a "continuing threat to society"—so he planned a trip. But once he arrived in Brownsville, a small city near where the border hits the Gulf of Mexico, he spoke with Castellano's lawyer James Stafford, who told him he shouldn't cross the border.

"Steve, [the witnesses] won't cooperate with you," Reis recalled Stafford saying. And a prosecutor seeking a death sentence against a

Mexican in the United States could easily find himself in danger. "You won't be safe."

Reis appreciated his concern. But when a member of the prosecution team tried to call a source in Mexico, the defense fired back, filing a motion arguing that Reis had violated Mexico's sovereignty. Recer was playing bad cop.

Reis sometimes thought about the cost of a trial, though he was not the sort to sully talk of justice with talk of money. And yet there was no way around it: A death penalty trial could cost as much as $2 million, and while big urban budgets could easily absorb the price tag, a small community could find its tax base devastated. Local officials compared them to floods and tornadoes. In counties with only one or two prosecutors, a capital trial could take weeks, effectively shutting the courthouse down and creating a backlog of smaller cases. A well-publicized example was the white supremacist truck-dragging murder of James Byrd, Jr., in Jasper, Texas, which had drawn attention from all over the world but ultimately became the financial responsibility of fewer than forty thousand taxpayers. When the costs of the death penalty trials for the three defendants climbed beyond $800,000, the county increased its tax rate nearly 12 percent.

In other parts of the country, a statewide fund might exist to pay for prosecution and defense in these cases, but Texas had no such fund. Small-town officials asked the Texas Legislature in 1999 to subsidize death penalty trials, and the legislature obliged, but the money wasn't enough to pay for everything. When the Supreme Court rejected death sentences for the intellectually disabled, defense lawyers had a stronger argument for why courts should pay for psychologists and neurologists. When the Court announced that juries should be able to hear mitigating evidence, defense lawyers could push for more money for investigation. It was a one-way ratchet; prosecutors didn't want to be caught with a lesser-credentialed expert, or with biological evidence that hadn't been tested for DNA—the growing number of exonerations made the cost of not testing all the more clear—so they paid up. In some states, including Texas, the cost began to chip away at conservative support for the death penalty. It was increasingly possible to see the death penalty as a government program that needlessly drained taxpayer dollars without touching the moral quagmire of whether someone "deserved" to die. From 2007 to 2016, seven states abolished the death penalty, and in all of them, the costs figured prominently in the conversion narratives of both liberal and conservative lawmakers.

As costs grew, death sentences declined. In the early 1990s, prosecutors in Texas counties with a population under three hundred thousand sought the death penalty an average of fifteen times per year across the state. A decade later, that number had dropped to four. Some of those prosecutors were a lot more blunt than Reis: "I know now that if I file a capital murder case and don't seek the death penalty, the expense is much less," said one in the Texas Panhandle in 2014, "While I know that justice is not for sale, if I bankrupt the county, and we simply don't have any money, and the next day someone goes into a daycare and guns down five kids, what do I say? Sorry?"

In 2005, a month after Francisco Castellano murdered his niece, small-town prosecutors went to the legislature and pushed for a new alternative to the death penalty: life without parole, or LWOP. At the time, anyone who was not sentenced to death would eventually be eligible to apply for release with the state's parole board. The board could always deny them, but that was not enough of a guarantee for some prosecutors and families of victims, who were afraid they'd have to spend the rest of their lives writing letter after letter asking the board to keep the person locked up.

Opponents of the death penalty had spent years trying to get an LWOP bill passed, but they failed in part because pro-death-penalty victims' groups and prosecutors from Dallas and Houston opposed it, fearing it would be a backdoor way to end capital punishment. But now, rural prosecutors were talking more about cost. "It simply will shut a small district attorney's office down to seek death," one told the legislators. This argument proved compelling, and Texas became one of the last states to adopt such sentences. Now a life sentence could mean, as one prosecutor put it, that defendants "are never, never, never going to come out except in a box."

Prosecutors and jurors were already seeking and giving the death penalty less often, but the availability of LWOP pushed the trend along. For defense lawyers, LWOP became a bargaining chip, a harsh alternative to death that could be presented as a win for both sides: Their client would avoid death, while the prosecutor would avoid a hugely expensive trial. The Texas Defender Service for years had its own trial consultant, a former Kentucky public defender named John Niland, who traveled around the state and helped defense lawyers negotiate for life sentences. Facing one direction, the lawyer would convince the client, who might be holding out hope of acquittal, that a guilty verdict was all but certain and a life sentence plea was a better option. Facing the other direction, the lawyer would show the DA that his case for death was weak and that he would be wasting scarce local tax resources on a trial he might lose.

Occasionally a case would come along and make the stakes painfully apparent. Prosecutors in the Panhandle spent around a million dollars trying to send Levi King to death row for killing three members of a family. It was a highly aggravated case—one victim was pregnant—but a single juror refused to vote for the death penalty, so King was sentenced to life without parole. But King was *already* serving life without parole for unrelated murders in Missouri. The county had needed to raise taxes and suspend raises for county employees in the years around the trial, and it technically made no difference to King's fate. Prosecutors often blamed defense attorneys for racking up the cost of trials—by spending too many hours investigating and hiring expensive experts—and some defenders would candidly admit this was intentional, a way of forcing the other side to negotiate. "Spend money," veteran trial lawyer Katherine Scardino would tell her peers at trainings. "That will get everybody's attention."

Even with the LWOP option, some prosecutors still sought death, and it was still tremendously expensive for their counties. In 2008, lawyers and judges in the Panhandle city of Lubbock hatched a plan to lessen the burden. They created a pool to fund a regional public defender office; counties would pay a small yearly fee based on their population and history of seeking death, and when a case arose, this office would handle the defense. The plan was nicknamed "murder insurance," which sounded more exciting than the eventual name, the West Texas Regional Public Defender for Capital Cases. Slowly, it grew into a network of offices encompassing more and more counties, eventually reaching roughly two-thirds of the state, including many counties that had never had a death penalty case, but paid as little as $1,000 per year just in case one came along. Speculating on why this idea began in a staunchly conservative rural area of the state, the office's director, Ray Keith, told a reporter that "a lot of farmers and ranchers are very aware of risk and reward."

The office brought an approach that was already used in other states and had much in common with Danalynn Recer's methods at GRACE, including working in teams and looking for mitigation evidence as early as possible, using the cheaper labor of non-lawyers—including law school students—to find it, and then negotiating a deal in which the defendant would plead guilty and receive a sentence less than death. By the summer of 2013, a study found that only 7 percent of cases handled by the public defenders were taken to trial, compared with more than 40 percent of capital cases handled by private, appointed attorneys.

Even lawyers who did not work for the office were gaining new tools for convincing prosecutors and jurors to forgo death, through the consulting and training sponsored by GRACE and TDS. At the University of Texas at Austin, a social work professor developed a program to help defense teams reach out to the family members of victims. The victims' rights groups who vocally supported the death penalty had been clustered in big cities like Houston, so they didn't hold as much sway in small towns, and sometimes it turned out that the victim's family was open to outcomes other than the death penalty. This could prove useful in negotiating with the DA. In 2005, defense lawyer Bobby Mims, with the help of a consultant from the Texas Defender Service, represented Johnny Lee Williams, who had killed nineteen-year-old Megan Holden after abducting her from the parking lot of the Wal-Mart where she worked. The family planned to sue Wal-Mart and the parking lot's security company. The defense team worked out a deal in which Williams would meet with Holden's family and answer their questions about her final hours, which would help them prove that the companies had been negligent. In return, the family asked prosecutors not to seek a death sentence. There were others ways, it turned out, of seeking closure.

Because Francisco Castellano had murdered his niece, the family of the defendant and the family of the victim were one and the same. Although the victim's mother had initially indicated her support for a death sentence, eventually the family approached Steve Reis and told him they didn't want Castellano to be executed. It was one more reason not to take the case to trial: Would he appear to be ignoring a grieving family's wishes? The defense team offered that Castellano would plead guilty in exchange for a life sentence, meaning there would be no trial or appeals. This would all be over. Reis took the deal, and Castellano went to prison.

Reis could not isolate a single reason for why he chose to spare Castellano. Talking about it later, he framed his decision as rational, as an estimation of how the competing narratives of prosecution and defense would play in front of a jury, without admitting whether the other side's narrative was compelling to him personally. But sometimes he did gesture toward empathy, saying of Castellano, "There was something broken, much earlier on than 'right now,' which had been broken in him years ago."

As rural counties increasingly opted for life without parole, the death penalty grew more concentrated in urban counties; by 2013, just fifteen counties were responsible for roughly a third of all executions in the United States. Harris County still topped the national list, with more than twice as many executions as number two, which was Dallas. In the big counties, DAs had deep enough pockets to seek death without thinking nearly as hard about the financial consequences. Recer was already beginning work on a case in Houston in which an undocumented immigrant had murdered a police officer. The DA was not willing to negotiate, so there would be a full trial.

12

RESPONDING TO THE LETTERS THEY RECEIVED IN THE MAIL, THE prospective jurors made their way to the twelfth floor of the Harris County courthouse in downtown Houston. They filled out questionnaires, and some were interviewed by the prosecution and the defense. Dan—not his real name, because he did not want it associated with the case, although it is in the public record—was a young professional, in his late twenties, a white man with boyish good looks and conservative politics.

Others who went on the stand that day in 2008 remembered the news story about the Mexican immigrant who had shot a police officer a couple of years earlier, but Dan did not.

"Do you think we ought to have the death penalty?" prosecutor Lyn McClellan asked him.

"Yes," Dan said. "If someone's indeed guilty of something and [the] punishment fits the crime." McClellan asked what sorts of crimes the death penalty would "fit." Dan wasn't sure, and answered vaguely: "I don't know really. Particularly your bloody crimes, or something like that . . ."

Although the transcript of their conversation is marked by Q's and A's, McClellan's questions were effectively short lectures. The prosecutor had been a longtime deputy of Johnny Holmes's and had helped Elsa Alcala send Edward Capetillo, among many others, to death row. He explained to Dan the intricacies of Texas law, occasionally pausing for a one-word answer.

He described how two jurors could look at the same evidence and come to different conclusions: "Juror one says . . . 'The defendant was high on drugs during the course of the crime. I think that mitigates towards a life sentence. When you're high on drugs you do things you would not ordinarily do.' Juror number two [says,] 'Time out. I've known people all my life who got high on drugs. They didn't go out and commit capital murder.' " It was obvious which juror McClellan would prefer. Dan needed to know it was okay to remain unconvinced by the defense's mitigation.

The prosecutor was followed by Danalynn Recer. "We represent Juan Eduardo Quintero Perez," she said. "How you doing up there?"

"As good as can be expected, I guess," Dan said.

"Little uncomfortable there in the hot seat?"

"A little bit."

She drew him out, asking about his parents. "I grew up in a conservative family," Dan told her. "My dad is one of those guys who would say, 'If he's convicted of capital murder, he should get death.' I guess I'm just not that black and white." Dan had been sued once—a woman ran a red light, hit his car, and then claimed he'd been the one to run the light—so he understood that you could be accused of something you didn't do. He thought he could be open-minded.

But if the defendant was guilty, Recer wanted to know, and if the death penalty was an option, how would he make up his mind? "It's a real hard thing to verbalize," Dan said. He'd consider the defendant's upbringing, whether the punishment would offer "closure" to the victim's family.

Recer started pushing. If Dan thought Quintero would pose a "continuing threat to society," and answered the "future dangerousness" question with a yes, would he really listen to the mitigating circumstances? Would stories about Quintero's life matter to him beyond just curiosity? He responded "yes" over and over as she kept asking nearly the same question in slightly different phrasings. Eventually the prosecutors objected and the judge forced her to move on.

In 1968, the Supreme Court had ruled that citizens could serve on a death penalty jury even if they had some misgivings about the punishment, but throughout the 1980s the Court made it clear that jurors had to say they felt capable of voting for death; anyone wholly opposed to capital punishment would be dismissed. Defense lawyers complained that people who were willing to hand down a death sentence were also more likely to find someone guilty. But slowly, they grew more adept at using the rules to their advantage.

One new resource was a massive bank of interviews showing how jurors made decisions. Academic researchers obtained a National Science Foundation grant to interview former jurors in death penalty cases, and they spoke to more than a thousand as part of the Capital Jury Project. Whereas before lawyers, on both sides, were limited to anecdotes about how jurors behaved behind closed doors, along with fictional portrayals like *Twelve Angry Men,* now they had data. It turned out, for example, that when jurors took an initial vote on whether to sentence someone to death, they were unanimous only 8 percent of the time, and people often switched their votes from life to death. A common reason jurors did so, these researchers learned, was the fear that the defendant would be dangerous in the future. The Texas law was priming jurors to see defendants as more deserving of the death penalty.

Defense lawyers needed to embolden jurors who had initially voted for life to hold to that vote. A death decision had to be unanimous, and one juror could single-handedly force a life sentence if he or she refused to be persuaded. In Colorado, a group of public defenders developed what became known as the Colorado Method, which involved ranking potential jurors on a scale of one to seven. David Lane, who was helping Recer defend Quintero, summed it up: "Ones are Gandhi, sevens are Hitler." "Ones" could never vote for the death penalty, so prosecutors were allowed to bar them from serving at all. Defense lawyers could counter by leading potential jurors through questions to get them to admit that despite their initial talk of fairness, they would not really consider the mitigation evidence—revealing them as "sevens" who could be dismissed.

Once the jury had been seated, defense lawyers would work to "isolate" and "insulate" each member, to encourage them to feel secure about their own opinions and not to pressure others to change theirs. These lawyers felt the Texas jury questions, particularly the one about future dangerousness, protected the jurors from feeling the full moral intensity of giving someone the death penalty. They wanted to rip out the cushion.

"Have you ever made such an important decision before, whether someone lives or dies?" Recer asked Dan.

"No, I never had to deal with that."

"Most people haven't. In making that decision, based on your morals, whatever they are, whether it's religion or ethics, whatever guides you in making the most important decisions in your life, would you be surprised if everybody in the jury room wasn't guided by exactly the same sort of . . . moral compass?"

"No, that wouldn't surprise me."

But once he had made up his mind, Recer wondered, would he tell someone else on the jury their decision was wrong?

"I mean, I could tell someone that I disagree with their opinion. I can't tell them that it's wrong. Everybody has their own reasons for thinking anything, you know."

Recer hammered this point. "Not only do you have your own reasons," she said, "you have a right to your own individual moral responsibility, don't you? Just like you wouldn't go to someone who made a moral decision, where to send their kids to school or who to marry, where to live, you wouldn't say, 'You're wrong, you should go to a different church. You should marry somebody different.' "

Dan seemed to get it. "I grew up in a conservative house where my dad was very much that way—he's right and if somebody thinks something else, then they're wrong. I don't believe that way."

"If that was happening, you would stick up for somebody even if you disagreed with them?"

"Yes."

Both sides agreed he could serve, though Lane rated him a five.

Juan Leonardo Quintero Perez had come to the United States from Mexico at age twenty. He had been arrested multiple times, for driving under the influence of alcohol and driving with a suspended license. In 1998 he was arrested for touching the breast of a twelve-year-old girl at a party and was deported to Mexico. He crossed the border again, married an American woman, and became the stepfather to her two daughters.

One night in September 2006, Houston police officer Rodney Johnson pulled him over for speeding and found he was driving without a license. Johnson called a tow truck and put Quintero in handcuffs, escorting him to the backseat of the police car. But while patting him down, he missed a 9 mm semiautomatic pistol that Quintero kept in his waistband. Wrestling his handcuffed hands under his pants, Quintero managed to pull it out, and he fired through the driver's seat. He hit Johnson seven times. When more officers arrived, they found the front door of the cruiser open, with Johnson slumped down, one foot on the ground.

The murder of Rodney Johnson sparked political outrage over Houston's immigration policies. The incident was mentioned in Congress, and Johnson's widow sued the city for not letting its officers check immigration status during arrests. A man who had employed Quintero was sent to prison for three months for "harboring an illegal immigrant," and Quintero's American wife was threatened with prosecution. His stepdaughters were interrogated at school. District Attorney Chuck Rosenthal announced he would prosecute Quintero's death penalty case himself.

After being retained by the Mexican government to represent Quintero, Recer began pushing Rosenthal to let him plead guilty in exchange for a life sentence, just as Steve Reis had allowed Francisco Castellano to do. When they met, she tried to present information about Quintero's past, but the DA was dismissive, shutting her down before she could begin. She was shocked. What prosecutor wouldn't want to hear the other side's evidence?

Then, a few months before the trial, Rosenthal was undone by scandal. He was involved in a federal lawsuit that led to many of his emails being made public, including romantic exchanges with his secretary. One email paired an image of a black man lying among watermelon scraps and fried chicken containers with the words "Fatal Overdose." Rosenthal blamed prescription drugs for impairing his judgment, and then stepped down from office. The trial would be handled by three of his top deputies.

As the trial began, the courtroom filled with spectators and television cameras. Recer's co-counsel, David Lane, looked back from his seat and noticed that the gallery was filled with police officers in uniform. He thought this would make the jury feel pressure to convict his client, so he objected and asked for a mistrial. When the judge denied him, he decided it would be a good issue on appeal. As he recalled, he stood on a chair, lifted up a camera, and told the officers to smile.

Later that day, the prosecutors told him that the police had agreed to wear civilian clothes in the future. But the victim's widow, Joslyn Johnson, was also a police officer, and she kept wearing her uniform to court, with her gun in a holster. Lane thought about how she'd be sitting for days near the man who killed her husband, listening to details about how he'd done it. He asked that she not be allowed to carry the gun. The judge, as he recalled, laughed: "Mr. Lane, this is Texas," she said. She merely asked the widow to keep her gun out of sight. A sheriff's deputy told Lane not to worry: If one of the many police officers in the courtroom tried to shoot Quintero, he would control the situation.

Lane was unnerved. "Am I the only person in this entire courtroom who doesn't have a fucking gun?" he asked.

"No," the deputy said. "Your client probably doesn't have one either."

There was no plausible way to argue that Quintero did not kill John-son, but that didn't mean the first part of the trial would be a formality, and to Dan it was clear that both sides were laying the groundwork for the punishment phase. This was the prosecution's chance to depict the full horror of Quintero's crime. In front of the judge's bench, they set up a life-sized replica of the inside of the police car, with bucket seats mounted on a wooden platform. The jurors passed around the gun Quintero had used. Prosecutor John Jordan dramatically pulled back the slide on the unloaded 9 mm three times, letting the sound echo through the courtroom.

Dan found this all draining. In the mornings he'd put in a few hours at work before driving to the courthouse, and he wasn't allowed to dis-cuss what he was hearing at trial. He couldn't even debrief with his girlfriend. The jurors, even as they ate meals together and made small talk, had to wait until the end of the trial to discuss the evidence.

Privately, they were diverging in their view of Quintero, though they were mostly arriving at a unified view of Recer: They found her irritating. One juror described her performance with the word "circus." Dan didn't dislike her, but he thought she seemed overmatched. She would stumble and seem flustered, unable to lead witnesses to the points she wanted them to make. She would forget to stand when addressing the judge.

Recer knew she wasn't a slick courtroom performer, but she was using this fact to her advantage. The idea was to create an atmosphere of forgiveness in the courtroom; if the jury saw her as human and flawed, they might be more likely to see her client that way. Many years later, when she learned of the jurors' negative feelings toward her, she smiled.

She let no detail go, questioning the testimony of officers who re-membered damning things about Quintero's behavior and bringing in psychologists to talk about how trauma warps memories. But the key to the defense was a legal strategy that would let her begin her plea for a life sentence as early as possible. Recer had Quintero plead not guilty by reason of insanity.

This was a long shot. Although the insanity defense has a long history in the American legal system, juries and lawmakers tend to be skeptical of it. The year Quintero went on trial, the Texas Court of Criminal Appeals published an opinion saying that under state law, "insanity" applied only in cases where the defendant did not know his acts were against the law. This was a very high bar: Someone could be diagnosed with schizophrenia, could believe aliens were instructing him to commit murder, and could believe his victim would come back from the dead, all the while technically knowing that murder was illegal.

But for Recer, the insanity defense was a strategy. It allowed her to introduce the jury to the idea that Quintero did not really understand what he was doing when he shot Johnson, and that the crime was the product of a "damaged and unmedicated brain," as she put it during her opening statement. She had learned through her investigation that at a young age, Quintero had fallen from a second-story roof onto a cement floor. For years afterward, he would stare into space for minutes on end, leading his friends to nickname him Nopal, or cactus. The damage to his frontal lobes diminished his ability to process panic and fear. For much of his life, he was terribly anxious, and he self-medicated with massive quantities of beer. In Recer's view, Quintero believed the officer arresting him was going to kill him, since in Mexico the police were known to be corrupt and dangerous. "He thought it was over," said psychologist Antonio Puente from the stand. "The end had come and everything he worked for was about to go down the drain." Fight or flight kicked in, and flight wasn't an option.

After the testimony, the jurors were shown down a hallway to a deliberation room, where they quickly agreed they didn't buy the insanity defense—Quintero was guilty. But Dan was not at ease. As they'd been walking to the room, he overheard a female juror say, "It's not like we're going to give this guy the death penalty."

He was shocked, and angry. He thought she was presumptuous, making assumptions about how the group would decide without even sitting through the punishment phase of the trial.

And yet Dan had also made up his own mind. He kept this to himself. He didn't think any of that stuff about a head injury made up for the fact that Quintero had killed a police officer. He planned to vote for death.

In the year leading up to the trial, Recer had assigned a young Spanish-speaking investigator named Matt Silverman to uncover Quintero's past. He visited Quintero at least once a week in jail, interviewed potential witnesses in Houston, and supervised multiple researchers in Mexico as they looked for anyone who had known him. At one point, they had more than eight hundred names, which they whittled down over months.

When it came time for the trial, Silverman enlisted a driver to pick up witnesses in Quintero's hometown of Celaya and bring them more than five hundred miles north to the border at Laredo. Silverman met them on the American side. The defense team jokingly called him the "coyote," the term for an illegal smuggler. He made this trip once for the guilt phase witnesses, and then, for the punishment phase, he did it again. Many witnesses had never left Mexico before, and they were amazed to see so many homes built of wood instead of cinder block. Once in Houston, they slept, cooked, and prepared for trial at a home for Dominican nuns.

The jurors saw none of this. In the courtroom, it just looked like a clean succession of friendly faces with stories about "Leo," about his childhood love of dance and soccer, about his devotion to Catholicism, about how he took the blame for his siblings' misdeeds and slowly became the black sheep in the eyes of their abusive father, who beat the children if they came home with poor grades and gave his son a terrible anxiety around math. "There came a time, from what he related to me, that he felt that the numbers were coming after him, were pursuing him," a cousin said. The narrative stretched back beyond his birth; Quintero's aunt said his maternal grandfather was also abusive, and his grandmother had taught his mother to be patient and tolerant. This helped explain why she hadn't intervened when Quintero's father hit him with brooms and belts. The abuse, some believed, had driven Leo to leave home and make his life in the United States.

The prosecution picked away at these stories, trying to show that his siblings had suffered the same misfortunes and none of them had gone on to kill a cop. They noted that after Quintero arrived in the United States, he "drove drunk all the time" and once left the scene of a car accident without giving his information. They brought up the "indecency with a minor" charge involving his daughter's friend. He had pleaded guilty and received "deferred adjudication," a form of probation that allows someone to avoid a conviction if they follow certain rules, but this was moot because he was deported. Then he chose to cross back into the country illegally.

In the battle over future dangerousness, each side confronts a logical conundrum. The prosecution needs to portray a defendant who has used his free will to get to a place where he committed a terrible crime but who is now beyond change for the better and will continue to hurt people. The defense, on the other hand, needs to portray a defendant who has been molded by the circumstances of his life to do something terrible but now has the ability to use his free will in order to choose not to do so again. Both sides need to downplay and amplify free will, only at different moments in their narratives.

Elizabeth Vartkessian, who had once worked as a mitigation specialist under Recer, went on to conduct interviews for the Capital Jury Project and analyze them for a 2011 dissertation. She found that the emphasis on future dangerousness in Texas gave an advantage to prosecutors because they could "convert" mitigation evidence, making it bolster their side. Whereas in other states, jurors heard good and bad things about the defendant and weighed them against each other, the future-dangerousness question helped prosecutors spin good *into* bad. Say the defendant was young; this might suggest he was impulsive but capable of rehabilitation. Or it could mean he had a long criminal future ahead of him. Say he had no criminal history, or came from a good family; that just meant he should have known right from wrong. If he had done drugs, he was irresponsible. If he had not done drugs, he was even more in control of his behavior. Future dangerousness was particularly unforgiving toward mental illness: In other states, a diagnosis might suggest he wasn't in control of his actions and deserved mercy. In Texas, it meant he wouldn't be able to stop himself from committing another crime. Instead of emotionally connecting with the defendant's struggles, the jurors were encouraged to think in rational terms: Would he kill again? Anything about the defendant could be marshaled toward a "yes." A couple of years after Vartkessian published her dissertation, the American Bar Association released a report saying that the future-dangerousness question had led to a situation in which "a death sentence would be deemed warranted in virtually every capital murder case."

When prosecutors didn't convert the mitigation evidence, they dismissed it as a paltry attempt to excuse the crime. A 2004 training book for Texas prosecutors warned that the defense would enlist "mitigation gypsies" to take jurors to "Truth Purgatory," presenting "testimony about the defendant being abused as a child, bullied in school, hit in the head in a Little League ball game, raised in a rich home or a poor home, that he is too young or too old, is left-handed or right-handed, has one parent or two parents and so on." At Quintero's trial, prosecutor John Jordan told the jury that Quintero "was smart, paid attention, was exceptional, brilliant at times. . . . He was different than all the rest because of his bad behavior. Think about that."

Defense lawyers need to present their mitigation evidence in a way that avoids these traps. Recer's solution was subtle. If one listened closely, some of the witnesses who testified on Quintero's behalf contradicted others. A cousin on his father's side said Quintero would often disobey his father by intentionally ignoring his studies. "A lot of us thought he was irresponsible," he said. But a cousin on the mother's side perceived Quintero and his siblings to be always studying. "They would not go out to play," he said.

This was all by design. Recer had worked hard to keep the two sides of the family apart, wanting them to present parallel visions that didn't feel neatly integrated. In other trials, when defense lawyers presented any mitigating evidence at all, they showed their clients as victims of terrible circumstances. It was natural that lawyers, who otherwise specialized in arguments featuring two sides, would present a clear, singular image of their client, but the result could be flat and easy to reject. To make your client human, you had to preserve the ways in which he did not make sense. In the process of resolving contradictions about him, a juror would—perhaps inadvertently and certainly not consciously—come to see him in three dimensions, making it harder to vote to kill him. Recer wanted jurors to have multiple routes to sympathy. It could even help if the jurors didn't like the lawyer; this would make them feel that they were coming to their conclusions on their own.

The prosecutors tried to close off the mental doors to mercy. "Some may say, well, let's just lock him up and throw away the key and put him in jail," John Jordan said at closing argument. "You know what? That's what Rodney thought: If you put him in the backseat of the patrol car . . . if he had him handcuffed, he wouldn't pose a threat. . . . Have you thought about a prison guard down the road who will not know what he's capable of as he ushers him into a cell block?" After 2005, when Texas lawmakers approved life-without-parole sentences, this had become a necessary argument for prosecutors to make: If the defendant was going to spend the rest of his life locked up, then they would need to show that he would be a "continuing threat to society" even if the society in question was prison. They would frequently bring in corrections experts to describe the violence of prison. Defense lawyers would respond by showing videos that portrayed prison life as tightly controlled.

The jurors also heard from the victim's children and widow. Joslyn Johnson felt it was partially her duty to encourage the jury to give Quintero a death sentence. "He was my soulmate," she told them. "I always thought we'd be together for the rest of our lives. You know, we had our share of problems, but we always worked through them. We were looking forward to all the kids getting out of the house and us enjoying ourselves and traveling and doing the things that we wanted to do as a couple together. Of course, that's no longer going to happen. He'll never be able to walk my daughter down the aisle, and his other two girls, you know, see them graduate from college." The testimony of Johnson and her children was far shorter than that of Quintero's family, and yet a decade later, it was their words that Dan would remember vividly.

Dan had mentioned disagreements with his father during jury selection, and though his father had not been abusive, Recer thought he might connect with Quintero's story of trying to escape paternal tyranny. She was wrong. To Dan, a series of siblings talking about abuse did not excuse what Quintero had done. And then there was Quintero himself: He showed no emotion in the courtroom. This struck Dan as strange and off-putting.

The jury had black, white, and Latinx members, old and young. When they entered deliberations they took an initial vote, and Dan was surprised to learn he was in the minority; more than half the jurors thought Quintero should receive a life sentence. They rewatched the video of his confession, discussing whether he would be a "continuing threat to society." A schoolteacher named Terry Harshaw thought it was "stupid" to think "society" could refer to prison; if some future prison officials allowed Quintero to be violent, that was their problem, not "society's." Harshaw, who taught science, was more receptive than Dan to the idea that Quintero's brain had reacted in the moment, that he had not planned to kill anyone. To her, his blank expression in the courtroom suggested something might be wrong with him. Other jurors who favored life without parole were particularly moved by the love expressed by Quintero's family and friends, but to Harshaw the key fact was that Johnson had missed the gun; in her mind this actually lessened Quintero's culpability. This was not a point the defense dwelled on; it was Harshaw's own analysis, so she was protective of it.

Dan and the dwindling death voters dug in, and the debate grew increasingly philosophical and emotional, less about Quintero than about whether the death penalty was just, and what believing in it or not believing in it said about you as a person. The longer it went on, the

more labels were meanly invoked: "liberal," "narrow-minded," "ignorant." When it became clear they wouldn't come to a consensus that
night, the jurors slept in a hotel, where they were sequestered.

The next morning, the discussion was calmer. There was a lot of
silence. It was becoming clear that the death voters would never convince everyone else; all they could do was engage in a kind of pointless
sit-in, forcing the jury to wait around all day, perhaps all week, until
the judge finally declared them hung, which would result in a life
sentence for Quintero, the very outcome they didn't want. Frustration
set in.

Dan—one of three pro-death-penalty jurors, in his recollection—
realized that any more discussion would be a waste of time, and so, to
push the group to finally commit and move on, he made an announcement: He was changing his vote. As he remembers it, this caused everyone to finally agree they could go back into the courtroom and
announce that Quintero would serve life in prison. The judge had them
share their votes one by one, and when it was Dan's turn, he almost
flipped back. But he didn't.

He began to cry. He felt he'd let Johnson's family down.

After the trial, the judge and the lawyers for both sides took turns
visiting with the jurors. When Recer came in, they criticized her performance. Afterward, walking to the parking garage, Dan thought to
himself that he hoped he never saw the other jurors ever again.

People asked him about the trial, but he didn't want to talk about it.
He saw John Jordan, the prosecutor, at a restaurant and considered
approaching him and apologizing, but he didn't want to force Jordan to
relive the experience. On his drives to work, he would pass a large tiered
arrangement of granite slabs that overlooked a major road; it was a
monument to fallen police officers. Seeing that monument every day,
Dan would well up with guilt.

Beyond helping lawyers, the Capital Jury Project demonstrated just
how much jurors are traumatized by their experiences in death penalty trials. More than four hundred jurors, about a third of one sample
set, said that either during or after a trial they had trouble sleeping or
eating. Many sought counseling. Some described drinking and taking

pills to cope. Dan's experience did cut against one key finding: The study found that 82 percent of female jurors regretted the jury's ultimate decision, while only 18 percent of men did. In general, women were more likely to describe being emotionally "upset" by their experience, although they may have just been more honest. A few months after the trial, a Capital Jury Project researcher interviewed Dan about his experience. She wrote in her notes:

> He appeared close to tears at certain times. . . . He would look down or away from me during these moments and shrug his shoulders. . . . Listening to this juror describe how he came to change his vote from death to life left me with the impression that he felt emasculated for having switched. He felt weak for not holding out even though he knew (in some way) that the defendant would receive [life without parole] if the jury was hung. He described his feelings about changing his vote as personally sickening. I just think he was traumatized, still trying to understand the experience himself.

Over time Dan learned to forget, but then, two years later, he came home and watched the news and heard Quintero's name again. It was reported that he and a group of prisoners—including a member of the MS-13 gang from Honduras—had attempted to escape from prison. The guilt returned.

There was also anger, though its source is somewhat mysterious. There's a memory Dan could vividly call forth even after a decade: After the trial concluded, when the judge visited the jury room to debrief, she told them that the police officers in the courtroom were there not only to show support for their fallen comrade. They were there to protect the jury from Quintero, who from his jail cell had threatened to kill them. The judge had a technical reason for not allowing this evidence to get to the jury earlier. "This man is not a good person, he's a bad person," Dan remembered her saying.

Only the judge didn't say that, and Quintero never made those threats. There is no mention of it in the record, and in later interviews, numerous other participants in the trial could not recall it. All of them—including the judge—agreed that such a threat would have been a big deal and certainly would have appeared in trial transcripts, if not in newspaper coverage.

Recer herself had showed the jurors how trauma distorts memory. It is possible that Dan was misremembering a threat made by someone else, perhaps a member of Quintero's family, but there is no evidence of that, either. It is possible that he was transmuting his guilt over his vote, or his anger toward Quintero. Whatever the source of this false memory, it sat in Dan's mind, curdling into a deep, bitter feeling toward the justice system as a whole. He resolved that if he saw the judge he might spit at her, and if he was asked to serve on a jury again, he would definitely refuse.

"What I fear," wrote Murray Newman, a former prosecutor with a blog about the Houston courts, regarding Quintero's life sentence, "is that today's verdict is more reflective of the changing attitude of our society. . . . When voices are more vocal in support of a child molester / cop killer than they are for one of the most honorable peace officers to ever hold a badge, what does that say about the shift in our values? . . . Do we really want to celebrate that somewhere Danalynn Recer is toasting her great success today, while the Johnson family is left to wonder what it was that made this crime somehow less deserving of the ultimate punishment?" Harris County had seen life sentences in infamous cases before, but the verdict seemed to validate the fears of big-city prosecutors, who just a few years earlier had opposed life without parole because they thought it would pull juries away from the death penalty. *The Texas Observer* used the Quintero case as the lead example in a trend story on the growing popularity of life without parole. But many outlets went further, seeing the trial's result as an anecdotal sign of a larger shift. *Time* magazine published the headline IS TEXAS CHANGING ITS MIND ABOUT THE DEATH PENALTY?

Recer didn't call reporters back. Still, the *Houston Press*—an alternative newsweekly—declared her criminal defense lawyer of the year for 2008. She had to bat away trolling online comments saying this was her first death penalty trial (she had been involved in one way or another with more than fifty by then) and that she took a six-figure salary as GRACE's director (she still made $38,000). But one day she got a call from the *New Yorker* writer Jeffrey Toobin. Having just published a bestselling book on the Supreme Court, he wanted to profile her for the magazine. She'd heard through the defense grapevine that he had initially wanted to profile her mentor Scharlette Holdman, but she had declined. Recer reluctantly agreed. The ensuing article, titled "The Mitigator," featured a photo of her standing against the austere brick of the Walls Unit in Huntsville.

Although the story was laudatory, Toobin recounted a clash between her and Greg Kuykendall, the head of the Mexican Capital Legal Assistance Program, who had accused her of overcharging the Mexican government, and said she was known to be "very difficult" to work with. Toobin delicately surmised, "Recer's peremptory manner and abundant self-confidence are familiar traits among entrepreneurs, and they are generally more often forgiven in men than in women."

Recer didn't like this analysis for a few reasons. One was practical: Now, if a lawyer didn't want to take her advice, he could point out that it was well known she was "difficult." She also thought it was simplistic to make it about misogyny. She had come to notice over the years that many men were uncomfortable with bossiness in women, but she didn't think it was because they looked down on them. She developed a theory that men are conditioned to see women as caretakers—mothers, teachers, nurses—and when women express disapproval, it feels especially crushing. It was classic Recer: a nuanced explanation that redefines roles and humanizes everyone.

Recer was uncomfortable with all this attention, with the idea that she was personally influential. She hated the phrase placed below *The New Yorker*'s headline: "A new way of looking at the death penalty." It implied that she had innovated, when really in her mind Texas was behind other states in terms of developing a strong culture of skilled defenders and she was just trying to get it to catch up. She knew that in the broader effort to stop the death penalty, it was not helpful for her or anyone else to be held out as uniquely brilliant; this would only serve to excuse the negligence of other lawyers.

Still, she recognized the importance of the Quintero verdict, writing in a law review article that it showed "that there was no crime so despicable and no defendant so far beyond the pale that a jury, even in Harris County, would not choose to value life if they were given an opportunity to look beyond anger and grief to see the 'diverse human frailties' of the man or woman whose life they hold in their hands." The phrase "diverse human frailties" had been written at the Supreme Court three decades earlier, as the justices tried to balance the desire to let individuals be judged as individuals with the principle that they were all equal before the law and should not live and die for arbitrary reasons. Can we be both unique and equal? The answer suggested by the Quintero case was yes: We are all equally unique, and equally able to be shown mercy, if only those who judge us know how to look at our diverse and frail lives.

This was still a radical notion, and Recer's reputation made her a target for those who saw this line of thinking as a way of letting people escape the justice they had earned by their choices. However much public sentiment had shifted, Recer was still very far from the center.

In 2011, still struggling to make its budget, GRACE tried to entice donors with T-shirts, one of which featured a drawing by Quintero. It wasn't the first time the organization had utilized art created by clients, but this time it sparked a backlash as the city's victim advocate, Andy Kahan, decried the shirts and Joslyn Johnson's lawyer said she was "aghast and angry." Recer apologized and said, "We will rethink our practice," sounding more than usual like a chastened executive.

She agreed to appear at the *New Yorker* festival in Manhattan a few months later, on a panel moderated by Toobin. On a stark set of black curtains and tables, she sat next to Marc Klaas, a prominent supporter of the death penalty whose daughter, Polly, had been murdered in 1993. He wore her picture on his lapel. Toobin brought up the T-shirts with Quintero's art. He mentioned a line he often heard from defense lawyers: My client may be a criminal, but he still has constitutional rights. He knew Recer thought differently—he clearly wanted to make this event more lively than the average panel discussion—and she delivered. "I don't do this just because I believe in the Constitution and think my clients are evil," she said. "I'm not going to apologize for loving my clients in all of their complexity." The point of sharing Quintero's artwork, she explained, was to show that criminal defendants are more than the worst act they had ever committed. "I think the reason that upsets people is they want the clients to be frozen in this one-dimensional image of just the day that they did the most horrible thing they ever did. . . . And mitigation is saying no, we're going to see all the minutes that came before and after."

Klaas interrupted. "The whole idea of just selling something that's been made by a convicted murderer is called 'murderabilia,'" he told her. "Quite frankly, putting this on the GRACE website and selling something that has absolutely no value—other than the fact that the person who created it had shot a cop in the back at point-blank range seven times—is a revictimization not only of the cop, but of the cop's family. I can only imagine what that cop's widow must have gone through when she found out that *you* were selling artwork produced by the guy that killed her husband."

There was scattered applause in the hall. Recer tried to answer, but he continued: "You say these people are somewhere where they can cause no more harm. Well, excuse me, but I think Quintero is in a place where he does continue to cause harm. He's selling T-shirts—*she's* selling his T-shirts and continuing to cause harm to the family of this man's victim."

"I need to clarify," Recer said, "that first of all we've never advertised any of our T-shirts or anything as being created by a *particular* client."

"But it's still murderabilia," Klaas said, repeating a word that was far more memorable than "mitigation."

"These are the sort of items that when people sign up to become monthly donors they receive," Recer said. Her answer continued, winding and technical, unable to disrupt the moral weight projected by this man who had lost his daughter.

"You're selling murderabilia," he said. "You're raising money for your organization off the so-called talent of somebody who has no other talent than the fact that he could shoot somebody in the back at point-blank range seven times."

"I think the point is that he has other talents," she said, suddenly finding her footing. "That is the point. That's not all there is to know about him. That is the point of mitigation."

"Wow," Klaas said, raising and turning his hands in a show of bewilderment. "No. That *is* all you need to know about him."

"Let's go to the next question," Toobin said.

13

AS EDWARD CAPETILLO NEARED THE END OF HIS EIGHTH YEAR ON death row, he was ordered to appear in a courtroom in Houston, where a judge told him he would be killed shortly after 6 P.M. on March 30, 2004. He understood his own mind better than he had as a teenager, and the isolation of death row, he discovered, reduced his emotional life to a binary of calm and anger. Now, in the courtroom, he could feel the latter prevailing. His lawyer Elizabeth DeRieux, who had never had an easy time getting him to open up during their visits, was shocked that he wouldn't even take her suggestion to ingratiate himself to the judge by being polite. "Fuck this," he said. She interpreted his rage as the product of his vulnerability, like he was "trying to prove to everyone he was this badass." But Capetillo saw it as resolve: If he could not avoid death, he would face it head-on. He thought of Vikings he'd read about in books, who believed that if they died with a weapon in hand, they would go to the warrior paradise of Valhalla. He felt the urge, he wrote later, "to spit in [death's] face and tell it, 'FUCK YOU!!!' "

After the hearing, he returned to death row, and less than a month later came another surprise: He would live, at least for a little longer. The Supreme Court announced it would hear arguments on whether to ban executions for prisoners who committed their crimes before age eighteen. Seventy-one death row prisoners across the country fell into this category, twenty-nine of them in Texas. Capetillo's lawyer had not told him much about the case, because she didn't think the argument would get traction in the courts, and because even if it did, there was little to discuss: His birthdate was his birthdate. Prosecutors were still trying to have him executed before the Supreme Court could rule, but she managed to get a stay from a lower court.

In March 2005, the case was decided in favor of the juveniles. Capetillo did not feel much at first. He was moved from death row to another prison, where the authorities decided he might be affiliated with a prison gang—they frequently put people in this category without definitive evidence—and kept him in solitary confinement. In a practical sense, his life was no different from day to day. But over time he felt that a weight had been lifted. He had been able to feel only calm and anger, which meant he had stopped feeling hope. Now he would have years to write poetry and draw and express himself in ways he could not even predict.

As the number of death sentences and executions declined, more and more prisoners were adjusting to the reality of living out the rest of their lives in prison. A group of prisoners in California started calling life in prison without a chance of parole the "other death penalty," seeing the fate as equivalent to facing execution—or even worse, because you were no longer going to have a lawyer work on your appeals. But because Capetillo's crime occurred before the Texas Legislature made life without parole a possibility, he would be eligible for release in 2036. He'd be fifty-eight years old. Maybe, he thought, he would get a GED and then put his drawing skills to work as a tattoo artist. Until then, he would keep improving himself, demonstrating that he was no longer the teenager who had ended two lives and devastated many more. "They call me an inmate, I call myself a monk," he wrote in a 2018 letter. "That shift of thinking allows me to live my life to a purpose. I may be doing time, but I'm not wasting time."

After so many years, Elsa Alcala was not particularly bothered to see Capetillo freed from death row. Her time as a lower court judge had given her a strong sense of deference to judges above her. She kept in touch with Allison Vickers, the sister and friend of Capetillo's victims. Even though they could email, they still sent each other physical letters, and Vickers kept some of the ones Alcala had sent her. Whenever she'd move to a new house and go through her belongings, she'd find them again. "Just a short note to let you know that I was thinking about you and hadn't forgotten about you," Alcala wrote in 2006. "Things are soooo busy here that sometimes I feel like I don't have time to breathe." They would catch up by phone, talking about their kids and jobs. When Alcala received a promotion, Vickers and sometimes her father would attend the festivities. Vickers was not happy with the news that Capetillo would never be executed, but she wasn't terribly upset either; she'd moved on and wanted to spend her mental energy remembering the people she loved rather than hating the man who killed them.

Elsa Alcala became a judge the same year she became a mother. Appointed by Governor George W. Bush, she began overseeing a trial court in Houston in January 1999, and that August, she gave birth to twins—a boy and a girl, Harlan and Lina. Three years later, right after giving birth to another daughter, Erin, she was asked by Governor Rick Perry's administration to join a court of appeals. Instead of running a courtroom, now she was reading trial transcripts and briefs and writing rulings, so she was alone more. "I guess I enjoy the quiet at work because home is very noisey [sic]," she wrote to Vickers. By the time she was elevated yet again, to the Court of Criminal Appeals—the highest court for criminal cases in the state—the twins were on the cusp of middle school, and her personal and professional lives were sometimes difficult to separate. One colleague noticed that she would compare judging the competing claims of lawyers to managing the quarrels of children.

On the lower appeals court, she had not ruled on death penalty cases—in Texas, these cases jump straight from the counties to the high court in Austin—so now her daily life took a surreal turn: A typical weekday calendar might include "3 P.M. Pick up kids," "5 P.M. Soccer game," and then, next to "6 P.M.," the name of someone set to be executed that night in Huntsville. She needed to be available all day to field last-minute pleas from defense lawyers and responses from prosecutors, and sometimes that meant dropping everything. Once, while helping her daughter volunteer at an animal shelter, she couldn't keep up with the dog they were walking because she was on her phone preparing a decision. Her daughter grew angry, and Alcala shot back that this was literally a matter of life and death. She later admitted, with regret, that of course her daughter was too young to understand what she meant.

At first she felt constantly overwhelmed, and she sometimes wondered why her eight colleagues on the court didn't seem to be struggling in the same way. Some were men—*How many dinners have they cooked?* she'd think. *How many dishes have they washed?*—or else were older women with adult children. Her family had recently moved to the outskirts of Houston so the twins could attend a better middle school. When she was appointed to the high court in Austin, she knew she would soon face an election, and it was risky to uproot everyone when she might not win. But then, after she did win a six-year term, it became clear that her husband, who worked in Houston, didn't want to move, and she didn't push it.

She had to be in Austin on Mondays and Wednesdays, so she moved into an apartment there with a fellow judge for the first half of each week, then drove the two and a half hours home for the rest of the week and weekend. After a year, she began to feel like an outsider within her family; it was always her husband signing the kids' school forms, helping them with homework. So she gave up the apartment and began commuting twice a week, getting up at five in the morning and arriving home around eight at night. She tried to reason away the exhaustion, telling herself that ten hours of driving per week was not uncommon for commuters. But then she'd get in the car and immediately be overtaken by a feeling of dread. Adrenaline would get her through, but she would be so sapped that it was impossible to accomplish much on Tuesdays and Thursdays, which made it all the more difficult to meet deadlines for opinion drafts at the end of the week. And there were a lot of deadlines. The nine justices received thousands of appeals from people convicted of crimes each year, facing more incoming cases than any comparable state court except one, in California.

A small number of these cases, maybe fifty a year, involved the death penalty. Capital case or not, the court usually rejected the defense's arguments and upheld the conviction.

Though she was often exhausted, Alcala also found herself bothered—not by the rejections, many of which seemed reasonable, but by the lack of explanation. More than 90 percent of the time, her new colleagues would reject a defense lawyer's argument without explaining what was wrong with it. Alcala thought these lawyers deserved to know why they had lost. So she began writing out her thoughts, which also forced her to think more for herself. On the lower courts she had always been bound by the views of the court above her, but now, within the state, there was nobody above her, nobody to whom she could defer.

Soon after she joined the court, Alcala had to rule on the case of Neal Hampton Robbins, who was serving life in prison for the murder of his girlfriend's seventeen-month-old daughter. Robbins had claimed he found the toddler unconscious, but a medical examiner noticed wounds on her chest and ruled the cause of death to be "asphyxiation," and Robbins was charged with murder. At his trial in 1999, the defense argued the toddler's wounds came from Robbins's failed attempts to revive her with CPR, but the jury didn't buy it.

Eight years later, a friend of Robbins asked another examiner to look at the autopsy. This new expert found that the evidence did not clearly indicate asphyxia. The original medical examiner admitted she may have been mistaken and changed her assessment of the cause of death to "undetermined." The results of the autopsy had been key not only to Robbins's conviction, but also to the idea that the child was murdered at all. Robbins asked for a new trial, and a local judge thought he should get one. But Alcala's court had the final say.

Five of her eight colleagues thought he should not get a new trial, because the original cause of death, asphyxiation, had not necessarily been proven false. In other words, nobody had definitively proven that

Robbins was innocent of murder. Judge Cathy Cochran dissented, writing that although Robbins's lawyers had not definitively proven his innocence, they had shown he "did not receive a fundamentally fair trial based upon reliable scientific evidence."

But the problem, Cochran thought, went deeper.

A prisoner's conviction could be overturned if his constitutional rights—to due process, to a lawyer, to a jury—were violated. It could also be overturned if new facts came to light that cast doubt on his guilt, like new DNA, or a new confession. But advances in forensic science do not necessarily produce new facts, just new ways of interpreting facts. "There is a fundamental disconnect between the worlds of science and of law," Cochran wrote. Scientists aim to be unbiased and to acknowledge uncertainty, whereas the legal system pits two openly biased sides against each other. The outcomes of courtrooms are generally final, but science changes. There were always going to be new ways of looking at autopsy results, to take just one of many examples, and how was the legal system supposed to handle that? In the end, Cochran wrote, "Despite every participant's honesty and good faith, this is a case that should be retried to ensure the accuracy of our verdicts and the integrity of our system."

Two other judges signed on to Cochran's opinion, but Alcala decided to write a solo dissent of her own. She was far more severe, writing that the original examiner was likely biased toward the prosecution and might have given her testimony in bad faith. Whether or not she was right, her tone captured the stakes of what in Cochran's writing could sound abstract and cerebral: This was about innocent people in prison.

Defense lawyers, especially those working for innocence projects, had long railed against "junk science" and its role in wrongful convictions, arguing that comparisons of teeth marks, hair, fibers, and other physical evidence were far more subjective than their promoters would admit. DNA had long been held up as a powerful, one-in-a-million method of matching a person to a crime, but even DNA turned out to have problems: A lab could contaminate samples, and someone's skin cells could travel to a crime scene without his ever having been there.

A 2009 report on forensic science by the widely respected National Academy of Sciences, created at the request of Congress, meant it wasn't just defense lawyers complaining about these problems; it was the scientific community as well.

In the wake of Bush's first presidential campaign, many Republicans in Texas had become more sensitive to the criminal justice system's flaws, and by the end of the decade, members of the Tea Party movement, offended by government overreach, became incensed at the idea that innocent people could be sent to prison. The state legislature created a commission named for Tim Cole, who had died in 1999 while in prison for a rape he did not commit. The journalist Pamela Colloff won national accolades for a set of lengthy, cinematic articles on wrongful convictions in *Texas Monthly*, and exonerees became a regular presence at the capitol building, telling harrowing stories of the moments they were plucked from otherwise normal lives and sent to prison.

As a new judge, Alcala saw herself as following rather than leading on these issues, and although she was receiving attention for writing solo opinions, it was Cochran's more moderate approach that proved influential. With her encouragement, Democrats and Republicans collaborated on a bill that explicitly allowed judges to overturn convictions based on changes in forensic science. Cochran spoke proudly of the way her court could encourage legislation through careful analysis and sober reasoning. "We are in the business of planting the seeds for change," she told *Texas Monthly*. "One of the jobs as a judge on the CCA is to be a teacher and to support positive changes in the rule of law without knocking on someone's door and specifically saying, 'Hey, do this.'"

This progress might have come earlier, if not for the death penalty.

In 2004, seven years before Alcala arrived, the Court of Criminal Appeals received a last-minute appeal from lawyers for Cameron Todd Willingham, who was about to be executed for setting a fire that had killed his three young daughters back in 1991. Willingham claimed he had not set the fire, but investigators believed the ash and wreckage left behind bore telltale signs of arson; on the floor they found patterns where they believed an accelerant had been poured, while the window glass was "crazed"—webbed with tiny cracks—which they said indicated a high temperature caused by fuel. As his execution neared, Willingham's pen pal contacted a world-renowned fire expert, who in turn declared that this analysis was nonsense: The glass had likely cracked when it was hit by water from a fire hose, and the patterns on the floor had nothing to do with accelerants. The expert filed a report with the Court of Criminal Appeals explaining that the fire was accidental; it could have been caused by a space heater or bad wiring.

The judges were unmoved, saying this did not count as "newly discovered evidence." Governor Rick Perry declined to stop the execution. "I am an innocent man convicted of a crime I did not commit," Willingham said from the gurney.

Shortly after his death, the *Chicago Tribune* quoted more experts who saw the same flaws in the arson investigation. In a different Texas case, a district attorney allowed Ernest Willis, whose conviction was based on similarly problematic evidence, to leave prison. The Texas Legislature was already in the process of forming a "forensic science commission" to deal with unrelated problems at crime laboratories, and the commission agreed to hire a new expert to look at the Willingham case. That expert also saw there was no scientific basis for finding Willingham guilty of arson. A decade earlier, Texas governor George W. Bush, while running for president, was accused of allowing the execution of Gary Graham despite strong claims of innocence. These accusations failed to gain enough traction to damage him politically, but now Perry had an eye on the presidency himself, and here was a taxpayer-funded agency on the cusp of announcing that he had let an innocent man go to his death. He replaced numerous members of the commission and installed as its new head a political ally who began holding meetings in far-flung locales, away from journalists and protesters. The final report on the Willingham case made recommendations for future fire investigations but said nothing of his innocence or guilt.

One of the many lessons of the Willingham scandal was that the death penalty remained politically toxic. More than other criminal justice matters, it could take otherwise quiet disputes among policymakers and destroy compromise by ratcheting up the political stakes. Supporters of the death penalty accused activists of using the Willingham case to try to abolish the punishment, and activists admitted as much, making it harder for scientists and lawyers to show how problems with forensic science affected scores of non-capital cases. "If this weren't a death penalty case where the defendant was already executed, I doubt Rick Perry would have bothered himself to intervene," wrote Scott Henson, a criminal justice blogger, adding that many innocent people in prison would "have to wait on justice awhile longer while the culture warriors slug it out."

It wasn't just in the political arena that the death penalty disrupted compromise. At the Court of Criminal Appeals, defense lawyers and judges were still often at each other's throats. In 2007, four years before Alcala joined, law professor David Dow tried to file a last-minute appeal to stop an execution, but he was having computer trouble. He asked the court to wait twenty minutes after their 5 P.M. deadline so he could deliver the appeal by hand. Chief judge Sharon Keller responded, "We close at five," and Dow's client was executed. Keller's four-word soundbite quickly spread as a symbol of her callousness; newspaper editorials called her Sharon Killer. Superficially, the dispute was about court deadlines, but under the surface it was clear that the animosity of the resource-center era had not totally dissipated.

A few years later, Dow was again accused of missing a deadline. He had taken on a death row prisoner's appeal at the last minute, after learning that previous lawyers had done a poor job (the original trial defender in the case called no witnesses). A majority of judges decided he should be suspended for a year, a rare and extreme punishment.

This time, Alcala was on the court, and she wasn't steeped in the old feuds. She thought Dow should just be fined and put on a form of probation, and she wrote that her colleagues' decision to suspend him was "ineffective, unwise, excessive, unjust to victims, and chilling to defendants and other attorneys." Instead of feeling bitter toward these zealous defense lawyers, she found she respected them for working so hard. She began to suspect that some of her peers could not sympathize with someone like Dow because they had jumped straight from being prosecutors to serving on this court and had not spent years on lower courts, as she had, or worked as defense lawyers.

Alcala especially liked Cathy Cochran, the dissenter who had called attention to the problems of science and the law. She had been a prosecutor, defense lawyer, professor, and policy adviser to Governor George W. Bush. She was conservative but not reactionary, and she shared Alcala's skepticism toward some of the pieties of their profession. It was becoming fashionable to compare judging to the task of a baseball umpire, whose job is simply to "call balls and strikes." This was how the Supreme Court's chief justice, John Roberts, described his work at a confirmation hearing in 2005, and the analogy was later invoked by nominee Brett Kavanaugh and several senators. Cochran pointed out that if this were true, "we could just use one computer to decide all cases." She and Alcala were becoming friends, able to be warm and cordial even when they didn't agree. When someone would ask Alcala how she developed her sense of fairness, she would point to her former mentor Johnny Holmes, who always told his prosecutors never to do anything that would produce "a damn fool result."

At the same time, Alcala was now starting to find faults in cases that her former boss had overseen.

In 2013, Alcala's court received a petition from the lawyers for a man named Duane Buck. He was facing execution for a crime he had committed in Houston in the summer of 1995, which happened to be right after Alcala sent one man to death row and right before she sent a second—meaning she could easily have been the one to send him there. She knew the lead prosecutor, Joan Huffman, who was now a state senator.

Early one morning, Buck had kicked open the door of his ex-girlfriend Debra Gardner's home, argued with her, taken some of his belongings, and left. A few hours later, when Gardner's friends were gathered, he came back with a rifle and shotgun, forced the door open again, and started firing. He shot Gardner, as well as Kenneth Butler, whom he accused of sleeping with her. Buck also shot Phyllis Taylor— his own sister.

Taylor survived, but both Gardner and Butler died from their wounds. After Buck left, his car wouldn't start, so he started walking away, which meant he had not gotten far when the police arrived. At trial, his defense lawyer called up a psychologist, Walter Quijano, to explain why Buck would not be dangerous in the future. Quijano said that Buck had a "dependent personality disorder," which made him excessively possessive. "These individuals can become very extreme in wanting to maintain that relationship and sometimes go to the point of thinking if I cannot have you, nobody else can," he explained. The crime, though horrific, was "unlikely to be repeated."

Quijano also looked at future dangerousness through the lens of statistics. By 1995, judges and other officials in the criminal justice system were increasingly using data to make decisions about whether people could be safely released from jails or prisons. In addition to age, gender, prior crimes, and other factors, Quijano looked at race. "It's a sad commentary that minorities, Hispanics and black people, are over-represented in the criminal justice system," he said.

On cross-examination, a prosecutor returned to this point and leaned into it: "You have determined that . . . the race factor, black, increases the future dangerousness for various complicated reasons. Is that correct?"

"Yes," Quijano replied.

Decades earlier, the lawyer Peggy Davis, working with Anthony Amsterdam at the NAACP Legal Defense Fund, suspected that the emphasis on future dangerousness in the Texas death penalty law would be especially perilous for black defendants because of a tendency in American culture to associate dark skin with violence. Over the decades, scholars had shown how racial bias could shape the perceptions of prosecutors, defenders, jurors, and judges. And while broad arguments about racial injustice seldom got much traction in the courts, judges were more willing to pay attention when a prosecutor or judge had explicitly invoked race. At one time, Texas officials had agreed that Buck's death sentence had been tainted by Quijano's testimony, but as his execution approached, they refused to agree with his defenders that he deserved a new trial.

By 2013, Buck had some of the best capital defense lawyers in the country working for him: Christina Swarns (of the NAACP LDF), Kathryn Kase (of the Texas Defender Service, the firm born out of the ashes of the Texas Resource Center), and Kate Black (who had been an intern at GRACE, working under Danalynn Recer). Fittingly, the brief they submitted to the Court of Criminal Appeals, which Alcala now had before her, tapped into numerous streams of thought in the capital defense community. They wrote sweepingly of entrenched racism in Houston's public schools, courts, and political institutions. They accused Johnny Holmes of overseeing the systematic exclusion of black residents from jury service and pointed to studies showing he was more likely to seek the death penalty against black defendants.

In her final opinion, Alcala wrote all this off, saying these lawyers had failed to show there was "discriminatory intent" in the decision to seek the death penalty for Buck, but she also found Quijano's testimony indefensible and thought Buck had suffered from years of substandard defense lawyering. She focused on the defense argument that Buck's trial defender had failed to investigate mitigating evidence.

The year before, she had found herself shocked by the case of a man who was on death row for killing a police officer; the officer had been out of uniform, and the man, though he had a long criminal record, appeared to have mistaken him for an intruder. When he learned of his victim's identity, he broke down in tears. During the punishment phase of the trial, in 1983, the man's defense lawyer did not argue that this should mitigate his sentence. Alcala's colleagues refused to overturn the death sentence, and Alcala dissented, citing numerous Supreme Court decisions about the importance of mitigating evidence. In private conversations, she found they had a limited view of what kinds of evidence juries would find convincing. Now she repeated a series of facts about Buck, uncovered in depth by his new team: Buck's father gave his son alcohol beginning at age five. He would also beat him "for any little reason or for no reason at all" with "electrical cords, belts, switches" and "spark plug wires," leaving welts all over his body. Buck was surrounded by drugs growing up, and as he got older, his family members sometimes thought he was "so high" that the "drugs were controlling him." Alcala wrote that if the jurors had heard all this, they might have spared his life. Her prose suggested that she herself would have done so.

The more time she spent on the court, the more uncomfortable she became with all the old Texas cases in which juries had never heard about all the reasons they might extend mercy. Even amid the legalese, a reader of Alcala's opinions could see she was moved by these portraits of people driven by terrible experiences toward terrible actions and terrible fates. Of course, she knew what it was like to have a difficult start in life.

It was increasingly clear to defense lawyers that Alcala was willing to part ways with her Republican peers. Even if it didn't ultimately change the outcome of a case—she was almost always in the minority—her ability to dissent without sparking much public controversy did represent a shift in what an elected Texas judge could say. Charlie Baird, a Democrat on the court in the 1990s, could still remember how dissenting in a death penalty case doomed him to electoral defeat, but Alcala skated through the 2012 election with barely any opposition. "I keep waiting for things to slow down," she wrote in a letter to Allison Vickers, "but, instead, it seems as though things get faster and faster."

As her confidence grew, some of the other judges began to follow her lead. Two colleagues joined her Duane Buck dissent. In 2014, she picked up three votes to halt the execution of Scott Panetti, a severely mentally ill man who had defended himself at trial and tried to call John F. Kennedy and Jesus Christ as witnesses and whose lawyers were now saying he was "incompetent to be executed." (His execution was eventually halted by a federal court.) In a non-capital case, she wrote scathingly about a lawyer who failed to find an interpreter for his Spanish-speaking client. Throughout her opinions, a theme was emerging: She thought her fellow judges were too quick to fall back on procedure—to say a particular legal claim had been brought too late, or in a technically incorrect way—in order to ignore legitimate arguments.

Dissenting so much took a toll. Sometimes the other judges would roll their eyes and huff and even shout at her. Sometimes they would talk over her, and even talk about her, in front of her, as if she were not in the room. A couple of times she emerged from closed-door meetings practically in tears. She would tell herself that some of her colleagues just couldn't rid themselves of their prosecutorial identities, that they resented her forcing them to do the work of responding to her dissents. At other times she would wonder if she was the one being too strident.

But she was also starting to receive vindication and encouragement from far beyond Texas. In June 2016, the Supreme Court announced it would hear arguments in two high-profile cases in which she had dissented. One was the case of Duane Buck; the Court was going to listen to his claim of racial bias. The other case concerned Bobby Moore, a death row prisoner who Alcala thought was intellectually disabled and thus could not be executed. Ever restrained, Alcala indulged in a tweet: "This makes my day!"

It was a good moment for encouragement, because she was preparing to go out on a limb.

The case of Julius Murphy—convicted of a 1998 robbery-murder in Texarkana, on the border with Arkansas—would have been unmemorable but for the radical claim his lawyers were making: that the entire Texas death penalty system violated the Constitution. It was the kind of argument that most judges dismiss out of hand, and yet Alcala and her clerks noticed that these lawyers' arguments reflected problems she had noticed in case after case. She decided to address the claim. She wrote that Murphy's lawyers should have an opportunity to gather evidence that the system was unconstitutional and bring it before a court. She noted her increasing discomfort with racial disparities and also discussed the harshness of solitary confinement on death row. "It should be evident from my numerous opinions on this subject that, in my view, the Texas scheme has some serious deficiencies that have, in the past, caused me great concern about this form of punishment as it exists in Texas today," she wrote. She wasn't saying the Texas death penalty violated the Constitution, but she was saying it was a reasonable question to ask.

Like Cathy Cochran, she was planting seeds. Justice Stephen Breyer at the Supreme Court had made similar arguments a year earlier, but he was a liberal, appointed by a Democratic president. One of Alcala's own former Republican colleagues on the Court of Criminal Appeals, Tom Price, had publicly written two years earlier that the death penalty should be abolished, but he was just two months out from retirement at that point, and critics suggested he might not have been so bold if he planned to face voters again. Here was a Republican—a protégé of Johnny Holmes, no less—talking this way with two years left in office and no plans to retire.

Alcala was surprised by the attention, but when reporters called from the Associated Press and *The Guardian*, she allowed herself to speak more directly, abandoning the dense legalese in her court opinions. "I was in my late twenties or early thirties when I was trying [death penalty cases]," she told a reporter. "Single, didn't have kids. Nowadays I think of the execution of a seventeen-year-old as barbaric. But back then I guess it just wasn't in my zone of reference." (She did not mention Eddie Capetillo, the seventeen-year-old she had worked to send to death row, by name.)

Her public moment was further proof that Americans were increasingly seeing the death penalty in a new light, and were willing to tolerate ambivalence in their elected officials. There was still some grumbling, of course; her former colleague Chuck Rosenthal started pestering her on Facebook about her true views on the death penalty, and she wondered if he was trying to get her to say something controversial, to stoke gossip and get her in trouble. She clung to an inspirational quote she heard once, spoken by a character in the sitcom *Girlfriends' Guide to Divorce:* "Nobody truly interesting is ever universally liked." She was becoming the voice of a new centrism on the death penalty, a political position that did not call for the full-scale abolition of the punishment but did think it merited a second look.

In February 2017, the Supreme Court ruled in Duane Buck's favor. Chief Justice John Roberts, who seldom voted in favor of death row prisoners, was outraged by the testimony about Buck's race. The comments in question represented just a couple of lines in thousands of pages of court transcript, but Roberts wrote that "some toxins can be deadly in small doses." While Alcala may have still been a gadfly on the CCA, she was finding herself in agreement with the conservative chief justice of the country's highest court.

Despite her long career as a judge, Alcala had never seen the Supreme Court in person. When the justices announced they would take oral arguments in the case of Bobby Moore, which she had studied in depth while preparing a dissent, it happened to be around the time that her older daughter, now at the end of high school, was considering a university in Baltimore. "We decided to combine a college visit with the oral arg. to hit two birds with one stone," she wrote in a lengthy Facebook post.

On the Tuesday after Thanksgiving in 2016, they stood in a long line and passed through a metal detector before entering the courtroom. She marveled at the formality and etiquette ("My daughter said that when she started closing her eyes, the marshals would stare her down") and described the justices with the reverence of a law student. Although still a Republican, she seemed especially starstruck by the justices appointed by Democrats:

> Justice Thomas leaned way back in his chair a lot of the time and said nothing. Justice Ginsburg was tiny, hoarse, and I could hardly see or hear her but she still seems very sharp. Justice Kagan was like a surgeon striking with precision. She was strong and brilliant. Justice Stephen Breyer was forceful in his questions, seemed to give a speech at one point, and very pragmatic. Justice Sotomayor was extremely prepared and familiar with the law and record. She was very confident with a lovely demeanor. . . . My daughter, a couple of lawyers, and I were all seated in different areas of the courtroom and each of

us said afterwards that we thought Justice Samuel Alito was looking at us. We joked that he was like the Mona Lisa painting with his eyes seeming to look at you no matter where you were. Ha . . . I was glad I went. Hope this was not too long but I will probably forget all the details by tomorrow!

The case concerned an issue that had come to dominate much litigation about the death penalty in the first decade of the millennium. In 2002, the Court had ruled in *Atkins v. Virginia* that intellectually disabled people could not be executed. But unlike the ruling that banned death sentences for anyone under eighteen, there was no simple way to decide who fit this category; "intellectual disability" was a diagnosis, and two doctors could disagree. The Court left it to the states to set guidelines on how to decide who was actually disabled.

In 2004, Judge Cathy Cochran asked the Texas Legislature to come up with such guidelines, but in the meantime, she wrote, her court would rely on a set of factors she thought most Texans might agree upon. To illustrate, she described Lennie Small, the character from John Steinbeck's 1937 novella *Of Mice and Men*. Lennie is a large, strong, and mentally slow migrant worker who loves rabbits but accidentally kills them. At the story's climax, he unwittingly kills his boss's daughter-in-law. "Most Texas citizens might agree that Steinbeck's Lennie should, by virtue of his lack of reasoning ability and adaptive skills, be exempt" from the death penalty, Cochran wrote. (In the novella, Lennie is executed not by the state but by his friend George, as a way of protecting him from a more violent death at the hands of others.)

Cochran listed seven questions a jury might consider: Is the defendant impulsive? Is he a leader or a follower? Can he lie effectively in his own interest? And so on. These became known as the Briseno factors, for the case in which Cochran had enumerated them.

Courts would hold hearings in which people who knew the defendant shared stories suggesting that he was or wasn't disabled. Scholars feared that the focus on anecdotes would allow stereotypes to override science, and in many cases, juries simply ignored the opinions of doctors to send men to death row. When John Steinbeck's son Thomas learned of Lennie's use in Texas courtrooms, he told a reporter, "I find the whole premise to be insulting, outrageous, ridiculous and profoundly tragic."

In 2014, the Supreme Court ruled in a Florida case that the state must pay attention to the views of clinicians. The next year, Alcala had to rule in the case of Bobby Moore, who was on death row for shooting an elderly supermarket clerk during a robbery in 1980. At a hearing more than three decades later, a judge, after learning that Moore had never been able to tell time or recite the days of the week, said he could not be executed, citing current medical guidelines. But Alcala's colleagues disagreed, saying the judge should not have departed from the Briseno factors. They pointed out that Moore was capable of filling out order slips to buy items from the prison commissary.

Alcala and her staff studied the nuances of intellectual disability. In the heavily controlled world of death row, she learned that someone might be able to function at a higher level, and though Moore was able to fill out commissary slips, those slips were full of arithmetical and spelling errors. In a dissent, she wrote that the Briseno factors violated the Constitution.

From her seat in the Supreme Court's gallery, she watched the faces of the justices as Moore's lawyer, with his back to her, made points similar to those she had made. When it was over, she had a good feeling. A month later, the Court indeed ruled in Moore's favor. In the majority opinion, Justice Ruth Bader Ginsburg criticized the Briseno factors and nodded to the Texas judge who had outlined all the same criticisms before, opening a long paragraph in the middle of the opinion with three words: "Judge Alcala dissented."

Soon after returning from Washington, Alcala, now confident in leading rather than following, went to the legislature herself to ask them to finally write guidelines on intellectual disability. Though she had attacked the Briseno factors, she did not blame Cochran for writing them, since they were only meant to be a temporary fix. Cochran "pleaded for the legislature to step in and come up with a test, and that didn't happen," Alcala told the legislators, on the edge of criticizing them for it. But then she held back. "In many ways I don't blame the legislature, because it's hard."

Democrat Terry Canales asked her how much time she spent on capital cases, and then he baited her: "Your job would be a whole bunch easier if we just abolished it, right?"

She laughed uncomfortably. "If the legislature did that I wouldn't quarrel with that. But I've never said that outright. What I have said is the death penalty is supposed to be [for] the worst of the worst, and from what I have seen, I don't necessarily see that we have targeted the worst of the worst."

"It'd be nice not to have to think about any of this stuff," he continued.

"I've always struggled with it," she responded. "You have people who are put into prison who, let's say, are dangerous to the prison guards, or are dangerous to the medical community in the prison, and my question is what do you do for that situation?"

She was being surprisingly candid for a judge, even vulnerable, and it seemed to suit her. She had a tendency in public to raise her voice in pitch and smile while delivering an argument she knew might rankle those around her. Usually that meant telling people who liked the death penalty about the system's problems, but now she was on the other side. "The only justification in my mind is whether we need the death penalty to truly target the mass terrorist, like the bomber at the Boston Marathon. . . . When I think of something like that, that is such a terroristic act against humanity as a whole, and you give that person the best possible trial attorney, the best possible appellate attorney . . . and if a jury hears all of that, and they get the best of everything, and he truly is the worst of the worst, then in my mind, I can see a law that society would approve of."

But then she pointed out that those who received the death penalty "seem to be the lesser educated, the poorer people, the people who didn't have as good representation." A liberal defense lawyer making the same argument would probably use words like "racist" and "classist," but Alcala didn't seem to be able to bear speaking in such tones. She wanted to be the reasonable, qualifying, sensible one in the room.

At the same time, she was finding she no longer enjoyed many aspects of being a judge. She hated campaigning for judicial positions: Voters knew little about judges, so the whole process could seem capricious. In 2012, she spent a day talking to voters at a county fair, only to lose the straw poll to a candidate who had not even shown up, just because he had the last name Law. She also felt abandoned by the Republican Party, which had once seemed so interested in cultivating her career as part of a larger effort to reach Latinx voters. Now Republicans were turning toward harsher immigration enforcement, and the country elected a man who wanted to build a wall on the border and separate parents from their children. Her term was set to end on December 31, 2018, and she decided that she would not run for another one. As her time on the court drew to a close, she experimented with a public, more openly political identity. On Twitter she especially liked to cheer on young female reporters.

At her retirement party in December 2018, her fellow judges presented her with a pen, handmade of maple and mesquite by a judge with a woodworking hobby. It featured a Texas flag. She wrote on Facebook that her court had overseen roughly one execution per month since she joined the court, and being exposed to so many stories of violence, while making decisions in which the stakes were life and death, had taken "a toll on me."

A couple of weeks later, she made a surprising announcement: She would spend the first half of 2019 working at the legislature on behalf of the Texas Defender Service, the organization that had grown out of the Texas Resource Center a generation earlier. The gig would last only a few months, and after that a new chapter of her life would begin. Her personal life was shifting, too: She and her husband had decided to divorce. Two of their kids were now in college, and a third would be going soon. Alcala was alone more often than she'd been in years, and a little apprehensive about how she'd spend her time, having worked essentially nonstop since finishing her education. Maybe she would write a book, she thought, or teach, or work on policy. She could really do anything.

EPILOGUE

ON EXECUTION DAYS IN HUNTSVILLE, PROTESTERS GATHER ON A small patch of grass in front of the Walls Unit and gaze up at the clock face above the entrance. Occasionally, hundreds of people fill the parking lot behind the grass and spill down the side streets, but usually there are fewer than ten. Along with some yellow caution tape and maybe a news truck, their presence is the only indication that something significant is happening inside the high brick walls. Gloria Rubac, a gravelly-voiced former elementary school teacher, is almost always there, having made the trip from her home in Houston for nearly every execution since the first, of Charlie Brooks, in 1982. When she and another activist named Joanne Gavin learned of the raucous pro-death-penalty demonstrations taking place that day, they drove up with their own posters and a megaphone. At some point over the next few decades, Rubac added a microphone and speakers, which she used to accuse whoever was governor of murder.

For most of these executions, the two women have been joined by Dennis Longmire, a criminologist who came to teach at the local college in 1984. He quietly prays the rosary and cups his hands around a candle. If asked about what is happening inside the prison, Rubac will say, "They're executing," as a rebel fighting power, while Longmire will say, "We're executing," as a citizen bearing witness. He's not much for all the shouting, and when on one occasion the wind blew over Rubac's speakers, he joked that his prayers had been answered.

She laughed. They had developed a warm rapport over the years. They'd been there together when executions were at midnight and when they were at 6 P.M., when Gary Graham's execution nearly provoked a street battle between black nationalists and white supremacists, when Karla Faye Tucker's execution attracted scores of Christian supporters, and when Michael Moore sent a marching band and cheerleaders to mock Governor George W. Bush. On quieter nights, they try to remain cordial to the loved ones of murder victims, comfort grieving relatives of those executed, and debate the finer points of deterrence and retribution with students from Longmire's college. They have seen countless defense lawyers stumble out after seeing their clients die.

When they aren't protesting, anti-death-penalty activists—who usually call themselves abolitionists, after those who fought to abolish slavery—organize clemency campaigns, testify at the capitol, befriend death row prisoners, and conduct research on cases. They are usually in a supporting role, because the Supreme Court's decisions to end and then revive the death penalty in the 1970s had the effect of placing lawyers at center stage.

So it was especially ironic when activists—from another country, no less—managed to disrupt the entire American death penalty system in a way that even Anthony Amsterdam probably could not have foreseen.

After working with Danalynn Recer in Louisiana, Clive Stafford Smith moved back to London in 2004 to run Reprieve, an organization that mounts international human rights campaigns and defends men held at the American detention center in Guantánamo Bay, Cuba. (After the World Trade Center attacks on September 11, 2001, some defense lawyers who felt a special calling to represent the least popular defendants moved from state death row prisoners to those accused of terrorism.) In 2010, Maya Foa, a former theater director with dual U.S.-British citizenship, began working there. She spoke fast and thought faster, the sort of person who borrows pens to scribble reminders on her hands. Stafford Smith asked her to look into the drugs that were being used to carry out executions, and she threw herself into the task, mastering the intricacies of pharmaceutical supply chains and regulatory schemes. Over the years, some drug manufacturers, owing to their ethical obligation to "do no harm," tried to stop prison officials from using their products in executions, and eventually European governments began restricting exports. The result was that states began looking to less official channels: Among Foa's early discoveries was that Arizona prison officials were importing a key execution drug, sodium thiopental, through a man operating alone out of the back of a London driving school.

States also began trading supplies with one another. Reporters discovered this emerging network and published embarrassing stories about a macabre behind-the-scenes scramble, full of prison officers going on road trips to purchase execution drugs with cash. Defense lawyers began challenging states on their sourcing, saying that using untested drugs on their clients would constitute "cruel and unusual punishment." State legislators passed laws to shield the drug manufacturers and middlemen from being named publicly, and they began discussing alternatives, most of which would represent a return to the past: firing squads, gas chambers, electric chairs. The efforts at secrecy, combined with the political reluctance to return to these older execution methods, suggested that while half of all Americans still support executions in theory, they continue to be ambivalent about the grisly reality. In the midst of all this was Maya Foa, who learned how to exploit the PR concerns of drug executives and help them enact distribution controls to keep their products away from prisons.

Cut off by multinational drug companies, states found a new source of execution drugs domestically. Oklahoma spent more than $50,000 to pay a small, secret pharmacy to produce a "compounded" form of pentobarbital, a barbiturate that could be used with no other accompanying drugs to kill a prisoner. (It is commonly used by veterinarians to put animals down.) This new source was so promising that officials from the Texas Department of Criminal Justice (TDCJ) asked their counterparts in Oklahoma for help getting the drug for their own executions. In emails later revealed by a reporter, Oklahoma officials complained that they had once asked Texas for similar assistance and been rebuffed. "Looks like they waited until the last minute and now need help from those they refused to help earlier," one government lawyer wrote to another. "So, I propose we help if TX promises to take a dive in the OU-TX game for the next 4 years." This was a reference to a famous football rivalry between universities in the two states. The second lawyer responded that he would "forgive and forget with sideline passes for Team Pentobarbital . . . to the 2011 OU-Texas game plus an on-field presentation of a commemorative plaque at halftime recognizing Oklahoma's on-going contributions to propping up the Texas system of capital punishment."

This mix of flippancy and chaos could not be further from the picture of sobriety and dignity that Carroll Pickett, Kenneth Dean, and so many other Texas prison officials had spent years cultivating. A lawyer for the Texas prison system now attacked Foa and Reprieve personally, saying the organization "crosses the line from social activists dedicated to their cause to authoritarian ideologues who menace and harass private citizens who decline to submit to Reprieve's opinion." She continued, "It is not a question of if but when Reprieve's unrestrained harassment will escalate into violence against a supplier," and went so far as to compare Reprieve's tactics to "practices by gangs . . . who intimidate and coerce rival gang members and which have erupted into prison riots." Stafford Smith demanded an apology and pointed out that he and Foa didn't need to harass anyone—the drug executives themselves opposed the use of their products in lethal injection.

The controversy didn't stop TDCJ from maintaining an active execution schedule, and by the summer of 2012 the agency was using pentobarbital from a secret compounding pharmacy while batting away lawsuits from defense lawyers who wanted to know the source. Doctors warned that poorly made pentobarbital could make prisoners feel immense pain as they died, and a few Texas prisoners said they felt a burning sensation as the drug began to enter their bloodstream. Eventually, the Associated Press obtained documents outing a small compounding pharmacy near Houston, and the pharmacist there angrily demanded that the drugs be returned. TDCJ found a new source, the lawsuits continued, the protests continued, the bad press continued, and the executions continued. Outside an execution in October 2013, Gloria Rubac held a cardboard sign reading TDCJ: LOOKING FOR DRUGS IN ALL THE WRONG PLACES.

In other states, the difficulties around sourcing led officials to try new drug combinations. Many states, including Texas, had seen executions go poorly over the years, leading scholars to categorize them as "botched"; the scramble for drugs led the media to watch more closely, and the public learned more about the horrific scenes taking place behind prison walls. In January 2014, an Ohio prisoner appeared to gasp repeatedly and clench his fist as he died, and that summer, an Arizona prisoner's execution lasted nearly two hours. But the biggest scandal took place in Oklahoma. Clayton Lockett was not publicly sympathetic—he'd been convicted of kidnapping, beating, raping, and fatally shooting a nineteen-year-old girl—but while he was being injected with midazolam, a drug that experts had warned against using, the IV dislodged, and Lockett bucked against the restraints, kicked his leg, clenched his teeth, rolled his head, opened an eye, and said, "Something is wrong." After forty minutes, he died of a heart attack. President Barack Obama called the incident "deeply troubling." Oklahoma then used the same drug to execute a second man, who calmly stated from the gurney, "My body is on fire."

Oklahoma's execution protocol went before the Supreme Court, where a dense discussion of pharmacology took a surprising turn. Justice Samuel Alito accused activists (like Maya Foa, though he didn't use her name) of mounting "guerrilla war against the death penalty," making it impossible to get drugs and then blaming the states when their workarounds had problems. (The attack echoed the moment two decades earlier when Justice Scalia accused the Texas Resource Center of abusing the legal system to stop executions.) In 2015, the Court ruled in Oklahoma's favor. "The Constitution does not require the avoidance of all risk of pain," Alito wrote. "After all, while most humans wish to die a painless death, many do not have that good fortune."

But the biggest surprise about the Oklahoma case was that Justice Stephen Breyer issued a lengthy dissent, not just about lethal injection but about the death penalty as a whole.

Breyer had been appointed in 1994 by Democratic president Bill Clinton, and he was known as a centrist—"the liberal Justice," one scholar wrote, "most likely to agree with his conservative colleagues." It appeared that, after two decades on the Court, something in him had cracked. "Rather than try to patch up the death penalty's legal wounds one at a time," he wrote, "I would ask for full briefing on a more basic question: whether the death penalty violates the Constitution." Though he was technically asking a question, he was also offering an answer. Over nearly fifty pages, he returned to the themes of the big cases of the 1970s, arguing that while the majority of the Supreme Court back then had hoped the states could find a fair way to administer the death penalty, four decades of evidence suggested they had failed: Innocent people had likely been executed, and among the guilty, there was little logic to why some people died and others did not. To the extent that there was a logic, it appeared to be unfair to racial minorities. In order to have a robust appeals process, to weed out the actually innocent people and those who suffered grossly unfair trials, prisoners had to live on death row for decades, often in solitary confinement. This alone, Breyer felt, might constitute cruel and unusual punishment.

The Court's conservatives fired back. Justice Clarence Thomas accused Breyer of being on a "ceaseless quest to end the death penalty through undemocratic means," noting that the justices, unlike jurors, "are not drawn from the community whose sense of security and justice may have been torn asunder by an act of callous disregard for human life." Justice Scalia called the dissent a "white paper devoid of any meaningful legal argument."

Breyer was not the first justice to question the death penalty in a dissent, but his big swing was mysterious for its timing: Why publish this now? The historian Evan Mandery—who had written the most comprehensive book on the major death penalty cases of the 1970s—

noticed that Breyer repeatedly cited prior opinions by Justice Anthony Kennedy. This seemed notable, because Justice Kennedy had been so pivotal in previous decisions to prevent the death penalty from being imposed on juveniles and the intellectually disabled. He had recently criticized a death row prisoner's placement in solitary confinement. He would likely be the swing vote should the death penalty system as a whole come before the Court. Was Breyer trying to convince Kennedy to join him? Was he signaling to defense lawyers that Kennedy might be newly swayable? A number of lawyers began filing petitions with the Court, arguing, just as Anthony Amsterdam had almost half a century before, that the entire death penalty system should again be thrown out, this time for good. Other lawyers urged caution: What if the Court agreed to address the issue but ruled against them? Such a decision would entrench the death penalty for another half century.

The Court declined to take any of these cases, and then came a moment of upheaval. In February 2016, Justice Scalia died while on a hunting trip in Texas. It seemed possible that Kennedy's views on the death penalty would no longer be so crucial, because President Barack Obama could replace the conservative Scalia with a justice who would provide a fifth vote to abolish the punishment. But then Senate Majority Leader Mitch McConnell announced that no nominees would be considered until a new president was sworn in, which wouldn't happen for nearly a year. Liberals were furious, but they consoled themselves with predictions that Hillary Clinton would win in November 2016.

Then Donald Trump was elected president. Many years earlier, after the arrests of the Central Park Five, a group of teenagers convicted of raping a woman who had been out jogging, Trump spent $85,000 placing full-page ads in multiple newspapers, calling for the return of the death penalty. When DNA eventually proved that these teenagers were innocent and they were released from prison, Trump said he didn't believe it. He said anyone who killed a police officer should be executed, too, and maybe even drug dealers.

Many conservatives had voted for Trump—despite his many public scandals and his ideological inconsistencies—because he promised to nominate conservative judges to the Supreme Court, and he delivered, nominating Neil Gorsuch and then, when Kennedy announced his retirement, Brett Kavanaugh, both of whom tended to vote against death row prisoners. Trump's first attorney general, Jeff Sessions, started telling federal prosecutors to seek the death penalty more often. In the summer of 2019, the Department of Justice announced it would attempt to carry out federal executions for the first time since 2003.

At the same time, in the years before and after Trump's election, the American public was beginning to question the policies that had given their country one of the largest prison systems in the world. Both liberals and conservatives began to realize that the laws enacted by Congress and state legislatures in the 1980s and 1990s had been an overblown and misguided response to the era's rise in crime. The term "mass incarceration" became shorthand for the idea that far too many people were spending far too long in prison. During President Obama's tenure, the deaths of young black men at the hands of police sparked protests in numerous cities, all under the banner of the #BlackLivesMatter movement. Libertarians began seeing oversized prisons and wrongful convictions as an example of big-government overreach. White evangelical Christians (many of whom still remembered Karla Faye Tucker) became more vocal in calling for a system that offered room for redemption. Many conservative states, including Texas, passed new laws that attempted to reduce the number of people in prison and guarantee more rights for people facing criminal charges. President Trump himself championed the First Step Act, which reduced some federal prison sentences, particularly for drug crimes.

Some prosecutors and conservative lawmakers believed these new state and federal laws went too far, while many liberal activists believed they did not go far enough. But it was still a sign of change that Trump—even as he oversaw the separation of immigrant children from parents at the border, and even as he sought the expansion of the death penalty—could say in his State of the Union address that past criminal justice laws "have wrongly and disproportionately harmed the African American community" and that "America is a nation that believes in redemption."

Even at its height, death sentences were a tiny fraction of the thousands of prison sentences handed out each year. Their power was in their symbolism; they were the pinnacle of a system and society that believed in retribution. So as the country turned its face—slowly, unevenly, and perhaps not permanently—away from retribution and toward other values, like rehabilitation and redemption, the death penalty lost its symbolic resonance. It was no longer a staple of the culture wars, along with abortion and gun control. Texas state senator Jerry Patterson found in the early 1990s that any voter who didn't know what to ask him would default to inquiring about his views on the death penalty. A generation later, this seemed unthinkable. In 2017, national support for the death penalty polled below 50 percent for the first time in decades, down from a peak of 80 percent in 1994. In 2018, the Washington State supreme court ruled the death penalty unconstitutional. Soon after, California's new governor, Gavin Newsom, announced that nobody would be executed during his tenure and had the state's execution chamber dismantled. Fewer than a dozen states were making a clear effort to carry out executions.

Executions continued—28 nationally in 2015, 20 in 2016, 23 in 2017, 25 in 2018, 22 in 2019—and they still occasionally garnered a great deal of press attention, but that attention was often far more negative than it had been in the 1990s. Whereas journalists once tended to load their stories with heinous details of crimes and macabre accounts of last meals, now many amplified the arguments of defense lawyers and watched executions with an eye for scandal. In 2019, *The Intercept*, a left-leaning online news site, published data showing that even as death sentences were decreasing, racial inequities were getting worse; prosecutors and jurors were giving a larger proportion of death sentences to people of color. Looking for an explanation, reporter Liliana Segura brought up the Texas "future dangerousness" question and quoted a lawyer who said the question "practically guarantees the death penalty for anyone who's black or Mexican." Even if a reader was skeptical of these arguments about race, the numbers pointed toward an overall systemic failure: Of the more than 7,335 people who had been sentenced to death around the country, only 1,448 had been executed. By June 2019, one innocent person had been freed from death row for every nine executions.

More public scandals erupted as drug companies continued to work with Maya Foa to fight with prison agencies over lethal injection drugs. The stop-start access to drugs meant that states would sometimes build up a number of eligible prisoners in a queue, and when, in 2017, Arkansas announced it would try to execute eight men in less than a month, the actor Johnny Depp showed up at the protests, and billionaire Richard Branson warned that the state would suffer economically because European companies wouldn't want to do business there. (In the end, four of the men were executed.) In late 2019, Texas set an execution date for Rodney Reed, who offered compelling new evidence of his innocence, and he attracted the support of Oprah Winfrey, Kim Kardashian West, Beyoncé Knowles-Carter, and other celebrities, just as their predecessors had lined up a generation earlier for Gary Graham. Dr. Phil McGraw personally interviewed Reed on death row and devoted two hours of his popular TV show to urging a stay of execution, which ultimately was granted by the Court of Criminal Appeals. Unlike in the Graham case, the backlash to the celebrity involvement was far more muted, and Texas senator Ted Cruz—who had once defended death sentences for the state before the Supreme Court—called upon the judicial system to carefully examine Reed's evidence.

Most cases did not receive such attention, and Texas continued to carry out a steady schedule of executions. The Texas Defender Service kept issuing reports showing that prosecutors were still withholding important information from defense lawyers and that death row prisoners were still being denied good lawyers at certain stages of their appeals. In 2010, the state legislature allocated money for a new statewide Office of Capital and Forensic Writs, which joined clinics at various law schools to ensure that death row prisoners would not drift toward execution without legal help as they had in the past.

But no matter how many changes were made in the appeals system, the more dramatic transformation was at the front end: In 1994, Texas juries sent forty-three people to death row. After 2014, that number never rose beyond ten, and in 2015 it dropped to two. In 2019, death rows around the country reached their smallest total population since 1992. (There were roughly two hundred prisoners in Texas, a few of whom had been there since the 1970s.) On the horizon was a possible future in which there would be very few prisoners to execute. Even the most publicly infamous murders—the nine people killed by Dylann Roof at a historic black church in Charleston, South Carolina; the seventeen people killed by Nikolas Cruz at a high school in Parkland, Florida; the eleven people killed by Robert Bowers at a synagogue in Pittsburgh, Pennsylvania—sparked debates about whether the death penalty was appropriate rather than overwhelming demands for it to be imposed.

In 2007, Dallasites had elected a black prosecutor named Craig Watkins as district attorney. Watkins's own great-grandfather had been executed by the state, and he set up a unit to root out wrongful convictions. He invited defense lawyers to make presentations long before trial about why their clients should not face death. He started noticing that even when he did pursue a death sentence, as many as half the potential jurors would say they couldn't serve because they didn't support the punishment. Over the following years, many urban counties, in Texas and elsewhere, joined the national criminal justice reform wave and voted in district attorneys who promised to seek the death penalty less often, if at all. Because death penalty prosecutions were so expensive, these counties tended to be the only ones who could afford them anymore, and so these urban political shifts had outsized effects on the death penalty's decline.

The decline could partially be attributed to public outrage over wrongful convictions, and partially to skilled defense lawyering. Partially it was libertarian talk of high costs and big government and Christian talk of human redemption and liberal talk of racial inequality. You could debate which of these factors were more or less influential, but all had played a role. Even if the death penalty were to remain legally viable for the long term, and even if executions continued, it would take an entirely new chapter in the country's political and cultural life to bring the punishment back to prominence.

In 2016, a police officer was murdered in San Antonio and a man was arrested. A hundred miles north, a judge named James Oakley took to Facebook and wrote, "Time for a tree and a rope." The defendant was black, and a screenshot of the post went viral. A state commission ordered Oakley to participate in "racial sensitivity training." The judge apologized, but also claimed "there was never anything racial about my comment."

In fact, he explained, he had been referencing an old television commercial. Ads for Pace salsa, which began running in the 1980s, featured a group of cowboys "somewhere in Texas" who learn that they're eating salsa that was made in New Jersey. One looks at the chef responsible and shouts, "Get a rope!" Oakley was on the board of a electricity cooperative, and at a meeting about how the board should respond, one defender of the judge said, "He wasn't talking about a lynching. He was talking about good West Texas justice." An employee of the cooperative responded, "For those ignorant of United States history, black men were lynched, to instill fear and compliance in the black population, for centuries."

Burnet County, where the judge presided, had been one of hundreds of lynching sites around the country; an 1893 magazine made reference to "the hanging at Burnet, Texas, upon the very slightest suspicion, of a colored girl who was afterwards found to be innocent." But the sort of historical ignorance invoked by the judge's comment was also facing a sustained attack: In 2018, the Equal Justice Initiative opened the National Memorial for Peace and Justice in Montgomery, Alabama, which featured more than eight hundred hanging steel columns, each bearing the names of victims of "racial terror" lynchings in a particular county. Duplicates of the columns were laid in rows nearby, waiting to be claimed by counties willing to display them. At a nearby museum, the organization explicitly compared lynchings to the contemporary death penalty. The organization behind the museum and memorial had been founded by the lawyer Bryan Stevenson to defend death row prisoners, shortly after the capital defense resource center in Alabama was defunded in 1995. He believed that the death penalty was "lynching's stepson" and that Americans would never truly question harsh punishments in the present until they had examined the historical roots of those punishments.

The connections are not all straight lines. Many of the most infamous people executed since the 1970s have been white: Timothy McVeigh, Ted Bundy, John Wayne Gacy. Even a society that never lynched or enslaved people based on the idea of race might have come to respond to violent violations of the social order with death sentences and long terms of incarceration. The desire for retribution has been a consistent feature of the human experience. But the "tree and a rope" comment reflected one story white Americans continue to tell themselves about their criminal justice system: that our taste for harsh punishment was inherited from the frontier rather than the plantation. Tracing the retributive thread in our culture back in time, it has been easy to look away from racially motivated lynchings, and one place our eyes have often rested upon instead is Texas, or rather "Texas," a half-imagined frontier society where harsh punishment was a regrettable necessity.

In Texas, our vision of the South, which many Americans associate with the worst racially motivated atrocities, meets the West, where we imagine a predominantly white population—atrocities against Mexicans and Native Americans are excised here—delivering efficient and honorable justice during the settling of the frontier. We cleanse a punishment of its roots in our darkest moments by tying it to our proudest. This vision remains seductive, and Texans continue to celebrate it and project it to the rest of the country. When Texas governor Rick Perry was running for president in 2011, he was asked at a debate about the 234 executions he had overseen, and before the moderator could even finish the question, the audience burst into applause. "If you come into our state and you kill one of our children, you kill a police officer," Perry responded as the applause died down, "you will face the ultimate justice in the state of Texas." Then he zoomed out: "I think Americans understand justice." We all could be Texans if we so desired.

But as Texas itself changes, these images lose their sheen. The cover of the fortieth anniversary issue of *Texas Monthly*, published in February 2013, displayed the state's signature shape covered in skyscrapers, and inside was the justifying statistic: 85 percent of the state's population now lived in cities. More and more Americans associate Texas not just with Republicans like Rick Perry and Ted Cruz but with Democrats like Beto O'Rourke and Julián Castro. The state's best-known musical export is now Beyoncé, not Willie Nelson or George Strait. Older American readers might associate Texas with white writers like Cormac McCarthy and Larry McMurtry, who tend to place their stories in rural settings, but younger readers are just as likely to know writers of color like Jia Tolentino and Bryan Washington, who lovingly portray Houston and its suburbs. "Some of the most marginalized populations in America take their coffee beside some of the country's richest and most privileged," Washington writes of his native city. "There's always the melting pot analogy, but, really, it's more like hot pot—a dish that's dipped in three, four, and five times, with less regard for the pleasantries than the experience." This is increasingly the Texas we are all getting to know.

The new vision represented a shift only in perception; the hot pot had always been there. In the summer of 2019, on her way to work at the GRACE office, Danalynn Recer saw artists painting a mural on the side of a building. It depicted four women, representing four groups that had settled the Old Sixth Ward in the nineteenth century: the formerly enslaved from Africa, along with immigrants from Italy, Mexico, and Germany. Each woman was holding up a house—bungalow, Victorian, shotgun—against a bright purple sky.

Not long after the Quintero trial, in 2009, Recer was diagnosed with breast cancer. After the surgery and radiation, she spent five years on drugs that often left her exhausted. GRACE survived, but the organization shrank to its smallest size since its inception a decade earlier. She finally married her fellow defense lawyer Morris Moon. It was as if a dam had broken and all the sickness and celebration that are normally scattered throughout a life came rushing in. When she took stock, it seemed like she had jumped from lynching to the death penalty two decades before and then tended to one life-or-death crisis after another. At the beginning, each case felt like a brief binge of work that would end with either an execution or a stay. Then the resource center closed and her peers quit the work or found a new, more sustainable rhythm while Recer threw herself into trials. "I didn't have hobbies, do sports, learn an instrument," she said. "This was everything. No book club. I was doing this: lynching and the death penalty and nothing else. There was this feeling of 'It's a short-term emergency,' so you didn't think about 'Is this what I want to do forever?'"

Over the next few years, Recer kept taking cases, but she was beginning to wonder whether it made sense to revive GRACE to full force, given that it might not be so long before the death penalty disappeared.

She experimented with other ways to promote a more merciful criminal justice system. In 2011 she took on a project that was surprising given her résumé: representing the victim of a crime. Raisuddin Bhuiyan had been shot in 2001 by a man named Mark Stroman, who had vowed retribution against Arabs in the wake of the September 11 attacks. He shot three men working at convenience stores in the Dallas area, all of whom were not Arab but South Asian. Two of them died, and Stroman received the death penalty, but Bhuiyan survived. He had come from Bangladesh to the United States to study (inspired, ironically, by a love for Wild West movies). After the shooting, his marriage ended and he lost his job.

He slowly rebuilt his life, and during a 2009 trip to Mecca for the Hajj pilgrimage he came to a realization: He wanted to forgive Mark Stroman, and to discuss with him, in person, what had transpired between them.

Texas has a victim-offender mediation program, and victims have a right under state law to meet those who harmed them. But Bhuiyan didn't learn this until Stroman was facing a March 2011 execution date. He enlisted a lawyer who happened to be a friend of Recer's husband, and she jumped in to help Bhuiyan meet Stroman. When prison officials refused to allow Bhuiyan into the mediation program, Recer's team sued the state for religious discrimination. The two never met face-to-face before Stroman's execution, although they did speak briefly by phone. Bhuiyan became a minor celebrity, showing how Americans might respond to crime with attitudes other than vengeance, and how executions could compound the trauma of victims.

Even if executions disappeared, any lawyer who thought that punishments in the United States were too harsh and racially biased would not soon run out of things to do. In 2012, the Supreme Court ruled that a person who committed a crime before age eighteen could not be sentenced to life in prison unless a jury or judge was given the chance to consider the specific circumstances of his or her life. When the ruling was made retroactive, hundreds of people who had been in prison since they were teenagers became eligible to have life history investigators join their defense teams.

At the same time, large numbers of defendants—more than had ever been sentenced to death—were receiving sentences of life without parole, which some felt was even harsher than the death penalty, and didn't have a right to such an investigator. But even without court funds, lawyers could push for a more merciful response to crime by looking at the life histories of those they were representing. Recer made presentations at trainings attended by social workers and lawyers who handled all kinds of cases—murders, rapes, thefts—who wanted to know how to research a defendant's background and use it to encourage a less punitive response from the courts. Even if they didn't ultimately win, they could slowly persuade judges—like Elsa Alcala—to see the "diverse human frailties" of the people before them and pull them to the cause of mercy.

In early 2019, Elsa Alcala threw herself into the Texas legislative session. She learned the art of getting fickle politicians to spend their limited time on you, and to find compromises you could count as wins. When a legislator tried to make it possible for people who killed children under age fifteen to get the death penalty without committing a second crime—previously it had been age ten—Alcala found that the family asking for the law to be changed was actually comfortable with life without parole, and she helped get the death penalty cut from the bill.

Alcala's primary goal was to pass a bill to fix some of the problems that had frustrated her as a judge, creating a better way for courts to decide which defendants could not face the death penalty because they were intellectually disabled. This effort failed; State Senator Joan Huffman—another former prosecutor under Johnny Holmes, who had sent Duane Buck to death row—fought Alcala. The proposed reforms gave judges more control, and she argued that they would make it too easy for an "activist judge" to cynically use the issue to take the death penalty off the table. The bill was whittled down to the point where it was largely symbolic. At a hearing, Alcala was visibly frustrated and disappointed. "It's not worth the paper it's written on," she said. Before she sat down, the committee's chair chastised her, saying she was "halfway rude." "You care, I understand," he said, "but you don't have a monopoly on caring, okay?"

"I agree," Alcala responded. Then she said, "I may just join you on the bench next time, to make sure that I prevail. In other words, maybe I'll just run and make sure I can have my voice heard more clearly."

In 2007, decades after his fights over the death penalty at the Supreme Court, Anthony Amsterdam made a rare public appearance at a luncheon for defense lawyers in Manhattan. Now in his seventies, with a large, bushy mustache and skeletal frame, he looked like an Old Testament prophet, and he was just as uninterested in small talk. "We have witnessed a subversion of the very idea that criminal defendants have rights," he thundered. "The blindfold that Justice is supposed to wear, to assure that cases are decided with indifference to the outcome, has been shredded." A writer for *The New Yorker* noted that Amsterdam's "pervasive gloominess left even the sympathetic crowd of lawyers disconcerted," and "when he finished, the applause was understated." He left without eating lunch.

At that moment, Amsterdam was working on at least forty separate capital cases, but never with his own name on the court filings. In the

1980s, he stopped showing his face before the Supreme Court, because he'd criticized the justices so much that he knew he wouldn't get a fair hearing. Behind the scenes, he was as active as ever, helping lawyers prepare for Supreme Court arguments, working on new frontiers of human rights law like the Guantánamo cases, and teaching law students. One lawyer called him an "oracle," and said, "You can sit around the table and fifty of us can say something, then he speaks and that is the end of the argument." (Amsterdam's response to this was "I don't shut up, so other people go to sleep. Naturally that will be the end of the argument.")

Over the course of his long career, Amsterdam had developed a key insight about lawyers that showed up in much of his writing and speaking: They are, more than most people realize, storytellers, and Amsterdam thought his peers could be a lot more effective if they studied the elements of good stories: genre, setting, character, plot, point of view. His students analyzed how courtroom speeches and briefs echoed famous narratives from *High Noon* to *The Great Gatsby*. "We now understand that stories are not just recipes for stringing together a set of 'hard facts,'" he wrote, "[but] that, in some profound, often puzzling way, stories *construct* the facts that comprise them." "Storytelling" and "narrative" can sound fluffy, or like a synonym for political spin, but they are actually "the way most people make sense of the world most of the time," and one can spend a life studying their construction.

A moment of violence demands a response, thus creating the seeds of a narrative: This person hurt me, and so I, or society, must do something. But what story do we look to tell?

At the trial of Juan Quintero, prosecutors told the story of a villain who kills the heroic police officer and will kill again unless the jury, the new heroes of the story, step in and vanquish him with a death sentence, delivering justice to Johnson's grieving family and saving the community from future harm. But the jury was drawn to Danalynn Recer's story, in which Quintero was the protagonist, struggling to escape the abuse of his alcoholic father and immigrating to the United States in hopes of making a better life, and then, threatened with the sudden undoing of that life, shooting the officer in a moment of panic.

It made sense to them that such a man would immediately feel remorseful and hope to spend the rest of his life making up for that terrible moment if only they showed him mercy. Neither story was objectively true; they were two different visions of the same information, each entangled in webs of personal beliefs and cultural influences, each shaped by forces only partially understood by the storyteller herself.

But a lawyer, Amsterdam writes, departs from a storyteller in one crucial way: A lawyer cannot conclude the story. She uses a story to lead the jury or the judge to favor the conclusion she wants, but then she must step back and wait for the conclusion: a decision in her favor, or not. Amsterdam was fond of a quote from the novelist William H. Gass: "Stories fly like arrows toward their morals." The murderer was acting out of free will, or he was responding to the world around him; justice means vengeance or justice means mercy; we are the proud descendants of the frontier or the chastened and searching descendants of the plantation. The lawyers start the story, but the ending is up to us.

ACKNOWLEDGMENTS

After Walter Long finished law school in 1994, he went to work defending death row prisoners at the Texas Resource Center, and after the center folded he continued working on capital cases. He often got to know the families of those he represented and was exposed to their trauma. "In my office, days before her son's execution, a mother went into a catatonic state," he wrote in an essay. "Another mother has told me, 'When my son's execution date was set, I successfully committed suicide, but the paramedics brought me back.'" At a certain point, he began to doubt whether he himself could "emotionally survive another client's execution."

But he also came to feel that the tools of law were inadequate for understanding and addressing what he believed were major failings in the way our society responds to crime. He came to see the death penalty as a public health problem, which radiates pain to communities in complex, little-understood ways. He zoomed out further, studying how other people in other times had led their societies away from violence. He noticed the way these movements relied on personal storytelling. "The abolitionists placed their hope not in sacred texts, but in human empathy," Adam Hochschild wrote of the eighteenth-century British activists who fought to end slavery. "We live with that hope still." Long told me he cried after reading those words.

Eventually Long founded the Texas After Violence Project, a small nonprofit organization that conducts oral histories with people affected by violence, especially murder and capital punishment. This was where we met. Shortly after college, I spent a year working for TAVP, driving around the state, setting up cameras, asking questions, and transcribing many hours of tape. It was not journalism—I did not write much about what I learned, and the interview subjects had ultimate control over the transcripts—but that year unlocked a passion for storytelling and its relationship to justice that led me into journalism and, a decade later, to this book.

I'm also grateful to Virginia Raymond, TAVP's director at the time I worked there, whose rare combination of intellectual rigor and desire to improve the world is an ongoing inspiration. Thank you to the editors who shaped my early stories on the Texas death penalty: Dave Mann, Ayan Mittra, Brandi Grissom Swicegood, Andrea Valdez, and Tana Wojczuk. Thank you, Pamela Colloff, Mike Hall, and Kate Rodemann, for all the encouragement over the years. Thank you, Micah Hauser and Asher Price, for the advice on pitching books, and Dana Goldstein, for the nudge to pitch this one.

Thank you to Neil Barsky for starting *The Marshall Project* and Bill Keller for giving me a professional home there and time to work on this book. I have been incredibly lucky to work with such supportive and thoughtful editors: Geraldine Sealey, Kirsten Danis, Susan Chira, Raha Naddaf, Tom Meagher, and Tim Golden. Thank you to my fellow writers, who have become my community: Alysia Santo, Christie Thompson, Eli Hager, Ken Armstrong, Keri Blakinger, Nicole Lewis, Joseph Neff, Beth Schwartzapfel, Andrew Cohen, Cary Aspinwall, Jamiles Lartey, Anna Flagg, Abbie VanSickle, and Simone Weichselbaum. Thanks as well to Ruth Baldwin.

Thank you to the J. Anthony Lukas Awards, administered by the Columbia Journalism School and the Nieman Foundation for Journalism at Harvard University, for the Work-in-Progress Award that funded the final stages of this book. Along with Walter Long, thank you to

Jordan Steiker, Carol Steiker, Joshua Reiss, Matt Puckett, Elizabeth Vartkessian, and Evan Mandery for reading drafts and offering comments.

Thank you to the archivists and clerks who helped me access files: Abel Acosta and Audrey Banda at the Texas Court of Criminal Appeals; Jodie Boyle at the University at Albany, SUNY; Tonia Wood at the Texas State Library and Archives Commission in Austin; Pilar Baskett at Texas A&M University; and Lisa M. Henry at the University of Oklahoma. I am especially grateful to Kendall Newton at the Dolph Briscoe Center for American History, University of Texas at Austin, for help finding material that had not yet been officially processed. Thank you to journalist Rachel Siegel, who tracked down Potter Stewart's papers at Yale University Library. Thank you, Evan Mandery, for helping me access key NAACP LDF documents.

Thank you to Julie Tate, who fact-checked the entire book.

At Crown, thank you to Aubrey Martinson, Emily Hotaling, Evan Camfield, Emily DeHuff, Jo Metsch, Richard Elman, and Amelia Zalcman.

When you write about living people, you ask them to grant you access to their inner lives without knowing how they will be rendered on the page. I am grateful to everyone I interviewed, but especially to Elsa Alcala and Danalynn Recer for agreeing to be primary figures in the book, as well as to Allison Vickers, Steven Reis, Robert Owen, Kenneth Dean, Buster McWhorter, Edward Capetillo, Elizabeth Vartkessian, "Dan," Craig Washington, Rebecca Gregory, David Gregory, Jr., and Shirley Gregory.

David Patterson, my agent, helped shape the vision for this book in ways large and small. Thank you as well to Aemilia Phillips and Hannah Schwartz.

Emma Berry, my editor at Crown and now a friend, is this book's second author. Her ethical standards, sense of history and storytelling, and attention to the art of a good sentence are reflected on every page of this book. I hope we work together again.

Before I met any of the people mentioned here, I was shaped by my mother, Lorraine Chammah. While caring for my father, the late Albert Chammah, she raised me to see the world as a place full of wonder, and supported me as I found my way of contributing.

Then I made a family of my own with Emily Smith Chammah, my partner in writing and everything else. She coached me through the many anxieties brought about by the research for this book, and read countless drafts—sometimes of a chapter, sometimes of a text message to a source. Most of all, she inspired me through her own ability to tell stories, and to keep in the front of one's mind why we do it: to grant people access to each other, so they will come to look at one another with love and curiosity rather than fear. It is a lesson I will be learning forever, and I am so grateful that I get to do it with her.

NOTES AND SOURCES

This book relies on more than two hundred interviews, most of which I conducted specifically for the book beginning in 2016, but some of which I conducted previously for *The Marshall Project*, *The Texas Observer*, *Texas Monthly*, and *The Texas Tribune*. I also relied on oral history interviews conducted by the Texas After Violence Project for both specific facts and broad perspective.

PROLOGUE

The account of the execution of Charlie Brooks is drawn from an interview with Carroll Pickett and his memoir *Within These Walls* (New York: St. Martin's Press, 2002), an interview with Dick J. Reavis and his article "Charlie Brooks' Last Words," *Texas Monthly* (February 1983), and interviews with Eric Freedman, Anita Ashton, and Joel Berger. I used press clippings in the papers of Randy Halperin, housed at the National Death Penalty Archive, M. E. Grenander Department of Special Collections and Archives, University Libraries, University at Albany, State University of New York. The material about the Brooks family is drawn from 2013 interviews conducted by the Texas After Violence Project (Texas After Violence Project Collection of Oral History Interviews, Human Rights Documentation Initiative, University of Texas Libraries, University of Texas at Austin). The material about the Gregory family is based on my 2017 interviews with David Gregory, Jr., Rebecca Gregory, and Shirley Gregory. Jack Pursley, reached via a family member, declined an interview, but to describe him I drew on Pickett's book as well as John DiIulio, Jr.'s *Governing Prisons* (New York: Free Press, 1990) and Jim Willett's *Warden: Texas Prison Life and Death from the Inside Out* (Houston: Bright Sky Press, 2005). Execution and death sentence numbers in this chapter and throughout the book are drawn from the Death Penalty Information Center, the Texas Judicial Council, the Bureau of Justice

Statistics at the federal Department of Justice, and the Texas Coalition to Abolish the Death Penalty.

3 **"We will soon be having an execution"**: Carroll Pickett, *Within These Walls* (New York: St. Martin's Press, 2002), 53.

4 **Pursley had been asked:** Jim Willett, *Warden: Texas Prison Life and Death from the Inside Out* (Houston: Bright Sky Press, 2005), 138.

4 **"I don't know a thing"**: Pickett, *Within These Walls*, 55.

4 **"all of the air"**: Ibid., 56.

4 **"framed in mint green"**: Ibid., 57.

4 **the smallest details:** John J. DiIulio, Jr., *Governing Prisons* (New York: Free Press, 1987), 141.

5 **"a scene like that"**: Pickett, *Within These Walls*, 59.

5 **"squirming, sparkle-eyed"**: Dick Reavis, "Charlie Brooks' Last Words," *Texas Monthly*, February 1983, texasmonthly.com/articles/charlie-brooks-last-words.

6 **"I decided to try Islam"**: Ibid.

7 **not uncommon:** Ken Armstrong, "Can Prosecutors Put the Same Gun in the Hands of More Than One Shooter?" *The Marshall Project*, November 6, 2017, themarshallproject.org/2017/11/06/can-prosecutors-put-the-same-gun-in-the-hands-of-more-than-one-shooter.

7 **invalidating his death sentence:** Loudres v. State, 614 S.W.2d 407 (Tex. Crim. App. 1980).

7 **spent that Thanksgiving holed up:** Joe Holley, "Death Race," *Texas Observer*, December 24, 1982, 1.

8 **"The merits of Brooks' claims"**: Brooks v. Estelle, 459 U.S. 1061 (1982).

8 **"In prison, you've got rights"**: Pickett, *Within These Walls*, 67.

9 **did not want to see them:** Ibid., 73.

9 **Joyce Brooks was at a friend's house:** Interview with Joyce Hazzard Easley, Texas After Violence Project Collection of Oral History Interviews, Human Rights Documentation Initiative, University of Texas Libraries, University of Texas at Austin, av.lib.utexas.edu/index.php?title=TAVP:Joyce_Hazzard_Easley.

9 **"prancing and going back and forth and crying"**: Ibid.

9 **Opponents of the death penalty:** "Organizations Will Meet to Protest Execution," *Huntsville Item*, December 6, 1982, 1A, Rick Halpern Papers, M. E. Grenander Department of Special Collections & Archives, University at Albany, State University of New York.

9 **Derrek thought:** Interview with Derrek Brooks, Texas After Violence Project Collection of Oral History Interviews, Human Rights Documentation Initiative, University of Texas Libraries, University of Texas at Austin, av.lib.utexas.edu/index.php?title=TAVP:Derrek_Brooks_1.

9 **a state official appeared:** Interview with Keith Brooks, Texas After Violence Project Collection of Oral History Interviews, Human Rights Documentation Initiative, University of Texas Libraries, University of Texas at Austin, av.lib.utexas.edu/index.php?title=TAVP:Keith_Brooks_1.

10 **"It's time to go"**: Pickett, *Within These Walls*, 73.

10 **Pursley had been in a car crash:** "Prison Warden's Trip Postponed," *Victoria Advocate*, January 21, 1983, 3C.

10 **A doctor had checked the prisoner:** Steve Carrell, "Execution Controversy Faces Physician," *American Medical News* 26, January 21, 1983, 25, cited in Deborah W. Denno, "The Lethal Injection Quandary: How Medicine Has Dismantled the Death Penalty," *Fordham Law Review* 49 (2007), ir.lawnet.fordham.edu/flr/vol76/iss1/3.

12 **conduct an autopsy:** Ron Creel, "Brooks' Body Claimed in Houston by Family," *Huntsville Item*, December 7, 1982, 1A.

12 **a cartoon in *The Huntsville Item*:** Doug Graham, "The Domino Theory," *Huntsville Item*, December 7, 1982, 4A.

12 **"I didn't know that I would feel this relief":** "Victim's Widow, Mother Are Relieved," Associated Press, December 7, 1982.

13 **"Now that I'm an adult":** Interview with Derrek Brooks, Texas After Violence Project Collection of Oral History Interviews.

13 **reveled in his father's status:** Interview with Keith Brooks, Texas After Violence Project Collection of Oral History Interviews.

15 **the long span of the human experience:** The British historian Richard Ward has written that capital punishment "has been practised at some point in the history of virtually all known societies and places." Richard Ward, *A Global History of Execution and the Criminal Corpse* (Basingstoke, U.K.: Palgrave Macmillan, 2015), ncbi.nlm.nih.gov/books/NBK379343/. The primatologist Richard Wrangham has looked even earlier, proposing that a version of capital punishment was crucial to the earliest forms of domestication among humans, as adult males banded together to kill those showing too much of the wrong type of aggressive behavior. The most extreme version of this argument places capital punishment at the very root of how humans began to conceptualize basic ideas about morality. Richard Wrangham, *The Goodness Paradox: The Strange Relationship Between Virtue and Violence in Human Evolution* (New York: Pantheon, 2019).

15 **"mildness":** Alexis de Tocqueville, *Democracy in America*, translated and edited by Harvey C. Mansfield and Delba Winthrop (Chicago: University of Chicago Press, 2002), 538.

15 **transformations in its cultural and sexual mores:** Steven Pinker, *The Better Angels of Our Natures: Why Violence Has Declined* (New York: Viking, 2011), 106–15.

16 **more people per capita:** "State Execution Rates," Death Penalty Information Center, accessed June 10, 2019, deathpenaltyinfo.org/state-execution-rates.

16 **other states sent more:** "Death Sentences per Capita by State," Death Penalty Information Center, accessed June 10, 2019, deathpenaltyinfo.org/death-sentences-capita-state.

16 **sat a smarmy politician:** "Texas Campaign 1," *Saturday Night Live*, March 17, 1990, nbc.com/saturday-night-live/video/texas-campaign-1/n9895.

16 **when a character on *The Simpsons*:** *The Simpsons*, "New Kid on the Block," season 8, episode 4, written by Conan O'Brien, directed by Wes Archer, Fox Network, November 1992, youtube.com/watch?v=Ki0BggwZL24.

17 **"If you come to Texas":** Ron White, "Ron White—Death Penalty," *Comedy Central* Video File, December 28, 2002, accessed June 10, 2019, cc.com/video

-playlists/kw3fjO/the-opposition-with-jordan-klepper-welcome-to-the-opposition
-w—jordan-klepper/5z52ao.

17 **"Down in parts of Texas"**: Robin Helene Conley, "Doing Death in Texas: Language and Jury Decision-Making in Texas Death Penalty Trials" (Ph.D. dissertation, University of California, Los Angeles, 2011), 51, ncjrs.gov/pdffiles1/nij/grants/236354.pdf.

17 **"expressions of the will"**: Franklin Zimring, *The Contradictions of Capital Punishment* (New York: Oxford University Press, 2004), 89.

17 **Their citizens don't necessarily get to choose**: A notable exception is Japan, another democratic country in which citizens choose to sentence people to death.

17 **the days of no trials at all**: The scholar David Garland has described the executions of the late twentieth century as "anti-lynchings," arguing that the rituals and legal process surrounding them appear designed to avoid an association with what came before. See David Garland, "The Peculiar Forms of American Capital Punishment," *Social Research* 74, no. 2 (Summer 2007): 458.

CHAPTER 1

I have drawn here on recordings of Supreme Court oral arguments, the Texas Legislature's debates on House Bill 200 (obtained from the Legislative Reference Library of Texas), and interviews with Donald Adams, Terry Doyle, John Green, Tom Hanna, Frank Maloney, Michael McCormick, Bill Meier, Jack Ogg, Max Sherman, Joe Spurlock, Bill Sullivant, Carol Vance, Craig Washington, Dain Whitworth, and Joseph Wyatt. An especially helpful analysis of their deliberations is in Eric F. Citron, "Sudden Death: The Legislative History of Future Dangerousness and the Texas Death Penalty," *Yale Law & Policy Review* 25, no. 1 (2006).

The best account of Anthony Amsterdam and the LDF's crusade against the death penalty is found in *A Wild Justice: The Death and Resurrection of Capital Punishment in America* by Evan Mandery. For a personal account, I recommend Michael Meltsner's *Cruel and Unusual: The Supreme Court and Capital Punishment* (New York: Random House, 1974). Much of the broader history about the American death penalty is drawn from Stuart Banner's *The Death Penalty: An American History* (Cambridge, Mass.: Harvard University Press, 2002) and Louis Masur's *Rites of Execution: Capital Punishment and the Transformation of American Culture, 1776–1865* (New York: Oxford University Press, 1991). Two useful Texas-specific sources were *The Rope, the Chair, and the Needle: Capital Punishment in Texas, 1923–1990*, by James W. Marquart, Sheldon Ekland-Olson, and Jonathan R. Sorensen (Austin: University of Texas Press, 1994), and *Lethal Injection: Capital Punishment in Texas During the Modern Era* by Jonathan R. Sorensen and Rocky LeAnn Pilgrim (Austin: University of Texas Press, 2006). I also found helpful press clippings, legislative recordings, and transcripts among Sorensen's papers at the National Death Penalty Archive in Albany.

23 **laughed and whooped**: "The Court on the Death Penalty," *Newsweek*, July 10, 1972, 20.

23 **wrapped a guard**: Martin Dyckman, "Life Arrives on Death Row in an Embrace," *St. Petersburg Times*, June 30, 1972, A1.

23 **wave of applause:** "What Happens Next Top Question for Texas Prisoners on Death Row," *Vernon Daily Record,* June 30, 1972, 3.

23 **stretched his arms out:** "Death Row Cheers Decision," *Austin American,* June 30, 1972, 1.

23 **above the fold:** "Supreme Court, 5–4, Bars Death Penalty as It Is Imposed Under Present Statutes," *New York Times,* June 30, 1972, A1.

23 **"If I ever get out":** "Happy Scene on Death Row in Huntsville," *San Antonio Express,* June 30, 1972, A3.

24 **a candidate for district attorney there openly questioned:** "On State Killings," *Texas Observer,* May, 6, 1960, 4.

24 **polls showed less than half:** "Death Penalty," Gallup, accessed June 11, 2019, gallup.com/poll/1606/death-penalty.aspx.

24 **dictate a brief from memory:** Nadya Labi, "A Man Against the Machine," *NYU Law Magazine,* Autumn 2007, 14.

25 **a brief statement:** Rudolph v. Alabama, 375 U.S. 889 (1963).

25 **sent students across the South:** Stuart Banner, *The Death Penalty: An American History* (Cambridge, Mass.: Harvard University Press, 2003), 251.

25 **"For each year the United States":** Michael Meltsner, *Cruel and Unusual: The Supreme Court and Capital Punishment* (New York: Random House, 1974), 107.

25 **struck down a federal law:** United States v. Jackson, 390 U.S. 570 (1968).

25 **declared that citizens who had "conscientious scruples":** Witherspoon v. Illinois, 391 U.S. 510 (1968).

25 **"Time is running out":** Richard Nixon, Presidential Nomination Acceptance Speech, Republican National Convention, Miami Beach, Florida, August 8, 1968, 4president.org/speeches/nixon1968acceptance.htm.

25 **ruled against a death row prisoner:** McGautha v. California, 402 U.S. 183 (1971).

25 **"This is an oblique attack":** Banner, *Death Penalty,* 256–57.

25 **thought it was perfectly constitutional:** Evan J. Mandery, *A Wild Justice: The Death and Resurrection of Capital Punishment in America* (New York: W. W. Norton, 2014), 114.

26 **others on Texas death row were apprehensive:** Clyde Walter, "Fate of 41 Men on Death Row Uncertain," *San Antonio Express,* June 30, 1972, A3.

27 **"gathered in a gym":** "The Court on the Death Penalty," *Newsweek.*

27 **Charles Manson and Sirhan Sirhan:** Jordan M. Steiker, "Penry v. Lynaugh: The Hazards of Predicting the Future," in *Death Penalty Stories,* edited by John Blume and Jordan M. Steiker (St. Paul: Foundation Press, 2009), 292–96.

27 **"In outlawing the death penalty":** "Patty Escapes!" *Texas Observer,* June 21, 1974, 8, archives.texasobserver.org/issue/1974/06/21#page=8.

27 **49 percent:** "Death Penalty," Gallup.

28 **"scab job":** Gary Brown, *Singin' a Lonesome Song: Texas Prison Tales* (Plano: Republic of Texas Press, 2001), 42.

28 **They pursued legislation:** Sam Kinch, Jr., "Sharpstown Stock-Fraud Scandal," *Handbook of Texas Online,* Texas Historical Association, accessed June 13, 2019, tshaonline.org/handbook/online/articles/mqs01.

28 **All that, and a new death penalty law:** In the preceding months, Texas governor Preston Smith had called a special session of the legislature to fix the death penalty law, but the lawmakers did not get anywhere, partially because it was such a complicated task. Eric F. Citron, "Sudden Death: The Legislative History of Future Dangerousness and the Texas Death Penalty," *Yale Law & Policy Review* 25, no. 1 (2006): 163.

29 **were considering a range of potential solutions:** Mandery, *Wild Justice*, 251.

30 **which types of murders:** The two primary bills before the House Committee on Criminal Jurisprudence were H.B. 229, by Frank Lombardino, which restricted the death penalty to only the killing of a policeman, and H.B. 200, which included a longer list of crimes.

31 **"Of those who have done extreme wrong":** Plato, *Plato in Twelve Volumes*, vol. 3, translated by W.R.M. Lamb (Cambridge, Mass.: Harvard University Press, 1967), perseus.tufts.edu/hopper/text?doc=Perseus%3Atext%3A1999.01.01 78%3Atext%3DGorg.%3Asection%3D525c.

31 **"All the people will hear":** Holy Bible, New International Version, Deuteronomy 17:12–13.

31 **a common feature:** David Garland et al., *America's Death Penalty: Between Past and Present* (New York: NYU Press, 2011), 30.

32 **Samuel Adams even believed:** Louis Masur, *Rites of Execution: Capital Punishment and the Transformation of American Culture, 1776–1865* (New York: Oxford University Press, 1989), 30.

32 **fifty thousand people:** Banner, *Death Penalty*, 25.

32 **"naturally brings with it":** Ibid., 12, 317n13.

32 **"The dreadful Deed":** Ibid., 42.

33 **"lessens the horror":** Benjamin Rush, *The Selected Writings of Benjamin Rush*, edited by Dagobert D. Runes (New York: Philosophical Library, 1947), http:// press-pubs.uchicago.edu/founders/documents/amendVIIIs16.html.

33 **had no clear effect on homicide rates:** A 2012 survey of numerous scholarly studies, by the National Research Council, found the evidence of deterrence largely inconclusive in either direction and advised against using it in policy debates. See Daniel S. Nagin and John V. Pepper, *Deterrence and the Death Penalty* (Washington, D.C.: National Academies Press, 2012), 2.

33 **Syrian immigrant family:** "Semaan Family History & Genealogy," *Ancient Faces*, accessed June 13, 2019, ancientfaces.com/surname/semaan-family-history/ 16641.

33 **"devastate a hostile witness":** "Remembering Charlie Butts," *San Antonio Lawyer*, January-February 2016, 18.

33 **"No client has ever":** "Barons of the Court," *Texas Monthly*, November 1974, texasmonthly.com/articles/barons-of-the-court/.

34 **"slang appendage":** Frederick Law Olmsted, *A Journey Through Texas; or, A Saddle-Trip on the Southwestern Frontier* (Lincoln: University of Nebraska Press, 2004), 124.

35 **"only in certain kinds":** Edward Ayers, *Vengeance and Justice: Crime and Punishment in the 19th-Century American South* (New York: Oxford University Press, 1984), 26.

35 **"the human hallmarks of most true frontiers"**: T. R. Fehrenbach, *Lone Star: A History of Texas and the Texans* (New York: Macmillan, 1968), 256.

35 **The first working model**: Ibid., 475.

35 **"no duty to retreat"**: Richard Maxwell Brown, *No Duty to Retreat: Violence and Values in American History and Society* (Norman: Oklahoma University Press, 1991), 26.

37 **hooked up to a lie detector**: "The 1991 Bum Steer Awards," *Texas Monthly*, January 1991, 85.

37 **forty-three-hour filibuster**: Manny Fernandez, "You Call That a Filibuster? Texas Still Claims Record," *New York Times*, July 3, 2013, nytimes.com/2013/07/04/us/politics/you-call-that-a-filibuster-texas-still-claims-record.html.

37 **"the element of mercy"**: Furman v. Georgia, 408 U.S. 238.

37 **Meier preferred letting juries**: Meier also wanted to let judges overrule juries in order to maintain consistency across the state. Discussions of Meier's approach are also found in Ana Otero, "The Death of Fairness: Texas's Future Dangerousness Revisited," *University of Denver Criminal Law Review* 4 (Summer 2014): 1–60. Another good resource is Michael Kuhn, "House Bill 200: The Legislative Attempt to Reinstate Capital Punishment in Texas," *Houston Law Review* 11 (1974): 410–23. Kuhn includes a helpful comparison of the House and Senate versions of the bill as well as the final outcomes of the particular policy disputes.

39 **"wins admirers"**: "The Ten Best and the Ten Worst Legislators," *Texas Monthly*, July 1981, 106.

39 **holding up a pair of jeans**: Rachel Graves, "Craig Washington Returns to the Spotlight," *Houston Chronicle*, March 6, 2005, chron.com/news/houston-texas/article/Craig-Washington-returns-to-the-spotlight-1654534.php.

39 **more than four thousand**: *Lynching in America: Confronting the Legacy of Racial Terror*, 3rd ed. (Montgomery, Ala.: Equal Justice Initiative, 2015), 4.

40 **day's outing and entertainment**: Philip Dray, *At the Hands of Persons Unknown: The Lynching of Black America* (New York: Modern Library, 2002), 17.

40 **"The things that influenced"**: Richard Wright, *Black Boy: A Record of Childhood and Youth* (London: Vintage, 2000), 173.

40 **white scholars touched lynching**: W. Fitzhugh Brundage, "Introduction," in *Under Sentence of Death: Lynching in the South*, edited by W. Fitzhugh Brundage (Chapel Hill: University of North Carolina Press, 1997), 10.

40 **Some sociologists**: Ibid., 8.

40 **more than eight hundred**: *Lynching in America*, 4.

40 **popular view of the state's origins**: Annette Gordon-Reed, "The Real Texas," *New York Review of Books*, October 24, 2019, nybooks.com/articles/2019/10/24/real-texas-history/.

41 **exported to the rest of the country**: Brundage, *Under Sentence*, 1.

41 **"I associated lynching"**: Joel Williamson, "Wounds Not Scars: Lynching, the National Conscience, and the American Historian," *Journal of American History* 83, no. 4 (March 1997): 1229. Williamson argued that the moral dilemma posed by the discovery of the Nazi death camps in 1945—How could this be us? How could this happen in a modern Western civilization?—fueled a refusal to

look lynching in the face, at least for his generation. International confrontations with Nazism and Communism pushed Americans to ignore parts of their history that would mar their sense of moral superiority on the world stage. "Arguably, southern whites lynching blacks in the turn-of-the-century South while northern whites looked on is as close as America has ever come to experiencing our own holocaust," he wrote. "And that, too, is a wound that will not heal, a wound, in fact, that we whites recurrently feel but prefer not to see."

41 **the NAACP LDF hired:** Patricia Bernstein, *The First Waco Horror: The Lynching of Jesse Washington and the Rise of the NAACP* (College Station: Texas A&M University Press, 2005).

41 **"The great ritual of state":** David Garland, *Peculiar Institution: America's Death Penalty in an Age of Abolition* (New York: Oxford University Press, 2010), 134.

41 **J. W. Thomas was elected to the Texas Senate:** James W. Marquart, Sheldon Eckland-Olson, and Jonathan R. Sorensen, *The Rope, The Chair, and the Needle: Capital Punishment in Texas, 1923–1990* (Austin: University of Texas Press, 1994), 13.

42 **The legislature appropriated $5,000:** Ibid.

42 **The warden of the prison resigned:** Ibid., 15.

42 **the first closed-door executions:** Ibid.

42 **"I can only be thankful":** "Dope and Death," *Texas Observer,* May 25, 1973, 8, archives.texasobserver.org/issue/1973/05/25#page=9.

42 **"seems to invite":** Garland, *Peculiar Institution,* 9–10.

43 **5,005 years:** J. D. Arnold, "Wretched Excess in Dallas," *Texas Observer,* May 11, 1973, 9, archives.texasobserver.org/issue/1973/05/11#page=9.

43 **With only three days left:** Citron, "Sudden Death," 162.

43 **Most of the room:** According to an interview with then-Rep. Terry Doyle, at first they sat down with three potential bills, one mandatory and two discretionary (one would give the final say on life or death to a jury, the other to a judge). Citron, "Sudden Death," 170; "Death Penalty Bill Goes to Conferees," *Houston Chronicle,* May 25, 1987; "In Search of a Formula," *Dallas Times Herald,* May 25, 1973; "Make It Straight Death," *Dallas Morning News,* May 16, 1973.

43 **Meier pleaded with them:** That night, he swayed fellow senator Jack Ogg (Citron, "Sudden Death," 171). Ogg confirmed this in an interview before his death in 2018.

43 **the next morning:** "Death Penalty Joint Panel Fails to Reach Compromise," *Austin American-Statesman,* May 26, 1973, A1.

43 **What if the death penalty was mandatory:** Citron, "Sudden Death," 171; "Compromise Bill Sought to Legalize Death Penalty," *Houston Chronicle,* May 27, 1973. This source says Meier arrived Saturday with the idea of exceptions. Meier also thought that if the Supreme Court decided in the end that the mandatory bill really was constitutional, they could simply lop off the part of the law about exceptions.

44 **"continuing threat to society":** There is no record of how Meier's idea of "exceptions" transformed into the "special questions" that juries would answer to determine death. Multiple sources present confirmed the basic dynamic of

prosecutors discussing what kinds of cases tended to produce a death sentence, and that this was the basis of the "future dangerousness" question. My sources did not remember the "exceptions" suggestion from Meier. And questions remain about who precisely came up with the questions. In an interview with me, as well as with Abbie VanSickle ("A Deadly Question," *Atlantic*, November 19, 2016, theatlantic.com/politics/archive/2016/11/a-deadly-question/ 508232/), Meier credited both himself and Rep. Terry Doyle, a former prosecutor, with the future-dangerousness question. In a previous interview, he gave Doyle more of the credit for the wording (*Lethal Injection: Capital Punishment in Texas During the Modern Era* by Jonathan R. Sorensen and Rocky LeAnn Pilgrim [Austin: University of Texas Press, 2006], 170n11). Law professor Ana Otero saw in the future-dangerousness question elements of Meier's earlier bill, which would allow juries to give weight to whether defendants had been convicted of violent crimes before. Sen. Jack Ogg, in an interview with me before his death, recalled being involved in the compromise that produced the questions. The *Austin American-Statesman*, at the time of writing, credited Rep. Robert Maloney with the compromise, which included the questions ("Panel Okays Death Bill with Life Sentence Option," *Austin American-Statesman*, May 28, 1973). Maloney told me that he wrote the questions, but he declined to give an interview. The scholar Jonathan Sorensen notes that the legislators would likely have seen a "Model Sentencing Act" drafted by the Council of Judges of the National Council on Crime and Delinquency, which listed dangerousness as a basis for sentencing.

44 **evened the playing field:** In interviews, Donald Adams said, "I think that gives the defendant a break—that's a hard burden of proof for the state," while Meier called their bill "a broad step away from the mandatory bill," and Jack Ogg said he thought it left "a broad range of judgment for the jury."

44 **spare especially sympathetic murderers:** Citron, "Sudden Death," 172.

44 **"hoped such a system":** Ibid.

44 **114–30 in the House, 27–4 in the Senate:** "Turn Out the Lights, the Party's Over," *Texas Observer*, June 15, 1973, 12, archives.texasobserver.org/issue/ 1973/06/15#page=12.

CHAPTER 2

Much of this chapter draws on Evan Mandery's *A Wild Justice*. In addition to Supreme Court oral arguments, along with court records from the Jurek case—at the Texas State Libraries and Archives Commission—I drew on interviews with Peggy Davis, Jerry Jurek, and Emmett Summers. Davis shared her memos. Anthony Amsterdam, David Kendall, and George Rutherglen answered emails. I drew on *John Hill for the State of Texas: My Years as Attorney General* (College Station: Texas A&M Press, 2008). An especially useful source on Amsterdam's strategy and its ramifications is found in Jordan M. Steiker, "*Penry v. Lynaugh:* The Hazards of Predicting the Future," in *Death Penalty Stories*, edited by John Blume and Jordan M. Steiker (St. Paul: Foundation Press, 2009).

Determining how Supreme Court justices reach their conclusions is difficult. Although the justices generally write out their reasoning in individual decisions at far more length than do members of the executive or legislative branches of government, they tend to say little publicly about the process that leads to those writings. Many former clerks are reticent when approached by reporters, and some are hostile; one former Rehnquist clerk wrote to me in an email that his service "included an express obligation of confidentiality regarding whatever I may have seen, heard, or done." He called my request for an interview "strange" and added, "Whatever may or may not have transpired 'behind the scenes' . . . cannot possibly have any legitimate value in our society."

In addition to Mandery's book, Bob Woodward and Scott Armstrong reported on the 1976 decisions in *The Brethren: Inside the Supreme Court* (New York: Simon & Schuster, 1979). Based on leaked documents and interviews with former clerks and a few of the justices themselves, this book was a bombshell when it was published in 1979. In the interest of source protection, the authors chose to forgo citations, so it is impossible to verify their claims—some of which were later disproved—or to determine who had a vested interest in making any particular fact known to the public. With a tone that sometimes feels gossipy, *The Brethren* can give the impression that the justices are more motivated by personal politics than by good-faith intellectual engagement. (Perhaps the Rehnquist clerk was so frosty because he thought I was looking for gossip.) For more, see George Anastaplo, "Legal Realism, the New Journalism, and *The Brethren,*" *Duke Law Journal,* vol. 1983, no. 5 (November 1983). In my account of the Jurek decision, I rely on both Mandery and Woodward-Armstrong in terms of analysis, but when there is disagreement, Mandery is the one to trust, since he cites the original documents, which I was able to check myself.

I consulted the papers of Lewis Powell, Jr., which are online, and his biography: John C. Jeffries, *Justice Lewis F. Powell, Jr.* (New York: Scribner, 1994). I accessed the drafts by Justice Potter Stewart, housed at Yale University Library, with the help of the journalist Rachel Siegel. The papers of John Paul Stevens are not yet public, though he has written on his regrets in *Five Chiefs: A Supreme Court Memoir* (New York: Little, Brown, 2011) and *The Making of a Justice: Reflections on My First 94 Years* (New York: Little, Brown, 2019).

46 **speeding down the road:** Jay Brakefield and Barry Boesch, "Death in Texas," *Texas Observer,* January 28, 1977, 4.

46 **shoeless and shirtless:** Ibid.

46 **One of the arresting officers:** Sara Sneath, "Special Report: A Life Sentence," *Victoria Advocate,* February 28, 2016, victoriaadvocate.com/news/local/special -report-a-life-sentence/article_bf6a9133-d7ee-5ea7-9919-836069de4c38.html.

47 **They pulled her into a muddy boat:** Ibid.

49 **"sociopathic":** Brakefield and Boesch, "Death in Texas," 4.

50 **"We may say there is a twenty percent":** Jurek v. State, 522 S.W.2d 934 (Tex. Crim. App. 1975).

51 **Gerald Ford and Jimmy Carter:** Mandery, *Wild Justice,* 321.

51 **would be a crucial indicator:** Ibid.

51 **actually involved too much discretion:** "Fowler v. North Carolina," *Oyez,* accessed June 26, 2019, oyez.org/cases/1975/73-7031.

53 **his eyes glassy and his speech slurred:** Mandery, *Wild Justice,* 319.

53 **The justices decided to hear five cases:** There were political dimensions to the choice of which cases to take. Chief Justice Warren Burger wanted to take the case of Timothy McCorquodale, a white man who had raped, tortured, mutilated, and killed a seventeen-year-old he accused of being a "nigger lover" and then desecrated her body. Taking this case would have helped Burger demonstrate that the new laws were succeeding in isolating the worst of the worst. It would also have undermined the LDF's position that the death penalty was primarily a product of white racism toward minorities. Mandery, *Wild Justice*, 345.

53 **"quasi-mandatory":** *Gregg v. Georgia*, Supreme Court Case Files Collection, Box 33, Powell Papers, Lewis F. Powell, Jr., Archives, Washington & Lee University School of Law, Virginia (hereafter: Powell Papers), scholarlycommons.law.wlu .edu/casefiles/97/, 74-6257 GreggGeorgia1976Jan8-12.pdf, 16.

53 **a lot of room for jury choice:** Ibid., 15.

54 **Many of the justices' clerks:** Mandery, *Wild Justice*, 355.

54 **"Maybe (I doubt it, but maybe)":** Ibid., 359.

54 **"We were sure if the Supreme Court had any balls":** Ibid.

54 **One of Amsterdam's assistants:** Ibid., 360.

54 **he would risk making matters worse:** For an extended discussion of Amsterdam's quandary, see Jordan M. Steiker, *"Penry v. Lynaugh:* The Hazards of Predicting the Future," in *Death Penalty Stories,* edited by John Blume and Jordan M. Steiker (St. Paul: Foundation Press, 2009), 292–96.

55 **There is no evidence:** Mandery, *Wild Justice*, 361.

55 **he relied on Davis:** Ibid., 357.

55 **"exotics":** Ibid., 375.

55 **dark rain clouds:** Ibid., 372.

56 **Amsterdam's opening:** "Jurek v. Texas," *Oyez,* accessed June 26, 2019, oyez .org/cases/1975/75-5394.

56 **"Amsterdam doesn't like these":** Powell Papers, 74-6257_GreggGeorgia1976 FebMar.pdf, 25.

56 **look like a compromiser:** Mandery, *Wild Justice*, 375.

56 **"fairly persuasive":** Powell Papers, 74-6257_GreggGeorgia1976FebMar. pdf, 27.

56 **Amsterdam is "not interested":** Ibid., 28.

56 **"right of legislatures":** Ibid., 27.

57 **lispy twang:** R. G. Ratcliffe, "Former Texas Chief Justice John Hill Dies," *Houston Chronicle,* July 9, 2007, chron.com/news/houston-texas/article/Former-Texas -Chief-Justice-John-Hill-dies-1829705.php.

57 **"My trial lawyer instincts pushed me":** *John Hill for the State of Texas: My Years as Attorney General* (College Station: Texas A&M Press, 2008), 178.

57 **sixty reported cases:** "Capital Murder Study," Texas Judicial Council, 1976, Executive Director Files, Box 1989/058-2, Criminal Justice Division records, Texas Office of the Governor, Archives and Information Services Division, Texas State Library and Archives Commission.

58 **"Strong jury speech!":** Powell Papers, 74-6257_GreggGeorgia1976FebMar. pdf, 29.

58 **it wasn't meant as one:** Mandery, *Wild Justice*, 381.

59 **pondering the what-might-have-beens:** Ibid., 397.

60 **"Now I know what it's like":** Ibid., 400.

60 **When the justices gathered two days later:** Del Dickson, *The Supreme Court in Conference (1940–1985): The Private Discussions Behind Nearly 300 Supreme Court Decisions* (New York: Oxford University Press, 2001), 620–22.

60 **how bloody the results:** Mandery, *Wild Justice*, 402.

60 **"lawless use of the legal system":** Journalists Bob Woodward and Scott Armstrong write that Stevens initially voted to strike down the Texas law, but this is contradicted by Powell's notes. See Bob Woodward and Scott Armstrong, *The Brethren: Inside the Supreme Court* (New York: Simon & Schuster, 1979), 434; Powell Papers, 74-6257_GreggGeorgia1976AprMay.pdf, 13.

60 **Powell also approved of the Texas law:** Powell Papers, 74-6257_GreggGeorgia1976AprMay.pdf, 14.

60 **"not at rest as to its validity":** Ibid., 10.

60 **had a tie of four to four:** Mandery, *Wild Justice*, 404.

60 **Chief Justice Burger picked Byron White:** Ibid.

61 **He was listening to one of his law clerks:** Ibid., 405.

61 **She had long thought:** Ibid., 343.

61 **Powell was an establishment figure:** Ibid., 346.

61 **"Wait until everyone else has spoken":** John C. Jeffries, *Justice Lewis F. Powell, Jr.* (New York: Scribner, 1994), 30.

62 **"a person cannot be both unique and equal":** Mandery, *Wild Justice*, 412.

62 **Powell, Stewart, and Stevens had lunch:** Ibid., 408–9.

62 **they worked out their differences:** Woodward and Armstrong (*Brethren*, 440) says Stewart and Stevens originally opposed the Louisiana law, setting up a compromise in which they persuaded Powell to go along with them and strike the law, while he persuaded them to uphold the Texas law. Mandery (*Wild Justice*, 409) says Stewart and Stevens supported the Louisiana law all along, which would mean there was no need for compromise. Mandery cites archival documents, suggesting Woodward is mistaken.

62 **was furious:** Mandery, *Wild Justice*, 414.

62 **"the diverse frailties of humankind":** Woodson v. North Carolina, 428 U.S. 280 (1976).

62 **The three justices believed:** Early drafts of the Jurek opinion reflect the justices' ambivalence about whether the Texas law should have been upheld. An early version found in the Potter Stewart Papers at Yale University reads: "In light of . . . the Texas Court's decision to interpret the second question in a way that allows consideration of mitigating factors in a manner similar to that approved in Gregg, it appears that the Texas capital sentencing procedures adequately guide and channel the jury's decision to impose the death penalty. These procedures minimize the risk that the death penalty will be imposed in an arbitrary or capricious manner in Texas." But the final text took out the reference to this all being "in light of" the Texas court's interpretation, which had made the approval sound provisional, and made no mention of any "risk." The final version also made no reference to the Texas "minimizing risk" provision.

62 **it was William Rehnquist:** Years later, Rehnquist made this point more force-fully: "It is hard to imagine a system of capital sentencing that leaves less dis-cretion in the hands of the jury while at the same time allowing them to consider the particular circumstances of each case—that is, to perform their assigned task at all." Adams v. Texas, 448 U.S. 38 (1980).

63 **"an expression of society's moral outrage":** Gregg v. Georgia, 428 U.S. 153 (1976).

63 **Brennan gave up in the middle:** Mandery, *Wild Justice*, 423.

63 **he suffered multiple heart attacks:** Ibid.

63 **his voice cracked and his hands trembled:** Woodward and Armstrong, *Breth-ren*, 441.

63 **Powell had tried to find a way:** Mandery, *Wild Justice*, 416.

64 **"we should have held the Texas statute":** "Sandra Day O'Connor Interviews John Paul Stevens," *Newsweek*, December 17, 2010, newsweek.com/sandra-day-oconnor-interviews-john-paul-stevens-69055.

64 **He said it was the only decision:** In a 2019 memoir, Justice Stevens explained that he had delegated the writing of the "statement of facts" in the Jurek opin-ion to one of his clerks. "If I had carefully stated the facts in *Jurek v. Texas*," he wrote, "I might well have changed my vote in that case. I should then have realized that a jury instruction required by the Texas statute had the practical consequence of converting what at first blush appeared to be a valid discretion-ary sentencing scheme into an invalid mandatory scheme." He now wrote that one clerk had "urged me to change my vote in that case and I have lived to re-gret my failure to do so," though he didn't think switching his position would have "affected the final outcome." This is a puzzling statement, since the vote in Jurek was 5–4. John Paul Stevens, *The Making of a Justice: Reflections on My First 94 Years* (New York: Little, Brown, 2019).

64 **"a cautionary tale about cause lawyering":** Steiker, *"Penry v. Lynaugh,"* 295.

64 **"tone deaf to the changing tune":** Edward Lazarus, *Closed Chambers: The Rise, Fall, and Future of the Supreme Court* (New York: Crown, 1998), 114.

64 **"narrowest factors of mitigation":** Powell Papers, 74-6257_GreggGeorgia-1976July22_Part3.pdf, 9. Amsterdam also wrote, "The only way in which [the Texas] statute can be read as permitting the consideration of mitigating cir-cumstances at all is by converting the statutory sentencing formula into an amorphous inkblot that provides no comprehensible 'guidance' to the jury."

64 **he declined her suggestion:** Mandery, *Wild Justice*, 426.

65 **five in 1983, twenty-one in 1984:** "Execution Database," Death Penalty Infor-mation Center, accessed June 26, 2019, deathpenaltyinfo.org/executions/execution-database.

65 **"A person like Jurek":** Jurek v. Estelle, 593 F.2d 672 (5th Cir. 1979).

66 **"I think that the death penalty":** Sneath, "Special Report."

CHAPTER 3

This chapter is based on interviews with Danalynn Recer and more than twenty of her peers at the Texas Resource Center, as well as interviews with others who helped the center (David Botsford, Steve Bright, George Kendall, Jordan Steiker) and those who fought it in legal and political arenas. Joe Ward shared memories of the Edward Ellis case. I also relied on records of the resource center held at the Dolph Briscoe Center for American History, University of Texas at Austin, and the Texas State Libraries and Archives Commission. To learn about Danalynn Recer's early life, I interviewed Major Espy (a relative of M. Watt Espy), Carey Hattic, Scott Henson, Kathy Mitchell, and Paul Recer. For insight into the Court of Criminal Appeals, I interviewed Charlie Baird, Cathy Cochran, Robin Norris, and Gary Taylor. I also spoke with Mark White, former governor of Texas, shortly before his death in 2017.

70 **lynchings in his native state of Kentucky:** George C. Wright, *Racial Violence in Kentucky, 1865–1940: Lynchings, Mob Rule, and "Legal Lynchings"* (Baton Rouge: Louisiana State University Press, 1996), xiii.

71 **Only about a quarter of lynchings:** *Lynching in America: Confronting the Legacy of Racial Terror,* 2nd ed. (Montgomery, Ala.: Equal Justice Initiative, 2015), 10.

71 **"gripped the southern imagination":** Jacquelyn Dowd Hall, *Revolt Against Chivalry: Jessie Daniel Ames and the Women's Campaign Against Lynching* (New York: Columbia University Press, 1993), 151.

71 **"lustful black brutes":** Ibid., 146.

71 **"denizens of the underworld":** Ibid., 129.

71 **"A new generation of blacks":** Ibid., 133.

72 **"made you forget that you were eaten up":** Lillian Smith, *Killers of the Dream* (New York: W. W. Norton, 1994), 170.

72 **the state led the country in burning victims alive:** Danalynn Recer, "Patrolling the Borders of Race, Gender and Class: The Lynching Ritual and Texas Nationalism, 1850–1994" (master's thesis, University of Texas at Austin, 1994), 5.

72 **"felt besieged by enemies on all sides":** Ibid., 56.

72 **"identity forged in fear":** Ibid., 6.

72 **"frontier vigilante justice with the ritualized codes":** Ibid., 57.

72 **at least 282 people of Mexican origin or descent:** William D. Carrigan and Clive Webb, "The Lynching of Persons of Mexican Origin or Descent in the United States, 1848 to 1928," *Journal of Social History* 37, no. 2 (Winter 2003): 415.

72 **the 1918 shooting:** Nashwa Bawab, "A Century After the Porvenir Massacre, Remembering One of Texas' Darkest Days," *Texas Observer,* January 31, 2018, texasobserver.org/century-porvenir-massacre-remembering-one-texas-darkest -days/.

73 **working from one in the afternoon to three in the morning:** Major Allen Espy, "Watt Espy, Keeper of the Museum of Death," YouTube video, 8:07, August 24, 2010, youtube.com/watch?v=8OZLYi6levk.

73 **The walls were yellow:** Michael Radelet, "M. Watt Espy, Jr.: America's Greatest Death Penalty Archivist," *Tomfoolery,* December 8, 2012, majorsensations .blogspot.com/2012/12/essay-on-watt-espy.html.

73 **he took the files back:** Ibid.

73 **scampering cockroaches:** Ibid.

74 **"properly under the law":** Recer, "Patrolling the Border," 180.

74 **"failing" to stop the mob:** Ibid., 181.

74 **preacher:** Paul N. Spellman, *Captain John H. Rogers, Texas Ranger* (Denton: University of North Texas Press, 2003), 135.

74 **"so thick it was difficult to move a hand or arm"**: "Garrett, Dick," M. Watt Espy Papers, 1730–2008, M. E. Grenander Department of Special Collections and Archives, University Libraries, University at Albany, State University of New York.

74 **Children were let out early**: Ibid.

74 **Garrett could hear hammers**: Ibid.

74 **"Y'all know about law and order"**: "Nixon's Hard-Won Chance to Lead," *Time*, November 15, 1968, 23.

74 **Nixon aide John Ehrlichman**: Dan Baum, "Legalize It All," *Harper's*, April 2016, 22.

75 **the execution of people who had committed rape**: Coker v. Georgia, 433 U.S. 584 (1977).

75 **The case concerned Warren McCleskey**: McCleskey v. Kemp, 481 U.S. 279 (1987).

75 **A Texas study found**: Sheldon Eckland-Olson, "Structured Discretion, Racial Bias, and the Texas Death Penalty: The First Decade After 'Furman' in Texas," *Political Science Quarterly* 69, no. 4 (December 1988): 853.

75 **"the Dred Scott decision"**: Mandery, *Wild Justice*, 429.

76 **the network was surprisingly successful**: In one Texas case, defense lawyers convinced the Supreme Court to overturn sentences in which a psychiatrist interviewed a defendant without a lawyer present and then testified against him at trial (Estelle v. Smith, 451 U.S. 454, 1981). In another case from the state, the Court struck down sentences in cases in which people had been excluded from jury service simply because they had some general qualms about the death penalty (Adams v. Texas, 448 U.S. 38, 1980).

76 **courts were reversing**: Jonathan R. Sorensen and Rocky LeAnn Pilgrim, *Lethal Injection: Capital Punishment in Texas During the Modern Era* (Austin: University of Texas Press, 2006), 160.

76 **he couldn't name the days**: Steiker, "*Penry v. Lynaugh*," 283.

76 **his mother had beaten him**: Penry v. Lynaugh, 492 U.S. 302 (1989).

76 **The decision forced the Texas Legislature**: In Oregon, lawmakers had copied much of the 1973 Texas law, but when the Supreme Court ruled against the law in the *Penry* case, Oregon overturned the sentences of all twenty-three people on death row, whereas Texas courts interpreted the law in ways that would preserve the death sentences. Carole S. Steiker and Jordan Steiker, *Courting Death: The Supreme Court and Capital Punishment* (Cambridge, Mass.: Harvard University Press, 2016), 125.

76 **They added explicit language**: For a thorough account of changes to the law over the years, see Ana M. Otero, "The Death of Fairness: Texas's Future Dangerousness Revisited," *University of Denver Criminal Law Review* 4, no. 1 (2014).

77 **jurors were not to be informed of this**: Brittany Fowler, "A Shortcut to Death: How the Texas Death-Penalty Statute Engages the Jury's Cognitive Heuristics in Favor of Death," *Texas Law Review* 96, no. 2 (2017): 379–98; Jolie McCullough, "Texas Death Penalty Juror Hopes to Change Law as Execution Looms," *Texas Tribune*, March 28, 2017, texastribune.org/2017/03/28/texas-death-penalty-juror-hopes-change-law-execution-looms/.

77 **he could beg by phone:** Robert Reinhold, "Lawyers, Citing Financial Losses, Shun Death Row Appeals," *New York Times*, September 22, 1986, A15, nytimes .com/1986/09/22/us/lawyers-citing-financial-losses-shun-death-row-appeals .html.

77 **Garcia found that her children:** Ibid.

78 **the ACLU sent:** This was Jim Rebholz.

78 **miss a birthday party:** David Margolick, "Death Row Appeals Are Drawing Sharp Rebukes from Frustrated Federal Judges in the South," *New York Times*, December 2, 1988, B9, nytimes.com/1988/12/02/us/law-bar-death-row -appeals-are-drawing-sharp-rebukes-frustrated-federal-judges.html.

78 **Death penalty supporters, including judges:** Edith Jones, "Death Penalty Procedures: A Proposal for Reform," *Texas Bar Journal* 8 (September 1990), 852.

78 **$30,000:** Lyz Entzeroth and Randall Coyne, "Report Regarding Implementation of the American Bar Association's Recommendations and Resolutions Concerning the Death Penalty and Calling for a Moratorium on Execution," *Georgetown Journal on Fighting Poverty* 4, no. 1 (Fall 1996): 22, digitalcommons .law.utulsa.edu/cgi/viewcontent.cgi?article=1285&context=fac_pub.

78 **Jordan Steiker:** Raymond Bonner, *Anatomy of Injustice: A Murder Case Gone Wrong* (New York: Alfred A. Knopf, 2012), 124.

79 **her yellow Cadillac:** Kathy Fair and T. J. Milling, "Man Facing Execution in Tub Slaying; Lawyers Claim New Proof of Innocence," *Houston Chronicle*, March 3, 1992, A9.

81 **"borderline mentally retarded":** Ibid.

81 **"It is not your role to sabotage":** Jim Zook and Kathy Fair, "Judge Irked at 11th-Hour Pleas for Condemned Man," *Houston Chronicle*, February 28, 1992, A30.

81 **admonishing the lawyers:** Ellis v. Collins, 788 F. Supp. 317 (S.D. Tex. 1992).

81 **a slow fax machine:** David R. Dow and Mark Dow, *Machinery of Death: The Reality of America's Death Penalty Machine* (New York: Routledge, 2002), 26.

81 **"self-perpetuating crime machine":** Fair and Milling, "Man Facing Execution," A9.

81 **"sorry sons of bitches":** "Offender: Edward Ellis #749," Texas Department of Criminal Justice, accessed June 28, 2019, tdcj.texas.gov/death_row/dr_info/ ellisedwardlast.html.

82 **his evidence of innocence wasn't enough:** Herrera v. Collins, 506 U.S. 390 (1993).

83 **"You are an extremely intelligent jury":** Romero v. Lynaugh, 884 F.2d 871, 875 (5th Cir. 1989).

83 **failed to raise a single objection:** Ex Parte Earvin 816 S.W.2d 379 (Tex. Crim. App. 1991).

83 **"wetback":** Ex Parte Guzmon, 730 S.W.2d 724 (Tex. Crim. App. 1987).

83 **In three separate cases:** The three men were Carl Johnson, Calvin Burdine, and George McFarland. See Stephen Bright, "Elected Judges and the Death Penalty in Texas: Why Full Habeas Corpus Review by Independent Federal Judges Is Indispensable to Protecting Constitutional Rights," *Texas Law Review* 78, no. 7 (2000): 1805–37; David R. Dow, "The State, the Death Penalty and Carl Johnson," *Boston College Law Review* 37, no. 4 (1996), lawdigitalcommons.bc.edu/ bclr/vol37/iss4/2; Janet Elliott, "New Trial Denied to Man Whose Lawyer

Slept in Court," *Houston Chronicle*, May 19, 2005, chron.com/news/houston -texas/article/New-trial-denied-to-man-whose-lawyer-slept-in-1563578.php; and Burdine v. Johnson, 231 F.3d 950 (5th Cir. 2000).

84 **fewer than ten hours:** Henry Weinstein, "A Sleeping Lawyer and a Ticket to Death Row," *Los Angeles Times*, July 15, 2000, articles.latimes.com/2000/jul/ 15/news/mn-53250.

84 **"It's boring":** John Makeig, "Asleep on the Job? Slaying Trial Boring, Lawyer Says," *Houston Chronicle*, August 14, 1992, A35.

84 **$11.84 per hour:** Martinez-Macias v. Collins, 979 F.2d 1067 (5th Cir. 1992).

84 **$600 a day:** J. Michael Kennedy, "Why Houston Leads in Death Row Cases," *Los Angeles Times*, July 2, 1992, articles.latimes.com/1992-07-02/news/mn -1903_1_death-row.

84 **"like greased lightning":** Leonard Pitts, "Justice Is Blind—Unless, of Course, You're Rich," *Chicago Tribune*, August 21, 2000, articles.chicagotribune.com/ 2001-08-21/news/0108210027_1_joc-frank-cannon-calvin-burdine-court -appointed-attorney.

84 **a Florida death case:** Strickland v. Washington, 466 U.S. 668 (1984).

84 **"dramatic ploy":** Romero v. Lynaugh, 884 F.2d 871 (5th Cir. 1989).

85 **"We've lost the streets to them":** Recer, "Patrolling," 223.

85 **shape-shifted but didn't disappear:** Ibid., 221.

85 **"Sweet and innocent":** Ibid., 222.

86 **twelve in 1992, seventeen in 1993:** "Execution Database," Death Penalty In-formation Center, accessed June 26, 2019, deathpenaltyinfo.org/executions/ execution-database.

86 **one hundred execution dates:** David Margolick, "As Texas Death Row Grows, Fewer Lawyers Help Inmates," *New York Times*, December 31, 1993, A1.

86 **sixteen lawyers:** Ibid.

CHAPTER 4

This chapter relies on interviews with Elsa Alcala and numerous prosecutors at the Harris County district attorney's office, including Luci Davidson, Rusty Hardin, Johnny Holmes, Rob Kepple, Jim Leitner, Lyn McClellan, Murray Newman, Chuck Rosenthal, Jane Waters, and Roe Wilson. Elsa's sisters Rita Alcala and Clara Trainor generously recounted their upbringing. I relied on an interview I conducted for the Texas After Violence Project with the late Arthur "Cappy" Eads for his story on the development of future-dangerousness testimony. On Dr. James Grigson and the Dal-las County DA's office, I interviewed Larry Baraka, Andy Beach, Ed Gray, Errol Mor-ris, the late Douglas Mulder, Toby Shook, and Craig Watkins. I developed some of the ideas on prosecutorial storytelling for my article "The Minority Report of David Pow-ell" (*Guernica*, March 1, 2013, guernicamag.com/the-minority-report-of-david -powell/) and also found helpful analysis in Paul Kaplan, *Murder Stories: Ideological Narratives in Capital Punishment* (Lanham, Md.: Lexington Books, 2012) and Austin Sarat, *When the State Kills: Capital Punishment and the American Condition* (Princeton, N.J.: Princeton University Press, 2001).

87 **in staggering numbers:** William D. Carrigan and Clive Webb write that "conser-vative estimates" of Mexicans killed by mobs "place the number in the thou-

sands." William D. Carrigan and Clive Webb, *Forgotten Dead: Mob Violence Against Mexicans in the United States, 1848–1928* (New York: Oxford University Press, 2013), 5.

87 **"It seems only necessary"**: Benjamin Heber Johnson, *Revolution in Texas: How a Forgotten Rebellion and Its Bloody Suppression Turned Mexicans into Americans* (New Haven, Conn.: Yale University Press, 2005), 3.

89 **Alcala ate so much tuna:** Keri Blakinger, "Listen: Former Texas Judge Raises Possibility of Death Penalty Moratorium," *Houston Chronicle: Behind the Walls*, podcast audio, January 9, 2019, houstonchronicle.com/local/behind-the -walls-podcast/article/Listen-Former-Texas-judge-raises-possibility-of-13520 701.php?t=8fcb936152#photo-15890320.

89 **the Reagan administration was pushing:** "Social Security Programs In the Reagan Presidency," *New York Times*, November 16, 1988, nytimes.com/1988/ 11/16/us/social-security-programs-in-the-reagan-presidency.html.

90 **forty-four felony cases in a single year:** Audrey Duff, "The Deadly DA," *Texas Monthly*, February 1994, 38.

91 **the big-city prosecutor as small-town sheriff:** Reporters would later chalk the Western trappings up to Holmes's early love for his uncle's Colorado ranch, where as a child he read books about the lawmen of the Old West. But as Holmes told it, he had once been dispatched to a rural county near Houston to help with a case, and he liked the handlebar worn by one of the deputies there. When he returned to Houston with his own mustache, as he recalled, some people "said I looked like a dope dealer, and that rubbed me the wrong way, so then I definitely didn't cut it." For an academic analysis of the Old West image of prosecutors, see Daniel LaChance, *Executing Freedom: The Cultural Life of Capital Punishment in the United States* (Chicago: University of Chicago Press, 2016), 129–54.

91 **"We've got to scratch the retribution itch":** Richard Willing, "Prosecutor Often Determines Which Way a Case Will Go," *USA Today*, December 20, 1999, A4.

91 **"would indict his own mother":** Duff, "Deadly DA," 38.

91 **"If I had a hit list":** Ibid.

91 **More than nine hundred thousand people:** Michael P. Malone and Richard W. Etulain, *The American West: A Twentieth-Century History* (Lincoln: University of Nebraska Press, 1989), 257.

91 **nationwide rise in crime:** Data analyzed by *The Marshall Project* shows the rate of homicides per hundred thousand people rose in Houston from 25.29 in 1975 to 40.38 in 1979. Gabriel Dance and Tom Meagher, "Crime in Context," *The Marshall Project*, August 18, 2016, themarshallproject.org/2016/08/18/ crime-in-context.

91 **number of burglaries alone nearly doubled:** Wayne King, "New Police Chief Battles Crime Boom in Houston," *New York Times*, January 14, 1983, A8, nytimes.com/1983/01/14/us/new-police-chief-battles-crime-boom-in-houston .html.

92 **more than 150 prisoners on death row:** Mike Tolson, "A Deadly Distinction, Part 1: Harris County Is a Pipeline to Death Row," *Houston Chronicle*, February 4, 2001, chron.com/news/article/Part-1-A-Deadly-Distinction-Harris -County-is-2002524.php.

92 **thirty-one other states:** Ibid.

92 **1 percent of the national population:** Ibid.

92 **"Johnny is a west-of-the-Pecos kind of guy":** Duff, "Deadly DA," 38.

92 **more likely to seek the death penalty:** Jonathan R. Sorensen and James W. Marquart, "Prosecutorial and Jury Decision-Making in Post-Furman Texas Capital Cases," *N.Y.U. Review of Law & Social Change* 18, no. 3 (1990): 744.

92 **"sexual degradation" of female victims:** Scott Phillips, Laura Potter Haas, and James E. Coverdill, "Disentangling Victim Gender and Capital Punishment: The Role of Media," *Feminist Criminology* 7, no. 2 (2012): 130–45.

92 **evidence of guilt is stronger:** Guy Goldberg and Gena Bunn, "Balancing Fairness and Finality: A Comprehensive Review of the Texas Death Penalty," *Texas Review of Law & Politics* 5, no. 1 (Fall 2000): 70.

93 **Holmes was three times more likely:** Ray Paternoster, "Racial Disparity in the Case of Duane Edward Buck," *NAACP LDF*, December 19, 2012, accessed June 30, 2019, naacpldf.org/files/case issue/Duane%20Buck-FINAL%20Signed%20Paternoster%20Report%20(00032221).PDF, 6.

93 **"doing God's work":** Buntion v. Quarterman, 555 U.S. 1176 (5th Cir. 2008).

93 **postcard depicting Judge Roy Bean:** Ibid.

95 **still had a bullet in his shoulder:** "Boy, 9, Tells Jury How Dad Fatally Shot Sister," *Houston Chronicle*, April 12, 1994, A30.

96 **relentless cheer:** Ron Rosenbaum, "Travels with Dr. Death," *Vanity Fair*, May 1990, archive.vanityfair.com/article/1990/5/travels-with-dr-death.

96 **to see whether they were mentally competent:** Ibid.

96 **particular murderers were incorrigible:** John Bloom, "Killers and Shrinks," *Texas Monthly*, July 1978, 66.

96 **twenty-six of the eighty-six men:** Ibid.

97 **He won unanimously:** Estelle v. Smith, 451 U.S. 454 (1981).

97 **was stumped:** "Interview with Arthur 'Cappy' Eads," *Texas After Violence Project*, accessed June 30, 2019, http://av.lib.utexas.edu/index.php?title=Category: Eads,_Arthur&gsearch=Eads.

98 **"Are you using just Dr. Grigson":** "Barefoot v. Estelle," *Oyez*, accessed June 30, 2019, oyez.org/cases/1982/82-6080.

98 **Ron Rosenbaum profiled:** Rosenbaum, "Travels."

99 **"Anyone can convict a guilty defendant":** Edward Gray, *Henry Wade's Tough Justice: How Dallas County Prosecutors Led the Nation in Convicting the Innocent* (Indianapolis: Dog Ear Publishing, 2010), 60.

99 **denied this characterization:** John Council, "Former ADAs Who Helped Convict Exonerated Men Reflect," *Texas Lawyer*, June 9, 2008, law.com/texaslawyer/almID/1202421991854/?slreturn=20190422074118.

99 **"If you ever put another nigger":** Steve McGonigle and Ed Timms, "Race Bias Pervades Jury Selection," *Dallas Morning News*, March 9, 1986, A1.

99 **remained in use:** Jim Atkinson, "The Law and Henry Wade," *D Magazine*, June 1977, dmagazine.com/publications/d-magazine/1977/june/the-law-and-henry-wade/.

100 **a person could not be excluded:** Batson v. Kentucky, 476 U.S. 79 (1986).

100 **judicially approved reasons to cut people:** Maurice Chammah, "Can Court-

room Prejudice Be Proved?" *The Marshall Project*, May 23, 2016, themarshall project.org/2015/11/02/can-courtroom-prejudice-be-proved.

100 **a training manual with racial stereotypes:** Miller-El v. Dretke, 545 U.S. 231 (2005).

100 **twenty-four death sentences:** Sally Giddens, "Mad Dog Mulder," *D Magazine*, April 1989, dmagazine.com/publications/d-magazine/1989/april/mad-dog -mulder/.

101 **threw the doctor's retirement party:** "Texas 'Dr. Death' Retires After 167 Capital Case Trials," *Washington Times*, December 20, 2003, washingtontimes .com/news/2003/dec/20/20031220-113219-5189r/.

101 **They were psychopaths:** Mark Singer, "Predilections," *New Yorker*, January 29, 1989, newyorker.com/magazine/1989/02/06/predilections.

101 **officially expelled:** Mike Tolson, "Effect of 'Dr. Death' and His Testimony Lingers," *Houston Chronicle*, June 17, 2004, chron.com/news/houston-texas/article/ Effect-of-Dr-Death-and-his-testimony-lingers-1960299.php.

101 **the prison records of 155 people:** *Deadly Speculation: Misleading Texas Capital Juries with False Predictions of Future Dangerousness* (Austin: Texas Defender Service, 2004), xiv. A. P. Merillat challenged many of the Texas Defender Service's findings in his book *Future Danger?* (Austin: Texas District & County Attorneys Association, 2004), 10, noting that TDS did not include attempted assaults as incidents of dangerousness, and that the men sentenced to death in its study had been held in far more restrictive conditions—thus having less of an opportunity to be violent—than they would have been had they not been sentenced to death.

102 **The doctors who came after Grigson:** One successor to Grigson, George Denkowski, was reprimanded by regulators after he was found to be inflating the intelligence scores of death row prisoners with intellectual disabilities in order to increase their chance of being executed. Brandi Grissom, "Psychologist Who Cleared Death Row Inmates Is Reprimanded," *New York Times*, April 14, 2011, nytimes.com/2011/04/15/us/15ttpsychologist.html.

102 **"He always had a good word":** "James Paul Grigson," *Dallas Morning News*, June 6, 2004, legacy.com/obituaries/dallasmorningnews/obituary.aspx?n= james-paul-grigson&pid=2300597.

102 **he beat up his young son:** Jennifer Liebrum, "Death Penalty Given to Man Who Killed Former Girlfriend, Tot," *Houston Chronicle*, April 19, 1994, A20.

104 **Ecclesiastes:** Merillat, *Future Danger?*

104 **"King Kong":** Andrew Cohen, "A Judge Overturned a Death Sentence Because the Prosecutor Compared a Black Defendant to King Kong," *The Marshall Project*, March 28, 2016, themarshallproject.org/2016/03/28/a-judge-overturned -a-death-sentence-because-the-prosecutor-compared-a-black-defendant-to -king-kong.

105 **Silver Needle Society:** Tolson, "Deadly Distinction."

105 **Death by Injection:** Keri Blakinger, "Death by Injection: The Band of Lawyers That Keeps Harris County DA Office Rocking," *Houston Chronicle*, May 31, 2018, houstonchronicle.com/entertainment/music/article/Death-By-Injection-the-band-of-lawyers-that-12957291.php.

105 **a novelty pen:** In an interview, Johnny Holmes said he stopped handing out these pens after someone in the office complained. "They thought it was in poor taste, and they were right," he said. He did not remember the Silver Needle Society. He did say a prosecutor made a T-shirt celebrating executions and Holmes told him, "Don't be doing that."

CHAPTER 5

In addition to Danalynn Recer and many of her Texas Resource Center colleagues, I am especially grateful to Rob Owen for sharing his recollections of the Carl Kelly case, explaining the legal issues involved, and sending case files. I accessed more case files at the Briscoe Center at the University of Texas and the Texas State Libraries and Archives Commission. I also relied a great deal on Tim Madigan's reporting on the case for the *Chicago Tribune* and *Fort Worth Star-Telegram* and on Susan Blaustein's article for *Harper's* ("Witness to Another Execution," May 1994). Some resource center alumni declined interviews because they did not want to revisit the trauma of the era. I am especially grateful to those alumni who, along with Owen and Recer, were willing to be candid about the work, including Sandra Babcock, Jeff Dworkin, Lynn Lamberty, Mauric Levin, Virginia Lindsay, Walter Long, Jim Marcus, Brent Newton, Rita Radostitz, Raoul Schonemann, Joel Schwartz, and Hilary Sheard. I also relied on the confidential interviews with capital defense lawyers by Susannah Sheffer in her book *Fighting for Their Lives: Inside the Experience of Capital Defense Attorneys* (Nashville: Vanderbilt University Press, 2013). Jerry Patterson recalled his battles with the resource center in an interview, and Jim Marcus helped shade in the picture. The material on how Texas diverged from other states draws on Carole S. Steiker and Jordan Steiker's *Courting Death: The Supreme Court and Capital Punishment* (Cambridge, Mass.: Harvard University Press, 2016).

106 **junk-cluttered porches:** Susan Blaustein, "Witness to Another Execution," *Harper's*, May 1994, harpers.org/archive/1994/05/witness-to-another-execution/.

106 EVERYONE LIVES LONGER IF SAFETY IS FIRST: Ibid.

106 **dropped their driver's licenses:** Barbara Bader Aldave, "My Journey with Caruthers," *University of Toledo Law Review* 35 (Spring 2004): 537.

106 **donated to a blood drive:** Ibid.

106 **separated by Plexiglas:** Ibid.

107 **It could get noisy:** Ibid.

107 **he'd fired a gun but missed:** Tim Madigan, "For One Inmate, Executioner's Song Lasts 11 Years," *Chicago Tribune*, November 9, 1992, chicagotribune.com/news/ct-xpm-1992-11-09-9204110636-story.html.

109 **the court thought this question:** Ex Parte Kelly 832 S.W.2d 44 (Tex. Crim. App. 1992).

109 **some "nexus" to the crime:** Mines v. State, 852 S.W.2d 941 (Tex. Crim. App. 1993).

109 **"Every move you make has consequences":** Tim Madigan, "Families Also Travel Road to Execution," *Chicago Tribune*, November 10, 1992, chicagotribune.com/news/ct-xpm-1992-11-10-9204110924-story.html.

109 **"You've been through this before":** Ibid.

110 **a raised-up red chair:** Madigan, "For One Inmate."

110 **"If you don't hear from me":** Ibid.

110 **"Michael Jordan is unbelievable":** Ibid.

111 **mitigation specialists were often enlisted:** Russell Stetler, "The Past, Present, and Future of the Mitigation Profession: Fulfilling the Constitutional Requirement of Individualized Sentencing in Capital Cases," *Hofstra Law Review* 46, no. 4 (2018): 1172–74.

112 **"I remember Richard whipping Gene":** During my own interviews in 2019, Kelly's siblings disputed the idea that Richard Stanford, who is now deceased, was "abusive," saying that he was "strict" and "rough." "He would whup," said his sister, Laura Thomas, "but I wouldn't say it was abuse." She added that her brother Carl "just would not listen, he was so hardheaded."

114 **"They were an inconvenience":** Myron A. Farber, "The Rule of Law Oral History Project: The Reminiscences of Richard H. Burr," Oral History Research Office, Columbia University, 2010, columbia.edu/cu/libraries/inside/ccoh _assets/ccoh_8626033_transcript.pdf.

114 **"But there's another surgeon":** Susannah Sheffer, *Fighting for Their Lives: Inside the Experience of Capital Defense Attorneys* (Nashville: Vanderbilt University Press, 2013), 72.

114 **"That's not him":** Ibid., 100.

114 **"and I'm awaiting the certainty":** Ibid., 98.

115 **"Texas is a very violent society":** "Texas Democratic Gubernatorial Primary Debate," C-SPAN, February 7, 1990, 1:23:13, c-span.org/video/?10966-1/ texas-democratic-gubernatorial-primary-debate&start=3593.

115 **Mark White released a campaign ad:** Richard Cohen, "Playing Politics with the Death Penalty," *Washington Post*, March 20, 1990, washingtonpost.com/ archive/opinions/1990/03/20/playing-politics-with-the-death-penalty/cfdad 065-9c2a-449d-bf66-c13aedc3bbba/.

115 **"juveniles and mentally retarded killers":** Jan Reid, *Let the People In: The Life and Times of Ann Richards* (Austin: University of Texas Press, 2012), 222.

115 **federal judges should rarely question:** Coleman v. Thompson, 501 U.S. 722 (1991).

115 **the justices restricted the ability:** McCleskey v. Zant, 499 U.S. 467 (1991).

116 **Each state had its own:** Carole S. Steiker and Jordan Steiker, *Courting Death: The Supreme Court and Capital Punishment* (Cambridge, Mass.: Harvard University Press, 2016), 117.

116 **more than twice the limit:** Ibid., 131.

116 **a defense lawyer could get $50,000 for investigation alone:** These were lawyers preparing a petition for a writ of habeas corpus, the second round of appeal. Ibid., 137.

116 **With the Supreme Court's blessing:** Graham v. Collins, 506 U.S. 461 (1993); Johnson v. Texas, 509 U.S. 350 (1993).

116 **This practically invites defense lawyers:** Franklin Zimring, *The Contradictions of Capital Punishment* (New York: Oxford University Press, 2004), 145–50.

117 **the DA charged Deckard:** Susan Warren, "Taking Offense at Death-Row Defense," *Houston Chronicle*, November 7, 1993, A20.

117 **One judge banned the center:** John Makeig, "Poe Bars Group from Death Row Cases in His Court," *Houston Chronicle*, June 8, 1994, A22.

117 **"leftist radical nut":** Madigan, "Families."

118 **"the Hollywood jury":** Terri Langford, "Death-Row Inmate's Opponents Tell Hollywood to Go Home," Associated Press, June 13, 1993.

118 **The *Houston Chronicle* took his side:** "Texas Resource Center Accountable for Public Money," *Houston Chronicle*, September 26, 1993, Editorials, page 2.

118 **produce three thousand words:** Warren, "Taking Offense," A20.

119 **to shame the system:** Michael McCormick, chief judge of the Texas Court of Criminal Appeals, wrote in the 1993 case of Michael Lee Lockhart: "By waiting until shortly before execution to request counsel and a stay, both the defendant and TRC are dangling his life in a perilous maneuver deliberately contrived to pressure the legal system to delay his execution." Ex Parte Lockhart, 868 S.W.2d 346 (Tex. Crim. App. 1993).

121 **"I know you're not supposed to hate":** Madigan, "For One Inmate."

121 **"she'll be crying before she gets in the doors":** Madigan, "Families."

121 **banged on pots and pans:** Blaustein, "Witness."

122 **"You're on the highway to hell":** Ibid.

122 **a rumpled blue pinstripe suit:** Tim Madigan, "An Odyssey of Anguish," *Fort Worth Star-Telegram*, August 29, 1993, A10.

122 **feel sad on his behalf:** Ibid.

122 **"Hey, Rob":** Ibid.

124 **As prosecutors saw it:** Warren, "Taking Offense," A20.

125 **"One need only drive":** Recer, "Patrolling the Borders," 227.

CHAPTER 6

My account of the murders is drawn from trial transcripts, found at the Texas State Libraries and Archives Commission, along with interviews with Elsa Alcala, Elizabeth DeRieux, Lyn McClellan, Allen Tanner, Allison Vickers, and Steve Vickers. The material on the Peña-Ertman murders is drawn from Corey Mitchell's *Pure Murder* (New York: Pinnacle Books, 2008), as well as an interview with Andy Kahan. Robin Kelley shared her memories. I learned more about the experience of victim families from Stephanie Frogge and Susannah Sheffer, as well as the most thorough study comparing experiences of victims in capital versus non-capital cases: Marilyn Peterson Armour and Mark S. Umbreit, "Assessing the Impact of the Ultimate Penal Sanction on Homicide Survivors: A Two State Comparison," *Marquette Law Review* 96, no. 1 (2012).

126 **the two runaway girls:** "Rape Claimed by Runaways," *Houston Chronicle*, January 16, 1995, A13.

126 **the store clerk beaten:** "Robbery Suspect Sought," *Houston Chronicle*, January 25, 1995, A18.

126 **shot and drowned by their father:** S. K. Bardwell and T. J. Milling, "2 Slain Youths Are Mourned; Ex-Police Officer Is Charged with Murder of Older Son," *Houston Chronicle*, January 27, 1995, A22.

126 **the homeless veteran:** Jennifer Liebrum, "14-Year-Old Found Guilty in 'Bum Bashing' Slaying," *Houston Chronicle*, January 21, 1995, A29.

128 **insurance money from a car accident:** Jennifer Liebrum, "Teen Who Led Killings Gets Death Sentence," *Houston Chronicle,* February 7, 1996, A15.

131 **"kids who have absolutely no respect":** John J. DiIulio, Jr., "The Coming of the Super-Predators," *Weekly Standard,* November 27, 1995, weeklystandard.com/john-j-dilulio-jr/the-coming-of-the-super-predators.

132 **it has been up to victims of crime:** John H. Langbein, "The Origins of Public Prosecution at Common Law," *American Journal of Legal History* 17 (1973): 313–35.

132 **a watchman to arrest someone:** W. F. McDonald, "Toward a Bicentennial Revolution in Criminal Justice: The Return of the Victim," *American Criminal Law Review* 13 (1976), 651.

133 **family members of victims could not testify:** Booth v. Maryland, 482 U.S. 496 (1987).

133 **overturning its own opinion in 1991:** Payne v. Tennessee, 501 U.S. 808 (1991).

134 **"prostitutes beaten senseless":** Lynne Henderson, "The Wrongs of Victim's Rights," *Stanford Law Review* 937 (1985): 951.

134 **Bill Clinton wrote letters:** Corey Mitchell, *Pure Murder* (New York: Pinnacle Books, 2008), 244.

134 **William F. Buckley penned a column:** Ibid., 242.

134 **"see these bastards fry":** Ibid., 224.

135 **"not even an animal":** Ibid., 285.

135 **"closure" grew in usage:** Zimring, *Contradictions,* 60–61.

136 **"satisfaction and closure":** "Public Ambivalence Fuels Support for a Halt in U.S. Executions," ABC News, May 2, 2011, abcnews.go.com/images/PollingUnit/851a1DeathPenalty.pdf.

136 **more than a dozen states:** Marilyn Peterson Armour and Mark S. Umbreit, "Assessing the Impact of the Ultimate Penal Sanction on Homicide Survivors: A Two State Comparison," *Marquette Law Review* 96, no. 1 (2012): 19.

136 **There has been very little scholarly research:** Ibid., 1.

136 **"higher levels of physical, psychological, and behavioral health":** Ibid., 98.

136 **they stopped telling her about his court dates:** Robert Renny Cushing and Susannah Sheffer, *Dignity Denied: The Experience of Murder Victims' Family Members Who Oppose the Death Penalty* (Cambridge, Mass.: Murder Victims' Families for Reconciliation, 2002), 12.

137 **showing favoritism to pro-death-penalty victims:** Scott Nowell, "Justice for Some," *Houston Press,* October 3, 2002, houstonpress.com/news/justice-for-some-6558074.

139 **owed $80,000:** Mary Rainwater, "Man Executed for Houston Triple Murder," *Huntsville Item,* September 22, 2009, A1.

140 **effectively ghostwritten by their former colleagues:** In Harris County, judges ruled with the prosecution's arguments against habeas petitions 95 percent of the time, often failing even to correct misspellings and other typographical errors. Prosecutors have pointed out that sometimes judges also side with the defense, and Alcala argued to the *Houston Chronicle* that there was nothing wrong with the practice as long as judges used their judgment and authentically agreed with the prosecutors. See Jordan Steiker, James Marcus, and Thea

J. Posel, "The Problem of 'Rubber-Stamping' in State Capital Habeas Proceedings: A Harris County Case Study," *Houston Law Review* 44, no. 4 (May 2018), houstonlawreview.org/article/3874-the-problem-of-rubber-stamping-in-state-capital-habeas-proceedings-a-harris-county-case-study, and Keri Blakinger, "In Houston Death Penalty Cases, Many Judges Carry a 'Rubber Stamp,' Lawyers Find," *Houston Chronicle*, July 19, 2018, houstonchronicle.com/news/houston-texas/houston/article/In-Houston-death-penalty-cases-many-judges-carry-13088591.php.

CHAPTER 7

Eddie Capetillo spoke about his life in an interview and numerous letters. Nathalie Pias discussed her correspondence with him and sent his poetry with his permission. I relied on interviews with his parents in the film *Les Chemins de Marie* (Monique LeBlanc, National Film Board of Canada, 2005, nfb.ca/film/chemins_de_marie/). In 2016, I sent letters seeking information about death row to men who had lived there and conducted correspondence over several months with those who responded. They include Arturo Aranda, Baby Ray Bennett, Anibal Canales, Charles Hood, Charles Mamou (whom I also interviewed in person), and Jonathan Reed. While reporting for *The Texas Tribune* in 2012 and 2013, I learned about death row during in-person interviews with Preston Hughes III, Robert Pruett, and Max Soffar. I also gained valuable insights from former death row prisoner Thomas Whitaker while working with him as part of PEN America's Writing for Justice Fellowship, 2018–2019. I relied on a Texas After Violence Project interview with former death row corrections officer Edgar Fincher. Many claims about life on the row, including Robert Pruett's description of rewired radios, were confirmed with a second source.

I gained valuable insight from Bruce Jackson and Diane Christian's book *In This Timeless Time* and the accompanying documentary *Death Row* (Chapel Hill, N.C.: University of North Carolina Press, 2012). I also consulted memoirs former by death row prisoners: Anthony Graves, *Infinite Hope: How Wrongful Conviction, Solitary Confinement, and 12 Years on Death Row Failed to Kill My Soul* (Boston: Beacon Press, 2018); Kerry Max Cook, *Chasing Justice: My Story of Freeing Myself After Two Decades on Death Row for a Crime I Didn't Commit* (New York: William Morrow, 2007); and Randall Dale Adams with William Hoffer and Marilyn Mona Hoffer, *Adams v. Texas* (New York: St. Martin's Press, 1991). Tassos Rigopoulos shared his 1997 documentary on death row, *Texas and the Death Penalty*. I accessed newspapers published by death row prisoners at the Dolph Briscoe Center for American History. Pamela Colloff's reporting for *Texas Monthly* was the source for much of the material on the escape of Martin Gurule ("The Getaway," February 1999), along with documents at the Texas State Libraries and Archives Commission.

141 **Until 1965:** "Death Row Information," Texas Department of Criminal Justice, accessed July 5, 2019, tdcj.state.tx.us/death_row/dr_facts.html.

142 **appeals grew longer and longer:** Jonathan Sorenson and Rocky LeAnn Pilgrim, *Lethal Injection: Capital Punishment in Texas During the Modern Era* (Austin: University of Texas Press, 2006), 2.

142 **11,000 acres:** "Ellis," Texas Department of Criminal Justice, accessed July 5, 2019, tdcj.state.tx.us/unit_directory/e.html.

142 **feel of the slave plantations:** Bruce Jackson, *Inside the Wire: Photographs from Texas and Arkansas Prisons* (Austin: University of Texas Press, 2013).

142 **"stepping back in time":** Anthony Graves, *Infinite Hope: How Wrongful Conviction, Solitary Confinement, and 12 Years on Death Row Failed to Kill My Soul* (Boston: Beacon Press, 2018), 126.

142 **408 prisoners on death row:** Tracy L. Snell, *Capital Punishment 1996* (Washington, D.C.: U.S. Department of Justice, Office of Justice Programs, Bureau of Justice Statistics, 1997), bjs.gov/content/pub/pdf/cp96.pdf.

142 **40 percent of death row:** Ibid. The numbers in Texas tracked with death rows across the country, which were 9 percent Hispanic and 42 percent black.

142 **12 percent of Texas:** "Texas Population, 1996," Texas Department of State Health Services, accessed September 19, 2019, dshs.state.tx.us/chs/popdat/ST1996.shtm.

142 **referred to as DRs:** Bruce Jackson and Diane Christian, *In This Timeless Time: Living and Dying on Death Row in America* (Chapel Hill: University of North Carolina Press, 2012), 143.

142 **two bright yellow lines:** Ibid., 148.

142 **more than twenty hours each day:** Ken Light and Suzanne Donovan, *Texas Death Row* (Jackson: University Press of Mississippi, 1997), 11.

142 **several stacked tiers of cells:** Jackson and Christian, *Timeless*, 17.

142 **pour water on the concrete floor:** Graves, *Infinite*, 150.

142 **small, enclosed yard:** Ibid.

142 **It smelled like feces:** Charles Hood, "Death Letters," *Texas Monthly*, September 2008, texasmonthly.com/articles/death-letters/.

143 **black steel mesh:** Nanon Williams, *Still Surviving* (Dallas: GoodMedia Press, 2013), 30.

143 **Breakfast here started:** Light and Donovan, *Texas*, 13.

143 **dinner around three thirty in the afternoon:** Kerry Max Cook, *Chasing Justice: My Story of Freeing Myself After Two Decades on Death Row for a Crime I Didn't Commit* (New York: William Morrow, 2007), 118.

143 **"The food wasn't quite rotten":** Graves, *Infinite*, 129.

143 **this greasy mush:** *Texas and the Death Penalty*, film, directed by Tassos Rigopoulos, 1997, provided to the author by the director.

143 **flushing and scraping:** Jackson and Christian, *Timeless*, 25.

143 **talking to imaginary friends:** Ibid., 158.

143 **to pass the time:** Ibid., 163.

143 **calls were rarely allowed:** Rigopoulos, *Texas*.

144 **rats as pets:** Hood, "Death Letters."

144 **sold his drawings of horses:** Jackson and Christian, *Timeless*, 135.

144 **converted to Judaism:** "Texas Death-Row Inmate Wraps Tefillin for First Time," *Times of Israel*, February 18, 2016, timesofisrael.com/texas-death-row-inmate-wraps-tefillin-for-first-time/.

144 **"timeless time":** Jackson and Christian, *Timeless*, 168.

144 **"When you go through life out there":** Light and Donovan, *Texas Death Row*, 14.

145 **very first man to be sentenced:** "Offenders No Longer on Death Row," Texas

Department of Criminal Justice, accessed July 5, 2019, tdcj.state.tx.us/death _row/dr_offenders_no_longer_on_dr.html.

145 **roughly a dozen death row prisoners:** Ibid.

145 **More than thirty gave up their appeals:** "Execution Volunteers," Death Penalty Information Center, last modified April 23, 2019, deathpenaltyinfo.org/ information-defendants-who-were-executed-1976-and-designated-volunteers.

145 **"If they don't want to take me":** Meredith Rountree, "'I'll Make Them Shoot Me': Accounts of Death Row Prisoners Advocating for Execution," *Law & Society Review* 46, issue 3 (2012), 589–90.

145 **they shared many traits:** John Blume, "Killing the Willing: 'Volunteers,' Suicide, and Competency," *Michigan Law Review* 103, issue 5 (2005), 962.

145 **studied the public statements:** Rountree, "I'll Make Them," 591.

145 **"death row syndrome":** Harold I. Schwartz, "Death Row Syndrome and Demoralization: Psychiatric Means to Social Policy Ends," *Journal of the American Academy of Psychiatry and Law* 33, issue 2 (2005).

146 **Capetillo came to realize:** *Les Chemins de Marie*, directed by Monique LeBlanc (Montreal: National Film Board of Canada, 2005), onf.ca/film/chemins_de _marie/.

146 **unacknowledged and disenfranchised:** Walter C. Long, "Trauma Therapy for Death Row Families," *Journal of Trauma & Dissociation* 12, issue 5 (2011), 482–94.

146 **"My impulse is to hug":** *Les Chemins de Marie*.

146 **fasted in solidarity:** Graves, *Infinite*, 142.

146 **they cheered:** Randall Dale Adams with William Hoffer and Marilyn Mona Hoffer, *Adams v. Texas* (New York: St. Martin's Press, 1991), 182.

147 **lit up the Colosseum:** Frances Kennedy, "Colosseum Lights Reflect Death Penalty Campaign," *Independent*, December 13, 1999, independent.co.uk/news/ world/colosseum-lights-reflect-death-penalty-campaign-1132220.html; Claire Heininger, "Rome's Colosseum Lit Up to Mark NJ's Abolishing Death Penalty," NJ.com, December 19, 2007, nj.com/news/2007/12/colosseum_lit _up_to_mark_un_nj.html.

147 **other European countries:** Emily Baucum, "Europeans Make Journey to Texas Death Row," News 4 San Antonio, May 17, 2016, news4sanantonio.com/ news/local/europeans-make-journey-to-texas-death-row.

148 **"aging out" of crime:** Dana Goldstein, "Too Old to Commit Crime?" *The Marshall Project*, March 20, 2015, themarshallproject.org/2015/03/20/too-old-to -commit-crime.

149 **"I don't like working":** Light and Donovan, *Texas*, 11.

150 **they used the prison chapel's sloped roof:** Pamela Colloff, "The Getaway," *Texas Monthly*, February 1999, texasmonthly.com/articles/the-getaway/.

151 **many had not seen cars:** Hood, "Death Letters."

151 **did not want his name:** *Texas Department of Criminal Justice* (Paducah, Ky.: Turner Publishing Company, 2004), 103.

151 **at least twenty-two hours a day:** "Designed to Break You: Human Rights Violations on Texas' Death Row," Human Rights Clinic at the University of Texas

School of Law, 2017, law.utexas.edu/wp-content/uploads/sites/11/2017/04/
2017-HRC-DesignedToBreakYou-Report.pdf, 5.

151 **group recreation:** Ibid., 17.

151 **religious services:** Ibid., 31.

151 **phone calls or television:** Ibid., 19.

151 **outdoor recreation:** Ibid., 17.

152 **struggled to advance past the age:** Graves, *Infinite*, 154.

152 **grown to 80,870:** Jean Casella and James Ridgeway, "How Many Prisoners Are
in Solitary Confinement in the United States?," *Solitary Watch*, February 1,
2012, solitarywatch.com/2012/02/01/how-many-prisoners-are-in-solitary
-confinement-in-the-united-states/.

152 **keep track of time:** "Designed," 21–22.

152 **guard applying handcuffs:** Ibid., 22.

152 **Suicides increased:** Dave Mann, "Solitary Men," *Texas Observer*, November 10,
2010, texasobserver.org/solitary-men/.

152 **dehumanizing nudity:** Alex Hannaford, "Inmates Aren't the Only Victims of
the Prison-Industrial Complex," *The Nation*, September 16, 2014, thenation
.com/article/inmates-arent-only-victims-prison-industrial-complex.

152 **couldn't touch their fathers:** Interview with Edgar Fincher, Texas After Violence Project Collection of Oral History Interviews, Human Rights Documentation Initiative, University of Texas Libraries, University of Texas at Austin, av
.lib.utexas.edu/index.php?title=Category:Fincher,_Edgar.

152 **final shower and meal:** Hannaford, "Inmates."

152 **little training:** Interview with Edgar Fincher.

152 **no counseling:** Ibid.

152 **black eyes:** Ibid.

153 **high blood pressure:** Hannaford, "Inmates."

153 **"PAWN TO ECHO FOUR!":** Hood, "Death Letters."

CHAPTER 8

Micki Dickoff, Steve Hall, and Bernadine Skillern told me about the Gary Graham
case, as did Graham's lawyers Richard Burr and Mandy Welch. See also Mandy
Welch and Richard Burr, "The Politics of Finality and the Execution of the Innocent:
The Case of Gary Graham," in *Machinery of Death: The Reality of America's Death
Penalty Machine*, edited by David R. Dow and Mark Dow (New York: Routledge,
2002), 127. I also consulted the Governor George W. Bush General Counsel execution case files at the George W. Bush Presidential Library in Dallas. I learned about
the legal situation in the mid-1990s through interviews with Pete Gallego, Michael McCormick, Yogi McKelvey, and Vincent Perini, an email exchange with Cathy
Cochran, recordings of Texas Legislature hearings from 1995 on Senate Bill 440, a
Texas After Violence Project interview with Roy Greenwood, Mike Hall's reporting
for *Texas Monthly* ("And Justice for Some," November 2004), and David R. Dow's
book *Executed on a Technicality: Lethal Injustice on America's Death Row* (Boston: Beacon Press, 2006), which details the cases of Cesar Fierro and Johnny Joe Martinez.

On the effects of the Anti-Terrorism and Effective Death Penalty Act of 1996, I
relied on Dow's two books mentioned above, as well as Ken Armstrong's reporting

for *The Marshall Project* ("Death by Deadline, Part One," November 15, 2014, themarshallproject.org/2014/11/15/death-by-deadline-part-one, and "Death by Deadline, Part Two," November 16, 2014, themarshallproject.org/2 014/11/16/ death-by-deadline-part-two). Ken graciously shared some of his transcripts and his own unpublished summaries of the congressional debates preceding passage, and Liliana Segura's reporting for *The Intercept* shed light on Bill Clinton's role ("Gutting Habeas Corpus," May 4, 2016, theintercept.com/2016/05/04/the-untold-story-of -bill-clintons-other-crime-bill/). Craig Washington recounted his time in Congress, and I also utilized reporting by Michael Berryhill in *The Trials of Eroy Brown: The Murder Case That Shook the Texas Prison System* (Austin: University of Texas Press, 2011). Danalynn Recer and Clive Stafford Smith recounted the Thibodeaux trial, and Recer shared the trial transcript. I accessed news stories about the trial through the archives of the Lake Charles *American Press.*

156 **they called Craig Washington:** Michael Berryhill, *The Trials of Eroy Brown: The Murder Case That Shook the Texas Prison System* (Austin: University of Texas Press, 2011), 61.

156 **save his own life:** Ibid., 108.

156 **"Washington wanted the jury":** Ibid., 92.

156 **he slipped:** Ibid.

156 **"No one wants to die":** Michael Berryhill, "The Trials of Eroy Brown," *Texas Observer,* November 1, 2011, texasobserver.org/the-trials-of-eroy-brown/.

156 **"no lie can live forever":** Ibid.

156 **Washington beat them:** Rachel Graves, "Craig Washington Returns to the Spotlight," *Houston Chronicle,* March 6, 2005, chron.com/news/houston -texas/article/Craig-Washington-returns-to-the-spotlight-1654534.php.

157 **never been much for compromise:** Paul Burka, Kaye Northcott, and Allison Cook, "1983: The Ten Best and the Ten Worst Legislators," *Texas Monthly,* July 1983, texasmonthly.com/politics/the-ten-best-and-the-ten-worst-legislators- 1983/.

157 **"Seldom has a member":** Ibid.

157 **called his peers racists:** Paul Burka, Kaye Northcott, Emily Yoffe, and Ellen Williams, "1987: The Ten Best and the Ten Worst Legislators," *Texas Monthly,* July 1987, texasmonthly.com/articles/the-best-and-the-worst-legislators-1987/.

157 **"haunted the House floor":** Burka et al., "1983."

157 **Washington was elected to his seat:** Berryhill, *Trials,* 204.

157 **$250,000 in back taxes:** Jim Zook, "Rep. Washington's Wife Files for Bankruptcy Protection," *Houston Chronicle,* November 5, 1991, A10.

157 **"affront to his constituents":** "Sorry Records; and a Sorry Excuse for It by Rep. Craig Washington," *Houston Chronicle,* December 29, 1993, A20.

158 **challenge prosecutors over race:** "House OKs Anti-Crime Measure," *St. Louis Post-Dispatch,* October 23, 1991, 1A.

158 **"Give 'em a fair trial":** Moss J. Jennings, "House Votes to Expand Capital Punishment," *Washington Times,* October 23, 1991.

158 **removing disparities in punishments:** Carol A. Bergman, "The Road to Reform," *Nation,* September 2, 1999, thenation.com/article/road-reform/.

158 *Washington Post* **editorial page:** "A Better Crime Bill," *Washington Post,* October

22, 1993, washingtonpost.com/archive/opinions/1993/10/22/a-better-crime-bill/a278c1a5-86f1-4216-82bd-da380e9b9f0b/?utm_term=.0053f4084e56.

158 **"We are trying to promote"**: Linda Feldmann, "Wrangling on Hill May Slow Passage of Crime Bill," *Christian Science Monitor,* October 26, 1993, csmonitor.com/1993/1026/26012.html.

158 **He moved to Bastrop:** Graves, "Craig Washington Returns."

159 **tag him as "soft":** Liliana Segura, "Gutting Habeas Corpus," *The Intercept,* May 4, 2016, theintercept.com/2016/05/04/the-untold-story-of-bill-clintons-other-crime-bill/.

160 **trying to broker a similar compromise:** Ken Armstrong, "Death by Deadline, Part One," *The Marshall Project,* November 15, 2014, themarshallproject.org/2014/11/15/death-by-deadline-part-one.

160 **solicited data from Columbia law professor James Liebman:** James S. Liebman, Jeffrey Fagan, and Valerie West, "A Broken System: Error Rates in Capital Cases, 1973–1995," Columbia Law School Public Law & Legal Theory Working Paper Group, Paper Number 15, June 12, 2000, 5.

160 **Liebman concluded both were right:** Ibid., Executive Summary.

160 **Clinton and his aides:** Segura, "Gutting."

160 **"No. Oklahoma":** Ibid.

161 **The complaints that had plagued:** South Carolina's attorney general, Charlie Condon, argued that they had become "lobbying groups against the death penalty." Henry J. Reske, "The Politics of Death," *ABA Journal,* November 1995, 20.

161 **complained that they had become "lobbying groups against the death penalty":** Henry J. Reske, "The Politics of Death," *ABA Journal,* November 1995, 20.

161 **voted to defund them:** Scott Pendleton, "Who Will Pay Now for Death-Row Appeals?" *Christian Science Monitor,* October 3, 1995, csmonitor.com/1995/1003/03031.html.

161 **money ran out in October 1995:** Ibid.

161 **death sentences had fallen by 80 percent:** David R. Dow and Eric Freedman, "The Effects of AEDPA on Justice," *Scholarly Commons at Hofstra Law* (2009), 261.

161 **Many lawyers missed:** Armstrong, "Death by Deadline."

161 **Prosecutors could seize on minor errors:** Ibid.

162 **$7,500:** Michael Hall, "And Justice for Some," *Texas Monthly,* November 2004, texasmonthly.com/politics/and-justice-for-some/.

162 **they tracked 84 cases:** *A State of Denial: Texas Justice and the Death Penalty* (Austin: Texas Defender Service, 2001), 4.

162 **160 cases involving forensic science:** Ibid., 4.

162 **6 cases of men executed:** Ibid., 8.

162 **251 habeas petitions:** *Lethal Indifference: The Fatal Combination of Incompetent Attorneys and Unaccountable Courts in Texas Death Penalty Appeals* (Austin: Texas Defender Service, 2001), 15.

163 **more than a hundred pages:** Ibid., 13.

163 **came in under thirty:** Ibid., 14.

163 **just two pages:** Ibid.

163 **same error of capitalization:** Chuck Lindell, "Death Row Inmates Share Identical Appeal," *Austin American-Statesman*, February 26, 2006, freerobwill.org/death-row-inmates-share-identical-appeal.

163 **urging members in 1998:** "TCDLA Urges Members to Pass on Accepting Habeas Cases," *Texas Lawyer*, June 22, 1998, 4.

163 **many did not listen:** Kathy Walt, "Lawyers Who Aid Condemned Paid $265,000," *Houston Chronicle*, October 3, 1997, A33.

163 **at least four hundred hours:** Stephen B. Bright, "Neither Equal nor Just: The Rationing and Denial of Legal Services to the Poor When Life and Liberty Are at Stake," *New York University School of Law Annual Survey of American Law* 1997 (1999): 14.

163 **no relevant experience:** David Dow, *Executed on a Technicality: Lethal Injustice on America's Death Row* (Boston: Beacon Press, 2006), 62.

163 **didn't accept the charges:** Ibid.

163 **"I am wondering about the due date":** Ibid., 67.

164 **seventeen lines of text:** Ibid., 63.

164 **"I know I'm fixing to die":** Ibid.

164 **Judge Cathy Cochran wrote for a majority:** Ex Parte Graves, 70 S.W.3d 103 (Tex. Crim. App. 2002). A dark irony of this opinion is that the death row prisoner in question, Anthony Graves, not only suffered terrible representation but was innocent of the crime for which he was sentenced to death. He was later exonerated.

164 **1996 opinion in the case of Cesar Fierro:** Ex Parte Fierro, 934 S.W.2d 370 (Tex. Crim. App. 1996).

164 **electric generator attached to their genitals:** Steve Mills and Ken Armstrong, "Justices Prove Reluctant to Nullify Cases," *Chicago Tribune*, June 12, 2000, 1.

164 **colluding with the Mexican police:** Michael Hall, "Death Isn't Fair," *Texas Monthly*, December 2002 texasmonthly.com/articles/death-isnt-fair/.

165 **he let his hair grow:** Dow, *Executed*, 48.

165 **"I used to think Fierro":** Ibid., 50.

165 **"a crime he had nothing to do with":** In December 2019, Cesar Fierro was finally resentenced to life in prison when the Court of Criminal Appeals vacated his sentence—citing problems in the instructions given to his jury—and a new district attorney in El Paso declined to seek another death sentence. See Jolie McCullough, "Cesar Fierro Spent 40 Years on Texas Death Row. A Court Tossed His Sentence Wednesday for Faulty Jury Instructions," *Texas Tribune*, December 18, 2019, texastribune.org/2019/12/18/texas-death-row-cesar-fierro-sentence-tossed/.

165 **mounting a vigorous defense at the trial stage:** Millard Farmer, "Death Row, U.S.A. Welcomes the State of Kansas as Its Newest Franchisee and Supplier," accessed July 4, 2019, goextranet.com/Seminars/BlackHole/DeathRowUSA/PrintFriendlydeath_rowPart1.htm.

166 **"Louisiana Crisis Assistance Center":** Clive Stafford Smith, "Killing the Death Penalty with Kindness," in Dow and Dow, *Machinery of Death*, 270.

168 **less than an hour:** Vincent Lupo, "Murderer Gets Life, Not Death," Lake Charles *American Press*, March 22, 1996, 1.

CHAPTER 9

George W. Bush, through a spokesperson, declined an interview. The material about him draws on his campaign memoir *A Charge to Keep* (New York: William Morrow, 1999) and on-background interviews with several former staffers. This and the following chapter rely primarily on interviews with corrections officers Frank AuBuchon, Kenneth Dean, Robert Lampert, Lance Lowry, and Buster McWhorter; lawyers David Dow, Maurie Levin, Jim Liebman, Walter Long, Jim Marcus, Robert McGlasson, Rita Radostitz, and Mac Secrest; and writers Ken Armstrong, Raymond Bonner, Beverly Lowry, and Sara Rimer. Lowry wrote an excellent book on the Karla Faye Tucker case, *Crossed Over: A Murder, a Memoir* (New York: Alfred A. Knopf, 1992). To learn about how other states sought help from Texas in their own execution protocols, I interviewed Gene Atherton of Colorado, John Hamm of Alabama, Gerges Scott of New Mexico, Duane Shillinger of Wyoming, and Daniel Vasquez of California. McWhorter provided the *Texas Monthly* letter written by his wife.

The material on the Board of Pardons and Paroles draws on interviews with Laura McElroy and a former board member who did not wish to be named.

Lawyer Sandra Babcock shared a transcript of the December 21–22, 1998, evidentiary hearing in *Joseph Stanley Faulder and Danny Lee Barber v. Texas Board of Pardons and Paroles, et al.* (United States District Court, Western District of Texas, Austin Division). The anecdote about John Bradley—who declined an interview—was related by Keith Hampton and confirmed by Michael Bernard and Michael Charlton. Robert Duncan and Lisa Kaufman also provided context on the 2011 legislative session.

171 **bristled at the intrusion:** Mandery, *Wild Justice*, 381.

172 **one execution per month:** "Executions by Year," *Texas Department of Criminal Justice*, April 25, 2019, tdcj.texas.gov/death_row/dr_executions_by_year .html.

172 **they executed forty people:** Ibid.

172 **three men in a single week:** Ibid.

172 **"I realized that the attitude":** Pickett, *Within These Walls*, 173.

173 **to see the sun go down:** Ibid., 172.

173 **James Autrey smoked a cigarette:** Ibid., 80.

173 **"Those innocent, childlike sounds":** Ibid., 175.

173 **image of DeLuna's eyes:** Alberta Phillips, "Questioning the Myth of a Painless Execution," *Austin American-Statesman*, December 11, 2003, A21.

173 **"How could I be a party":** Pickett, *Within These Walls*, 60.

173 **At least fifteen states:** This number is based on interviews with numerous prison officials around the country and some news articles. The following states took at least some lessons from Texas: Alabama, Arkansas, California, Colorado, Florida, Indiana, Kansas, Louisiana, Nevada, New Mexico, Oklahoma, Oregon, Pennsylvania, Wyoming, and Washington.

174 **"implies there is something inhuman":** In Re Kemmler, 136 U.S. 436 (1890).

174 **roughly 3 percent:** Austin Sarat, *Gruesome Spectacles: Botched Executions and America's Death Penalty* (Palo Alto, Calif.: Stanford University Press, 2014), 5.

174 **a television reporter from Dallas:** Garrett v. Estelle, 556 F.2d 1274 (1977).

175 **"When we did our very first execution":** Testimony of Donald Courts in *Louisiana v. Code*, case no. 138,850, March 18, 2003, cited in "So Long as They Die: Lethal Injections in the United States," *Human Rights Watch*, vol. 18, no. 1, April 2006, 17.

175 **play a role in killing someone:** Pickett, *Within These Walls*, 115.

175 **He started seeing in his mind:** *Into the Abyss: A Tail of Death, a Tale of Life*, film, directed by Werner Herzog (Hollywood: Creative Differences Productions, 2011).

176 **"Does it get worse":** "Karla Faye Tucker: Born Again on Death Row," CNN, March 26, 2007, edition.cnn.com/2007/US/03/21/larry.king.tucker/.

176 **exposed to heroin by age ten:** Linda Strom, *Karla Faye Tucker Set Free: Life and Faith on Death Row* (Colorado Springs: WaterBrook Press, 2000), 18; Beverly Lowry, "The Good Bad Girl," *New Yorker*, February 9, 1998, 60.

176 KILL THEM ALL: Beverly Lowry, *Crossed Over: A Murder, a Memoir* (New York: Alfred A. Knopf, 1992), 31.

176 **"I come with every stroke":** Ibid., 65.

176 THE EMBODIMENT OF EVIL: Ibid., 13.

176 **a puppet show put on by a Christian ministry:** "Born Again on Death Row."

177 **they could eat together:** Lowry, *Crossed Over*, 192.

177 **sold to prison employees:** "Born Again on Death Row."

177 **Evangelical Christians in the United States:** Maurice Chammah, "Are Evangelicals Ditching the Death Penalty?," *The Marshall Project*, August 14, 2016, themarshallproject.org/2016/08/14/are-evangelicals-ditching-the-death-penalty.

177 **the primary basis for the death sentence:** Walter Long, "Karla Faye Tucker: A Case for Restorative Justice," *American Journal of Criminal Law* 27 (Fall 1999): 117.

178 **"Faith changes lives":** George W. Bush, *A Charge to Keep* (New York: William Morrow, 1999), 139.

178 **Mark White had rarely done:** Mark White, "Why I Changed My Mind on the Death Penalty," *Politico*, May 5, 2014, politico.com/magazine/story/2014/05/capital-punishment-106364.

178 **Ann Richards never did:** Gregory Curtis, "Seven Women," *Texas Monthly*, October 1997, texasmonthly.com/politics/seven-women/.

178 **"ample opportunity":** Bush, *Charge to Keep*, 141.

178 **Bush openly admitted:** Ibid., 151.

178 **"They didn't tell me":** The board member in question asked not to be named in this book.

178 **Those who did go on record:** Sara Rimer and Raymond Bonner, "Capital Punishment in Texas; Bush Candidacy Puts Focus on Executions," *New York Times*, May 14, 2000, nytimes.com/2000/05/14/us/record-capital-punishment-texas-bush-candidacy-puts-focus-executions.html.

179 **The effort to make the board more transparent:** Federal judge Sam Sparks upheld the Texas procedure, following a 1998 Supreme Court decision, *Woodard v. Ohio Adult Parole Authority* (523 U.S. 272), that required only "minimal procedural safeguards." Still, Sparks wrote, "It is abundantly clear the Texas clem-

ency procedure is extremely poor and certainly minimal. Legislatively, there is a dearth of meaningful procedure. Administratively, the goal is more to protect the secrecy and autonomy of the system rather than carrying out an efficient legally sound system. The board would not have to sacrifice its conservative ideology to carry out its duties in a more fair and accurate fashion."

179 **He was troubled:** Bush, *Charge to Keep*, 142.

179 **getting lots of pressure:** Ibid., 144.

179 **"If my execution is the only thing":** Ibid., 148.

179 **"I can't bring back the lives I took":** Ibid., 150.

180 **"Don't worry":** Timothy Carter, *The Executioner's Redemption: My Story of Violence, Death, and Saving Grace* (St. Louis: Concordia Publishing House, 2016), 49.

180 **"help them to find my vein":** Strom, *Karla Faye Tucker Set Free*, 15.

181 **no extra pay:** Sara Rimer, "Working Death Row: A Special Report," *New York Times*, December 17, 2000, A1.

181 **he found the routine itself:** Ibid.

182 **thinking of their own mothers:** Ibid.

182 **feel more bothered:** Ibid.

183 **the words of Jim Willett:** Patrick Beach, "Jim Willett: What I've Learned," *Esquire*, January 29, 2007, esquire.com/news-politics/interviews/a1753/esq0302-mar-wil/.

184 **challenges to this script:** Another example of a death row exoneration in Texas that gained widespread public attention was the saga of Clarence Brandley. He was convicted in Conroe, in East Texas, for the 1980 rape and murder of Cheryl Ferguson, a sixteen-year-old student at the high school where he worked as a janitor. During the investigation a Texas Ranger called him the n-word. The state's Court of Criminal Appeals overturned his sentence, saying his trial had lacked "the rudiments of fairness," and he was freed in 1990. Local officials chose not to retry him, but because he was never formally cleared of the crime, he did not receive compensation from the state. See Nick Davies, *White Lies: The True Story of Clarence Brandley, Presumed Guilty in the American South* (London: Chatto & Windus, 1991).

184 **Orange Socks:** In 2019, the victim of the "Orange Socks" case was identified by law enforcement as twenty-three-year-old Debra Jackson of Abilene.

184 **"my office":** Cynthia Gorney, "Anatomy of a Killer," *Washington Post*, October 11, 1984, washingtonpost.com/archive/lifestyle/1984/10/11/anatomy-of-a-killer/0f8e6d66-2905-4235-a771-9a80f71a6643/?utm_term=.bf33ac60 1824.

184 **assassinate President Jimmy Carter:** Gísli H. Guðjónsson, *The Psychology of Interrogations and Confessions: A Handbook* (Hoboken, N.J.: Wiley, 2003), 555.

185 **"refreshed" his memory:** Pamela Colloff, "The Innocent Man: Part 1," *Texas Monthly*, November 2012, texasmonthly.com/politics/the-innocent-man-part-one/.

185 **hundreds of miles:** Cynthia Gorney and Paul Taylor, "The Killer Who Recanted," *Washington Post*, April 15, 1985, washingtonpost.com/archive/

lifestyle/1985/04/15/the-killer-who-recanted/93193008-374f-47a6-8673-3
04c7a8f258a/?utm_term=.a7aa3ab5d181.

185 **held up three fingers:** Carlton Stowers, "Dead Wrong," *Dallas Observer,* May 17,
2001, dallasobserver.com/content/printView/6392124.

185 **"the most prolific serial confessor":** Guðjónsson, *Psychology of Interrogations
and Confessions,* 554.

185 **"Everybody was paying attention":** Ibid., 559.

186 **"Even if they don't believe":** Colloff, "Innocent Man."

186 **wrote Bush a long letter:** Bush, *Charge to Keep,* 160–61.

186 **Bush's own advisers:** Ibid., 157.

186 **"unusual or exceptional circumstances":** Ibid., 163.

186 **"I take this action":** Allen R. Myerson, "Citing Facts, Bush Spares Texas Inmate
on Death Row," *New York Times,* June 27, 1998, nytimes.com/1998/06/27/
us/citing-facts-bush-spares-texas-inmate-on-death-row.html.

187 **claims of personal limitation:** Bush's clemency record was the subject of an
investigative feature that challenged many of his assertions about his record.
Alan Berlow, "The Texas Clemency Memos," *The Atlantic,* August 12, 2003,
theatlantic.com/magazine/archive/2003/07/the-texas-clemency-memos/30
2755/.

187 **"this was not 1920":** Ricardo C. Ainslie, *Long Dark Road: Bill King and Murder in
Jasper, Texas* (Austin: University of Texas Press, 2009), 118.

187 **"Black residents who had never supported":** Joyce King, *Hate Crime: The Story
of a Dragging in Jasper, Texas* (New York: Anchor, 2003), 48.

187 **No white man had been executed:** Michael Graczyk, "Hayes First White Executed in 21 Years for Killing a Black," *Victoria Advocate,* September 15,
2003, 7A.

188 **A representative of the NAACP:** Faulkner Fox, "Justice in Jasper," *Texas Observer,* September 17, 1999, texasobserver.org/275-afterword-justice-in
-jasper/.

188 **"You can't fight murder":** Karen Brooks, "Victim's Son Objects as Texas Sets
Execution in Hate Crime Death," Reuters, September 21, 2011, reuters.com/
article/us-texas-execution-son/victims-son-objects-as-texas-sets-execution-in
-hate-crime-death-idUSTRE78K35B20110921.

189 **"awkward political decision":** Paul Duggan, "Texas Hate-Crimes Bill Dies,"
Washington Post, May 15, 1999, washingtonpost.com/wp-srv/politics/
campaigns/wh2000/stories/bush051699.htm.

CHAPTER 10

See header to chapter 9 notes section above.

190 **a profile of George W. Bush:** Tucker Carlson, "Devil May Care," *Talk,* September
1999, 106.

191 **"suggests an atmosphere of adolescence":** George F. Will, "Bush's Revealing
Interview," Baltimore *Sun,* August 12, 1999, baltimoresun.com/news/bs-xpm
-1999-08-12-9908120344-story.html.

191 **"You could actually see":** Lauren Kern, "Stand Up and Holler," *Houston Press,*

February 3, 2000, houstonpress.com/news/stand-up-and-holler-6565798. The segment appeared in season 2, episode 2 of Michael Moore's show *The Awful Truth.*

192 **"The vision of American criminal law":** Edmund Pearson, "Hauptmann and Circumstantial Evidence," *New Yorker,* March 9, 1935, 41.

192 **"Had the state of Illinois":** Don Terry, "Survivors Make the Case Against Death Row," *New York Times,* November 16, 1998, nytimes.com/1998/11/16/us/survivors-make-the-case-against-death-row.html.

192 **"public relations counterattack":** Ibid.

193 **"new breed of death penalty abolitionists":** Byron York, "The Death of Death," *American Spectator,* April 2000, 33.

193 **"Capital punishment is a government program":** George F. Will, "Innocent on Death Row," *Washington Post,* April 6, 2000, A23.

193 **In 1999, the *Chicago Tribune*:** "How the Death Penalty Was Abolished in Illinois," *Chicago Tribune,* May 15, 2018, chicagotribune.com/news/ct-met-illinois-death-penalty-timeline-gfx-20180514-htmlstory.html.

193 **"I cannot support a system":** Alan Berlow, "Death in Texas," *Washington Post,* February 13, 2000, B5, washingtonpost.com/wp-srv/WPcap/2000-02/13/075r-021300-idx.html.

194 **"we should not have automobiles":** Banner, "Death Penalty," 304.

195 **Defense lawyers began receiving flurries of calls:** Dow and Dow, *Machinery of Death,* 3.

195 **"How would we know?":** Rimer and Bonner, "Capital Punishment in Texas."

195 **"a promiscuous girl":** Ofra Bikel, "The Case for Innocence," Frontline #1808 (transcript), January 11, 2000, pbs.org/wgbh/pages/frontline/shows/case/etc/script.html.

195 **"laughingstock":** Hall, "Death Isn't Fair."

195 **incredulous at the question:** Jim Yardley, "Bush Stance on Bias Crimes Emerges as Campaign Issue," *New York Times* October 13, 2000, A25.

195 **"The man is out":** "Text: GOP Debate in Los Angeles," *Washington Post,* March 2, 2000, washingtonpost.com/wp-srv/politics/campaigns/wh2000/stories/text030200.htm.

195 **appeared to smile:** Richard Cohen, "And Bush Smiles," *Washington Post,* October 17, 2000, washingtonpost.com/archive/opinions/2000/10/17/and-bush-smiles/d380f784-341d-4b6a-8396-d0e8be7c65a2/?utm_term=.e694995e1f38.

195 **NAACP-funded ad:** Yardley, "Bush Stance."

195 **"I hope you're not laughing":** Yvonne Abraham, " 'Late Show' No Joke for Bush," *Boston Globe,* October 20, 2000, A28.

195 **the cover of *Newsweek*:** Mark Miller, "A Life or Death Gamble," *Newsweek,* May 28, 2000, 22–28.

196 **1 in 65 quadrillion chance:** Stevenson Swanson, "Results from DNA Testing Keep Texan on Death Row," *Chicago Tribune,* August 16, 2000, 52.

196 **subconsciously led to identify him:** Mandy Welch and Richard Burr, "The Politics of Finality and the Execution of the Innocent: The Case of Gary Graham," in Dow and Dow, *Machinery of Death,* 136.

197 **Mock Wing:** Sara Rimer and Raymond Bonner, "Texas Lawyer's Death Row Record a Concern," *New York Times*, June 11, 2000, A1.

197 **The Congressional Black Caucus:** "Housebroken," *Newsweek*, November 28, 1993, newsweek.com/housebroken-191504.

197 **Roman Catholic bishops:** "Foes of Execution Contest a Texas Case," *New York Times*, June 2, 1993, A16.

197 **Kenny Rogers:** "NAACP Head Asks Governor to Reopen Graham Case," UPI, July 24, 1993, upi.com/Archives/1993/07/24/NAACP-head-asks-governor -to-reopen-Graham-case/4984743486400/.

197 **forty thousand Quaaludes:** Welch and Burr, "Politics of Finality," 138.

197 **stymied at every turn:** Ibid., 138–41.

197 **grant him a hearing:** Ibid., 141.

198 **Bush was able to sell Cornyn's decision:** "Bush Comments on Death Row Case," Associated Press, June 6, 2000, apnews.com/17db3e6e18b2667b46c4410 dbb28f08e.

199 **"Visiting days here":** J. Michael Kennedy, "Texas Murder Case Turns Into a Media Drama," *Los Angeles Times*, September 7, 1993, latimes.com/archives/la -xpm-1993-09-07-mn-32488-story.html.

199 **"he changed his first name":** Journalists continued to refer to him as Graham, and I have opted to continue to do so after this point in the timeline for clarity.

199 **"highly charged debate":** "Jew Don Boney on the Maury Povich Show Discuss- ing Gary Graham Execution," YouTube video, 5:39, "Hon. Jew Don Boney," April 20, 2015, youtube.com/watch?v=Mym6b0aCcys.

199 **"He pulled out a 12-gauge":** "Does Gary Graham Deserve to Be Executed?," *Larry King Live* (transcript), June 22, 2000, http://transcripts.cnn.com/ TRANSCRIPTS/0006/22/lkl.00.html.

200 **brought in to manage the crowds:** "Gary Graham Case: Texas Board of Pardons and Paroles to Make Final Deliberation," *Early Edition* (transcript), June 22, 2000, cnn.com/TRANSCRIPTS/0006/22/ee.04.html.

200 **"Fuck you":** "Gary Graham Demonstrations—Huntsville, Texas—22 June 2000," YouTube video, 35:25, NARDO, August 22, 2012, youtube.com/watch ?v=K5YwU5Xw4AI.

200 **"We fired up":** "Gary Graham Execution Protest," YouTube video, 33:41, Pre- cious Opie, March 29, 2016, youtube.com/watch?v=TSfDIx8BXi8.

200 **spat in Chaplain Pickett's face:** Pickett, *Within These Walls*, 191.

200 **"You can step out":** Willett, *Warden*, 210.

200 **outfitted in leg irons:** Ibid., 212.

200 **"There's nothing in his eyes":** Ibid., 210.

201 **paper clothing to wear:** Ibid., 211.

201 **"I need you to move up":** Ibid., 215.

201 **shoulders and waists:** Ibid.

201 **Dean recovered and pinned:** Ibid.

202 **noticed bruises on his arm:** "USA: Texas: Gary Graham Executed," YouTube video, 3:00, AP Archive, July 21, 2015, youtube.com/watch?v=BRpNzzSgA6Q. Kenneth Dean, speaking with fact checker Julie Tate, denied that there were bruises.

202 **strapped down with Velcro:** Ibid.

202 **nearly exposing his genitals:** Willett, *Warden*, 215.

202 **"What is happening here":** "Final Statement of Shaka Sankofa (Gary Graham)," *The Ethical Spectacle*, July 2000, spectacle.org/0700/shakastate.html.

202 **long line of horrid spectacles:** "CNBC—Gary Graham," YouTube video, 2:11, Rodney Ellis, April 24, 2009, youtube.com/watch?v=ZVe-p838L1w.

202 **"like anti-death-penalty wishful thinking":** Julie Mason, "Death Penalty Not Haunting Bush as Predicted," *Houston Chronicle*, July 2, 2000.

202 **eight points around the time:** Ibid.

202 **obtained confidential memos:** Berlow, "Texas Clemency Memos."

203 **"All of us wonder":** Rimer, "Working Death Row," A1.

204 **a story by Nate Blakeslee:** Nate Blakeslee, "The Color of Justice," *Texas Observer*, June 23, 2000, texasobserver.org/611-the-color-of-justice/.

206 **given that he'd be surrounded by men:** Richard Goldstein, "Queer on Death Row," *Village Voice*, March 13, 2001, villagevoice.com/2001/03/13/queer-on -death-row/.

206 **Pitts sarcastically compared:** Leonard Pitts, "Giving New Meaning to 'Dream Team'; Does the Trial Count If Your Lawyer Nods Off?" *Chicago Tribune*, June 13, 2000, 17.

206 **"After my first trial":** Henry Weinstein, "Attorney in 'Sleeping Lawyer' Case Hits Roadblock in Texas," *Los Angeles Times*, July 21, 2002, articles.latimes.com/ 2002/jul/21/nation/na-lawyer21.

207 **She also rounded up fifty:** "Danalynn Recer," *Petra*, accessed July 17, 2019, petrafoundation.org/fellows/danalynn-recer/.

207 **Rosenthal agreed to let Burdine:** Henry Weinstein, "Inmate in Texas Sleeping-Lawyer Case Pleads Guilty," *Los Angeles Times*, June 20, 2003, latimes.com/ archives/la-xpm-2003-jun-20-na-sleep20-story.html.

208 **$6,800:** Jeffrey Toobin, "The Mitigator," *New Yorker*, May 9, 2011, newyorker .com/magazine/2011/05/09/the-mitigator.

CHAPTER 11

This chapter relies on interviews with John Niland, Danalynn Recer, Steven Reis, Matt Silverman, James Stafford, Clive Stafford Smith, and Elizabeth Vartkessian. Reis and Stafford shared documents on the Francisco Castellano case. The mother of the victim in the case declined an interview. James Sidney Crowley did not respond to multiple phone calls in 2017 and 2018, and he died in 2019. Many early GRACE newsletters are online (gracelaw.org). I consulted Jeffrey Toobin's profile of Recer, titled "The Mitigator," in the May 2, 2011, issue of *The New Yorker* and Brandon Garrett's book *End of Its Rope: How Killing the Death Penalty Can Revive Criminal Justice* (Cambridge, Mass.: Harvard University Press, 2017). Some of the reporting in this chapter was done for previous articles: "To Kill? Or Not to Kill?" *Texas Observer*, April 23, 2014, texasobserver .org/to-kill-or-not-to-kill/; "The Slow Death of the Death Penalty," *The Marshall Project*, December 17, 2014, themarshallproject.org/2014/12/17/the-slow-death-of-the -death-penalty; "How Mexico Saves Its Citizens from the Death Penalty in the U.S.," *The Marshall Project*, September 22, 2016, themarshallproject.org/2016/09/22/how -mexico-saves-its-citizens-from-the-death-penalty-in-the-u-s; and "Scharlette Holdman, Voice for the Defense on Death Row, Dies at 70," *New York Times*, July 22, 2017, nytimes.com/2017/07/22/us/scharlette-holdman-dead.html.

209 **Reis exuded none:** Maurice Chammah, "To Kill? Or Not to Kill?" *Texas Observer*, April 23, 2014, texasobserver.org/to-kill-or-not-to-kill/.

210 **"Maybe law is not":** Ibid.

211 **"gun messed up":** Robbie Byrd, "Man Executed in Death of Bay City Woman," *Huntsville Item*, August 15, 2007, itemonline.com/news/local_news/man -executed-in-death-of-bay-city-woman/article_89444db3-ee5a-5b59-a0d4 -f74477020ece.html.

215 **expanded the meaning of this phrase:** Lockett v. Ohio, 438 U.S. 586 (1978); Eddings v. Oklahoma, 455 U.S. 104 (1982).

215 **said their trial lawyers failed:** Williams v. Taylor, 529 U.S. 420 (2000); Wiggins v. Smith, 539 U.S. 510 (2003); Rompilla v. Beard, 545 U.S. 374 (2005).

215 **expected of all competent lawyers:** John H. Blume and Stacey D. Neumann, "It's Like Deja Vu All Over Again": Williams v. Taylor, "Wiggins v. Smith, Rompilla v. Beard and a (Partial) Return to the Guidelines Approach to the Effective Assistance of Counsel," *Cornell Law Faculty Publications Paper* 38 (2007); Russell Stetler and W. Bradley Wendel, "The ABA Guidelines and the Norms of Capital Defense Representation," *Hofstra Law Review* 41 (2013): 635.

215 **"change of heart":** Carol Steiker and Jordan Steiker, "Justice Kennedy: He Swung Left on the Death Penalty but Declined to Swing for the Fences," *SCOTUSblog*, July 2, 2018, scotusblog.com/2018/07/justice-kennedy-he -swung-left-on-the-death-penalty-but-declined-to-swing-for-the-fences/.

215 **a handful of prisoners:** These cases were Penry v. Johnson, 532 U.S. 782 (2001); Tennard v. Dretke, 542 U.S. 274 (2004); Abdul-Kabir v. Quarterman, 550 U.S. 297 (2007); and Smith v. Texas, 550 U.S. 297 (2007). To some scholars, these new decisions proved once and for all that the Texas death penalty law created in 1973 should have been rejected along with other overly rigid "mandatory" death penalty laws back in 1976, and that for decades it had allowed the state to get away with executing people without letting juries really make a fully informed decision about whether they deserved the ultimate punishment. See Lucas A. Powe, Jr., *America's Lone Star Constitution: How Supreme Court Cases from Texas Shape the Nation* (Berkeley: University of California Press, 2018), 198–236.

215 **challenge ineffective trial defense lawyering:** Martinez v. Ryan, 566 U.S. __ (2012), Trevino v. Thaler, 569 U.S. 413 (2013).

215 **later stages of appeal:** Davila v. Davis, 582 U.S. __ (2017).

215 **abolished the death penalty for people:** Atkins v. Virginia, 536 U.S. 304 (2002).

215 **"the mind of a child":** Connie Mabin, "Prosecutors Fear Flood of Death Penalty Appeals After Supreme Court Ruling," Associated Press, June 21, 2002.

216 **"bully":** Michael Fleishman, "Reciprocity Unmasked: The Role of the Mexican Government in Defense of Its Foreign Nationals in United States Death Penalty Cases," *Arizona Journal of International and Comparative Law* 20, no. 2 (2003): 373.

216 **At the International Court of Justice:** Case Concerning Avena and Other Mexican Nationals (Mexico v. United States), no. 128 (I.C.J. Feb. 5, 2003).

216 **Supreme Court ruled it was not binding:** Medellín v. Texas, 552 U.S. 491 (2008).

216 **solicitor general Ted Cruz:** "Medellín v. Texas," *Oyez*, accessed April 14, 2020, oyez.org/cases/2007/06-984.

216 **95 percent:** Gregory J. Kuykendall, Alicia Amezcua-Rodriguez, and Mark Warren, "Mitigation Abroad: Preparing a Successful Case for Life for the Foreign National Client," *Hofstra Law Review* 36, no. 3 (2008): 12.

217 **Reis recalled Stafford saying:** Stafford did not recall this conversation when asked in April 2020.

218 **as much as $2 million:** Christy Hoppe, "Executions Cost Texas Millions: Study Finds It's Cheaper to Jail Killers for Life," *Dallas Morning News*, March 8, 1992.

218 **compared them to floods and tornadoes:** Maurice Chammah, "The Slow Death of the Death Penalty," *The Marshall Project*, December 17, 2014, the marshallproject.org/2014/12/17/the-slow-death-of-the-death-penalty.org.

218 **increased its tax rate nearly 12 percent:** W. Gardner Selby, "Ron Paul Says Death Penalty Trial Fueled Texas County's Tax Hike," *Politifact*, July 9, 2015, politifact.com/factchecks/2015/jul/09/ron-paul/ron-paul-says-death-penalty -trial-fueled-texas-tax/.

219 **From 2007 to 2016, seven states:** These were New Jersey, New York, Maryland, New Mexico, Connecticut, Delaware, and Illinois.

219 **an average of fifteen times:** David McCord, "What's Messing with Texas Death Sentences?" *Texas Tech Law Review* 43 (2011): 607.

220 **"are never, never, never":** Chammah, "Slow Death."

220 **"Spend money":** Ibid.

221 **"murder insurance":** Maria Sprow, "Murder Insurance," *County Magazine*, September/October 2008, 18.

221 **$1,000 per year:** Maria Sprow, "The 3 E's of Capital Defense," *County Magazine*, September/October 2008, 42.

221 **including law school students:** Sprow, "Murder Insurance," 21.

221 **negotiating a deal:** Dottie Carmichael, "Judgment and Justice: An Evaluation of the Texas Regional Public Defender for Capital Cases," Public Policy Research Institute at Texas A&M University, 2013, rpdo.org/publications/posts/ 2013/june/judgment-and-justice/, 58–60.

221 **only 7 percent of cases:** Ibid., 53.

222 **just fifteen counties:** Richard C. Dieter, *The 2% Death Penalty: How a Minority of Counties Produce Most Death Cases at Enormous Costs to All* (Washington, D.C.: Death Penalty Information Center, 2013), 7.

CHAPTER 12

This chapter relies on interviews with Joan Campbell, Terry Harshaw, David Lane, David Lida, Lyn McClellan, Danalynn Recer, Brian Rogers, Matt Silverman, Franklin Singer, and "Dan," who asked not to be named. I examined the records of the Capital Jury Project at the National Death Penalty Archive in Albany and worked with project researchers to keep some identifying information confidential. Most of all, I have relied on a trial transcript prepared by court reporter Louise Steckler, who had the arduous task of retrieving it from old floppy disks. I obtained the names of jurors from Steckler's transcript and local media accounts. The *Houston Chronicle* published numerous useful articles on the trial. Jaime Zamora, a longtime cameraman for KTRK (ABC13) in Houston, helped me access news broadcasts from the trial and shared his memories. For more on the laborious process of getting trial transcripts, see Emma Eisenberg, "Public Record, Astronomical Price," *The Marshall Project*, March 21, 2017, themarshallproject.org/2017/03/21/public-record-astronomical-price.

223 **Dan—not his real name:** In addition to honoring this juror's desire to be unnamed, I was bound by restrictions set by the Capital Jury Project, which interviewed this juror and has protocols related to research with human subjects designed to keep those they interview unnamed in archived materials.

224 **"We represent Juan Eduardo Quintero Perez":** Perez was Juan Quintero's mother's last name, and it is customary in Mexico to add it to the end of the full name, but he was referred to during the trial as Quintero.

225 **even if they had some misgivings:** The term the Court used was "conscientious scruples." Witherspoon v. Illinois, 391 U.S. 510 (1968)

225 **wholly opposed to capital punishment:** Lockhart v. McCree, 476 U.S. 162 (1986); Wainwright v. Witt, 470 U.S. 1039 (1985).

225 **also more likely to find someone guilty:** C. L. Cowan, W. C. Thompson, and P. C. Ellsworth, "The Effects of Death Qualification on Jurors' Predisposition to Convict and on the Quality of Deliberation," *Law and Human Behavior* 8 (1984): 53.

225 **Capital Jury Project:** "What Is the Capital Jury Project?" University at Albany, State University of New York, accessed June 29, 2019, albany.edu/scj/13189 .php.

225 **unanimous only 8 percent of the time:** Scott Sundby, "War and Peace in the Jury Room: How Capital Juries Reach Unanimity," *Hastings Law Review* 62 (2010): 107.

225 **fear that the defendant would be dangerous:** John Blume, Theodore Eisenberg, and Stephen P. Garvey, "Lessons from the Capital Jury Project," in *Beyond Repair? America's Death Penalty* (Durham, N.C.: Duke University Press, 2003), 167.

225 **"Ones are Gandhi":** *The Life Penalty*, film, directed by David Quint (Wildberry Productions, 2008), available on DVD.

226 **revealing them as "sevens":** Matthew Rubenstein, "Overview of the Colorado Method of Capital Voir Dire," *The Champion*, November 2010, 18.

226 **"isolate" and "insulate":** Ibid.

227 **seven times:** Danalynn Recer et al., "Representing Foreign National Capital Defendants," *University of Memphis Law Review* (Summer 2012), 965–66.

227 **mentioned in Congress:** Armando Villafranca, "Some Say Immigrants Fear Shooting Will Cause a Backlash," *Houston Chronicle*, September 26, 2006, chron.com/news/article/Some-say-immigrants-fear-shooting-will-cause-a-18 72751.php.

227 **"harboring an illegal immigrant":** "Business Owner Convicted of Harboring an Illegal Alien Sentenced," United States Attorney's Office, Southern District of Texas, May 10, 2010, justice.gov/archive/usao/txs/1News/Releases/2010 %20May/051010%20Camp.htm.

227 **interrogated at school:** Recer, et al. "Representing," 966.

227 **Chuck Rosenthal announced:** Brian Rogers et al., "Rosenthal Steps Up in Officer's Death," *Houston Chronicle*, September 26, 2006, B1.

228 **What prosecutor wouldn't want:** "Danalynn Recer on the Quintero Verdict," *Grits for Breakfast*, May 25, 2008, http://gritsforbreakfast.blogspot.com/2008/05/danalynn-recer-on-quintero-verdict.html.

228 **romantic exchanges with his secretary:** "Fight over Harris County DA's Emails," *ABC13*, December 28, 2007, abc13.com/archive/5858347/.

228 **"Fatal Overdose":** Ralph Blumenthal, "New Investigation in Texas E-Mail Case," *New York Times*, January 9, 2008, A12, nytimes.com/2008/01/09/us/09texas.html.

228 **blamed prescription drugs:** Brian Rogers, "Rosenthal Cites Prescription Drugs in Resignation as DA," *Houston Chronicle*, February 15, 2008, chron.com/news/houston-texas/article/Rosenthal-cites-prescription-drugs-in-resignation-1600712.php.

229 **set up a life-sized replica:** Brian Rogers, "DA Rejects Plea for Illegal Immigrant who Shot Officer," *Houston Chronicle*, April 27, 2008, chron.com/news/houston-texas/article/DA-rejects-plea-for-illegal-immigrant-who-shot-1765538.php.

230 **"insanity" applied only in cases:** Ruffin v. State, nos. PD-1482-07 through PD-1489-07 (Tex. Crim. App. 2008).

230 **"He thought it was over":** "Quintero Defense Tries to Prove Insanity," *ABC13*, May 6, 2008, http://abc13.com/archive/6123508/.

231 **more than eight hundred names:** Toobin, "Mitigator."

232 **moments in their narratives:** Often the portrayals of defendants in death penalty trials would hew to tropes. The scholar Paul Kaplan lists common themes in how defense lawyers portrayed their clients ("The onetime screwup," "The guy with a terrible life," "The addict") and how the prosecutors portrayed them ("The gang-banger," "The lurking rapist," "The sociopath"). Paul Kaplan, *Murder Stories: Ideological Narratives in Capital Punishment* (Lanham, Md.: Lexington Books, 2012), 80.

232 **"convert" mitigation evidence:** Elizabeth Vartkessian, "Fatal Distraction: Does the Texas Capital Sentencing Statute Discourage the Consideration of Mitigating Evidence?," Doctoral Thesis, University of Oxford, 2011.

233 **"Truth Purgatory":** Merillat, *Future Danger?* 86.

233 **"testimony about the defendant":** Ibid., 78.

234 **showing videos that portrayed:** Mitigation specialist Vince Gonzales told me he helped produce such a video back in 1999. "We began showing it to jurors in Texas death penalty cases," he said. "It is my belief that the use of that video led to a direct decline in the number of death sentences handed out in Texas."

235 **moved by the love:** Brian Rogers and Dale Lezon, "Quintero's Life Sentence Shocks Victim's Family," *Houston Chronicle*, May 21, 2008, chron.com/news/article/Quintero-s-life-sentence-shocks-victim-s-family-1783060.php.

236 **monument to fallen police officers:** "Houston Police Memorial Guard Post + Visitor's Entrance," *Brave Architecture*, accessed June 30, 2019, bravearchitecture.com/work/civic/houston-police-memorial-guard-post/.

236 **More than four hundred jurors:** Michael E. Antonio, "Stress and the Capital

Jury: How Male and Female Jurors React to Serving on a Murder Trial," *Justice System Journal* 29, no. 3 (2008): 399–405.

236 **sought counseling:** Ibid.

236 **drinking and taking pills to cope:** Ibid.

237 **82 percent of female jurors:** Ibid.

237 **"upset" by their experience:** Ibid.

237 **attempted to escape from prison:** Vanesa Brashier, "Cop Killer Among Five Involved in Failed Prison Escape," *Courier,* January 30, 2010, yourconroenews .com/neighborhood/moco/news/article/Cop-killer-among-five-involved-in-failed -prison-9250895.php.

238 **"What I fear":** Murray Newman, "The Quintero Verdict," *Life at the Harris County Criminal Justice Center,* May 20, 2008, http://harriscountycriminaljustice .blogspot.com/2008/05/quintero-verdict.html.

238 **life sentences in infamous cases before:** Rosanna Ruiz and Brian Rogers, "Killer of Houston Policeman Surprised He Won't Go to Death Row," *Houston Chronicle,* May 21, 2008, chron.com/news/houston-texas/article/Killer-of-Houston -policeman-surprised-he-won-t-go-1756280.php.

238 **anecdotal sign of a larger shift:** John Moritz, "The Life Penalty," *Texas Observer,* November 28, 2008, 14.

238 *Time* **magazine published the headline:** Hilary Hylton, "Is Texas Changing Its Mind About the Death Penalty?" *Time,* December 23, 2008, content.time.com/ time/nation/article/0,8599,1868145,00.html.

238 **criminal defense lawyer of the year:** "Best of Houston 2008," *Houston Press,* accessed June 30, 2019, houstonpress.com/best-of/2008/people-and-places/ best-criminal-defense-attorney-6606260.

239 **she still made $38,000:** Mark Bennett, "The Best Criminal Defense Lawyer in Houston," *Defending People,* October 11, 2008, blog.bennettandbennett.com/ 2008/10/the-best-criminal-defense-lawyer-in-houston/.

239 **featured a photo of her standing:** Toobin, "Mitigator."

240 **"We will rethink our practice":** Peggy O'Hare, "Cop Killer's T-shirt for Sale, Under Fire in Houston," *Houston Chronicle,* January 17, 2011, chron.com/ news/houston-texas/article/Cop-killer-s-T-shirt-for-sale-under-fire-in-16849 99.php.

240 **On a stark set of black:** "Capital Punishment—The New Yorker Festival—The New Yorker," YouTube Video, published July 22, 2014, youtube.com/watch?v =PSGlUpkABT0.

CHAPTER 13

In addition to Elsa Alcala, Eddie Capetillo, Elizabeth DeRieux, and Allison Vickers, I interviewed Alcala's former staff lawyer Ingrid Grobey and clerk Sarah Tompkins, as well as others who worked at the court. Along with Alcala's opinions and her Twitter account (twitter.com/TexasElsa), I relied on analysis by Scott Henson on his indispensable blog *Grits for Breakfast.*

Steve Mills and Maurice Possley of the *Chicago Tribune* were the first to call national attention to the Cameron Todd Willingham case ("Man Executed on Disproved Forensics," December 9, 2004), and David Grann followed them with a lengthy, literary account of the case in *The New Yorker* ("Trial by Fire," September 7, 2009). I also relied here on the film *Incendiary: The Willingham Case* (Joe Bailey, Jr., and Steve Mims, Yokel, 2011).

244 **Seventy-one death row prisoners:** "The Juvenile Death Penalty Prior to Roper v. Simmons," *Death Penalty Information Center,* accessed July 9, 2019, deathpenaltyinfo.org/juvenile-offenders-who-were-death-row#streibstats.

244 **favor of the juveniles:** Roper v. Simmons, 543 U.S. 551 (2005).

247 **received thousands of appeals:** *Annual Statistical Report for the Texas Judiciary, Fiscal Year 2017* (Austin, Texas: Office of Court Administration, 2017), 107.

247 **more incoming cases than any comparable:** "2012 Overview—Appellate Court," Court Statistics Project DataViewer, accessed July 21, 2019, popup .ncsc.org/CSP/CSP_Intro.aspx.

247 **maybe fifty a year:** "Court of Criminal Appeals Activity: FY 2011," *Texas Judicial Branch,* accessed July 21, 2019, txcourts.gov/All_Archived_documents/ JudicialInformation/pubs/AR2011/cca/2-cca-activity.pdf, 1.

247 **usually rejected the defense's arguments:** From 1995 to 2000 the court ordered eight new trials and affirmed 270 death sentences. Ken Armstrong and Steve Mills, "Gatekeeper Court Keeps Gates Shut; Justices Prove Reluctant to Nullify Cases," *Chicago Tribune,* June 12, 2000, 1.

247 **More than 90 percent of the time:** "Court of Criminal Appeals Activity: FY 2011," 2.

247 **The original medical examiner admitted:** Craig Malisow, "Judge Blasts Autopsy in Baby-Killer Case; New Trial May Happen," *Houston Press,* January 22, 2010, houstonpress.com/news/judge-blasts-autopsy-in-baby-killer-case-new-trial -may-happen-6747217.

247 **local judge thought:** Ibid.

247 **Five of her eight colleagues thought:** Ex Parte Neal Hampton Robbins, AP-76,464 (Tex. Crim. App. 2011).

248 **A lab could contaminate:** Katie Worth, "The Surprisingly Imperfect Science of DNA Testing," *The Marshall Project,* June 24, 2015, themarshallproject.org/ 2015/06/24/the-surprisingly-imperfect-science-of-dna-testing.

249 **A 2009 report on forensic science:** *Strengthening Forensic Science in the United States: A Path Forward* (Washington, D.C.: National Academies Press, 2009).

249 **changes in forensic science cast doubt:** Maurice Chammah, "Bill Aims to Address Changing Science in Criminal Appeals," *Texas Tribune,* February 4, 2013, texastribune.org/2013/02/04/criminal-justice-advocates-renew-call-flawed -scien/.

249 **"We are in the business":** Michael Hall, "The Reformer," *Texas Monthly,* January 9, 2015, texasmonthly.com/politics/the-reformer/.

249 **setting a fire that had killed:** David Grann, "Trial by Fire," *New Yorker,* September 7, 2009, newyorker.com/magazine/2009/09/07/trial-by-fire.

250 **quoted more experts who saw the same flaws:** Steve Mills and Maurice Possley, "Texas Man Executed on Disproved Forensics," *Chicago Tribune,* December 9, 2004, chicagotribune.com/news/ct-xpm-2004-12-09-0412090169-story .html.

251 **"If this weren't a death penalty case":** Scott Henson, "Willingham Debate

Not Focused on Arson Science," *Grits for Breakfast*, October 4, 2009, gritsforbreakfast.blogspot.com/2009/10/willingham-debate-not-focused-on -arson.html.

251 **the death penalty disrupted compromise:** Former Supreme Court clerk Edward Lazarus bemoaned how, in the 1980s, capital cases wounded the Supreme Court's culture of civility. "There are some disagreements so deep that the disputants share no moral ground and have no mutually recognized obligations to meet," he wrote. "Neither side can shake the other's conviction, and both are reduced to exchanging accusations of hypocrisy and bad faith." Edward Lazarus, *Closed Chambers: The Rise, Fall, and Future of the Modern Supreme Court* (New York: Penguin, 2005), 165.

251 **"ineffective, unwise":** In Re David Dow and Jeffrey R. Newberry WR-61,939-01 & WR-61,939,02 (Tex. Crim. App. 2015).

253 **associate dark skin with violence:** In 1976, the same year the Supreme Court approved the Texas law and the future-dangerousness question, the University of California psychologist Birt L. Duncan published a study that suggested as much. He gathered more than a hundred white students, paid them each $1.50, and showed them all a videotape of an argument that leads to one person shoving another. There were four versions of the video that varied the races of the people involved. The students perceived the shove as "more violent" when the shover was black. Birt L. Duncan, "Differential Social Perception and Attribution of Intergroup Violence: Testing the Lower Limits of Stereotyping of Blacks," *Journal of Personality and Social Psychology* 34, no. 4 (1976): 590–98. See also Jennifer L. Eberhardt et al., "Looking Deathworthy: Perceived Stereotypicality of Black Defendants Predicts Capital-Sentencing Outcomes," *Cornell Law Faculty Publications* 41 (2006).

254 **"discriminatory intent":** Ex Parte Duane Edward Buck, 418 S.W.3d 98, 113 (Tex. Crim. App. 2013).

254 **he broke down in tears:** Ex Parte Arthur Lee Williams, no. AP-76,455 (Tex. Crim. App. 2012).

255 **halt the execution of Scott Panetti:** Ex Parte Scott Louis Panetti, no. WR-37,145-04 (Tex. Crim. App. 2014).

255 **interpreter for his Spanish-speaking client:** Ex Parte Irving Magana Garcia, no. WR-83,681-01 (Tex. Crim. App. 2016).

257 **"form of punishment as it exists in Texas today":** Ex Parte Julius Jerome Murphy, 495 S.W.3d 282 (Tex. Crim. App. 2016).

257 **Tom Price, had publicly written:** Ex Parte Scott Louis Panetti, no. WR-37,145-04 (Tex. Crim. App. 2014).

257 **"I was in my late twenties or early thirties":** Tom Dart, "Texas Judge Confronts 'Serious Deficiencies' in Death Penalty Cases," *Guardian*, October 6, 2016, theguardian.com/us-news/2016/oct/06/texas-judge-elsa-acala-death -penalty-cases-execution-barney-fulle.

258 **"some toxins can be deadly":** Buck v. Davis, 580 U.S. __ (2017).

259 **The Court left it to the states:** Hensleigh Crowell, "The Writing Is on the Wall: How the Briseno Factors Create an Unacceptable Risk of Executing Persons with Intellectual Disability," *Texas Law Review* 94, no. 4 (2016): 747–48.

259 **most Texans might agree upon:** Ex Parte Briseno 135 S.W.3d 1 (Tex. Crim. App. 2004).

259 **Scholars feared that the focus:** Crowell, Writing Is on the Wall," 751.

260 **"I find the whole premise":** Robert Mackey, "Steinbeck Family Outraged That Texas Judge Cited 'Of Mice and Men' in Execution Ruling," *New York Times*, August 8, 2012, thelede.blogs.nytimes.com/2012/08/08/steinbeck-family -outraged-texas-judge-cited-of-mice-and-men-in-execution-ruling/?_r=0.

260 **Alcala's colleagues disagreed:** Ex Parte Moore, 470 S.W.3d 481 (2015).

260 **Justice Ruth Bader Ginsburg criticized:** Moore v. Texas, 581 U.S. __ (2017).

262 **he had the last name Law:** Emma Platoff and Alexa Ura, "In Texas Republican Judicial Primaries, Do Hispanic-Sounding Surnames Spell Loss?" *Texas Tribune*, March 1, 2018, texastribune.org/2018/03/01/texas-highest-courts-have-few -hispanic-judges-some-attribute-surname-c/.

EPILOGUE

I interviewed Dennis Longmire and Gloria Rubac and witnessed their protesting for *Texas Monthly* ("Executions Are So Common, Even Protesting Them Has Become Routine," November 12, 2013, texasmonthly.com/the-culture/executions-are-so -common-even-protesting-them-has-become-routine/). I also relied on interviews with both, conducted by the Texas After Violence Project. I interviewed Maya Foa and Clive Stafford Smith about her work. Foa was also profiled by the podcast *More Perfect* ("Cruel and Unusual," June 2, 2016).

I am especially grateful to Anthony Amsterdam for sharing material on story-telling and its relevance to the work of lawyers.

265 **tried to stop prison officials:** Justine Sharrock, "Undercutting Executions," *Mother Jones*, December 28, 2001, motherjones.com/politics/2001/12/ undercutting-executions/.

265 **European governments began restricting:** Jeffrey Stern, "The Execution of Clayton Lockett," *Atlantic*, June 2015, theatlantic.com/magazine/archive/ 2015/06/execution-clayton-lockett/392069/.

265 **distribution controls:** Ibid.

265 **more than $50,000:** Ibid.

266 **"Looks like they waited":** Katie Fretland, "Records Show Oklahoma Officials Wanted Perks for Helping Texas in Search for Scarce Lethal Injections," *Colorado Independent*, March 18, 2014, coloradoindependent.com/2014/03/18/ oklahoma-scrambles-to-find-lethal-injections-for-two-imminent-executions/.

266 **"crosses the line from social activists":** Ed Pilkington, "Texas Accuses Anti-Death Penalty Charity Reprieve of Fomenting Violence," *Guardian*, March 28, 2012, theguardian.com/world/2012/mar/28/death-penalty-texas-reprieve.

266 **immense pain as they died:** A Harvard anesthesiologist told reporters that if a compounding pharmacy had allowed any small contaminants to remain in the drug, it would "cause an inmate immense pain in his veins" that could be "compared to rubbing sandpaper on an open wound." Molly Redden, "New Lethal Injections Could Cause Extreme Pain, Make Deaths 'Drag On' for Hours," *Mother Jones*, November 7, 2013, motherjones.com/politics/2013/11/ohio -lethal-injection-cocktail-execution-drugs.

266 **burning sensation:** Manny Fernandez and John Schwartz, "Confronted on Execution, Texas Proudly Says It Kills Efficiently," *New York Times*, May 12, 2014, A1.

266 **angrily demanded the drugs be returned:** Carey Gillam, "Texas Says Won't Return Execution Drugs to Pharmacy Facing Scrutiny," Reuters, October 8, 2013, reuters.com/article/us-usa-execution-drug/texas-says-wont-return -execution-drugs-to-pharmacy-facing-scrutiny-idUSBRE9960W320131007 ?feedType=RSS&feedName=domesticNews.

267 **Looking for Drugs:** Maurice Chammah, "Executions Are So Common, Even Protesting Them Has Become Routine," *Texas Monthly*, November 12, 2013, texasmonthly.com/the-culture/executions-are-so-common-even-protesting -them-has-become-routine/.

267 **"deeply troubling":** "Botched Execution 'Deeply Troubling,' Says Barack Obama," *Guardian*, May 3, 2014, theguardian.com/world/2014/may/03/ botched-execution-deeply-troubling-says-barack-obama.

267 **"My body is on fire":** The prisoner who said these words, Charles Warner, began describing pain before the drugs were administered, which led to theories that he was exaggerating in order to bolster the legal claims of others facing execution. Sean Murphy, "Dying Oklahoma Inmate's Last Words Stir Questions," Associated Press, January 15, 2015, apnews.com/fbd81caf836e45e9abdbca57 381691d6. See also tulsaworld.com/news/local/crime-and-courts/oklahoma -executes-charles-warner-in-20-minute-procedure-state-says/article _134dd8b3-0024-574e-a732-f3b466274f1c.html.

268 **Breyer issued a lengthy dissent:** Glossip v. Gross, 576 U.S. ___ (2015).

268 **"the liberal Justice":** David Cole, "Justice Breyer v. the Death Penalty," *New Yorker*, June 30, 2015, newyorker.com/news/news-desk/justice-breyer-against -the-death-penalty.

269 **prior opinions by Justice Anthony Kennedy:** Evan Mandery, "What Was Justice Breyer Really Saying?," *The Marshall Project*, July 2, 2015, themarshallproject .org/2015/07/02/what-was-justice-breyer-really-saying.

269 **placement in solitary confinement:** Davis v. Ayala, 576 U.S. ___ (2015).

269 **began filing petitions with the Court:** Maurice Chammah, "Could One of These Cases Spell the End of the Death Penalty?" *The Marshall Project*, January 12, 2016, themarshallproject.org/2016/01/12/could-one-of-these-cases-spell-the -end-of-the-death-penalty.

271 **50 percent for the first time:** J. Baxter Oliphant, "Support for Death Penalty Lowest in More Than Four Decades," *Pew Research Center*, September 29, 2016, pewresearch.org/fact-tank/2016/09/29/support-for-death-penalty-lowest-in -more-than-four-decades/.

271 **"anyone who's black or Mexican":** Liliana Segura, "Death and Texas," *Intercept*, December 3, 2019, theintercept.com/2019/12/03/death-penalty-race-texas/.

272 **1,448 had been executed:** Liliana Segura and Jordan Smith, "Counting the Condemned," *The Intercept*, December 3, 2019, theintercept.com/2019/12/ 03/death-penalty-capital-punishment-data/.

272 **Texas Defender Service kept issuing reports:** *Lethally Deficient: Direct Appeals in Texas Death Penalty Cases* (Austin: Texas Defender Service, 2016), http:// texasdefender.org/wp-content/uploads/TDS-2016-LethallyDeficient-Web.pdf.

272 **forty-three people to death row:** "Death Sentences in the United States Since 1977," Death Penalty Information Center, accessed November 17, 2019, deathpenaltyinfo.org/facts-and-research/sentencing-data/death-sentences-in -the-united-states-from-1977-by-state-and-by-year.

274 **"Time for a tree and a rope":** Debra Cassens Weiss, "Texas Judge Is Repri-manded After Explaining His 'Tree and Rope' Facebook Comment," *ABA Jour-nal*, May 8, 2017, abajournal.com/news/article/judge_is_reprimanded_after _explaining_his_tree_and_a_rope_facebook_comment/.

274 **salsa that was made in New Jersey:** A later version of the ad used "New York City."

274 **"For those ignorant of United States history":** Daniel Clifton, "PEC Holds Emo-tional Meeting over James Oakley's 'Tree and Rope' comment," *DailyTrib.com*, December 1, 2016, dailytrib.com/2016/12/01/pec-holds-emotional-meeting -james-oakleys-tree-rope-comment/.

274 **"the hanging at Burnet, Texas":** J. Castell Hopkins, "Canadian Hostility to An-nexation," *Forum*, vol. 16 (New York: Forum Publishing Co., September–November 1893), 331.

275 **Americans would never truly question:** " 'Death Penalty Is Lynching's Stepson': Bryan Stevenson on Slavery, White Supremacy, Prisons & More," *Democ-racy Now!*, May 1, 2018, democracynow.org/2018/5/1/the_death_penalty_is _lynching_s.

275 **harsh punishment was a regrettable necessity:** The legal scholar James Q. Whitman has argued that Germany and France, societies with strong class di-vides, eventually made efforts to punish people from the lower classes in the nicer ways once reserved for the aristocrats, while Americans, who never had formal aristocrats, seemed to want to pull everyone down to the harshest pun-ishments. James Q. Whitman, *Harsh Justice: Criminal Punishment and the Widen-ing Divide Between America and Europe* (New York: Oxford University Press, 1995).

275 **"I think Americans understand justice":** Adam Serwer, "Rick Perry's 'Ultimate Justice,' " *Mother Jones*, September 8, 2011, motherjones.com/crime-justice/ 2011/09/rick-perrys-ultimate-justice/.

276 **"Some of the most marginalized":** Bryan Washington, "Houston and Its Di-verse Hubs Made Me Who I Am," *Catapult*, January 10, 2018, catapult.co/ stories/bayou-diaries-how-houstons-diverse-hubs-made-me-who-i-am.

276 **artists painting a mural:** Tracy Maness, "New Mural Project Debuts at Arts Dis-trict Houston," *Houston Chronicle*, August 30, 2019, chron.com/neighborhood/ bellaire/news/article/New-mural-project-debuts-at-Art-District-Houston-144 03052.php.

278 **a person who committed a crime before age eighteen:** Miller v. Alabama, 567 U.S. 460 (2012); Graham v. Florida, 560 U. S. __ (2010).

278 **some felt was even harsher:** James Ridgeway and Jean Casella, "What Death Penalty Opponents Don't Get," *The Marshall Project*, November 30, 2014, themarshallproject.org/2014/11/30/what-death-penalty-opponents-don-t-get.

279 **where it was largely symbolic:** Elizabeth Byrne and Jolie McCullough, "Despite Bipartisan Support, Texas Bill Tackling Intellectual Disability in Death Penalty

Cases Fails," *Texas Tribune,* May 26, 2019, texastribune.org/2019/05/26/Texas-death-penalty-intellectual-disability-fails/.

279 **a luncheon for defense lawyers:** Jeffrey Toobin, "Comeback," *New Yorker,* March 19, 2007, newyorker.com/magazine/2007/03/26/comeback-8.

279 **forty separate capital cases:** Ibid.

280 **"I don't shut up":** "The Reminiscences of Anthony G. Amsterdam," interview by Myron A. Farber, April 1, 2009, session 1, The Rule of Law Oral History Project, Oral History Research Office, Columbia University, columbia.edu/cu/libraries/inside/ccoh_assets/ccoh_8616918_transcript.pdf, 229.

280 **"We now understand that stories are not just recipes":** Anthony Amsterdam and Jerome Bruner, *Minding the Law* (Cambridge, Mass.: Harvard University Press, 2000), 111.

280 **"the way most people make sense of the world":** Anthony G. Amsterdam, Randy Hertz, and Robin Walker-Sterling, "Introduction," *Clinical Law Review* 12, no. 1 (2005): 5.

INDEX

LET
THE LORD
SORT THEM

THE RISE AND FALL OF THE DEATH PENALTY

Maurice Chammah

A READER'S GUIDE

1. What was your experience reading *Let the Lord Sort Them*? Was there anything you learned that surprised you? If so, what? Which scenes or stories did you find emotionally resonant or overwhelming, and why?

2. Whose perspectives are often left out of media coverage and public discussions of death penalty cases? What is the importance of including them?

3. How does race play a role in death penalty rulings? What does the fact that black people are overrepresented on death rows across the United States say about our country? What steps can be taken to resolve this disparity?

4. In the prologue, Maurice Chammah writes that the focus of this book is lawyers, since they are "helping us answer some of our deepest questions about our own society: Can a person be evil? What does 'justice' mean?" (19). What are your thoughts on this focus and these questions?

5. Do you agree that justice should be "local": determined by state legislatures, and then handled by local prosecutors and juries? Should someone receive or avoid the death penalty based on what county or state they committed the crime in? If so, why? If not, what would be a better system?

6. In Chapter Two, Chammah walks readers through the Supreme Court's decision to approve the Texas death penalty law, which directed juries to decide whether defendants would be dangerous in the future. Did the court make the right ruling? Please explain.

7. Are prosecutors responsible for executions because they seek death sentences, or are they simply doing what the public wants them to do? Discuss Kenneth Dean and the "tie-down team." Are they responsible for executions because they carry out the punishment directly? Where does their responsibility begin and end?

8. What do you make of Eddie Capetillo? Do you think he could be called "rehabilitated" or "redeemed" after his years on death row? Should the fact that he was seventeen years old at the time of the murders have been taken into account by the courts?

9. If you had been in Elsa Alcala's shoes, would you have sought a death sentence for Eddie Capetillo? Explain your decision.

10. Should those who commit murder as a hate crime—like the perpetrators in the case of James Byrd, Jr., in Jasper, Texas—receive harsher punishments than others who commit murder? Why or why not?

11. Should the cost of the death penalty dictate whether someone receives the sentence? Why or why not?

12. If you had been a juror in the trial of Juan Quintero, what would you have brought up in the jury room? Is Quintero's crime, murdering a police officer, "all you need to know about him" (242), or is there more to the story?

13. Do you have a different view of the death penalty than you did twenty or thirty years ago? From when you started reading *Let the Lord Sort Them*? If so, how have your views changed?

14. Do you think the United States will still have the death penalty in 2040? Why or why not?

PHOTO: © TAMIR KALIFA

MAURICE CHAMMAH is a journalist and staff writer for The Marshall Project, where he shared a Pulitzer Prize for National Reporting. His coverage of the criminal justice system has been published by *The New Yorker, The New York Times, The Atlantic,* and other publications. He received the 2019 J. Anthony Lukas Work-in-Progress Award for *Let the Lord Sort Them.* He lives in Austin, Texas, where he and his wife, Emily Chammah, co-organize the Insider Prize, a fiction and essay contest for incarcerated writers sponsored by *American Short Fiction.*